●Dráma T H R A C E ●Komotiní

Kavála●

Alexandroúpoli●

NORTHERN GREECE
Pages 232–257

A R O U N D
A T H E N S
● ATHENS
A T T I C A
Lávrio ●

ATHENS
Pages 62–135

AROUND ATHENS
Pages 140–157

EYEWITNESS TRAVEL GUIDES

GREECE
ATHENS & THE MAINLAND

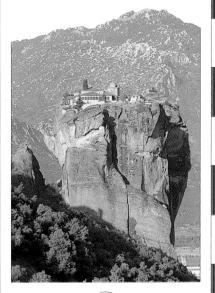

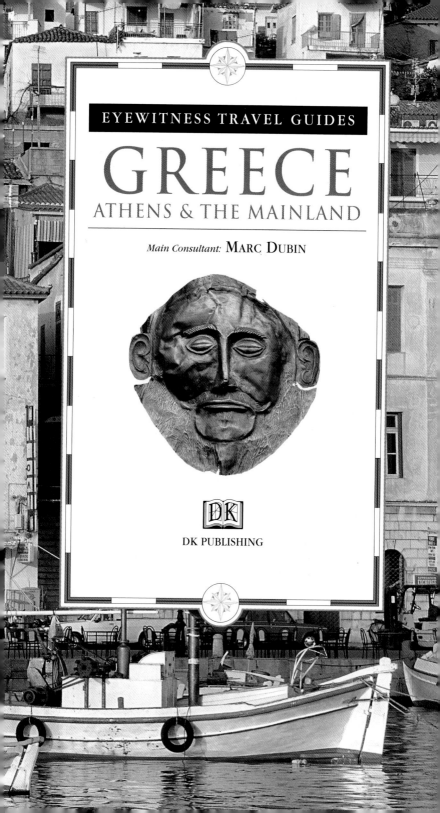

EYEWITNESS TRAVEL GUIDES

GREECE
ATHENS & THE MAINLAND

Main Consultant: MARC DUBIN

DK PUBLISHING

LONDON • NEW YORK • MUNICH
MELBOURNE • DELHI

PROJECT EDITOR Jane Simmonds
ART EDITOR Stephen Bere
EDITORS Isabel Carlisle, Michael Ellis, Simon Farbrother,
Claire Folkard, Marianne Petrou, Andrew Szudek
US EDITORS Michael Wise, Mary Sutherland
DESIGNERS Jo Doran, Paul Jackson, Elly King, Marisa Renzullo
MAP CO-ORDINATORS Emily Green, David Pugh
VISUALIZER Joy Fitzsimmons
LANGUAGE CONSULTANT Georgia Gotsi

CONTRIBUTORS AND CONSULTANTS
Rosemary Barron, Marc Dubin, Mike Gerrard, Andy Harris,
Lynette Mitchell, Colin Nicholson, Robin Osborne, Barnaby
Rogerson, Paul Sterry, Tanya Tsikas

MAPS
Gary Bowes, Fiona Casey, Christine Purcell (ERA-Maptec Ltd)

PHOTOGRAPHERS
Joe Cornish, John Heseltine, Rob Reichenfeld, Peter Wilson,
Francesca Yorke

ILLUSTRATORS
Stephen Conlin, Paul Guest, Steve Gyapay, Maltings Partnership,
Chris Orr & Associates, Paul Weston, John Woodcock

Reproduced by Colourscan (Singapore)
Printed and bound by L. Rex Printing Company Limited, China

First American Edition, 1997
02 03 04 05 10 9 8 7 6 5 4 3 2 1

Published in the United States by
DK Publishing, Inc., 375 Hudson Street,
New York, New York 10014

Reprinted with revisions 1998, 1999, 2000, 2001, 2002, 2003

Copyright © 1997, 2003 Dorling Kindersley Limited, London

Library of Congress Cataloging-in-Publication Data
Greece, Athens, & the Mainland / main consultant, Marc Dubin.
p. cm. –– (DK eyewitness travel guides)
Originally published: Great Britain: Dorling Kindersley Limited, 1997.
Includes index.
ISBN 0-7894-9426-4 (alk. paper)
1. Greece –– Guidebooks. I. Title: Greece, Athens, and the Mainland.
II. Dubin, Marc S. (Marc Stephen) III. Eyewitness travel guides

DF716.G71333 2003
914.9504'76 –– dc21   2002031411

FLOORS ARE REFERRED TO THROUGHOUT IN ACCORDANCE WITH EUROPEAN USAGE;
IE THE "FIRST FLOOR" IS THE FLOOR ABOVE GROUND LEVEL.

See our complete product line at
www.dk.com

**The information in this
DK Eyewitness Guide is checked annually.**
Every effort has been made to ensure that this book is as up-to-date as
possible at the time of going to press. Some details, however, such as
telephone numbers, opening hours, prices, gallery hanging
arrangements and travel information are liable to change. The publishers
cannot accept responsibility for any consequences arising from the use
of this book, nor for any material on third party websites, and cannot
guarantee that any website address in this book will be a suitable source
of travel information. We value the views and suggestions of our readers
very highly. Please write to: Publisher, DK Eyewitness Travel Guides,
Dorling Kindersley, 80 Strand, London WC2R 0RL, Great Britain.

◁ **Morning at Gýtheio harbor in the Peloponnese**

CONTENTS

HOW TO USE THIS GUIDE 6

**Black-figure bowl depicting
the god Dionysos**

INTRODUCING ATHENS AND MAINLAND GREECE

ANCIENT GREECE

Tower houses at Vátheia, Inner Máni in the Peloponnese

Fresco at Varlaám monastery at Metéora, Central Greece

Greek salad

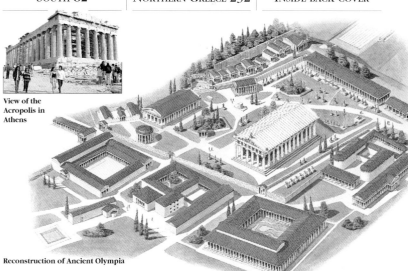

View of the Acropolis in Athens

Reconstruction of Ancient Olympia

HOW TO USE THIS GUIDE

THIS GUIDE helps you to get the most from your visit to Mainland Greece. It provides expert recommendations and practical information. *Introducing Athens and Mainland Greece* maps the country and sets it in its historical and cultural context. *Ancient Greece* gives a background to the many remains and artifacts to be seen. The four regional chapters, plus *Athens*, describe important sights, with maps and illustrations. Restaurant and hotel recommendations can be found in *Travellers' Needs*. The *Survival Guide* has tips on everything from using a Greek telephone to transport.

ATHENS

Athens has been divided into two sightseeing areas. Each has its own chapter, opening with a list of the sights described. All sights are numbered on an area map, and are described in detail on the following pages.

Sights at a Glance gives a categorized list of the chapter's sights: Museums and Galleries; Squares, Parks and Gardens; Churches and Historic Buildings.

All pages relating to Athens have red thumb tabs.

A locator map shows you where you are in relation to the rest of Athens.

1 Area Map
The sights are numbered and located on a map. Sights in the city centre are also shown on the Athens Street Finder *on pages 122–35.*

2 Street-by-Street Map
This gives an overhead view of the key areas in central Athens. The numbering on the map ties in with the area map and the fuller descriptions that follow.

Story boxes highlight special aspects of a particular sight.

Stars indicate the sights that no visitor should miss.

A suggested route for a walk is shown in red.

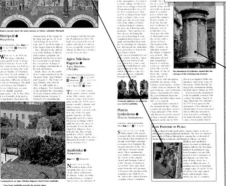

3 Detailed Information
The sights within Athens are described individually. Addresses, telephone numbers, opening hours and information concerning admission charges and wheelchair access are given for each entry. Map references to the Athens Street Finder are also provided for orientation.

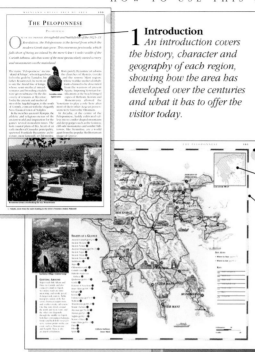

THE PELOPONNESE

[introductory text of the sample page]

1 Introduction
An introduction covers the history, character and geography of each region, showing how the area has developed over the centuries and what it has to offer the visitor today.

MAINLAND GREECE AREA BY AREA

Mainland Greece has been divided into four regions, each of which has a separate chapter. A map of these areas can be found inside the front cover of the book.

Each region can be identified by its colour coding, shown on the inside front cover.

A locator map shows you where you are in relation to the other regions in the book.

2 Pictorial Map
This shows the region covered in the chapter. The main sights are numbered on the map. The major roads are marked and there are useful tips about the best ways of getting around the area.

3 Detailed Information
All the important towns and areas to visit are described individually. They are listed in order, following the numbering on the Pictorial Map. Within each entry there is detailed information on all the major sights.

Ancient Olympia

Stadium Entrance
Late in the 3rd century BC the stadium entrance acquired a vaulted ceiling, part of which survives. The existing stadium was the third built out of Olympia.

Visitors' Checklist
[practical information block]

A Visitors' Checklist provides the practical information you will need to plan your visit.

4 Greece's Top Sights
These are given one or more full pages. Historic buildings are dissected to reveal their interiors. Many of the ancient sites are reconstructed to supplement information about the site as it is seen today.

INTRODUCING
ATHENS AND
MAINLAND GREECE

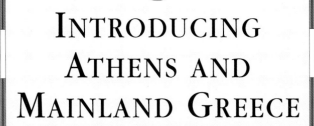

Putting Greece on the Map

OCCUPYING THE SOUTHERNMOST TIP of the Balkan peninsula, Greece divides into over 2,000 islands stretching from the Ionian Sea in the west to the Aegean Sea and Turkey in the east. The mainland has borders with Albania, Bulgaria, Turkey and Macedonia and is home to most of the country's 10.2 million people, with a third of these in the capital, Athens.

KEY

⛴ Main international ferry service

✈ International airport

═ Motorway, dual-carriageway

═ Major road

── Railway line

∙-∙ National boundary

PRAGUE — **CZECH REPUBLIC** — Brno — **SLOVAKIA** — **POLAND** — Kraków

VIENNA — **AUSTRIA** — **BRATISLAVA** — **BUDAPEST** — Oradea

Graz — Dunav — Szeged

SLOVENIA — **LJUBLJANA** — **HUNGARY** — Timişoara

Milano — Venezia — Trieste — **ZAGREB** — Drava — **CROATIA**

Torino — Po — **BELGRADE**

Genova — Bologna — Sana — Sava — **BOSNIA AND HERZEGOVINA** — **SERBIA AND MONTENEGRO**

Nice — Pisa — Firenze — Ancona — **SARAJEVO** — Niš

Calvi — Bastia — Split

Ajaccio — **CORSICA** — Dubrovnik — Podgorica

Olbia — **ROME** — **ITALY** — Bari — **TIRANA** — **FYR OF MACEDONIA**

SARDINIA — Napoli — Taranto — Brindisi — **ALBANIA**

Cagliari — Ioánnina — **G**

Corfu — Igoumenitsa

Préveza

Trapani — Palermo — Messina — Kefalloniá — Pát

TUNIS — Reggio di Calabria — Zákynthos — Kyllíni

SICILY — Catania — Kalamáta

TUNISIA — Sousse

VALLETTA — **MALTA**

Sfax

TRIPOLI — Banghāzī — **LIBYA**

Adriatic Sea

Tyrrhenian Sea

Ionian Sea

Mediterranean

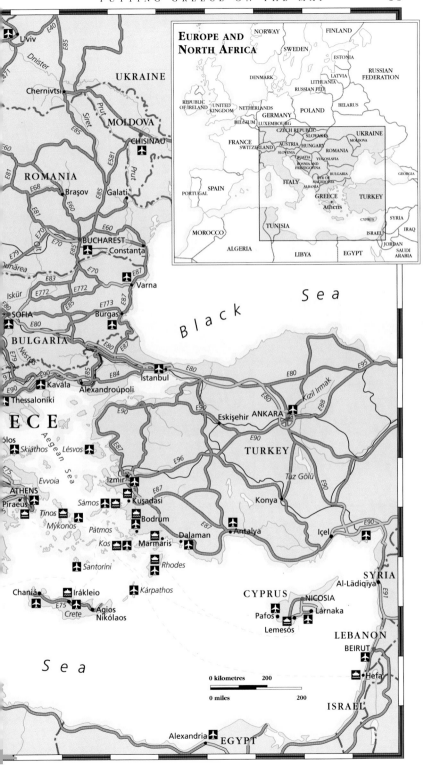

L'viv

Dnister

UKRAINE

Chernivtsi

Siret

Prut

MOLDOVA

CHISINAU

ROMANIA

Braşov

Galaţi

Prut

BUCHAREST

Constanţa

Dunărea

Varna

Iskŭr

SOFIA

Burgas

BULGARIA

Néstos

Kavála

Alexandroúpoli

Thessaloníki

Black   Sea

Istanbul

Eskişehir

ANKARA

Kizil Irmak

E C E

Aegean Sea

Skiáthos

Lésvos

Evvoia

ATHENS

Piraeus

TURKEY

Izmir

Sámos

Kuşadası

Konya

Tinos

Bodrum

Mýkonos

Pátmos

Antalya

İçel

Kos

Marmaris

Dalaman

Santorini

Rhodes

Chaniá

Irákleio

Kárpathos

SYRIA

Al-Lādiqīya

CYPRUS

NICOSIA

Crete

Agios
Nikólaos

Pafos

Lárnaka

Lemesós

LEBANON

BEIRUT

Sea

Hefa

0 kilometres   200

0 miles   200

ISRAEL

Alexandria

EGYPT

**EUROPE AND
NORTH AFRICA**

NORWAY

FINLAND

SWEDEN

ESTONIA

DENMARK

LATVIA

RUSSIAN
FEDERATION

LITHUANIA

RUSSIAN FED.

REPUBLIC
OF IRELAND

UNITED
KINGDOM

NETHERLANDS

BELGIUM

LUXEMBOURG

GERMANY

POLAND

BELARUS

CZECH REPUBLIC

SLOVAKIA

UKRAINE

FRANCE

SWITZERLAND

AUSTRIA

HUNGARY

MOLDOVA

SLOVENIA

CROATIA

ROMANIA

BOSNIA AND
HERZEGOVINA

YUGOSLAVIA

GEORGIA

BULGARIA

PORTUGAL

SPAIN

ITALY

ALBANIA

FYR OF
MACEDONIA

GREECE

Athens

TURKEY

CYPRUS

SYRIA

IRAQ

MOROCCO

TUNISIA

ISRAEL

JORDAN

SAUDI
ARABIA

ALGERIA

LIBYA

EGYPT

A PORTRAIT OF MAINLAND GREECE

REECE IS ONE OF THE MOST VISITED *European countries, yet one of the least known. The modern Greek state dates only from 1830 and bears little relation to the popular image of ancient Greece. At a geographical crossroads, Greece combines elements of the Balkans, Middle East and Mediterranean.*

For a relatively small country, less than 132,000 sq km (51,000 sq miles) in area, Greece possesses marked regional differences in topography. Nearly three-quarters of the land is mountainous, uninhabited or uncultivated. Fertile agricultural land supports tobacco farming in the northeast, with orchard fruits and vegetables grown further south. A third of the population lives in the capital, Athens, the cultural, financial and political centre, in which ancient and modern stand side by side.

Fresco from Moní Frankavílla, Amaliáda

Rural and urban life in contemporary Greece have been transformed this century despite years of occupation and conflict, including a bitter civil war *(see p42)* that would surely have finished off a less resilient people. The society that emerged was supported with US aid, yet Greece remained relatively under-developed until the 1960s.

Rural areas lacked paved roads and even basic utilities, prompting extensive, unplanned urban growth and emigration. It has been said, with some justice, that there are no architects in Greece, only civil engineers.

For centuries a large number of Greeks have lived abroad: currently there are over half as many Greeks outside the country as in. This

Backgammon players at the flea market around Plateía Monastirakíou in Athens

◁ **Leading a mule on the streets of Monemvasía**

The Píndos mountain range, from above the village

diaspora occurred in several stages prompted by changes in the Ottoman Empire late in the 17th century. Most recently, emigration has been to Africa, the Americas and Australia.

RELIGION, LANGUAGE AND CULTURE

During the centuries of domination by Venetians and Ottomans (*see pp38–9*) the Greek Orthodox Church preserved the Greek language, and with it Greek identity, through its liturgy and schools. Today, the Orthodox Church is still a powerful force despite the secularizing reforms of the first democratically elected PASOK government of 1981–85. The

...s (Are you ...synonymous ...you ...lf-...d ...h ...or ...r-...y ...i-...

Sunday Mass is very popular with women, who often use the services as meeting places for socializing much in the same way as men do the *kafeneía* (cafés).

Votive offerings in the Pantánassas convent

Parish priests, often recognizable by their tall stovepipe hats and long beards, are not expected to embody the divine, but to transmit it at liturgy. Many marry and have a second trade (a custom that helps keep up the numbers of entrants to the church). There has also been a

Greek priests leading a religious procession in Athens

recent renaissance in monastic life, perhaps in reaction to the growth of materialism since World War II.

Tavernas in the town of Náfplio

The subtle and beautiful Greek language, another great hallmark of national identity, was for a long time a field of conflict between *katharévousa*, an artificial, written form hastily devised around the time of Independence, and the slowly evolved *dimotikí*, or everyday speech, with its streamlined grammar and words borrowed from several other languages. The dispute acquired political overtones, with the Right tending to champion *katharévousa*, the Left, *dimotikí*, with blood even being shed at times.

Today's prevalence of the more supple *dimotikí* was perhaps a foregone conclusion in an oral culture. The art of storytelling is still as prized in Greece as in Homer's time, with conversation pursued for its own sake in *kafeneía* and at dinner parties. The bardic tradition has remained alive with the poet-lyricists such as Mános Eleftheríou, Apóstolos Kaldarás and Níkos Gátsos. The continuous efforts made to produce popular and accessible art have played a key role in helping to keep *dimotikí* alive from the 19th century until the present day.

Both writers and singers, the natural advocates of *dimotikí*, have historically been important to the Greek public. During recent periods of censorship under the dictatorship or in times of foreign occupation, they carried out an essential role as one of the chief sources of coded information and morale-boosting.

DEVELOPMENT AND DIPLOMACY

Compared to most of its Balkan neighbours, Greece is a wealthy and stable country,

An archaeologist helping to restore the Parthenon

but by Western economic indicators Greece languishes at the bottom of the EU league table, and will be a net EU beneficiary for some years to come. The persistent negative trade deficit is aggravated by imports of luxury goods, an expression of *xenomanía* or belief in the inherent superiority of all things foreign. Cars are most conspicuous among these, since Greece is one of the very few European countries not to manufacture its own.

Greece still bears the hallmarks of a developing economy, with agriculture and the service sector accounting for two-thirds of the GNP. Blurred lines

Selling fish at Vólos harbour, the Pílio

Barrels in the Achaïa Klauss winery at Pátra

between work and living space are the norm, with professional brass plates alternating with personal bell-buzzer tags in any apartment block. There is a tenacious adherence, despite repeated campaigns against it, to the long afternoon siesta. As a result, some workers have to endure commuting twice a day.

With EU membership since 1981 and a nominally capitalist orientation, Greece has now overcome its resemblance to pre-1989 Eastern Europe. The state no longer invests heavily in antiquated industries nor is the civil service of today overstaffed as part of a full-employment policy. Instead, recent years have seen a number of improvements: loss-making state enterprises have been sold off, inflation has dipped to single figures for the first time since 1973 and interest rates have fallen. However, the drachma suffered on entry to the ERM and unemployment

remains stubbornly high. Tourism ranks as the largest hard-currency earner, offsetting the depression in world shipping and the fact that Mediterranean agricultural products are duplicated within the EU. Greece's historically lenient entry requirements for refugees, and its pre-eminent status in the Balkans, have made it a magnet for Arabs, Africans, Kurds, Poles and Albanians for a number of years. Now protectionist procedures, such as stringent frontier clamp-downs and the deportation of all undocumented individuals, have been introduced.

The fact that the Greek state is less than 200 years old, and that this century has been marked by political instability, means that there is little faith in government institutions. Life operates on networks of personal friendships and official contacts. The classic designations of Right and Left have only

Statue of Athena standing beside the Athens Academy

acquired their conventional meanings since the 1930s. The dominant political figure of the first half of the 20th century was Elefthérios Venizélos, an anti-royalist Liberal. The years following World War II

Rooftops of Náfplio and Boúrtzi islet from the Palamídi fortress

House in the village of Psarádes, beside the Préspa lakes

have been largely shaped by the influence of two men: the late Andréas Papandréou, three times premier as head of the Panhellenic Socialist Movement (PASOK), and the late conservative premier Konstantínos Karamanlís.

With the Cold War over, Greece looks likely to assert its underlying Balkan identity in many ways. Relations with Albania have improved since the collapse of the Communist regime in 1990. Greece is already the biggest investor in Bulgaria, and after a recent rapprochement with Skopje, it seems poised to be a regional power, with Thessaloníki's port (second largest in the Mediterranean) seen as the future gateway to the southern Balkans.

Man with a shepherd's crook in the village of Métsovo

HOME LIFE

The family is still the basic Greek social unit. Traditionally, one family could sow, plough and reap its own fields, without need of cooperative work parties. Today, family-run businesses are still the norm in urban settings. Family life and social life are usually one and the same, and tend to revolve around eating out, which is done more often than in most of Europe. Arranged marriages and granting of dowries, though officially banned, persist; most single young people live with their parents or another relative until married, and outside the largest cities, few couples dare to cohabit. Despite the renowned Greek love of children, Greece has the lowest birth rate in Europe after Italy: less than half its pre-World War II levels. Owing in part to the recent reforms in family and inheritance law, urban Greek women have been raised in status. Better represented in medicine and the law, many women run their own businesses. In the country, however, macho attitudes persist and women often forgo the chance of a career for the sake of the house and children. New imported notions and attitudes have begun to creep in, especially in the larger cities, but generally tradition remains strong and no amount of innovation or outside influence is likely to jeopardize the Greek way of life.

Wednesday market in Argos

Byzantine Architecture

MEDIEVAL CHURCHES are virtually all that have survived from a millennium of Byzantine civilization in Greece. Byzantine church architecture was concerned almost exclusively with a decorated interior. The intention was to sculpt out a holy space where the congregation would be confronted with the true nature of the cosmos, cleared of all worldly distractions. The mosaics and frescoes portraying the whole body of the Church, from Christ downwards, have a dual purpose: they give inspiration to the worshipper and are windows to the spiritual world. From a mountain chapel to an urban church there is great conformity of design, with structure and decoration united to a single purpose.

THE BEST OF BYZANTINE ARCHITECTURE

1. Thessaloníki *p248*
2. Mount Athos *pp252–4*
3. Arta *p213*
4. Monastery of Osios Loúkas *pp222–3*
5. Pátra *p169*
6. Moní Kaïsarianís *pp150–51*
7. Monastery of Dafní *pp152–3*
8. Athens *p80, p105, p108*
9. Mystrás *pp192–3*
10. Geráki *p189*

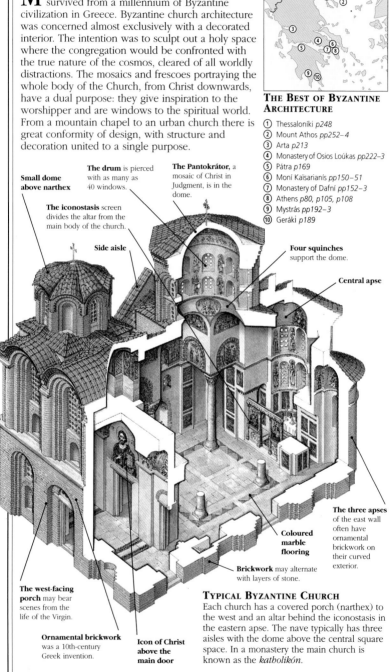

Small dome above narthex

The drum is pierced with as many as 40 windows.

The iconostasis screen divides the altar from the main body of the church.

The Pantokrátor, a mosaic of Christ in Judgment, is in the dome.

Side aisle

Four squinches support the dome.

Central apse

The three apses of the east wall often have ornamental brickwork on their curved exterior.

Coloured marble flooring

Brickwork may alternate with layers of stone.

The west-facing porch may bear scenes from the life of the Virgin.

Ornamental brickwork was a 10th-century Greek invention.

Icon of Christ above the main door

TYPICAL BYZANTINE CHURCH

Each church has a covered porch (narthex) to the west and an altar behind the iconostasis in the eastern apse. The nave typically has three aisles with the dome above the central square space. In a monastery the main church is known as the *katholikón*.

Understanding Frescoes in a Byzantine Church

The frescoes and mosaics in churches' interiors were organized according to a standard scheme. Symbolically, images descended from heaven (Christ Pantokrátor in the dome) to earth (the saints on the lowest level). The Virgin was shown in the semi-dome of the apse, with the fathers of the church below her.

Choirs of angels

Windows in drum

Christ Pantokrátor

The dome is symbolically filled by the figure of Christ in Judgment, the Pantokrátor. Choirs of angels swirl around Him, and outside them stand the Old Testament prophets. This dome comes from Moní Perivléptou in Mystrás (see p192).

Prophets

The Virgin and Child are in the curve of the apse, symbolically between heaven (the dome) and earth (the nave).

Archangels Michael and Gabriel, dressed like courtiers of a Byzantine emperor, honour the Virgin.

The Fathers of Orthodoxy, here in their episcopal robes, defined Orthodoxy in the early centuries.

The apse is often hidden from public view by an elaborate iconostasis screen, through whose doors only the clergy are admitted. This apse is from Agios Stratigós in the Máni (see pp194–9).

Upper register of saints

Lower register of saints

Sand-filled tray for votive candles

The side walls are decorated in registers. On the lowest level stand life-size portrayals of the saints, their heads illuminated with haloes. More complex scenes portraying incidents from the Gospels or the Day of Judgment fill the upper walls and vaults. This church is at Miliés in the Pílio (see pp218–20).

The Virgin Mary

Icons of the Virgin Mary abound in every Orthodox church, where she is referred to as Panagía, the All Holy. Her exceptional status was confirmed in 431 when she was awarded the title Theotókos "Mother of God", in preference to just "Mother of Christ".

Eleoúsa, *meaning "Our Lady of Tenderness", shows the Virgin Mary brushing cheeks with the Christ Child.*

***The Virgin seated on a throne**, flanked by two arch-angels, is a depiction usually found in the eastern apse.*

Odigítria, *meaning the "Conductress", shows the Virgin indicating the Christ Child with her right arm.*

Vernacular Architecture in Mainland Greece

M OST OF THE SURVIVING masterpieces of vernacular architecture in mainland Greece date from the 18th century, when improved conditions within the Ottoman Empire permitted the rise of a non-Muslim bourgeoisie. Sumptuous mansions, or *archontiká*, relying heavily on Ottoman and Byzantine designs, were built by Orthodox Christians returning from Italy, Central Europe and Constantinople. The stonemasons, woodworkers and mural painters came mainly from remote mountain villages in Epirus, now a region divided between Greece and Albania.

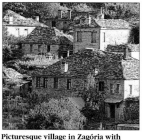

Picturesque village in Zagória with schist-slab roofs

Decorated plasterwork

The *sachnisí* juts out on wooden buttresses.

Protective iron grille on lower windows

The Kanatsoúlis mansion in Siátista is representative of those here and in nearby Kastoriá (see p240). Lavishly decorated on their upper storeys with stained glass and painted wood, they reflect the prosperity of local fur merchants in the 17th and 18th centuries.

Chatília, or bands of wood, divide masonry sections.

Main door studded with heavy nails

Arched windows with masoned lintels

Sloping roof of tiles or schist

Round turrets at the corners of the roof acted as sentry posts or *klouviá.*

Reversed conical supports

The upper floors were for sleeping, living and guests.

The ground floor was for storage and stabling.

The small **balcony** was made of wood or wrought iron.

Arched doorway, often low

Small windows for firing through

Stone farmhouse

Arcadian mansions in the mountainous central Peloponnese were built of local stone. Small windows and wooden floors and ceilings were for warmth. On steep slopes, one side of the building could have two or three storeys, the other up to five.

Access to the tower was often through the attached house.

Máni tower houses are found in the south-central spur of the Peloponnese. (see pp194–9) The Máni was historically occupied by feuding families who used the stone towers for both shelter and attack. The attached two-storey building was occupied in peacetime.

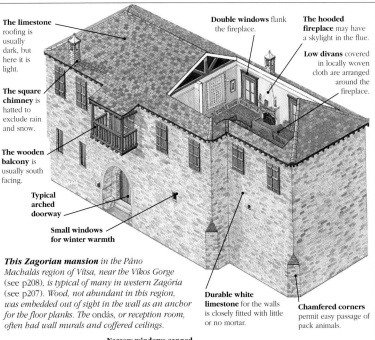

The limestone roofing is usually dark, but here it is light.

The square chimney is hatted to exclude rain and snow.

The wooden balcony is usually south facing.

Typical arched doorway

Small windows for winter warmth

Double windows flank the fireplace.

The hooded fireplace may have a skylight in the flue.

Low divans covered in locally woven cloth are arranged around the fireplace.

Durable white limestone for the walls is closely fitted with little or no mortar.

Chamfered corners permit easy passage of pack animals.

This Zagorian mansion in the Páno Machalás region of Vítsa, near the Víkos Gorge (see p208), is typical of many in western Zagória (see p207). Wood, not abundant in this region, was embedded out of sight in the wall as an anchor for the floor planks. The ondás, or reception room, often had wall murals and coffered ceilings.

Tiled roofs with corner ornaments

Narrow windows capped with pediments

Iron balcony supported on stone corbels

Pilasters at corners

Wrought-iron fanlight

Stone cladding on ground floor

Secondary doors with horizontal slats

The Neo-Classical revival style became popular in Greece in the 19th century with the rule of Bavarian King Otto. At first it was confined to public buildings such as schools, courthouses and libraries in the capital. Later it spread to wealthy provincial towns and into domestic use. This generic Peloponnesian structure is late 19th century.

LOCAL BUILDING METHODS AND MATERIALS

Stone, usually limestone, is used across the mainland for lower storeys, because of its strength in weight-bearing and fortification. *Tsatmás* and *bagdatí* (lath and plaster) suffice for upper storeys, both for interior partition walls, and in *sachnisiá* (airy overhangs) which add extra space but little extra weight. Wood, in the former times when it was plentiful in Thessaly, Macedonia and Thrace, was used for balustrades and lattice work around a *chagiáti* or upstairs covered porch, window grilles and clapboard siding. More recently, iron has been used instead of wood.

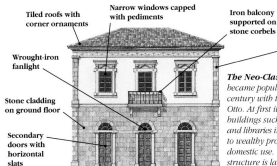

White limestone exterior wall

Wooden *sachnisí* (overhang)

Roof tiled with slates

***Tsatmás* (timber and rubble) wall**

Ornate iron window grille

Roof of clay canal tiles

The Landscape of Mainland Greece

GREECE IS A LAND of rugged beauty. The narrow coastal belt is backed by cliffs in places while inland there are massive mountain ranges, gorges and cliffs, the haunt of eagles and vultures. The fantastic array of vegetation, including many species of spring wild flowers, is strongly influenced by the Mediterranean climate of long, hot and dry summers and mild, wet winters. Clearance of forests for agriculture and timber has produced a mosaic of flower-rich fields and areas of shrubs. This shrubland habitat is of two kinds: the dense aromatic bushes of *maquis* and the sparser *phrygana* with lower and more compact plants. Although the country's millions of goats destroy the vegetation with their constant grazing, one of the most romantic sights in Greece is that of flocks being herded through olive groves full of archaeological remains, as at Sparta in the Peloponnese.

Common poppy

Abandoned areas of cultivation soon revert to the wild. Larks and pipits feed and nest here and, in spring, wild flowers and butterflies are abundant.

Phrygana often covers bare slopes and rocky outcrops.

***Hilly landscapes** with stately cypress trees standing tall and dark against the steep slopes are closely associated with Greece's archaeological sites. These, including the Byzantine town of Mystrás above, are worth visiting for their wildlife alone and in particular the spring wild flowers that mix rare orchids with daisies, poppies and marigolds.*

Olive trees harbour numerous birds and insects among their silvery-green foliage.

Spring flowers such as poppies and irises have a brief but prolific season.

MAQUIS AND PHRYGANA

Maquis shrubland dominates the landscape in this view of Mycenae. It is a mixture of rockroses and aromatic herbs. The more barren *phrygana*, in the far distance, has clumps of spiny vetches.

***Olive groves** are found all over Greece at low altitudes; this one is at Argalastí in the Pílio. In spring, flowers grow in profusion in the shade of trees and attract a wealth of butterflies and beetles. Lizards hunt for insects in the twisted trunks that also provide nesting places for birds such as masked shrikes.*

Wetland areas, such as the margins of Lake Stymfalia in the Peloponnese, are often used for farming. Usually fairly dry underfoot, they are rich in birds, amphibians and plants.

Areas of *maquis* provide ideal habitats for nesting birds such as warblers, serins and hoopoes.

Between the shrubs in open areas of *maquis*, orchids, tulips and other native flowers appear in the spring.

WILD FLOWERS OF GREECE

Greece is blessed with an extraordinary wealth of flowering plants. At least 6,000 species grow in the country, quite a few of them found nowhere else in the world. The floral richness is due in part to the country's diversity of habitats, ranging from wetlands, coastal plains and lowland *maquis* to snow-capped mountain tops. The growing period for many plants is winter, the dampest, coolest season, and the flowering periods run from March to early June, and again in September. Coastal areas of the Peloponnese are perhaps the richest in wild flowers.

The wild gladiolus has several varieties that are among the most showy spring flowers.

The tassel hyacinth is aptly named for its appearance. It grows on open ground and flowers in May.

Cytinus hypocistus is a parasite plant found growing close to the base of colourful cistus bushes *(see below)*.

Sage-leaved cistus is widespread in *maquis* habitats. Its colourful flowers attract pollinating insects.

White asphodel is often seen growing on roadside verges in many parts of Greece. Tall spikes of white flowers appear from April to June.

ORCHIDS

One of the botanical highlights of a visit to Greece is the range of wild orchid species that can be found in bloom between late February and May. All have strangely shaped, and sometimes colourful, flowers whose purpose is to attract pollinating insects.

The four-spotted orchid has spots on the flower lip. A plant of open hillsides, it flowers in April.

The naked man orchid has a dense head of pale pinkish flowers and favours open woodland.

The Greek spider orchid looks more like a bumblebee than a spider. It is found in *maquis* in early spring.

THE HISTORY
OF GREECE

Alexander the Great, by the folk artist Theófilos

THE HISTORY of Greece is that of a nation, not of a land: the Greek idea of nationality is governed by language, religion, descent and customs, not so much by location. Early Greek history is the story of internal struggles, from the Mycenaean and Minoan cultures of the Bronze Age to the competing city-states that emerged in the 1st millennium BC.

After the defeat of the Greek army by Philip II of Macedon at Chaironeia in 338 BC, Greece soon became absorbed into Alexander the Great's new Asian empire. With the defeat of the Macedonians by the Romans in 168 BC, Greece became a province of Rome. As part of the Eastern Empire she was ruled from Constantinople and in the 11th century became a powerful element within the new, Orthodox Christian, Byzantine world.

After 1453, when Constantinople fell to the Ottomans, Greece disappeared altogether as a political entity. Eventually the realization that it was the democracy of Classical Athens which had inspired so many revolutions abroad gave the Greeks themselves the courage to rebel and, in 1821, to fight the Greek War of Independence. In 1832 the Great Powers that dominated Europe established a protectorate over Greece which marked the end of Ottoman rule. Although Greece re-established itself as a sizeable state, the "Great Idea" – the ambition to re-create Byzantium – ended in a disastrous defeat by Turkey in 1922.

The instability of the ensuing years was followed by the dictatorship of Metaxás and then by the war years of 1940–8, during which half a million people were killed and one in ten was made homeless. The present boundaries of the Greek state have only existed since 1948, when Italy returned the Dodecanese. Now, as an established democracy and member of the European Union, Greece's fortunes seem to have come full circle after 2,000 years of foreign rule.

A map of Greece from the 1595 Atlas of Abraham Ortelius called *Theatrum Orbis Terrarum*

◁ **The beginning of the 1821 Greek Revolution as shown in 1825 by L Dupré**

Prehistoric Greece

Mycenaean gold brooch

DURING THE BRONZE AGE three separate civilizations flourished in Greece: the Cycladic, during the 3rd millennium; the Minoan, based on Crete but with an influence that spread throughout the Aegean islands; and the Mycenaean, which was based on the mainland but spread to Crete in about 1450 BC when the Minoans went into decline. Both the Minoan and Mycenaean cultures found their peak in the Palace periods of the 2nd millennium when they were dominated by a centralized religion and bureaucracy.

PREHISTORIC GREECE

☐ *Areas settled in the Bronze Age*

Neolithic Head *(3000 BC)*
This figure was found on Alónnisos in the Sporades. It probably represents a fertility goddess who was worshipped by farmers to ensure a good harvest. These figures indicate a certain stability in early communities.

The town is unwalled, showing that inhabitants did not fear attack.

Cycladic Figurine
Marble statues such as this, produced in the Bronze Age from about 2800 to 2300 BC, have been found in a number of tombs in the Cyclades.

Multistorey houses

Minoan "Bathtub" Sarcophagus
This type of coffin, dating to 1400 BC, is found only in Minoan art. It was probably used for a high-status burial.

TIMELINE

200,000 BC	5000 BC	4000 BC	3000 BC	2000
	7000 Neolithic farmers in northern Greece	**3200** Beginnings of Bronze Age cultures in Cyclades and Crete	**2000** Arrival of first Greek-speakers on mainland Greece	
200,000 Evidence of Palaeolithic civilization in northern Greece and Thessaly		*"Frying Pan" vessel from Sýros (2500–2000 BC)*	**2800–2300** Kéros-Sýros culture flourishes in Cyclades	
			2000 Building of palaces begins in Crete, initiating First Palace period	

Mycenaean Death Mask

Large amounts of worked gold were discovered at wealthy Mycenae, the city of Agamemnon. Masks like this were laid over the faces of the dead.

Forested hills

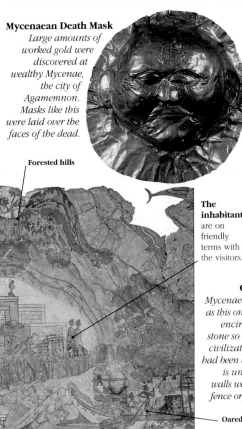

The inhabitants are on friendly terms with the visitors.

WHERE TO SEE PREHISTORIC GREECE

The Museum of Cycladic Art in Athens *(see pp74–5)* has Greece's leading collection of Cycladic figurines. The remains at Mycenae are extensive *(pp178–80)* and the museum at Náfplio *(p182)* displays finds from the site, as does the National Archaeological Museum, Athens *(pp68–71)*. Excavations at so-called Nestor's Palace *(p201)* uncovered tablets written in Linear B script. These earliest examples of Greek language can be seen in the museum at nearby Chóra, together with frescoes and pottery from the palace.

Cyclopean Walls

Mycenaean citadels, such as this one at Tiryns, were encircled by walls of stone so large that later civilizations believed they had been built by giants. It is unclear whether the walls were used for defence or just to impress.

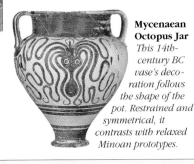

Oared sailing ships

MINOAN SEA SCENE

The wall paintings on the island of Santoríni were preserved by the volcanic eruption at the end of the 16th century BC. This section shows ships departing from a coastal town. In contrast to the warlike Mycenaeans, Minoan art reflects a more stable community which dominated the Aegean through trade, not conquest.

Mycenaean Octopus Jar

This 14th-century BC vase's decoration follows the shape of the pot. Restrained and symmetrical, it contrasts with relaxed Minoan prototypes.

1750–1700 Start of Second Palace period and golden age of Minoan culture in Crete	**1525** Volcanic eruption on Santoríni devastates the region	**1250–1200** Probable destruction of Troy, after abduction of Helen *(see p54)* **1450** Mycenaeans take over Knosós; use of Linear B script	*Helen of Troy*
1800 BC	**1600 BC**	**1400 BC**	**1200 BC**
1730 Destruction of Minoan palaces; end of First Palace period		*Minoan figurine of a snake goddess, 1500 BC*	**1200** Collapse of Mycenaean culture
1600 Beginning of high period of Mycenaean prosperity and dominance			**1370–50** Palace of Knosós on Crete destroyed for second time

The Dark Ages and Archaic Period

Silver coin from Athens

IN ABOUT 1200 BC, Greece entered a period of darkness. There was widespread poverty, the population decreased and many skills were lost. A cultural revival in about 800 BC accompanied the emergence of the city-states across Greece and inspired new styles of warfare, art and politics. Greek colonies were established as far away as the Black Sea, present-day Syria, North Africa and the western Mediterranean. Greece was defined by where Greeks lived.

Koúros *(530 BC)*
Kouroi *were early monumental male nude statues (see p70). Idealized representations rather than portraits, they were inspired by Egyptian statues, from which they take their frontal, forward-stepping pose.*

Bronze breastplate

MEDITERRANEAN AREA, 479 BC

☐ *Areas of Greek influence*

The double flute player kept the men marching in time.

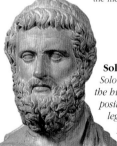

Solon *(640–558 BC)*
Solon was appointed to the highest magisterial position in Athens. His legal, economic and political reforms heralded democracy.

Bronze greaves protected the legs.

HOPLITE WARRIORS

The "Chigi" vase from Corinth, dating to about 750 BC, is one of the earliest clear depictions of the new style of warfare that evolved at that period. This required rigorously trained and heavily armed infantrymen called hoplites to fight in a massed formation or phalanx. The rise of the city-state may be linked to the spirit of equality felt by citizen hoplites fighting for their own community.

TIMELINE

Vase fragment showing bands of distinctive geometric line patterns

900 Appearance of first Geometric pottery

1100 BC	1000 BC	900 BC
1100 Migrations of different peoples throughout the Greek world	**1000–850** Formation of the Homeric kingdoms	

6th-Century Vase
This bowl (krater)
*for mixing wine
and water at
elegant feasts is an
early example of the
art of vase painting.
It depicts mythological
and heroic scenes.*

WHERE TO SEE ARCHAIC GREECE

Examples of *koúroi* can be found in the National Archaeological Museum *(see pp68–71)* and in the Acropolis Museum *(p97)*, both in Athens. The National Archaeological Museum also houses the national collection of Greek Geometric, red-figure and black-figure vases. The first victory over the Persians in 490 BC was commemorated by the mound of Athenian dead which still dominates the plain at Marathon *(p145)*. The museum at Sparta *(p189)* contains a bust of Leonidas, the Spartan king, who with his 300 hoplite soldiers was massacred by the Persians at Thermopylae in 480 BC.

Spears were used for thrusting.

Bronze helmets for protection

The phalanxes shoved and pushed, aiming to maintain an unbroken shield wall, a successful new technique.

Gorgon's head decoration

Characteristic round shields

Hunter Returning Home *(500 BC)*
*Hunting for hares, deer,
or wild boar was an
aristocratic sport
pursued by Greek nobles
on foot with dogs, as
depicted on this cup.*

Darius I *(ruled 521–486 BC)*
*This relief from Persepolis shows
the Persian king who tried to
conquer the Greek mainland,
but was defeated at the battle
of Marathon in 490.*

---

776 Traditional date for the first Olympic Games

675 Lykourgos initiates austere reforms in Sparta

600 First Doric columns built at Temple of Hera, Olympia

Doric capital

490 Athenians defeat Persians at Marathon

800 BC	700 BC	600 BC	500 BC

750–700 Homer records epic tales of the *Iliad* and *Odyssey*

770 Greeks start founding colonies in Italy, Egypt and elsewhere

Spartan votive figurine

546 Persians gain control over Ionian Greeks; Athens flourishes under the tyrant, Peisistratos, and his sons

630 Poetess Sappho writing in Lésvos

480 Athens destroyed by Persians who defeat Spartans at Thermopylae; Greek victory at Salamis

479 Persians annihilated at Plataiaí by Athenians, Spartans and allies

Classical Greece

Trading amphora

THE CLASSICAL PERIOD has always been considered the high point of Greek civilization. Around 150 years of exceptional creativity in thinking, writing, theatre and the arts produced the great tragedians Aeschylus, Sophocles and Euripides as well as the great philosophical thinkers Socrates, Plato and Aristotle. This was also a time of warfare and bloodshed, however. The Peloponnesian War, which pitted the city-state of Athens and her allies against the city-state of Sparta and her allies, dominated the 5th century BC. In the 4th century Sparta, Athens and Thebes struggled for power only to be ultimately defeated by Philip II of Macedon in 338 BC.

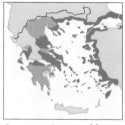

CLASSICAL GREECE, 440 BC
- Athens and her allies
- Sparta and her allies

Theatre used in
Pythian Games

Temple of
Apollo

Siphnian
Treasury

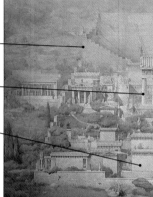

Fish Shop
This 4th-century BC Greek painted vase comes from Cefalù in Sicily. Large parts of the island were inhabited by Greeks who were bound by a common culture, religion and language.

Perikles
This great democratic leader built up the Greek navy and masterminded the extensive building programme in Athens between the 440s and 420s, including the Acropolis temples.

THE SANCTUARY OF DELPHI

The sanctuary *(see pp228–9)*, shown in this 1894 reconstruction, reached the peak of its political influence in the 5th and 4th centuries BC. Of central importance was the Oracle of Apollo, whose utterances influenced the decisions of city-states such as Athens and Sparta. Rich gifts dedicated to the god were placed by the states in treasuries that lined the Sacred Way.

TIMELINE

Detail of the Parthenon frieze

462 Ephialtes's reforms pave the way for radical democracy in Athens

431–404 Peloponnesian War, ending with the fall of Athens and start of 33-year period of Spartan dominance

c.424 Death of Herodotus, historian of the Persian Wars

475 BC	450 BC	425 BC

478 With the formation of the Delian League, Athens takes over leadership of Greek cities

451–429 Perikles rises to prominence in Athens and launches a lavish building programme

447 Construction of the Parthenon begins

Bust of Herodotus, probably of Hellenistic origin

Gold Oak Wreath from Vergína
By the mid-4th century BC, Philip II of Macedon dominated the Greek world through diplomacy and warfare. This wreath comes from his tomb.

WHERE TO SEE CLASSICAL GREECE

Athens is dominated by the Acropolis and its religious buildings, including the Parthenon, erected as part of Perikles's mid 5th-century BC building programme *(see pp94–9)*. The Marmaria, just outside the sanctuary at Delphi, features the remains of the unique circular *tholos* *(p230)*. In the Peloponnese, the town of Messene dates from 396 BC *(p201)*; the best-preserved theatre is at Epidaurus *(pp184–5)*. Philip II's tomb can be seen at Vergína in Macedonia *(p242)*.

Votive of the Rhodians

Stoa of the Athenians

Sacred Way

Athenian Treasury

Slave Boy *(400 BC)*
Slaves were fundamental to the Greek economy and used for all types of work. Many slaves were foreign; this boot boy came from as far as Africa.

Athena Lemnia
This Roman copy of a statue by Pheidias (c.490–c.430 BC), the sculptor-in-charge at the Acropolis, depicts the goddess protector of Athens in an ideal rather than realistic way, typical of the Classical style in art.

387 Plato founds Academy in Athens

Sculpture of Plato

337 Foundation of the the League of Corinth legitimizes Philip II's control over the Greek city-states

359 Philip II becomes King of Macedon

400 BC | **375 BC** | **350 BC**

399 Trial and execution of Socrates

371 Sparta defeated by Thebes at Battle of Leuktra, heralding a decade of Theban dominance in the area

338 Greeks defeated by Philip II of Macedon at Battle of Chaironeia

336 Philip II is assassinated at Aigai and is succeeded by his son, Alexander

Hellenistic Greece

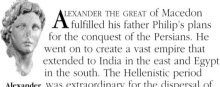

ALEXANDER THE GREAT of Macedon fulfilled his father Philip's plans for the conquest of the Persians. He went on to create a vast empire that extended to India in the east and Egypt in the south. The Hellenistic period was extraordinary for the dispersal of Greek language, religion and culture throughout the territories conquered by Alexander. It lasted from after Alexander's death in 323 BC until the Romans began to dismantle his empire, early in the 2nd century BC. For Greece, Macedonian domination was replaced by that of Rome in AD 168.

Alexander the Great

Relief of Hero-Worship *(c.200 BC)*
The worship of heroes after death was a feature of Greek religion. Alexander, however, was worshipped as a god in his lifetime.

Péla was the birthplace of Alexander and capital of Macedon.

The Mausoleum of Halicarnassus was one of the Seven Wonders of the Ancient World.

Issus, in modern Turkey, was the site of Alexander's victory over the Persian army in 333 BC.

BLACK SEA

• Péla

• Athens

ASIA MINOR

Mausoleum of Halicarnassus

• Issus

MEDITERRANEAN SEA

Alexander Defeats Darius III
This Pompeiian mosaic shows the Persian leader overwhelmed at Issus in 333 BC. Macedonian troops are shown carrying their highly effective long pikes.

Ammon •

Lighthouse at Alexandria

EGYPT

Ishtar Gate Babylon

Alexander died in Babylon in 323 BC.

ARABIA

RED SEA

The Ammon oracle declared Alexander to be divine.

Terracotta Statue
This 2nd-century BC statue of two women gossiping is typical of a Hellenistic interest in private rather than public individuals.

Alexandria, founded by Alexander, replaced Athens as the centre of Greek culture.

KEY

– – – Alexander's route

▨ Alexander's empire

▨ Dependent regions

TIMELINE

333 Alexander the Great defeats the Persian king, Darius III, and declares himself king of Asia

323 Death of Alexander, and of Diogenes

301 Battle of Ipsus, between Alexander's rival successors, leads to the break-up of his empire into three kingdoms

268–261 Chremonidean War, ending with the capitulation of Athens to Macedon

325 BC	300 BC		275 BC	250 BC

322 Death of Aristotle

331 Alexander founds Alexandria after conquering Egypt

287–275 "Pyrrhic victory" of King Pyrros of Epirus who defeated the Romans in Italy but suffered heavy losses

Diogenes, the Hellenistic philosopher

Fusing Eastern and Western Religion
This plaque from Afghanistan shows the Greek goddess Nike, and the Asian goddess Cybele, in a chariot pulled by lions.

Susa, capital of the Persian Empire, was captured in 331 BC. A mass wedding of Alexander's captains to Asian brides was held in 324 BC.

Alexander chose his wife, Roxane, from among Sogdian captives in 327 BC.

CASPIAN SEA

Roxane
• Alexandropolis

SOGDIANI

• Taxil

BACTRIA

PERSIA

• Susa

War elephant

Sculpture from Persepolis

Beas

INDIA

GEDROSIA

PERSIAN GULF

ARABIAN SEA

Battle elephants were used against the Indian King Poros in 326 BC.

Alexander's army turned back at the River Beas.

The Persian religious centre of Persepolis, in modern Iran, fell to Alexander in 330 BC.

Alexander's army suffered heavy losses in the Gedrosia desert.

WHERE TO SEE HELLENISTIC GREECE

The royal palace at Pélla *(see p243)*, capital of Macedon and birthplace of Alexander, and the palace of Palatítsia *(p242)* are exceptional. Pélla has outstanding mosaics, one of which depicts Alexander. Goldwork and other finds are in the museum at Pélla and the Archaeological Museum at Thessaloníki *(pp246–7)*. In Athens, the Stoa of Attalos *(pp90–91)* in the Greek Agora was given by Attalos of Pergamon (ruled 159 to 138 BC). The Tower of the Winds *(pp86–7)* in the Roman Agora, built by the Macedonian astronomer Andronikos Kyrrestes, incorporates a water clock.

ALEXANDER THE GREAT'S EMPIRE

In forming his empire Alexander covered huge distances. After defeating the Persians in Asia he moved to Egypt, then returned to Asia to pursue Darius, and then his murderers, into Bactria. In 326 his troops revolted in India and refused to go on. Alexander died in 323 in Babylon.

The Death of Archimedes
Archimedes was the leading Hellenistic scientist and mathematician. This mosaic from Renaissance Italy shows his murder in 212 BC by a Roman.

227 Colossus of Rhodes destroyed by earthquake

Colossus of Rhodes

197 Romans defeat Philip V of Macedon and declare Greece liberated

146 Romans sack Corinth and Greece becomes a province of Rome

225 BC	200 BC	175 BC	150 BC

222 Macedon crushes Sparta

217 Peace of Náfpaktos: a call for the Greeks to settle their differences before "the cloud in the west" (Rome) settles over them

168 Macedonians defeated by Romans at Pydna

Roman coin commemorating Roman victory over the Macedonians in 196 BC

Roman Greece

ROMAN PROVINCES, AD 211

AFTER THE ROMANS GAINED final control of Greece with the sack of Corinth in 146 BC, Greece became the cultural centre of the Roman Empire. The Roman nobility sent their sons to be educated in the schools of philosophy in Athens *(see p57)*. The end of the Roman civil wars between leading Roman statesmen was played out on Greek soil, finishing in the Battle of Actium in Thessaly in 31 BC. In AD 323 the Emperor Constantine founded the new eastern capital of Constantinople; the empire was later divided into the Greek-speaking East and the Latin-speaking West.

Mark Antony

Mithridates
In a bid to extend his territory, this ruler of Pontus, on the Black Sea, led the resistance to Roman rule in 88 BC. He was forced to make peace three years later.

Bema, or raised platform, where St Paul spoke

Roman basilica

Bouleuterion

Springs of Peirene, the source of water

Notitia Dignitatum *(AD 395) As part of the Roman Empire, Greece was split into several provinces. The proconsul of the province of Achaïa used this insignia.*

RECONSTRUCTION OF ROMAN CORINTH

Corinth *(see pp162–6)* was refounded and largely rebuilt by Julius Caesar in 46 BC, becoming the capital of the Roman province of Achaïa. The Romans built the forum, covered theatre and basilicas. St Paul visited the city in AD 50–51, working as a tent maker.

Baths of Eurycles

TIMELINE

A coin of Cleopatra, Queen of Egypt

49–31 BC Rome's civil wars end with the defeat of Mark Antony and Cleopatra at Actium, in Greece

AD 49–54 St Paul preaches Christianity in Greece

AD 124–131 Emperor Hadrian oversees huge building programme in Athens

| 100 BC | | AD 1 | | AD 10 |

86 BC Roman commander, Sulla, captures Athens

46 BC Corinth refounded as Roman colony

St Paul preaching

AD 66–7 Emperor Nero tours Greece

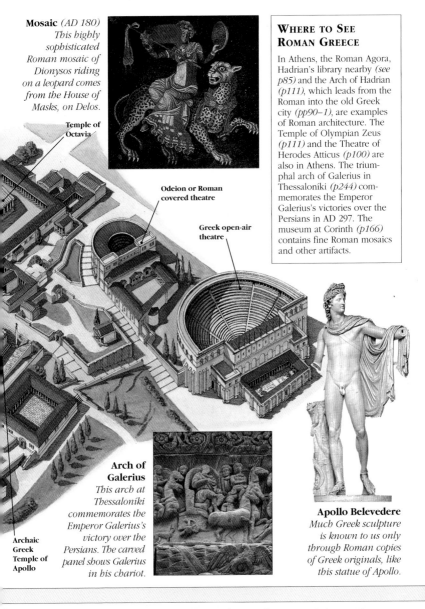

Mosaic *(AD 180)*
This highly sophisticated Roman mosaic of Dionysos riding on a leopard comes from the House of Masks, on Delos.

Temple of Octavia

Odeion or Roman covered theatre

Greek open-air theatre

Archaic Greek Temple of Apollo

WHERE TO SEE ROMAN GREECE

In Athens, the Roman Agora, Hadrian's library nearby *(see p85)* and the Arch of Hadrian *(p111)*, which leads from the Roman into the old Greek city *(pp90–1)*, are examples of Roman architecture. The Temple of Olympian Zeus *(p111)* and the Theatre of Herodes Atticus *(p100)* are also in Athens. The triumphal arch of Galerius in Thessaloníki *(p244)* commemorates the Emperor Galerius's victories over the Persians in AD 297. The museum at Corinth *(p166)* contains fine Roman mosaics and other artifacts.

Arch of Galerius
This arch at Thessaloníki commemorates the Emperor Galerius's victory over the Persians. The carved panel shows Galerius in his chariot.

Apollo Belevedere
Much Greek sculpture is known to us only through Roman copies of Greek originals, like this statue of Apollo.

170 Pausanias completes guide to Greece for Roman travellers

267 Goths pillage Athens

323 Constantine becomes sole emperor of Roman Empire and establishes his capital in Constantinople

395 Goths devastate Athens and Peloponnese

390 Emperor Theodosius I makes Christianity state religion

AD 200   **AD 300**

Coin of the Roman Emperor Galerius

293 Under Emperor Galerius, Thessaloníki becomes second city to Constantinople

393 Olympic games banned

395 Death of Theodosius I; formal division of Roman Empire into Latin West and Byzantine East

Byzantine and Crusader Greece

Byzantine court dress arm band

U NDER THE BYZANTINE EMPIRE, which at the end of the 4th century succeeded the old Eastern Roman Empire, Greece became Orthodox in religion and was split into administrative *themes*. When the capital, Constantinople, fell to the Crusaders in 1204 Greece was again divided, mostly between the Venetians and the Franks. Constantinople and Mystrás were recovered by the Byzantine Greeks in 1261, but the Turks' capture of Constantinople in 1453 was a significant part of the demise of the Byzantine Empire. It left a legacy of hundreds of churches and a wealth of religious art.

BYZANTINE GREECE IN THE 10TH CENTURY

Chapel

Watch-tower of Tsimiskís

Refectory

GREAT LAVRA
This monastery is the earliest (AD 963) and largest of the religious complexes on Mount Athos *(see pp252–4)*. Many parts of it have been rebuilt, but its appearance remains essentially Byzantine. The monasteries became important centres of learning and religious art.

Two-Headed Eagle
In the Byzantine world, the emperor was also patriarch of the church, a dual role represented in this pendant of a two-headed eagle.

Defence of Thessaloníki
The fall of Thessaloníki to the Saracens in AD 904 was a blow to the Byzantine Empire. Many towns in Greece were heavily fortified against attack from this time.

TIMELINE

578–86 Avars and Slavs invade Greece

Gold solidus of the Byzantine Empress Irene, who ruled AD 797–802

400	600	800

529 Aristotle's and Plato's schools of philosophy close as Christian culture supplants Classical thought

680 Bulgars cross Danube and establish empire in northern Greece

726 Iconoclasm introduced by Pope Leo III (abandoned in 843)

841 Parthenon becomes a cathedral

Constantine the Great

The first eastern emperor to recognize Christianity, Constantine founded the city of Constantinople in AD 324. Here he is shown with his mother, Helen.

Cypress tree of Agios Athanásios

Christ Pantokrátor

This 14th-century fresco of Christ as ruler of the world is in the Byzantine city and monastic centre of Mystrás.

WHERE TO SEE BYZANTINE AND CRUSADER GREECE

In Athens, both the Benáki (pp78–9) and the Byzantine (p76) museums contain sculpture, icons, metalwork and textiles. The medieval city of Mystrás (pp192–3) has a castle, palaces, houses and monasteries. The churches of Thessaloníki (p248), and the monasteries of Dafní (pp152–3) and Osios Loúkas (pp222–3) contain fine Byzantine mosaics and frescoes, as do the monasteries of Mount Athos (pp252–4). Chlemoútsi (p169), built in 1223, is one of Greece's oldest Frankish castles. There are important fortresses at Acrocorinth (p166) and Monemvasía (pp186–8).

Chapel of Agios Athanásios, founder of Great Lávra

Combined library and treasury

Fortified walls

The katholikón, the main church in Great Lávra, has the most magnificent post-Byzantine murals on Mount Athos.

1054 Patriarch of Constantinople and Pope Leo IX excommunicate each other

Frankish Chlemoútsi Castle

1081–1149 Normans invade Greek islands and mainland

1354 Ottoman Turks enter Europe, via southern Italy and Greece

1390–1450 Turks gain power over much of mainland Greece

1000	1200	1400

Basil the Bulgar Slayer, Byzantine emperor (lived 956–1025)

1204 Crusaders sack Constantinople. Break-up of Byzantine Empire as result of occupation by Franks and Venetians

1210 Venetians win control over Crete

1261 Start of intellectual and artistic flowering of Mystrás; Constantinople re-occupied by Byzantines

1389 Venetians in control of much of Greece and the islands

Venetian and Ottoman Greece

Venetian lion of St Mark

FOLLOWING THE OTTOMANS' momentous capture of Constantinople in 1453, and their conquest of almost all the remaining Greek territory by 1460, the Greek state effectively ceased to exist for the next 350 years. Although the city became the capital of the vast Ottoman Empire, it remained the principal centre of Greek population and the focus of Greek dreams of resurgence. The small Greek population of what today is modern Greece languished in an impoverished and underpopulated backwater, but even there rebellious bands of brigands and private militias were formed. The Ionian Islands, Crete and a few coastal enclaves were seized for long periods by the Venetians – an experience more intrusive than the inefficient tolerance of the Ottomans, but one which left a rich cultural and architectural legacy.

GREECE IN 1493

▨ Areas occupied by Venetians

▧ Areas occupied by Ottomans

Battle of Lepanto *(1571)*
The Christian fleet, under Don John of Austria, decisively defeated the Ottomans off Náfpaktos, halting their advance westwards (see p225).

ARRIVAL OF TURKISH PRINCE CEM ON RHODES

Prince Cem, Ottoman rebel and son of Mehmet II, fled to Rhodes in 1481 and was welcomed by the Christian Knights of St John. In 1522, however, Rhodes fell to the Ottomans after a siege.

Cretan Painting
This 15th-century icon is typical of the style developed by Greek artists in the School of Crete, active until the Ottomans took Crete in 1669.

TIMELINE

1453 Mehmet II captures Constantinople which is renamed Istanbul and made capital of the Ottoman Empire

1503 Ottoman Turks win control of the Peloponnese apart from Monemvasía

1571 Venetian and Spanish fleet defeats Ottoman Turks at the Battle of Lepanto

1500	1550	1600

1460 Turks capture Mystrás

1456 Ottoman Turks occupy Athens

1522 The Knights of St John forced to cede Rhodes to the Ottomans

Cretan chain mail armour from the 16th century

Shipping

Greek merchants traded throughout the Ottoman Empire. By 1800 there were merchant colonies in Constantinople and as far afield as London and Odessa. This 19th-century embroidery shows the Turkish influence on Greek decorative arts.

The Knights of St John defied the Turks until 1522.

The massive fortifications eventually succumbed to Turkish artillery.

The Knights supported Turkish rebel, Prince Cem.

WHERE TO SEE VENETIAN AND OTTOMAN ARCHITECTURE

Náfplio contains many examples of the Venetian presence, especially the Naval Warehouse (now a museum) and the Palamídi fortress (*see p183*). Following a pattern familiar throughout the Balkan states, enormous efforts were made after Independence to remove or disguise all Ottoman buildings. However, in Athens there are small but well-preserved Ottoman quarters in the Pláka district, and the Tzistarákis Mosque (now the Ceramics Museum, *p86*) is also Ottoman. The White Tower in Thessaloníki (*p244*) was built by the Turks in the 15th century. In Kavála (*p255*), there is an aqueduct built in the reign of Suleiman the Magnificent, and in Ioánnina (*p210*) the Aslan Pasha Mosque.

Dinner at a Greek House in 1801
Nearly four centuries of Ottoman rule profoundly affected Greek culture, ethnic composition and patterns of everyday life. Greek cuisine incorporates Turkish dishes still found thoughout the old Ottoman Empire.

1687 Parthenon seriously damaged during Venetian artillery attack on Turkish magazine

1715 Turks reconquer the Peloponnese

Ali Pasha (1741–1822), a governor of the Ottoman Empire

1814 Britain gains possession of Ionian Islands

1650	1700	1750	1800

Parthenon blown up

1684 Venetians reconquer the Peloponnese

1778 Ali Pasha becomes Vizier of Ioánnina and establishes powerful state in Albania and northern Greece

1801 Frieze on Parthenon removed by Lord Elgin

1814 Foundation of *Filikí Etaireía*, Greek liberation movement

The Making of Modern Greece

Flag with the symbols of the *Filikí Etaireía*

THE GREEK WAR of Independence marked the overthrow of the Ottomans and the start of the "Great Idea", an ambitious project to bring all Greek people under one flag *(énosis)*. The plans for expansion were initially successful, and during the 19th century the Greeks succeeded in doubling their national territory and reasserting Greek sovereignty over many of the islands. However, an attempt to take Asia Minor by force after World War I ended in disaster. In 1922 millions of Greeks were expelled from Smyrna in Turkish Anatolia, ending thousands of years of Greek presence in Asia Minor.

THE EMERGING GREEK STATE

- Greece in 1832
- Areas gained 1832–1923

Klephts (mountain brigands) were the basis of the Independence movement.

Massacre at Chíos
This detail of Delacroix's shocking painting Scènes de Massacres de Scio *shows the events of 1822, when Turks took savage revenge for an earlier killing of Muslims.*

Weapons were family heirlooms or donated by philhellenes.

Declaration of the Constitution in Athens
Greece's Neo-Classical parliament building in Athens was the site of the Declaration of the Constitution in 1843. It was built as the Royal Palace for Greece's first monarch, King Otto, during the 1830s.

TIMELINE

1824 The poet Lord Byron dies of a fever at Mesolóngi

1831 President Kapodístrias assassinated

1832 Great Powers establish protectorate over Greece and appoint Otto, Bavarian prince, as king

1834 Athens replaces Náfplio as capital

German archaeologist Heinrich Schliemann

1830	1840	1850	1860	1870

1827 Battle of Navaríno

1828 Ioánnis Kapodístrias becomes first President of Greece

King Otto (ruled 1832–62)

1862 Revolution drives King Otto from Greece

1874 Heinrich Schliemann begins excavation of Mycenae

1821 Greek flag of independence raised on 25 March; Greeks massacre Turks at Tripolitsá in Morea

1864 New constitution makes Greece a "crowned democracy"; Greek Orthodoxy made the state religion

Life in Athens
By 1836 urban Greeks still wore a mixture of Greek traditional and Western dress. The Ottoman legacy had not totally disappeared and is visible in the fez worn by men.

FLAG RAISING OF **1821** REVOLUTION
In 1821, the Greek secret society *Filikí Etaireía* was behind a revolt by Greek officers which led to anti-Turk uprisings throughout the Peloponnese. Tradition credits Archbishop Germanós of Pátra with raising the rebel flag near Kalávryta *(see p168)* on 25 March. The struggle for independence had begun.

WHERE TO SEE 19TH-CENTURY GREECE
Independence was proclaimed at the Moní Agías Lávras, near Kalávryta *(see p168)*. Lord Byron died at Mesolóngi *(p225)*. Ioánnis Kapodístrias was assassinated at the church of Agios Spyrídon in Náfplio *(p182)*. Pýlos is the site of the battle of Navaríno *(p200)*.

Corinth Canal
This spectacular link between the Aegean and Ionian seas opened in 1893 (see p167).

Elefthérios Venizélos
This great Cretan politician and advocate of liberal democracy doubled Greek territory during the Balkan Wars (1912–13) and joined the Allies in World War I.

1893 Opening of Corinth Canal

1896 First Olympics of modern era, held in Athens

1908 Crete united with Greece

1919 Greece launches offensive in Asia Minor

1917 King Constantine resigns; Greece joins World War I

1922 Turkish burning of Smyrna signals end of the "Great Idea"

1880	1890	1900	1910	1920

Spyrídon Loúis, Marathon winner at the first modern Olympics

1899 Arthur Evans begins excavations at Knosós

1912–13 Greece extends its borders during the Balkan Wars

1920 Treaty of Sèvres gives Greece huge gains in territory

1923 Population exchange agreed between Greece and Turkey at Treaty of Lausanne. Greece loses previous gains

Twentieth-Century Greece

THE YEARS after the 1922 defeat by Turkey were terrible ones for Greek people. The influx of refugees contributed to the political instability of the interwar years. The dictatorship of Metaxás was followed by invasion in 1940, then Italian, German and Bulgarian occupation and, finally, Civil War between 1946 and 1949, with its legacy of division. After experiencing the Cyprus problem of the 1950s and the military dictatorship of 1967 to 1974, Greece is now an established democracy and expected to become a member of the European Economic and Monetary Union.

1947 Internationally acclaimed Greek artist, Giánnis Tsaroúchis, holds his first exhibition of set designs, in the Romvos Gallery, Athens

1938 Death of sculptor Giannoúlis Chalepás, best known for his *Sleeping Girl* funerary statue

1946 Government institutes "White Terror" against Communists

1945 Níkos Kazantzákis publishes *Zorba the Greek*, later made into a film

1958 USSR threatens Greece with economic sanctions if NATO missiles installed

1957 Mosaics found by chance at Philip II's 300 BC palace at Pélla

1925	1935	1945	1955
1925	1935	1945	1955

1933 Death of Greek poet, Constantine (C P) Cavafy

1951 Greece enters NATO

1955 Greek Cypriots start campaign of violence in Cyprus against British rule

1948 Dodecanese becomes part of Greece

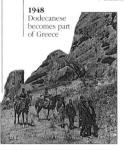

1932 Aristotle Onassis purchases six freight ships, the start of his shipping empire

1939 Greece declares neutrality at start of World War II

1946–9 Civil War between Greek government and the Communists who take to the mountains

1925 Mános Chatzidákis, who wrote music for the film *Never on Sunday*, is born

1944 Churchill visits Athens to show his support for Greek government against Communist Resistance

1960 Cyprus declared independent

OI HPΩIΔEΣ TOY 1940

1940 Italy invades Greece. Greek soldiers defend northern Greece. Greece enters World War II

1963 Geórgios Papandréou's centre-left government voted into power

1981 Melína Merkoúri appointed Minister of Culture. Start of campaign to restore Elgin Marbles to Greece

1993 Andréas Papandréou wins Greek general election for the third time

1973 University students in Athens rebel against dictatorship and are crushed by military forces. Start of decline in power of dictatorship

1994 Because of the choking smog *(néfos)* central Athens introduces traffic restrictions

1974 Cyprus is partitioned after Turkish invasion

1967 Right-wing colonels form Junta, forcing King Constantine into exile

1975 Death of Aristotle Onassis

1988 Eight million visitors to Greece; tourism continues to expand

1998 Karamanlís dies. Kostis Stefanopoulos succeeds him

1965	1975	1985	1995	2000

1965	1975	1985	1995	2000

1990 New Democracy voted into power; Konstantínos Karamanlís becomes President

2002 Euro becomes sole legal currency

1971 Nobel poet laureate George Seféris dies

1974 Fall of Junta; Konstantínos Karamanlís elected Prime Minister

1973 Greek bishops give their blessing to the short-lived presidency of Colonel Papadópoulos

1981 Andréas Papandréou's left-wing PASOK party forms first Greek Socialist government

1997 Athens is awarded the 2004 Olympics

1996 Andréas Papandréou dies; Kóstas Simítis succeeds him

1994 European leaders meet in Corfu under Greek presidency of the EU

ATHENS AND MAINLAND GREECE THROUGH THE YEAR

May Day wild flower wreath

REDOMINANTLY RURAL, Greece is deeply attached to its locally produced food and wine, and chapels dotting the countryside serve as the focus for culinary, as well as religious, celebrations. Festivals of the Orthodox Church are deeply identified with Greekness, no more so than on 25 March, a date which commemorates both the Feast of the Annunciation and the start of the Independence uprising in 1821. Summer festivals are celebrated widely in rural villages, and expatriate Greeks return from across the globe. Organized arts events are a more recent phenomenon, paralleling the rise of tourism.

SPRING

SPRING is a glorious time in Greece. The lowland landscape, parched for much of the year, luxuriates in a carpet of green, and wild flowers abound. But the weather does not stabilize until late spring, with rainy or blustery days common in March and April. Artichokes ripen in March, and May sees the first strawberries. The fishing season lasts to the end of May, overlapping with the start of the tourist season. Spring festivities focus on Easter.

MARCH

Apókries, Carnival Sunday *(first Sun before Lent)*. Carnivals take place for three weeks leading up to this climax of pre-Lenten festivities. There are parades and costume balls in many large cities, and the port of Pátra *(see p169)* hosts one of the most exuberant celebrations.
Katharí Deftéra, Clean Monday *(immediately after "Cheese Sunday" – seven Sundays before Easter)*. Kites are flown in the countryside.
Independence Day and **Evangelismós** *(25 Mar)*. A national holiday, with parades and dances nationwide celebrating the 1821 revolt against the Ottoman Empire. The religious festival, one of the most important for the Orthodox Church, marks the Angel Gabriel's announcement to the Virgin Mary that she was to become the Holy Mother.

25 March, Independence Day

CELEBRATING EASTER IN GREECE

Greek Orthodox Easter can fall up to three weeks either side of Western Easter. It is the most important religious festival in Greece and Holy Week is a time for Greek families to reunite. It is also a good time to visit Greece, to see the processions and church services and to sample the Easter food. The ceremony and symbolism is a direct link with Greece's Byzantine past, as well as with earlier and more primitive beliefs. The festivities reach a climax at midnight on Easter Saturday. As priests intone "Christ is risen", fireworks are lit, the explosions ushering in a Sunday devoted to feasting, music and dance. Smaller, more isolated towns, such as Andrítsaina and Koróni in the Peloponnese, and Polýgyros (the capital of Chalkidikí), are particularly worth visiting during Holy Week for the Friday and Saturday night services.

Priests in their richly embroidered Easter robes

Christ's bier, decorated with flowers and containing His effigy, is carried in solemn procession through the streets at dusk on Good Friday.

Candle lighting takes place at the end of the Easter Saturday mass. In pitch darkness, a single flame is used to light the candles held by worshippers.

Banners raised during a workers' May Day rally in Athens

APRIL

Megáli Evdomáda, Holy Week *(Apr or May)*, including *Kyriakí ton Vaḯon* (Palm Sunday), *Megáli Pémpti* (Maundy Thursday), *Megáli Paraskeví* (Good Friday), *Megálo Savváto* (Easter Saturday), and the most important date in the Orthodox calendar, *Páscha* (Easter Sunday).

Agios Geórgios, St George *(23 Apr)*. One of the most important feast days in the Orthodox calendar, commemorating the patron saint of shepherds, and traditionally marking the start of the grazing season. Celebrations are nationwide, and are particularly festive at Aráchova, near Delphi *(see p221)*.

MAY

Protomagiá, May Day, *(1 May)*. Also known as Labour Day, this is given over to a national holiday. Traditionally, families go to the countryside and pick wild flowers, which are made

Firewalkers in a Macedonian village, 21 May

into wreaths with garlic. These are then hung on doors, balconies, fishing boats and even car bonnets to ward off evil. In major towns and cities across the country, there are also parades and workers' rallies to mark Labour Day, usually led by the Communist Party.

Agios Konstantínos kai Agía Eléni *(21 May)*. A celebration throughout Greece for Constantine and his mother, Helen, the first Orthodox Byzantine rulers *(see p37)*. Firewalking ceremonies may be seen in some Macedonian villages.

Análipsi, Ascension *(40 days after Easter; usually late May)*. This is another important religious feast day.

Easter biscuits celebrate the end of Lent. Another Easter dish, magerítsa *soup, is made of lamb's innards and is eaten in the early hours of Easter Sunday.*

The procession of candles *in the very early hours of Easter Day, here at Lykavittós Hill in Athens, celebrates Christ's resurrection.*

Egg loaves, made of sweet plaited dough, contain eggs with shells dyed red to symbolize the blood of Christ. Red eggs are also given separately as presents.

Lamb roasting *is traditionally done in the open air on giant spits over charcoal, for lunch on Easter Sunday. The first retsina wine from the previous year's harvest is opened. After lunch young and old join hands to dance, Greek-style.*

SUMMER

WARM DAYS in early June signal the first sea-baths for Greeks (traditionally after Análipsi, Ascension Day). The peak tourist season begins, and continues until late August; after mid-July it can be difficult to find hotel vacancies in the more popular resorts. June sees the arrival of cherries, plums and apricots, and honey can start to be collected from hives. The last green leaf vegetables are soon totally replaced by tomatoes, melons and cucumbers. By July much of the Aegean is buffeted by the notorious *meltémi*, a high-pressure northerly wind, which – though more severe on the islands – can be felt along the mainland coast.

Various cultural festivals – programmed with an eye on the tourist audience, but no less impressive for that – are hosted in major cities and resorts. Outdoor cinemas are also well attended *(see p119)*. Urban Greeks retreat to mountain villages, often the venues for musical and religious fairs.

Beehives for summer honey production, near Mount Parnassus

Consecrated bread, baked for festivals

JUNE

Pentikostí, Pentecost or Whit Sunday *(seven weeks after Orthodox Easter)*. This important Orthodox feast day is celebrated throughout Greece.

Agíou Pnévmatos, Feast of the Holy Spirit or Whit Monday *(the following day)*. A national holiday.
Athens Festival *(mid-Jun to mid-Sep)*. A cultural festival encompassing a mix of modern and ancient theatre, ballet, opera, classical music and jazz. It takes place at various venues, including the Herodes Atticus Theatre *(see p119)* and the Lykavittós Theatre *(see p72)*. The Herodes Atticus Theatre, on the slopes of the Acropolis, hosts performances of ancient tragedies, concerts by international orchestras and ballet. The Lykavittós Theatre, spectacularly situated on Lykavittós Hill, with extensive views across Athens, hosts performances of modern music – jazz and folk – as well as drama and dance.

Concert at Herodes Atticus Theatre during the Athens Festival

Epidaurus Festival *(Jun–Aug)*. Affiliated to the Athens Festival, though sited 150 km (90 miles) from the capital at the Epidaurus Theatre *(see p184)* in the Peloponnese, this festival includes open-air performances of Classical drama.
Agios Ioánnis, St John's Day *(24 Jun)*. A day celebrated throughout Greece commemorating the birth of St John the Baptist. However, it is on the evening of the 23rd that bonfires are lit in most areas, and May wreaths consigned to the flames. Older children jump over the fires. This is an equivalent celebration to midsummer's eve.
Agioi Apóstoloi Pétros kai Pávlos, Saints Peter and Paul *(29 Jun)*. A widely celebrated name day for Pétros and Pávlos.

JULY

Agía Marína *(17 Jul)*. This day is widely celebrated in rural areas, with feasts to honour the saint, an important protector of crops.
Ioánnina's Cultural Summer *(through Jul and Aug)*. A wide range of music, arts and cultural events.
Profítis Ilías, the Prophet Elijah *(18–20 Jul)*. Widely celebrated at hill-top shrines, the best known being Mount Taÿgetos, near the town of Spárti. Name day for Ilías.
Agía Paraskeví *(26 Jul)*. There are many big village festivals on this day, but it is particularly celebrated in the Epirus region.

Agios Panteleímon
(27 Jul). As a doctor-saint, he is celebrated as the patron of many hospitals, and as a popular rural saint he is celebrated in the countryside. Name day for Pantelís and Panteleímon.

AUGUST

Metamórfosi, Transfiguration of Christ *(6 Aug).* For the Orthodox church

Girl in national dress for 15 August festivities

this is an important feast day. Name day for Sotíris and Sotiría.

Koímisis tis Theotókou, Assumption of the Virgin Mary *(15 Aug).* A national holiday, and an important and widely celebrated feast day. This is traditionally a day when Greeks return to celebrate in their home villages. It is also a name day for Mary, María, Pános and Panagiótis.

Pátra Summer Festival *(Aug–Sep).* This festival offers events such as Classical drama and art exhibitions, as well as concerts in the Roman theatre.

Vlachopanagía *(19 Aug).* A day of celebration in many Vlach villages located in the mountainous Epirus region.

Apotomí Kefalís Ioánnou Prodrómou, beheading of John the Baptist *(29 Aug).* The occasion for festivals at the many country chapels that bear his name.

Strings of tomatoes hanging out to dry in the autumn sunshine

AUTUMN

BY SEPTEMBER most village festivals have finished. The sea is at its warmest for swimming and, though the crowds have gone, most facilities are still available. There is a second, minor blooming of wild flowers, and the fine, still days of October are known as the "little summer of St Dimitrios",

randomly punctuated by stormy weather. Grapes, and the fat peaches *germádes,* are virtually the only fruit to ripen since the figs of August, and strings of onions, garlic and tomatoes are hung up to dry for the winter. The hills echo with the sound of the September quail shoot and dragnet fishing resumes.

SEPTEMBER

Génnisis tis Theotókou, birth of the Virgin Mary *(8 Sep).* An important religious feast day in the calendar of the Orthodox church.

Ypsosis tou Timíou Stavroú, Exaltation of the True Cross *(14 Sep).* This is an important Orthodox feast day, and, although it is almost autumn, it is regarded as the last of Greece's major outdoor summer festivals.

OCTOBER

Agios Dimítrios *(26 Oct).* This traditionally marks the end of the grazing season, when sheep are brought down from the hills. Celebrations for Dimítrios are particularly lively in Thessaloníki, where he is the patron saint. Name day for Dimítris and Dímitra.

Ochi Day *(28 Oct).* A national holiday, with patriotic parades in cities and plenty of dancing. It commemorates the Greek reply to the 1940 ultimatum from Mussolini calling for Greek surrender: an emphatic no *(óchi).*

Ceremonial dress on Ochi Day

NOVEMBER

Ton Taxiarchón Archangélou Michaïl kai Gavriíl *(8 Nov).* Ceremonies at the many rural monasteries and churches named after Archangels Gabriel and Michael. It is also name day for Michális and Gavriíl.

Eisódia tis Theotókou, Presentation of the Virgin in the Temple *(21 Nov).* An important feast day in the Orthodox calendar, celebrated throughout Greece.

Agios Andréas, St Andrew *(30 Nov),* Pátra. A long liturgy is recited for Pátra's patron saint in the opulent cathedral named after him.

Parade in Thessaloníki for Agios Dimítrios, 26 October

View over a snow-covered Herodes Atticus Theatre, Athens

WINTER

MANY MOUNTAIN VILLAGES assume a ghostly aspect in winter, with their seasonal inhabitants returned to the cities. Deep snow accumulates at higher altitudes and skiing can begin; elsewhere, rain falls several days of the week. Fishing is in full swing, and at the markets kiwi fruits and exotic greens abound. Cheese shops display a full range of goat and sheep products, and olives are pressed for oil. The major festivals cluster to either side of the solstice. New Year and Epiphany are the most fervently celebrated festivals during winter.

Branch of olives

DECEMBER

Agios Nikólaos, St Nicholas *(6 Dec)*. The patron saint of seafarers, travellers, children and orphans is celebrated at seaside churches. Name day for Nikólaos and Nikolétta.

Christoúgenna, Christmas *(25 Dec)*. A national holiday and, though less significant than Easter, it still constitutes an important religious feast day.

Sýnaxis tis Theotókou, meeting of the Virgin's entourage *(26 Dec)*. A religious celebration and national holiday.

JANUARY

Agios Vasíleios, also known as *Protochroniá*, or New Year *(1 Jan)*. A national holiday. Gifts are exchanged on this day and the traditional new year greeting is *Kalí Chroniá*.
Theofánia, or Epiphany *(6 Jan)*. A national holiday and an important feast day. Blessing of the waters ceremonies take place by rivers and coastal locations throughout Greece. Youths dive to recover a cross that is thrown into the water by a priest.

Gynaikokratía *(8 Jan)*, Thrace. Matriarchy is celebrated by women and men swapping roles for the day in some villages of Thrace.

FEBRUARY

Ypapantí, Candlemas *(2 Feb)*. An Orthodox feast day all over Greece, at a quiet time, prior to pre-Lenten carnivals.

Diving for a cross at a blessing of the waters ceremony, 6 January

Women playing cards on Gynaikokratía day, Thrace

NAME DAYS

Most Greeks do not celebrate birthdays past the age of about 12. Instead they celebrate their name day, or *giortí*, the day of the saint after whom they were named when baptized. Children are usually named after their grandparents, though in recent years it has become fashionable to give children names deriving from Greece's history and mythology. When someone celebrates their name day you may be told, *Giortázo símera* (I'm celebrating today), to which the traditional reply is *Chrónia pollá* (many years). Friends tend to drop in, bearing small gifts, and are given cakes and sweet liqueurs in return.

The Climate of Mainland Greece

Summer visitors

THE MAINLAND CLIMATE varies most between the coastal lowlands and the mountainous inland regions. The mountains of western Greece and the Peloponnese get heavy snow in winter, rain during autumn and spring, and hot days in summer. The Ionian coast has milder temperatures, but is the wettest part of Greece. In Macedonia and Thrace rainfall is spread more evenly across the year, with the North Aegean exerting a moderating influence on coastal temperatures. Around Athens, temperatures are hot in summer and rarely drop below freezing in winter, when rainfall is at its greatest.

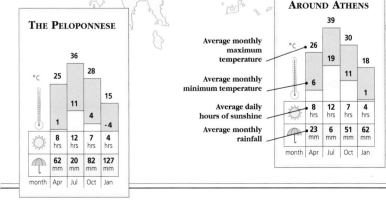

NORTHERN GREECE

°C				
		38		
	26		28	
		17		16
	4		7	
				-4
☼	8 hrs	12 hrs	6 hrs	4 hrs
☂	41 mm	22 mm	57 mm	44 mm
month	Apr	Jul	Oct	Jan

CENTRAL AND WESTERN GREECE

°C				
		40		
			33	
	27			
		15		16
	2		5	
				-6
☼	8 hrs	11 hrs	5 hrs	3 hrs
☂	80 mm	19 mm	80 mm	84 mm
month	Apr	Jul	Oct	Jan

ATHENS AND AROUND ATHENS

Average monthly maximum temperature

Average monthly minimum temperature

Average daily hours of sunshine

Average monthly rainfall

°C				
		39		
	26		30	
		19		18
	6		11	
				1
☼	8 hrs	12 hrs	7 hrs	4 hrs
☂	23 mm	6 mm	51 mm	62 mm
month	Apr	Jul	Oct	Jan

THE PELOPONNESE

°C				
		36		
	25		28	
		11		15
	1		4	
				-4
☼	8 hrs	12 hrs	7 hrs	4 hrs
☂	62 mm	20 mm	82 mm	127 mm
month	Apr	Jul	Oct	Jan

NORTHERN GREECE

CENTRAL AND WESTERN GREECE

ATHENS AND AROUND ATHENS

THE PELOPONNESE

ATHENS

ANCIENT GREECE

Gods, Goddesses and Heroes

THE GREEK MYTHS that tell the stories of the gods, goddesses and heroes date back to the Bronze Age when they were told aloud by poets. They were first written down in the early 6th century BC and have lived on in Western literature. Myths were closely bound up with Greek religion and gave meaning to the unpredictable workings of the natural world. They tell the story of the creation and the "golden age" of gods and mortals, as well as the age of semi-mythical heroes, such as Theseus and Herakles, whose exploits were an inspiration to ordinary men. The gods and goddesses were affected by human desires and failings and were part of a divine family presided over by Zeus. He had many offspring, both legitimate and illegitimate, each with a mythical role.

Hades and Persephone *were king and queen of the Underworld (land of the dead). Persephone was abducted from her mother Demeter, goddess of the harvest, by Hades. She was then only permitted to return to her mother for three months each year.*

Zeus was the father of the gods and ruled over them and all mortals from Mount Olympos.

Eris was the goddess of strife.

Clymene, a nymph and daughter of Helios, was mother of Prometheus, creator of mankind.

Poseidon, *one of Zeus's brothers, was given control of the seas. The trident is his symbol of power, and he married the sea-goddess Amphitrite, to whom he was not entirely faithful. This statue is from the National Archaeological Museum in Athens (see pp68–71).*

Hera, sister and wife of Zeus, was famous for her jealousy.

Athena was born from Zeus's head in full armour.

Paris was asked to award the golden apple to the most beautiful goddess.

Paris's dog helped him herd cattle on Mount Ida where the prince grew up.

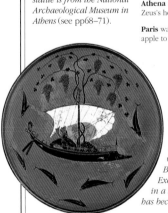

Dionysos, *god of revelry and wine, was born from Zeus's thigh. In this 6th-century BC cup painted by Exekias he reclines in a ship whose mast has become a vine.*

A DIVINE DISPUTE

This vase painting shows the gods on Mount Ida, near Troy. Hera, Athena and Aphrodite, quarrelling over who was the most beautiful, were brought by Hermes to hear the judgment of a young herdsman, the Trojan prince, Paris. In choosing Aphrodite, he was rewarded with the love of Helen, the most beautiful woman in the world. Paris abducted her from her husband Menelaos, King of Sparta, and thus the Trojan War began (see pp54–5).

Artemis, the virgin goddess of the hunt, was the daughter of Zeus and sister of Apollo. She can be identified by her bow and arrows, hounds and group of nymphs with whom she lived in the forests. Although sworn to chastity, she was, in contrast, the goddess of childbirth.

Happiness, here personified by two goddesses, waits with gold laurel leaves to garland the winner. Wreaths were the prizes in Greek athletic and musical contests.

Helios, the sun god, drove his four-horse chariot (the sun) daily across the sky.

Hermes was the gods' messenger.

Aphrodite, the goddess of love, was born from the sea. Here she has her son Eros (Cupid) with her.

Apollo, son of Zeus and brother of Artemis, was god of healing, plague and also music. Here he is depicted holding a lyre. He was also famous for his dazzling beauty.

THE LABOURS OF HERAKLES

Herakles (Hercules to the Romans) was the greatest of the Greek heroes, and the son of Zeus and Alkmene, a mortal woman. With superhuman strength he achieved success, and immortality, against seemingly impossible odds in the "Twelve Labours" set by Eurystheus, King of Mycenae. For his first task he killed the Nemean lion, and wore its hide ever after.

Killing the Lernaean hydra was the second labour of Herakles. The many heads of this venomous monster, raised by Hera, grew back as soon as they were chopped off. As in all his tasks, Herakles was helped by Athena.

The huge boar that ravaged Mount Erymanthus was captured next. Herakles brought it back alive to King Eurystheus who was so terrified that he hid in a storage jar.

Destroying the Stymfalian birds was the sixth labour. Herakles rid Lake Stymfalia of these man-eating birds, which had brass beaks, by stoning them with a sling, having first frightened them off with a pair of bronze castanets.

The Trojan War

Ajax carrying the body of the dead Achilles

T HE STORY of the Trojan War, first narrated in the *Iliad*, Homer's 8th-century BC epic poem, tells how the Greeks sought to avenge the capture of Helen, wife of Menelaos, King of Sparta, by the Trojan prince, Paris. The Roman writer Virgil takes up the story in the *Aeneid*, where he tells of the sack of Troy and the founding of Rome. Recent archaeological evidence of the remains of a city identified with ancient Troy in modern Turkey suggests that the myth may have a basis in fact. Many of the ancient sites in the Peloponnese, such as Mycenae and Pylos, are thought to be the cities of some of the heroes of the Trojan War.

Achilles binding up the battle wounds of his friend Patroklos

GATHERING OF THE HEROES

W HEN PARIS *(see p52)* carries Helen back to Troy, her husband King Menelaos summons an army of Greek kings and heroes to avenge this crime. His brother, King Agamemnon of Mycenae, leads the force; its ranks include young Achilles, destined to die at Troy.

At Aulis their departure is delayed by a contrary wind. Only the sacrifice to Artemis of Iphigéneia, the youngest of Agamemnon's daughters, allows the fleet to depart.

FIGHTING AT TROY

T HE ILIAD OPENS with the Greek army outside Troy, maintaining a siege that has already been in progress for nine years. Tired of fighting, yet still

hoping for a decisive victory, the Greek camp is torn apart by the fury of Achilles over Agamemnon's removal of his slave girl Briseis. The hero takes to his tent and refuses adamantly to fight.

Deprived of their greatest warrior, the Greeks are driven back by the Trojans. In desperation, Patroklos persuades his friend Achilles to let him borrow his armour. Achilles agrees and Patroklos leads the Myrmidons, Achilles's troops, into battle. The tide is turned, but Patroklos is killed in the fighting by Hector, son of King Priam of Troy, who mistakes him for Achilles. Filled with remorse at the news of his friend's death, Achilles returns to battle, finds Hector, and kills him in revenge.

King Priam begging Achilles for the body of his son

PATROKLOS AVENGED

R EFUSING HECTOR's dying wish to allow his body to be ransomed, Achilles instead hitches it up to his chariot by the ankles and drags it round the walls of Troy, then takes it back to the Greek camp. In contrast, Patroklos is given the most elaborate funeral possible with a huge pyre, sacrifices of animals and Trojan prisoners and funeral games. Still unsatisfied, for 12 days Achilles drags the corpse of Hector around Patroklos's funeral mound until the gods are forced to intervene over his callous behaviour.

PRIAM VISITS ACHILLES

O N THE INSTRUCTIONS of Zeus, Priam sets off for the Greek camp holding a ransom for the body of his dead son. With the help of the god Hermes he reaches Achilles's tent undetected. Entering, he pleads with Achilles to think of his own father and to show mercy. Achilles relents and allows Hector to be taken back to Troy for a funeral and burial.

Although the Greek heroes were greater than mortals, they were portrayed as fallible beings with human emotions who had to face universal moral dilemmas.

Greeks and Trojans, in bronze armour, locked in combat

ACHILLES KILLS THE AMAZON QUEEN

Penthesileia was the Queen of the Amazons, a tribe of warlike women reputed to cut off their right breasts to make it easier to wield their weapons. They come to the support of the Trojans. In the battle, Achilles finds himself face to face with Penthesileia and deals her a fatal blow. One version of the story has it that as their eyes meet at the moment of her death, they fall in love. The Greek idea of love and death would be explored 2,000 years later by the psychologists Jung and Freud.

Achilles killing the Amazon Queen Penthesileia in battle

THE WOODEN HORSE OF TROY

As was foretold, Achilles is killed at Troy by an arrow in his heel from Paris's bow. With this weakening of their military strength, the Greeks resort to guile.

Before sailing away they build a great wooden horse, in which they conceal some of their best fighters. The rumour is put out that this is a gift to the goddess Athena and that if the horse enters Troy, the city can never be taken. After some doubts, but swayed by supernatural omens, the Trojans drag the horse inside the walls. That night, the Greeks sail back, the soldiers creep out of the horse and Troy is put to the torch. Priam, with many others, is murdered. Among

An early image of the Horse of Troy, from a 7th-century BC clay vase

the Trojan survivors is Aeneas who escapes to Italy and founds the race of Romans: a second Troy. The next part of the story (the *Odyssey*) tells of the heroes' adventures on their way home to Greece.

DEATH OF AGAMEMNON

Klytemnestra, the wife of Agamemnon, had ruled Mycenae in the ten years that he had been away fighting in Troy. She was accompanied by Aigisthos, her lover. Intent on vengeance for the death of her daughter Iphigéneia, Klytemnestra receives her husband with a triumphal welcome and then brutally murders him, with the help of Aigisthos. Agamemnon's fate was a result of a curse laid on his father, Atreus, which was finally expiated by the murder of both Klytemnestra and Aigisthos by her son Orestes and daughter Elektra. In these myths, the will of the gods shapes and overrides that of heroes and mortals.

GREEK MYTHS IN WESTERN ART

From the Renaissance onwards, the Greek myths have been a powerful inspiration for artists and sculptors. Kings and queens have had themselves portrayed as gods and goddesses with symbolic attributes of love or war. Myths have also been an inspiration for artists to paint the nude or Classically draped figure. This was true of the 19th-century artist Lord Leighton, whose depiction of the human body reflects the Classical ideals of beauty. His tragic figure of Elektra is shown here.

Elektra mourning the death of her father Agamemnon at his tomb

Greek Writers and Philosophers

Playwrights Aristophanes and Sophocles

THE LITERATURE OF GREECE began with long epic poems, accounts of war and adventure, which established the relationship of the ancient Greeks to their gods. The tragedy and comedy, history and philosophical dialogues of the 5th and 4th centuries BC became the basis of Western literary culture. Much of our knowledge of the Greek world is derived from Greek literature. Pausanias's *Guide to Greece*, written in the Roman period and used by Roman tourists, is a key to the physical remains.

Hesiod with the nine Muses who inspired his poetry

EPIC POETRY

AS FAR BACK as the 2nd millennium BC, before even the building of the Mycenaean palaces, poets were reciting the stories of the Greek heroes and gods. Passed on from generation to generation, these poems, called *rhapsodes,* were never written down but were changed and embellished by successive poets. The oral tradition culminated in the *Iliad* and *Odyssey* *(see pp54–5),* composed around 700 BC. Both works are traditionally ascribed to the same poet, Homer, of whose life

nothing reliable is known. Hesiod, whose most famous poems include the *Theogony,* a history of the gods, and the *Works and Days,* on how to live an honest life, also lived around 700 BC. Unlike Homer, Hesiod is thought to have written down his poems, although there is no firm evidence available to support this theory.

PASSIONATE POETRY

FOR PRIVATE OCCASIONS, and particularly to entertain guests at the cultivated drinking parties known as *symposia,* shorter poetic forms were developed. These poems were often full of passion, whether love or hatred, and could be personal or, often, highly political. Much of this poetry, by writers such as Archilochus, Alcaeus, Alcman, Hipponax and Sappho, survives only in quotations by later writers or on scraps of papyrus that have been preserved by chance from private libraries in Hellenistic and Roman Egypt. Through these fragments we can gain glimpses

of the life of a very competitive elite. Since *symposia* were an almost exclusively male domain, there is a strong element of misogyny in much of this poetry. In contrast, the fragments of poems discovered by the authoress Sappho, who lived on the island of Lésvos, are exceptional for showing a woman competing in a literary area in the male-dominated society of ancient Greece, and for describing with great intensity her passions for other women.

HISTORY

UNTIL THE 5th century BC little Greek literature was composed in prose – even early philosophy was in verse. In the latter part of the 5th century, a new tradition of lengthy prose histories, looking at recent or current events, was established with Herodotus's account of the great war between Greece and Persia (490–479 BC). Herodotus put the clash between Greeks and Persians into a context, and included an ethnographic account of the vast Persian Empire. He attempted to record objectively what people said about the past. Thucydides took a narrower view in his account of the long years of the Peloponnesian War

Herodotus, the historian of the Persian wars

between Athens and Sparta (431–404 BC). He concentrated on the political history, and his aim was to work out the "truth" that lay behind the events of the war. The methods of Thucydides were adopted by later writers of Greek history, though few could match his acute insight into human nature.

An unusual vase-painting of a *symposion* for women only

The orator Demosthenes in a Staffordshire figurine of 1790

ORATORY

Public argument was basic to Greek political life even in the Archaic period. In the later part of the 5th century BC, the techniques of persuasive speech began to be studied in their own right. From that time on some orators began to publish their speeches. In particular, this included those wishing to advertise their skills in composing speeches for the law courts, such as Lysias and Demosthenes. The texts that survive give insights into both Athenian politics and the seamier side of Athenian private life. The verbal attacks on Philip of Macedon by Demosthenes, the 4th-century BC Athenian politician, became models for Roman politicians seeking to defeat their opponents. With the 18th-century European revival of interest in Classical times, Demosthenes again became a political role model.

DRAMA

Almost all the surviving tragedies come from the hands of the three great 5th-century BC Athenians: Aeschylus, Sophocles and Euripides. The latter two playwrights developed an interest in individual psychology (as in Euripides' *Medea*). While 5th-century comedy is full of direct references to contemporary life and dirty jokes, the "new" comedy developed in the 4th century BC is essentially situation comedy employing character types.

Vase painting of two costumed actors from around 370 BC

GREEK PHILOSOPHERS

The Athenian Socrates was recognized in the late 5th century BC as a moral arbiter. He wrote nothing himself but we know of his views through the "Socratic dialogues", written by his pupil, Plato, examining the concepts of justice, virtue and courage. Plato set up his academy in the suburbs of Athens.

His pupil, Aristotle, founded the Lyceum, to teach subjects from biology to ethics, and helped to turn Athens into one of the first university cities. In 1508–11 Raphael painted this vision of Athens in the Vatican.

Aristotle, author of the *Ethics*, had a genius for scientific observation.

Euclid laid the rules of geometry in around 300 BC.

Plato saw "the seat of ideas" in heaven.

Epicurus advocated the pursuit of pleasure.

Socrates taught by debating his ideas.

Diogenes, the Cynic, lived like a beggar.

Temple Architecture

Temples were the most important public buildings in ancient Greece, largely because religion was a central part of everyday life. Often placed in prominent positions, temples were also statements about political and divine power. The earliest temples, in the 8th century BC, were built of wood and sun-dried bricks. Many of their features were copied in marble buildings from the 6th century BC onwards.

Pheidias, sculptor of the Parthenon, at work

TEMPLE CONSTRUCTION

This drawing is of an idealized Doric temple, showing how it was built and used.

The pediment, triangular in shape, often held sculpture.

The cella, or inner sanctum, housed the cult statue.

The cult statue was of the god or goddess to whom the temple was dedicated.

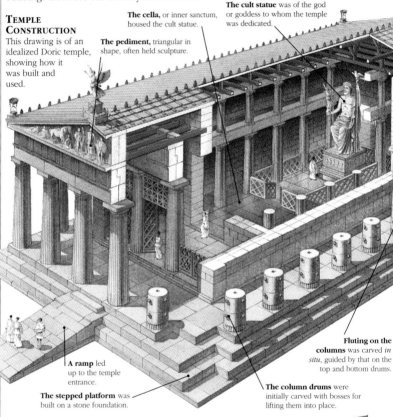

Fluting on the columns was carved *in situ*, guided by that on the top and bottom drums.

A ramp led up to the temple entrance.

The column drums were initially carved with bosses for lifting them into place.

The stepped platform was built on a stone foundation.

TIMELINE OF TEMPLE CONSTRUCTION

700 First temple of Poseidon, Ancient Isthmia (Archaic; *see p167*) and first Temple of Apollo, Corinth (Archaic; *see p162*)

550 Second temple of Apollo, Corinth (Doric; *see p162*)

520 Temple of Olympian Zeus, Athens, begun (Doric; completed Corinthian 2nd century AD; *see p111*)

6th century Temple of Artemis, Ancient Brauron (Doric; *see pp146–7*)

Detail of the Parthenon pediment

700 BC	600 BC	500 BC	400 BC	300 BC

7th century Temple of Hera, Olympia (Doric; *see p170*)

460 Temple of Zeus, Olympia (Doric; *see p171*)

447–405 Temples of the Acropolis, Athens: Athena Nike (Ionic), Parthenon (Doric), Erechtheion (Ionic) (*see pp94–9*)

445–425 Temple of Apollo, Bassae (Doric with Ionic; *see p177*)

4th century Temple of Apollo, Delphi (Doric; *see p229*); Temple of Athena Aléa, Tegéa (Doric and 1st Corinthian capital; *see p177*)

440–430 Temple of Poseidon, Soúnio (Doric; *see pp148–9*)

The gable ends of the roof were surmounted by statues, known as *akroteria*, in this case of a Nike or "Winged Victory". Almost no upper portions of Greek temples survive.

The roof was supported on wooden beams and covered in rows of terracotta tiles, each ending in an upright *akroteria*.

Stone blocks were smoothly fitted together and held by metal clamps and dowels: no mortar was used in the temple's construction.

The ground plan was derived from the megaron of the Mycenaean house: a rectangular hall with a front porch supported by columns.

Caryatids, or figures of women, were used instead of columns in the Erechtheion at Athens' Acropolis. In Athens' Agora (see pp90–91), tritons (halffish, halfhuman creatures) were used.

THE DEVELOPMENT OF TEMPLE ARCHITECTURE

Greek temple architecture is divided into three styles, which evolved chronologically, and are most easily distinguished by the column capitals.

Doric *temples were surrounded by sturdy columns with plain capitals and no bases. As the earliest style of stone buildings, they recall wooden prototypes.*

Triangular pediment filled with sculpture

Guttae imitated the pegs for fastening the wooden roof beams.

Triglyphs resembled the ends of cross beams.

Metopes could contain sculpture.

Doric capital

Ionic *temples differed from Doric in their tendency to have more columns, of a different form. The capital has a pair of volutes, like rams' horns, front and back.*

Akroteria, at the roof corners, could look Persian in style.

The frieze was a continuous band of decoration.

The Ionic architrave was subdivided into projecting bands.

The Ionic frieze took the place of Doric *triglyphs* and *metopes*.

Ionic capital

Corinthian *temples in Greece were built under the Romans and only in Athens. They feature columns with slender shafts and elaborate capitals decorated with acanthus leaves.*

The pediment was decorated with a variety of mouldings.

Akroterion in the shape of a griffin

The cella entrance was at the east end.

The entablature was everything above the capitals.

Acanthus leaf capital

Vases and Vase Painting

Donkey cup

THE HISTORY OF GREEK vase painting continued without a break from 1000 BC to Hellenistic times. The main centre of production was Athens, which was so successful that by the early 6th century BC it was sending its high-quality black- and red-figure wares to every part of the Greek world. The Athenian potters' quarter of Kerameikós can still be visited today (see pp88–9). Beautiful works of art in their own right, the painted vases are the closest we can get to the vanished paintings with which ancient Greeks decorated the walls of their houses. Although vases could break during everyday use (for which they were intended) a huge number still survive intact or in reassembled pieces.

This 6th-century BC black-figure vase shows pots being used in an everyday situation. The vases depicted are hydriai. *It was the women's task to fill them with water from springs or public fountains.*

The white-ground lekythos *was developed in the 5th century BC as an oil flask for grave offerings. They were usually decorated with funeral scenes, and this one, by the Achilles Painter, shows a woman placing flowers at a grave.*

The naked woman *holding a* kylix *is probably a flute-girl or prostitute.*

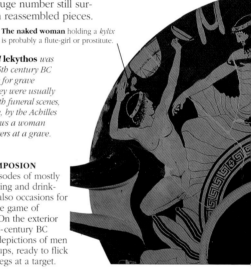

THE SYMPOSION
These episodes of mostly male feasting and drinking were also occasions for playing the game of *kottabos*. On the exterior of this 5th-century BC *kylix* are depictions of men holding cups, ready to flick out the dregs at a target.

THE DEVELOPMENT OF PAINTING STYLES
Vase painting reached its peak in 6th- and 5th-century BC Athens. In the potter's workshop, a fired vase would be passed to a painter to be decorated. Archaeologists have been able to identify the varying styles of many individual painters of both black-figure and red-figure ware.

The body of the dead man *is carried on a bier by mourners.*

The geometric design *is a proto-type of the later "Greek-key" pattern.*

Chariots and warriors *form the funeral procession.*

Geometric style characterizes the earliest Greek vases, from around 1000 to 700 BC, in which the decoration is in bands of figures and geometric patterns. This 8th-century BC vase, placed on a grave as a marker, is over 1 m (3 ft) high and depicts the bier and funeral rites of a dead man.

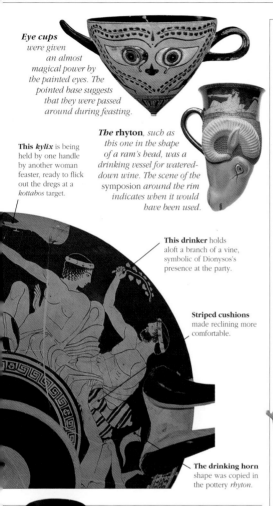

Eye cups *were given an almost magical power by the painted eyes. The pointed base suggests that they were passed around during feasting.*

This kylix is being held by one handle by another woman feaster, ready to flick out the dregs at a *kottabos* target.

The rhyton, *such as this one in the shape of a ram's head, was a drinking vessel for watered-down wine. The scene of the symposion around the rim indicates when it would have been used.*

This drinker holds aloft a branch of a vine, symbolic of Dionysos's presence at the party.

Striped cushions made reclining more comfortable.

The drinking horn shape was copied in the pottery *rhyton.*

Black-figure style *was first used in Athens around 630 BC. The figures were painted in black liquid clay on to the iron-rich clay of the vase which turned orange when fired. This vase is signed by the potter and painter Exekias.*

Red-figure style *was introduced in c.530 BC. The figures were left in the col-our of the clay, silhouetted against a black glaze. Here a woman pours from an oinochoe (wine jug).*

VASE SHAPES

Almost all Greek vases were made to be used; their shapes are closely related to their intended uses. Athenian potters had about 20 different forms to choose from. Below are some of the most commonly made shapes and their uses.

The amphora *was a two-handled vessel used to store wine, olive oil and foods pre-served in liquid such as olives. It also held dried foods.*

This krater *with curled handles or "volutes" is a wide-mouthed vase in which the Greeks mixed water with their wine before drinking it.*

The hydria *was used to carry water from the fountain. Of the three handles, one was vertical for holding and pouring, two horizontal for lifting.*

The lekythos *could vary in height from 3 cm (1 in) to nearly 1 m (39 in). It was used to hold oil both in the home and as a funerary gift to the dead.*

The oinochoe, *the standard wine jug, had a round or trefoil mouth for pouring, and just one handle.*

The kylix, *a two-handled drinking cup, was one shape that could take in-terior decoration.*

ATHENS
AREA BY AREA

Athens at a Glance

ATHENS HAS BEEN A CITY for 3,500 years but its
greatest glory was during the Classical period
of ancient Greece from which so many buildings
and artifacts still survive. The 5th century BC in
particular was a golden age, when Perikles oversaw
the building of the Acropolis. Within the Byzantine
Empire and under Ottoman rule, Athens played
only a minor role. It returned to prominence in
1834, when it became the capital of Greece. Today
it is a busy and modern metropolitan centre.

The Kerameikós quarter
(see pp88–9) *was once the potters'*
district of ancient Athens and site
of the principal cemetery,
whose grave monuments
can still be seen.
Tranquil and
secluded, it lies
off the main
tourist track.

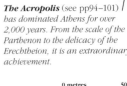

The Agora (see
pp90–91), *or market*
place, was the ancient
centre of commercial
life. The Stoa of Attalos
was reconstructed in
1953–6 on its original,
2nd-century BC foun-
dations. It now houses
the Agora Museum.

The Tower of the Winds
(see pp86–7) *stands beside*
the Roman forum, but this
small, octagonal building
is Hellenistic in style. The
tower – built as a water
clock, with a compass,
sundials and weather vane
– has a relief on each side
depicting the wind from
that direction.

The Acropolis (see pp94–101)
has dominated Athens for over
2,000 years. From the scale of the
Parthenon to the delicacy of the
Erechtheion, it is an extraordinary
achievement.

0 metres	500
0 yards	500

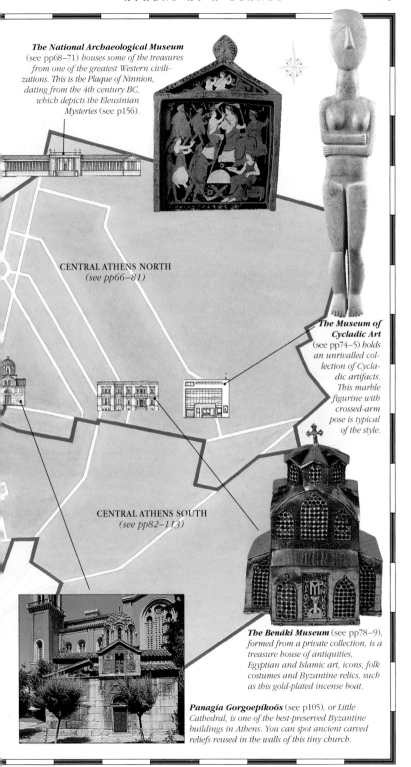

The National Archaeological Museum (see pp68–71) houses some of the treasures from one of the greatest Western civilizations. This is the Plaque of Ninnion, dating from the 4th century BC, which depicts the Eleusinian Mysteries (see p156).

CENTRAL ATHENS NORTH
(see pp66–81)

The Museum of Cycladic Art (see pp74–5) holds an unrivalled collection of Cycladic artifacts. This marble figurine with crossed-arm pose is typical of the style.

CENTRAL ATHENS SOUTH
(see pp82–113)

The Benáki Museum (see pp78–9), formed from a private collection, is a treasure house of antiquities, Egyptian and Islamic art, icons, folk costumes and Byzantine relics, such as this gold-plated incense boat.

Panagía Gorgoepíkoös (see p105), or Little Cathedral, is one of the best-preserved Byzantine buildings in Athens. You can spot ancient carved reliefs reused in the walls of this tiny church.

CENTRAL ATHENS NORTH

INHABITED FOR 7,000 YEARS, Athens was the birthplace of European civilization. It flourished in the 5th century BC when the Athenians controlled much of the eastern Mediterranean. The buildings from this era, including those in the ancient Agora and on the Acropolis, lie largely in the southern part of the city. The northern half has grown since the early 1800s when King Otto made Athens the new capital of Greece. When the king's architects planned the new, European-style city, they included wide, tree-lined avenues, such as Panepistimíou and Akadimías, that were soon home to many grand

Icon of the Archangel Michael, from the Byzantine Museum

Neo-Classical public buildings and mansion houses. Today, these edifices still provide elegant homes for all the major banks, embassies and public institutions, such as the University and the Library.

The chic residential area of Kolonáki is located in the north of the city centre, as is the cosmopolitan area around Patriárchou Ioakeím and Irodótou. These streets have excellent shopping and entertainment venues. Most of Athens' best museums, including the National Archaeological Museum, are also found in this area of the city. For information on getting around Athens, see pages 322–5.

SIGHTS AT A GLANCE

Museums and Galleries
Benáki Museum pp78–9 ⑩
Byzantine Museum ⑦
City of Athens Museum ⑫
Museum of Cycladic Art pp74–5 ⑧
National Archaeological Museum pp68–71 ①
National Gallery of Art ⑤
National Historical Museum ⑬
Theatrical Museum ⑪
War Museum ⑥

Squares, Parks and Gardens
Exárcheia and Stréfi Hill ②
Lykavittós Hill ③
Plateía Kolonakíou ⑨

Churches
Kapnikaréa ⑭

Historic Buildings
Gennádeion ④

KEY

M Metro station

P Parking

🛈 Tourist Information

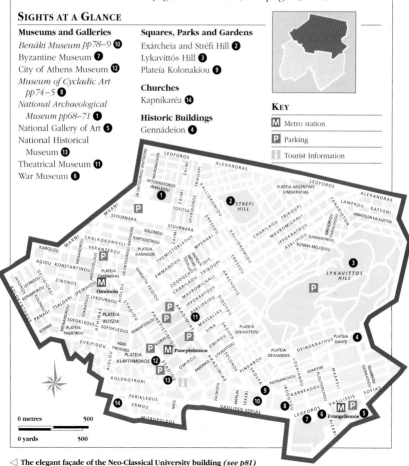

◁ **The elegant façade of the Neo-Classical University building** *(see p81)*

National Archaeological Museum ❶
Εθνικό Αρχαιολογικό Μουσείο

Hellenistic bronze head from Delos

O PENED IN 1891, this superb museum, often known simply as the National Museum, brought together a collection that had previously been stored all over the city. New wings were added in 1939. The priceless collection was then dispersed and buried underground during World War II to protect it from possible damage. The museum reopened in 1946, but it took a further 50 years of renovation and reorganization finally to do justice to its formidable collection. With the combination of such unique exhibits as the Mycenaean gold, along with the unrivalled amount of sculpture, pottery and jewellery on display, this is without doubt one of the world's finest museums.

Neo-Classical entrance to the National Archaeological Museum on Patission

GALLERY GUIDE

On the ground floor, Mycenaean, Neolithic and Cycladic finds are followed by Geometric, Archaic, Classical, Roman and Hellenistic sculpture. Smaller collections of bronzes, Egyptian artifacts, the Eléni Stathátou jewellery collection and the Karapános collection are also on the ground floor. The first floor houses a collection of pottery.

Bronze collection

Dipylon Amphora
This huge Geometric vase was used to mark an 8th-century BC woman's burial and shows the dead body surrounded by mourning women. It is named after the location of its discovery near the Dipýlon Gate in Athens' Kerameikós (see pp88–89).

Sculpture garden

Main entrance hall

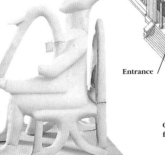

Harp Player
The minimalist Cycladic style of sculpture flourished in the 3rd millennium BC and originated in the Cyclades. The simple lines and bold forms of the marble figurines influenced many early 20th-century artists, including the British sculptor Henry Moore.

Entrance

Ground floor

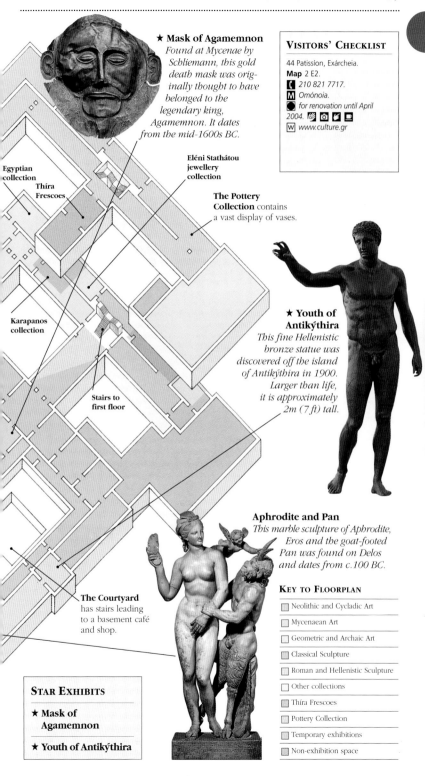

★ Mask of Agamemnon
Found at Mycenae by Schliemann, this gold death mask was originally thought to have belonged to the legendary king, Agamemnon. It dates from the mid-1600s BC.

VISITORS' CHECKLIST

44 Patission, Exárcheia.
Map 2 E2.
📞 210 821 7717.
Ⓜ Omónoia.
⬤ for renovation until April 2004. ♿ 🅿 ✔ 🖥
🌐 www.culture.gr

Egyptian collection

Thíra Frescoes

Eléni Stathátou jewellery collection

The Pottery Collection contains a vast display of vases.

Karapanos collection

★ Youth of Antikýthira
This fine Hellenistic bronze statue was discovered off the island of Antikýthira in 1900. Larger than life, it is approximately 2m (7 ft) tall.

Stairs to first floor

Aphrodite and Pan
This marble sculpture of Aphrodite, Eros and the goat-footed Pan was found on Delos and dates from c.100 BC.

KEY TO FLOORPLAN

- ☐ Neolithic and Cycladic Art
- ☐ Mycenaean Art
- ☐ Geometric and Archaic Art
- ☐ Classical Sculpture
- ☐ Roman and Hellenistic Sculpture
- ☐ Other collections
- ☐ Thíra Frescoes
- ☐ Pottery Collection
- ☐ Temporary exhibitions
- ☐ Non-exhibition space

The Courtyard has stairs leading to a basement café and shop.

STAR EXHIBITS

- ★ Mask of Agamemnon
- ★ Youth of Antikýthira

Exploring the National Archaeological Museum's Collection

DISPLAYING ITS TREASURES in chronological order, the museum presents an impressive and thorough overview of Greek art through the centuries. Beginning with early Cycladic figurines and continuing through the Greek Bronze Age, the exhibits end with the glories of Hellenistic period bronzes and a collection of busts of Roman emperors. High points in between include the numerous gold artifacts found at Mycenae, the elegant Archaic *koúroi* statues and the many examples of fine Classical sculpture.

Mycenaean head of a sphinx

NEOLITHIC AND CYCLADIC ART

THE DAWNING of Greek civilization (3500–2900 BC) saw primitive decorative vases and figures. This collection also contains terracotta figurines, jewellery and a selection of weapons.

The vibrant fertility gods and goddesses, such as the *kourotróphos* (nursing mother) with child, are particularly well preserved. Of exceptional importance are the largest known Cycladic marble figurine, from Amorgós, and the earliest known figures of musicians – the *Flute Player* and *Harp Player* both from Kéros. Later finds from Mílos, such as the painted vase with fishermen, reveal the changes in pot shapes and colour that took place in the late Cycladic Bronze Age.

Neolithic clay vases with simple painted decoration

MYCENAEAN ART

IT IS NOT DIFFICULT to understand the allure of the museum's most popular attraction, the Hall of Mycenaean Antiquities, with its dazzling array of 16th-century BC gold treasures. Other exhibits in the collection include frescoes, ivory sculptures and seal rings made out of precious stones.

From the famous shaft graves *(see p180)* came a procession of daggers, cups, seals and rings as well as a number of regal death masks, including the justly famous *Mask of Agamemnon*. Two superb *rhytons*, or wine jugs, are also on display: one in the shape of a bull's head, made in silver with gold horns, and one in gold shaped like a lion's head. Equally rich finds from sites other than Mycenae have since been made. These include two gold bull cups found at Vafeió, in Crete, a gold phial entwined with dolphins and octopuses (excavated from a royal tomb at Déntra), clay tablets with the early Linear B script from the Palace of Nestor *(see p201)* and a magnificent sword from the Tomb of Stáfylos on the island of Skópelos.

Mycenaean bronze dagger, inlaid with gold

THE DEVELOPMENT OF GREEK SCULPTURE

Sculpture was one of the most sophisticated forms of Greek art. We are able to trace its development from the early *koúroi* to the great works of named sculptors such as Pheidias and Praxiteles in Classical times. Portraiture only began in the 5th century BC; even then most Greek sculptures were of gods and goddesses, heroes and athletes and idealized men and women. These have had an enormous influence on Western art down the centuries.

The Marathon Boy *(340 BC), like many other Greek bronzes, was found on the sea floor. The dreamy expression and easy pose of the figure are characteristic of the works of Praxiteles, the leading late Classical sculptor. An example of the "heroic nude", it shows a great naturalism and perfect balance.*

The Volomándra Koúros *was discovered in Attica and dates from the mid-6th century BC. The highly stylized koúroi (statues of naked youths) first appear in the mid-7th century BC. Derived from Egyptian art, these figures share a common pose and proportions. Clothed kórai are the female counterpart.*

Hellenistic bronze known as the *Horse with the Little Jockey*

GEOMETRIC AND ARCHAIC ART

FAMED FOR ITS monumental burial vases, such as the *Dipylon Amphora*, the Geometric period developed a more ornate style in the 7th century BC with the introduction of mythological and plant and animal motifs. By the 6th century BC the full artistry of the black-figure vases had developed. Two rare examples from this period are a *lekythos* depicting Peleus, Achilles and the centaur, Cheiron, and the sculptured heads known as *aryballoi*.

Warrior from Boiotia, early 7th century BC

CLASSICAL SCULPTURE

THE COLLECTION OF Classical sculpture contains both fine statues and a selection of grave monuments, mostly from the Kerameikós. These include the beautiful *stele* (c.410 BC) of Hegeso *(see p88)*. Classical votive sculpture on display includes parts of a statue of the goddess

This "valedictory stele" *(mid-4th century BC) shows a seated woman bidding farewell to her family. The figures express a dignified suffering found in many Greek funerary reliefs.*

Hera, from the Argive Heraion in the Peloponnese, and many statues of the goddess Athena, including the *Varvakeion Athena*, a reduced copy of the original ivory and gold statue from the Parthenon *(see p99)*.

ROMAN AND HELLENISTIC SCULPTURE

ALTHOUGH A LARGE number of Greek bronzes were lost in antiquity, as metal was melted down in times of emergency for making weapons, the museum has some excellent pieces on display. These include the famous bronzes *Poseidon* and the *Horse with the Little Jockey*, both found at Cape Artemísion on Evvoia, and the *Youth of Antikýthira*, found in the sea off that island. Another of the best known sculptures is the *Marathon Boy*.

OTHER COLLECTIONS

THE MUSEUM also houses several smaller collections, many donated by private individuals. Among these is the glittering **Eléni Stathátou jewellery collection**, which covers the Bronze Age through to the Byzantine period. The **Karapános collection**, which is composed mainly from discoveries made at the site at Dodóni *(see p211)*, contains many fine bronzes, including *Zeus Hurling a Thunderbolt*. Also on display are small decorative and votive pieces, and strips of lead inscribed with questions for the oracle at Dodóni.

Gold Hellenistic ring from the Eléni Stathátou collection

Other collections include the recently opened **Egyptian collection** and the **Bronze collection** which comprises many small pieces of statuary and decorative items discovered on the Acropolis.

THIRA FRESCOES

THREE OF THE FAMOUS frescoes discovered at Akrotíri on the island of Thíra (Santoríni) in 1967, and originally thought to be from the mythical city of Atlantis, are displayed in the museum. The rest remain on Santoríni. Dating from 1500 BC, they confirm the sophistication of late Minoan civilization. The colourful, restored images depict a naval expedition, elegant women, children, naked fishermen, animals and flowers.

POTTERY COLLECTION

THE STRENGTH of this vast collection lies not only in its size, but in the quality of specific works, representing the flowering of Greek ceramic art. The real gems belong to the 5th century BC when red-figure vases and white-ground *lekythoi* became the established style *(see p60)* and were produced in vast numbers. Expressive painting styles and new designs characterize this period. The most poignant pieces are by the "Bosanquet Painter" and the "Achilles Painter" who portrayed young men by their graves.

View northeast to Lykavittós Hill from the Acropolis

Exarcheía and Stréfi Hill ❷

Εξάρχεια
Λόφος Στρέφη

Map 2 F2 & 3 A2. Ⓜ *Omónoia.*

UNTIL RECENTLY, the area around Plateía Exarcheíon was renowned as a hotbed of anarchist activity. Prior to the invasion of students, Exárcheia was a very attractive area and the 19th-century Neo-Classical buildings still stand as testament to this. Today, the area is picking up again and although parts of it are still rather run-down, an influx of new gentrification has brought many fashionable cafés, bars and *ouzerí* to the area. Themistokléous, which leads off the square down to Omónoia, is pleasant to wander along; the local food stores and small boutiques make a refreshing change from the noisy bars. Plateía Exarcheíon is especially lively at night when the outdoor tavernas and the open-air cinema, the Riviera, in the streets that climb towards Stréfi, attract many visitors.

Every year a demonstration takes place on 17 November, marking the date in 1973 when many students were killed by the Junta *(see p43)* during a sit-in.

The nearby park of Stréfi Hill, with its intriguing maze of paths, is quiet and peaceful by day but comes to life at night when its cafés are full. Stréfi Hill is one of the many green areas in Athens that provide welcome relief from the noise and grime of the city, particularly in the oppressive heat of summer.

The restaurant on Lykavittós Hill, overlooking Athens

Lykavittós Hill ❸

Λόφος Λυκαβηττού

Map 3 C3. **Funicular:** *from Ploutárchou, 8:45am–12:45pm Mon–Wed & Fri–Sun, 10:30am–12:45pm Thu.*

THE PEAK of Lykavittós (also known as Lycabettus) reaches 277 m (910 ft) above the city, and is its highest hill. It can be climbed on foot by various paths or by the easier, albeit vertiginous, ride in the funicular from the corner of Ploutárchou. On foot, it should take about 45 minutes. The hill may derive its name from a combination of the words *lýki* and *vaino*, meaning "path of light". The ancient belief was that this was the rock once destined to be the Acropolis citadel, accidentally dropped by the city's patron goddess, Athena. Although it is without doubt the most prominent hill in Athens, surprisingly little mention is made of Lykavittós in Classical literature; the exceptions are passing references in Aristophanes's *Frogs* and Plato's *Kritías*. This landmark is a favourite haunt for many Athenians, who come for the panoramic views of the city from the observation decks that rim the summit.

The small whitewashed chapel of **Agios Geórgios** crowns the top of the hill. It was built in the 19th century on the site of an older Byzantine church, dedicated to Profítis Ilías (the Prophet Elijah). Both saints are celebrated on their name days (Profítis Ilías on 20 July and Agios Geórgios on 23 April). On the eve of Easter Sunday, a spectacular candlelit procession winds down the peak's wooded slopes *(see p45)*.

Lykavittós Hill is also home to a summit restaurant, some cafés and the open-air **Lykavittós Theatre**, where contemporary jazz, pop and dance performances are held annually during the Athens Festival *(see p46)*.

Gennádeion **4**
Γεννάδειον

American School of Classical Studies, Souidías 61, Kolonáki.
Map 3 C4. 210 721 0536.
M *Evangelismos.* 3, 7, 8, 13.
9am–5pm Mon– Fri, 9am–2pm Sat. Aug, main public hols.

T HE GREEK DIPLOMAT and bibliophile, Ioánnis Gennádios (1844–1932), spent a lifetime accumulating rare first editions and illuminated manuscripts. In 1923, he donated his collection to the American School of Classical Studies. The Gennádeion building, named after him, was designed and built between 1923 and 1925 by the New York firm Van Pelt and Thompson to house the collection. Above its façade of Ionic columns is an inscription which translates as "They are called Greeks who share in our culture" – from Gennádios's dedication speech at the opening in 1926.

Researchers need special permission to gain access to over 70,000 rare books and manuscripts and no items are allowed to be removed from the library. Casual visitors may look at selected exhibits that are on show, and books, posters and postcards are for sale at the souvenir stall.

Exhibits in the main reading room include 192 Edward Lear sketches purchased in 1929. There is also an eclectic mix of Byron memorabilia, including the last known portrait of the poet made before his death in Greece in 1824 *(see p149).*

The imposing Neo-Classical façade of the Gennádeion

National Gallery of Art **5**
Εθνική Πινακοθήκη

Vasiléos Konstantínou 50, Ilísia.
Map 7 C1. 210 723 5937. M *Evangelismos.* 3, 13.
9am–3pm Mon–Sat, 10am–2pm Sun. main public hols.

O PENED IN 1976, the National Gallery of Art is housed in a modern low-rise building which contains a permanent collection of European and Greek art. The ground floor stages travelling exhibitions and opens out on to a sculpture garden. The first floor, with the exception of five impressive works by El Greco (1541–1614), is devoted to a minor collection of non-Greek, European art. Alongside works of the Dutch, Italian and Flemish schools, there are studies, engravings and paintings by Rembrandt, Dürer, Brueghel, Van Dyck, Watteau, Utrillo, Cézanne and Braque, among others. These

include Caravaggio's *Singer* (1620), Eugène Delacroix's *Greek Warrior* (1856) and Picasso's Cubist-period *Woman in a White Dress* (1939).

A changing display of Greek modern art from the 18th to the 20th century is featured on the second floor. The 19th century is represented mainly by numerous depictions of the War of Independence and seascapes, enlivened by portraits such as Nikólaos Gýzis's *The Loser of the Bet* (1878), *Waiting* (1900) by Nikifóros Lýtras and *The Straw Hat* (1925) by Nikólaos Lýtras. There are many fine works by major Greek artists including Chatzimichaïl, Chatzikyriákos-Gkíkas, Móralis and Tsaroúchis.

War Museum **6**
Πολεμικό Μουσείο

Corner of Vasilíssis Sofías & Rizári, Ilísia. **Map** 7 C1. 210 725 2975.
M *Evangelismos.* 3, 7, 8, 13.
9am–2pm Tue–Sun. main public hols.

T HE WAR MUSEUM was opened in 1975 after the fall of the military dictatorship *(see p43).* The first nine galleries are chronologically ordered, and contain battle scenes, armour and plans from as far back as ancient Mycenaean times through to the more recent German occupation of 1941. Other galleries contain a miscellany of items including a selection of different uniforms and Turkish weapons.

Spartan bronze helmet

There is a fine display of paintings and prints of leaders from the Greek War of Independence *(see pp40–41),* such as General Theódoros Kolokotrónis (1770–1843). His death mask can also be seen in the museum. A sizeable collection of fine oils and sketches by the artists Floras-Karavías and Argyrós vividly captures the hardships of the two world wars.

Modern sculpture outside the National Gallery of Art

Museum of Cycladic Art ⓼

Μουσείο Κυκλαδικής Τέχνης

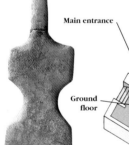

Cycladic marble head

OPENED IN 1986, this modern museum offers the world's finest collection of Cycladic art. It was initially assembled by Nikólas and Dolly Goulandrí and has expanded with donations from other Greek collectors. The museum now has an excellent selection of ancient Greek art, the earliest from about 5,000 years ago.

The Cycladic figurines, dating from the 3rd millennium BC, have never enjoyed quite the same level of popularity as Classical sculpture. However, the haunting simplicity of these marble statues has inspired many 20th-century artists and sculptors, including Picasso, Modigliani and Henry Moore.

LOCATOR MAP

The third floor houses temporary exhibitions.

Second floor

Red-Figure Kylix

This 5th-century BC drinking cup depicts a boxing match between two young male athletes, supervised by their instructor.

First floor

Main entrance

Ground floor

Violin-Shaped Figurine

This 13-cm (5-in) high, Cycladic, white marble statuette is thought to be a stylized human figure. Most figurines of this shape come from Páros and Antíparos.

Stairs to toilets and café

Walkway leading to Stathátos Mansion

GALLERY GUIDE

In the main building, the Cycladic collection is on the first floor. Ancient Greek art is on the second, and the third shows temporary exhibitions. The fourth floor houses the Charles Polítis collection. In the Stathátos Mansion is the Greek art collection of the Athens Academy.

STAR EXHIBITS

★ **Cycladic Figurine**

★ **White Lekythos**

★ **Cycladic Figurine**

This "Folded Arm" type statue of a woman is 39 cm (15 in) tall. It has only four toes on each foot and a swollen abdomen, indicating pregnancy.

Terracotta Figurine
This elegant figure of a woman is one of many that were thought to have been produced at Tanágra, in Boiotia, Central Greece. It dates from 330–320 BC.

VISITORS' CHECKLIST

Neofýtou Doúka 4, Kolonáki (entrance to Stathátos Mansion at Irodótou 1). Map 7 B1.
210 722 8321. 3, 7, 8, 13. 10am–4pm Mon, Wed–Fri, 10am–3pm Sat. main public hols. limited. www.cycladic-m.gr

KEY

☐ Shop and ticket office
☐ Cycladic art
☐ Ancient Greek art
☐ Temporary exhibitions
☐ Charles Polítis collection

Fourth floor

Stairs and lifts connecting all floors

★ **White Lekythos**
This fine clay lekythos (funerary vase) is an example of white-ground vase painting (see p60) and was used to contain embalming oil. It depicts a mourning woman taking offerings to a grave, and dates from c.450 BC.

Bronze Askos
This elegant Hellenistic bronze wine jar dates from the 2nd century BC. The jar is so named because of its resemblance to the shape of a goat skin, or askos.

Entrance to main building via walkway

The first floor houses temporary exhibitions.

The original porch is the entrance to the Stathátos Mansion.

The ground floor is home to the Greek art collection of the Athens Academy. The glass conservatory-style roof at the back makes this a very light and airy floor.

STATHATOS MANSION
The "new" wing of the Museum of Cycladic Art was opened in 1992. It is housed in this elegant Neo-Classical building, once the home of Otto and Athína Stathátos. It was designed and built by the architect Ernst Ziller in 1895.

The lower ground floor has a café in the courtyard between the two buildings.

A 14th-century icon of St Michael in the Byzantine Museum

Byzantine Museum 7
Βυζαντινό Μουσείο

Vasilíssis Sofías 22, Plateía Rigílis, Kolonáki. **Map** 7 B1. **☎** *210 723 1570.* **M** *Evangelismos.* **☎** *3, 8, 7, 13.* **☐** *8:30 am– 3pm Tue –Sun.* **●** *main public hols.* **☒** **&** *ground floor only.*

ORIGINALLY CALLED the Villa Ilissia, this elegant Florentine-style mansion was built between 1840 and 1848 by Stamátis Kleánthis for the Duchesse de Plaisance (1785–1854). This eccentric woman, wife of one of Napoleon's generals, was a key figure in Athens society during the mid-19th century and a dedicated philhellene.

Collector Geórgios Sotiríou converted the house into a museum in the 1930s with the help of architect Aristotélis Záchos. They transformed the entrance into a monastic court, incorporating a copy of a fountain from a 4th-century mosaic in Dafní *(see pp152–3).* A modern annexe (which is now nearing completion) will soon enable the whole collection of icons and mosaics, sculptures and frescoes, and ecclesiastical silverware to be on permanent display in the museum.

Spanning over 1,500 years of Byzantine art and architecture from the Greek diaspora, the ground floor exhibits run in chronological order. Three rooms have been cleverly created from fragments of now lost Byzantine churches. They are of three different periods: an early 5th-century three-aisled basilica, an 11th-century domed cruciform structure and a post-Byzantine church. Icons are on display in these rooms. Elsewhere on

Funerary stele showing Orpheus with his lyre

the ground floor, the exhibits range from early Christian 4th-century basilica fragments from the Acropolis to ornate 15th-century sculptures from the Frankish occupation of Greece. Fine pieces to watch out for include a 4th–5th-century BC funerary stele from Aigina, depicting Orpheus surrounded by wild animals, and an unusual 10th–11th-century marble plaque of three apostles from Thessaloníki.

The first floor is devoted to ecclesiastical *objets d'art*, including the *Epitaphios of Salonika*, an intricate 14th-century gold-threaded embroidery. There are also some magnificent frescoes that have been rescued from churches in Náxos, Oropós and Delphi. In addition, the first floor houses an unsurpassed collection of icons from the Greek diaspora. Two of the most stunning icons are the *Galaktotrophousa* (Virgin Nursing the Child), painted in 1784 by Makários of Galatísta, a monk from Mount Athos, and the famous 14th-century mosaic icon, the *Episkepsis*, from Bithynia.

The *Episkepsis*, from the Byzantine Museum, depicting the Virgin and Child

ICONS IN THE ORTHODOX CHURCH

The word icon simply means "image" and has come to signify a holy image through association with its religious use. Subjects range from popular saints such as St Andrew and St Nicholas to lesser known martyrs, prophets and archangels. The image of the Virgin and Child is easily the most popular and exalted. Icons are a prominent feature in the Greek Orthodox religion and appear in many areas of Greek life. You will see them in taxis and buses, on boats and in restaurants, as well as in homes and churches. An icon can be in fresco, a mosaic, or made from bone or metal. The most common form is a portable painting, in wax-based paints applied to wooden boards treated with gesso. The figures are arranged so that the eyes are clearly depicted and appear to be looking directly at the viewer of the icon. These works, often of great artistic skill, are unsigned, undated and share a rigid conformity, right down to details of colour, dress, gesture and expression *(see pp18–19).* The icon painter is careful to catch every detail of a tradition that stretches back hundreds of years.

Puppet Theatre from the Theatrical Museum

Museum of Cycladic Art ❽

See pp74–5.

Plateía Kolonakíou ❾
Πλατεία Κολωνακίου

Kolonáki. **Map** 3 B5. 🚌 *3, 7, 8,13.*

KOLONAKI SQUARE and its neighbouring side streets are the most chic and sophisticated part of Athens. The area is often missed by those who restrict themselves to the ancient sites and the popular flea markets of Monastiráki. Also known as Plateía Filikís Etaireías, the square is named after a small ancient column (*kolonáki*) found in the area. Celebrated for its designer boutiques and fashionable bars and cafés, smart antique shops and art galleries, sumptuous *zacharoplastéia* (pastry shops) and *ouzerí*, it revels in its status as the city's most fashionable quarter (*see p116*). The lively pavement cafés around the square each attract a particular devoted clientele. At one there may be rich kids drinking *frappé* (iced coffee) perched on their Harley Davidson motorbikes. Another, such as the *Lykόvrissi*, will be full of an older crowd of intellectuals sipping coffee and discussing the ever-popular subject of politics.

Benáki Museum ❿

See pp78–9.

Theatrical Museum ⓫
Μουσείο και Κέντρο Μελέτης του Ελληνικού Θεάτρου

Akadamías 50, Kéntro. **Map** 2 F4. 📞 *210 362 9430.* Ⓜ *Panepistimio.* 🚌 *3, 8, 13.* ⏱ *9am–2:30pm Mon–Fri.* ⚫ *Aug, 17 Nov, main public hols.* ♿ *limited.* 📷

HOUSED IN THE BASEMENT of a fine Neo-Classical building, this small museum traces Greek theatrical history from Classical times to present day. There are displays of original posters, programmes, costumes and designs from productions by influential directors such as Károlos Koun. There is also a colourful puppet theatre. The dressing rooms of famous Greek actresses such as Eléni Papadáki and Elli Lampéti have been recreated to give an insight into their lives.

Perikles, from the Theatrical Museum

City of Athens Museum ⓬
Μουσείο της Πόλεως των Αθηνών

Paparrigopoúlou 7, Plateía Klafthmónos, Sýntagma. **Map** 2 E5. 📞 *210 324 6164.* Ⓜ *Panepistimio.* 🚌 *1, 2, 4, 5, 9, 11, 12, 15, 18.* ⏱ *9:30am–3pm Mon, Wed, Fri & Sat.* ⚫ *main public hols.* 📷

KING OTTO and Queen Amalía (*see p40*) lived here from 1831, until their new palace, today's Voulí parliament building (*see p112*), was completed in 1838. It was joined to the neighbouring house to create what was known as the Old Palace.

The palace was restored in 1980 as a museum devoted to royal memorabilia, furniture and family portraits, maps and prints. It offers a delightful look at life during the early years of King Otto's reign.

Exhibits include the manuscript of the 1843 Constitution, coats of arms from the Frankish (1205–1311) and Catalan (1311–88) rulers of Athens, and a scale model of the city as it was in 1842, made by architect Giánnis Travlós (1908–1985).

The museum also has a fine art collection, including Nikólaos Gýzis's *The Carnival in Athens* (1892) and a selection of watercolours by the English artists Edward Dodwell (1767–1832), Edward Lear (1812–88) and Thomas Hartley Cromek (1809–73).

Upstairs sitting room recreated in the City of Athens Museum

Benáki Museum ⑩
Μουσείο Μπενάκη

THIS OUTSTANDING MUSEUM was founded in 1931 by Antónis Benákis (1873–1954), the son of Emmanouíl, a wealthy Greek who made his fortune in Egypt. Housed in an elegant Neo-Classical mansion, which was once the home of the Benákis family, the collection contains a diverse array of Greek arts and crafts, paintings and jewellery, local costumes and political memorabilia that spans over 5,000 years, from the Neolithic era to the 20th century.

Flag of Hydra
The imagery symbolizes the island of Hydra's supremacy in sea warfare as it was Greece's most powerful naval community.

Bridal Cushion
This ornate embroidered cushion comes from Epirus and dates from the 18th century. It depicts a bridal procession, with ornamental flowers in the background.

★ Detail of Wood Decoration
This intricately painted and carved piece of wooden panelling comes from a mansion in Kozáni, in western Macedonia. It dates from the 18th century.

Silver Ciborium
Used to contain consecrated bread, this elegant piece of ecclesiatical silverware is dated 1667 and comes from Edirne, in Turkey.

Lecture hall

Second floor

Roof garden

Auditorium

Atrium

Entrance

KEY TO FLOORPLAN
- ☐ Ground floor
- ☐ First floor
- ☐ Second floor
- ☐ Third floor
- ☐ Non-exhibition space

Third floor

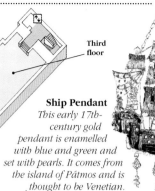

Ship Pendant
This early 17th-century gold pendant is enamelled with blue and green and set with pearls. It comes from the island of Pátmos and is thought to be Venetian.

VISITORS' CHECKLIST

Corner of Koumpári & Vassilísis Sofías, Sýntagma.
Map 7 A1.
📞 210 367 1000.
Ⓜ Sýntagma. 🚌 3, 7, 8, 13.
🕐 9am–5pm Mon, Wed, Fri & Sat, 9am–midnight Thu, 9am–3pm Sun.
⬤ 1 Jan, 25 Mar, Good Fri am, Easter Sun, 1 May, 25, 26 Dec.
💳 (free Thu) 🚻 ♿ 🍴 🛒

GALLERY GUIDE

The ground floor collection is arranged into different periods and ranges from Neolithic to late-Byzantine art and Cretan icon painting. The first floor exhibits are organized geographically and are from Asia Minor, mainland Greece and the Greek islands. There is also a collection of ecclesiastical silverware and jewellery. The second floor displays items relating to Greek spiritual, economic and social life, and the third floor concentrates on the Greek War of Independence (see pp40–41) and modern political and cultural life.

First floor

Ground floor

★ **Icon of St Anne**
The icon of St Anne was painted in the 15th century. She is carrying the Virgin Mary as a child, who is holding a white lily, symbol of purity.

Bowl from Paphos
Dating from the 13th century AD, this colourful bowl originates from Cyprus. The dancing figure is holding rattles.

★ **El Faiyûm Portrait**
This Hellenistic portrait of a man, painted on linen, dates from the 3rd century AD.

STAR EXHIBITS

★ **El Faiyûm Portrait**

★ **Icon of St Anne**

★ **Detail of Wood Decoration**

Neo-Classical façade of the National Historical Museum

National Historical Museum ⓭
Εθνικό Ιστορικό Μουσείο

Stadíou 11, Sýntagma. **Map** 2 F5. 210 323 7617. Sýntagma. 1, 2, 4, 5, 9, 10, 11, 18. 9am–2pm Tue–Sun. main public hols.

DESIGNED BY French architect François Boulanger (1807–75), this museum was originally built as the first home of the Greek parliament. Queen Amalía laid the foundation stone in 1858, but it was 13 years later that it became the first permanent site of the Greek parliament. The country's most famous prime ministers have sat in the imposing chamber of the Old Parliament of the Hellenes, including Chárilaos Trikoúpis and Theódoros Deligiánnis, who was assassinated on the steps at the front of the building in 1905. The parliament moved to its present-day site in the Voulí building on Plateía Syntágmatos (*see p112*) after the Voulí was renovated in 1935.

In 1961, the building was opened as the National Historical Museum, owned by the Historical and Ethnological Society of Greece. Founded in 1882, the purpose of the society is to collect objects that illuminate the history of modern Greece. The museum

Statue of General Theódoros Kolokotrónis

covers all the major events of Greek history from the Byzantine period to the 20th century in a chronological display. Venetian armour, traditional regional costumes and jewellery and figureheads from the warships used during the Revolution in 1821 are just some examples of the many exhibits on show.

The collection also focuses on major parliamentary figures, philhellenes and leaders in the War of Independence, displaying such items as Byron's sword, the weapons of Theódoros Kolokotrónis (1770–1843), King Otto's throne and the pen that was used by Elefthérios Venizélos to sign the Treaty of Sèvres in 1920. The revolutionary memoirs of General Makrigiánnis (1797–1864) can also be seen. Among the numerous paintings on view is a fine rare woodcut of the Battle of Lepanto (1571), the work of Bonastro.

Outside the building is a copy of Lázaros Sóchos's statue of Kolokotrónis on horseback, made in 1900, the original of which is in Náfplio (*see pp182–3*), the former capital of Greece. There is a dedication on the statue in Greek, which reads "Theódoros Kolokotrónis 1821. Ride on, noble commander, through the centuries, showing the nations how slaves may become free men."

Kapnikaréa ⓮
Καπνικαρέα

Corner of Ermoú & Kalamiótou, Monastiráki. **Map** 6 D1. 210 322 4462. Monastiráki. 8am–2pm Mon, Wed & Sat, 4:30–7:30pm Tue, Thu & Fri; 7–10:15am Sun. main public hols.

THIS CHARMING 11th-century Byzantine church was rescued from demolition in 1834, thanks to the timely intervention of King Ludwig of Bavaria. Stranded in the middle of a square between Ermoú and Kapnikaréa streets, it is surrounded by the modern office blocks and shops of Athens's busy garment district.

Traditionally called the Church of the Princess, its foundation is attributed to Empress Irene, who ruled the Byzantine Empire from AD 797 to 802. She is revered as a saint in the Greek church for her efforts in restoring icons to the Empire's churches.

The true origins of the name "Kapnikaréa" are unknown, although according to some sources, the church was named after its founder, a "hearth-tax gatherer" (*kapnikaréas*). Hearth tax was imposed on buildings by the Byzantines.

Restored in the 1950s, the dome of the church is supported by four Roman columns. Frescoes by Fótis Kóntoglou (1895–1965) were painted during the restoration, including one of the Virgin and Child. Much of Kóntoglou's work is also on display in the National Gallery of Art (*see p73*).

The dome and main entrance of the Byzantine Kapnikaréa

Athenian Neo-Classical Architecture

NEO-CLASSICISM flourished in the 19th century, when the architects who were commissioned by King Otto to build the capital in the 1830s turned to this popular European style. Among those commissioned were the Hansen brothers, Christian and Theophil, and also Ernst Ziller. As a result of their planning, within 50 years a modern city had emerged, with elegant administrative

National Bank, built in the 1890s

buildings, squares and tree-lined avenues. In its early days Neo-Classicism had imitated the grace of the buildings of ancient Greece, using marble columns, sculptures and decorative detailing. In later years, it evolved into an original Greek style. Grand Neo-Classicism is seen at its best in the public buildings along Panepistimíou; its domestic adaptation can be seen in the houses of Pláka.

Schliemann's House *(also known as Ilíou Mélathron, the Palace of Ilium, or Troy) was built in 1878 by Ziller. The interior is decorated with frescoes and mosaics of mythological subjects. It is now home to the Numismatic Museum (***Map** 2 F5*).*

The National Theatre *was built between 1882 and 1890. Ernst Ziller used a Renaissance-style exterior with arches and Doric columns for George I's Royal Theatre. Inspired by the Public Theatre of Vienna, its interior was very modern for its time (***Map** 2 D3*).*

The National Library *was designed by Danish architect Theophil Hansen in 1887 in the form of a Doric temple with two side wings. Built of Pentelic marble, it houses over half a million books, including many illuminated manuscripts and rare first editions (***Map** 2 F4*).*

Athens Academy *was designed by Theophil Hansen and built between 1859 and 1887. Statues of Apollo and Athena, and seated figures of Socrates and Plato, convey a Classical style, as do the Ionic capitals and columns. Inside the building, the Academy hall has beautiful frescoes that depict scenes from the myth of Prometheus (***Map** 2 F4*).*

The University of Athens *was designed by Christian Hansen. This fine building, completed in 1864, has an Ionic colonnade and a portico frieze depicting the resurgence of arts and sciences under the reign of King Otto. A symbol of wisdom, the Sphinx is connected with Athens through the Oedipus legend (see p221). Oedipus, who solved the riddle of the Sphinx, later found sanctuary in enlightened Athens. Other statues on the façade include Patriarch Gregory V, a martyr of the War of Independence (***Map** 2 F4*).*

CENTRAL ATHENS SOUTH

Southern Athens is dominated by the Acropolis and is home to the buildings that were at the heart of ancient Athens. Pláka and Monastiráki still revel in their historical roots as the oldest inhabited areas of the city, and are full of Byzantine churches and museums. Nestling among the restored Neo-Classical houses are grocery stores,

Relief from Panagía Gorgoepíkoös

icon painters and open-air tavernas. In the busy streets of Monastiráki's flea market, food vendors, gypsies and street musicians provide the atmosphere of a Middle Eastern bazaar. Southeast of Plateía Syntágmatos are the National Gardens, the city centre's tree-filled park. For information on getting around Athens, see pages 322–5.

SIGHTS AT A GLANCE

Museums and Galleries
Greek Folk Art Museum ⑯
Jewish Museum of Greece ⑰
Kanellópoulos Museum ⑧
Kyriazópoulos Folk Ceramic
  Museum ❶
Municipal Art Gallery ❹
Museum of Greek Popular
  Musical Instruments ⑩
University of Athens
  Museum ⑨

Ancient Sites
Acropolis pp94–101 ❼
Ancient Agora pp90–91 ❻
Kerameikós pp88–9 ❺
Temple of Olympian Zeus ⑱
Tower of the Winds pp86–7 ❷

Churches
Agios Nikólaos Ragavás ⑬
Mitrópoli ⑫
Panagía Gorgoepíkoös p105 ⑪
Russian Church of
  the Holy Trinity ⑲

Historic Districts
Anafiótika ⑭

Markets
Flea Market ❸

Squares and Gardens
National Gardens ㉑
Plateía Lysikrátous ⑮
Plateía Syntágmatos ⑳

**Historic Buildings
and Monuments**
Kallimármaro Stadium ㉓
Presidential Palace ㉒

Cemeteries
First Cemetery of Athens ㉔

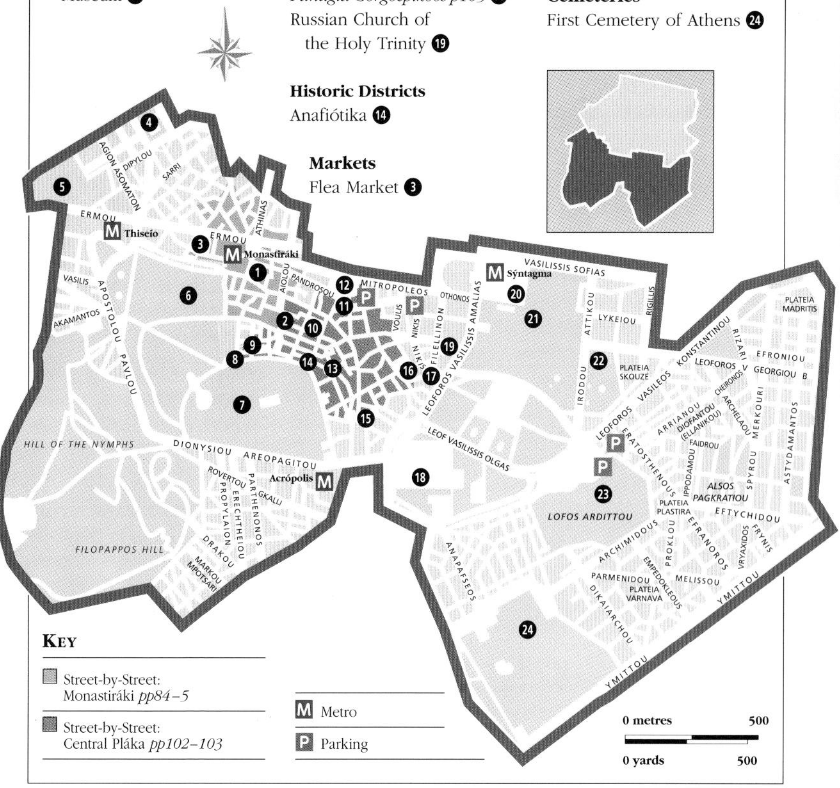

KEY

■ Street-by-Street:
  Monastiráki *pp84–5*

■ Street-by-Street:
  Central Pláka *pp102–103*

Ⓜ Metro

Ⓟ Parking

| 0 metres | 500 |
| 0 yards | 500 |

◁ **The remaining columns of the ancient Temple of Olympian Zeus**

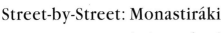

Street-by-Street: Monastiráki

THIS OLD AREA OF THE CITY takes its name from the little sunken monastery in Plateía Monastirakíou. The former heart of Ottoman Athens, Monastiráki is still home to the bazaar and market stalls selling everything from junk to jewellery. The Fethiye Mosque and the Tzistarákis Mosque, home of the Kyriazópoulos Museum, stand as reminders of the area's eastern past. Roman influences are also strong in Monastiráki. The area borders the Roman Agora and includes the remains of Emperor Hadrian's library and the unique Tower of the Winds, a Hellenistic water clock. Monastiráki mixes the atmospheric surroundings of ancient ruins with the excitement of bargaining in the bazaar.

Flea Market
Plateía Avissynías is the heart of the flea market, which extends through the surrounding streets. It is particularly popular on Sundays ❸

KEY

– – –   Suggested route

STAR SIGHT

★ **Tower of the Winds**

0 metres   50
0 yards   50

Ifaístou is named after Hephaistos, the god of fire and metal craftsmanship. Areos is named after Ares, the war god.

Monastiráki metro station

The Fethiye Mosque is situated in the corner of the Roman Agora. It was built by the Turks in the late 15th century to mark Mehmet the Conqueror's visit to Athens.

Ancient Agora
(see pp90–91)

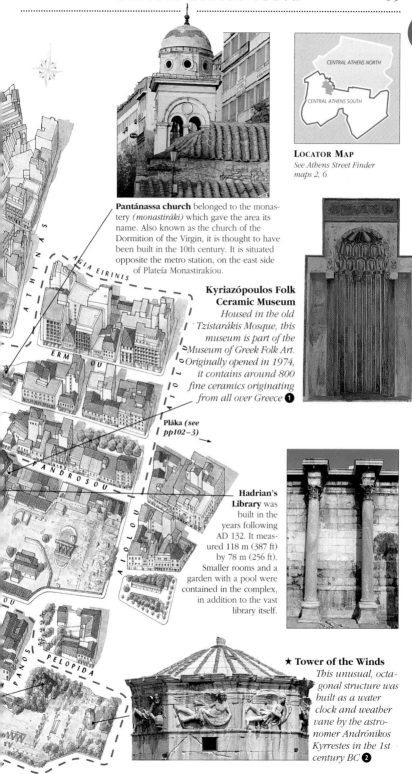

Pantánassa church belonged to the monastery *(monastiráki)* which gave the area its name. Also known as the church of the Dormition of the Virgin, it is thought to have been built in the 10th century. It is situated opposite the metro station, on the east side of Plateía Monastirakíou.

Kyriazópoulos Folk Ceramic Museum
Housed in the old Tzistarákis Mosque, this museum is part of the Museum of Greek Folk Art. Originally opened in 1974, it contains around 800 fine ceramics originating from all over Greece ❶

Pláka *(see pp102–3)*

Hadrian's Library was built in the years following AD 132. It measured 118 m (387 ft) by 78 m (256 ft). Smaller rooms and a garden with a pool were contained in the complex, in addition to the vast library itself.

★ Tower of the Winds
This unusual, octagonal structure was built as a water clock and weather vane by the astronomer Andrónikos Kyrrestes in the 1st century BC ❷

Kyriazópoulos Folk Ceramic Museum ❶

Μουσείο Ελληνικής Λαϊκής Τέχνης, Συλλογή Κεραμικών Β. Κυριαζοπούλου

Tzistarákis Mosque, Areos 1, Monastiráki. **Map** 6 D1. **℡** 210 324 2066. **Ⓜ** Monastiráki. **◑** 9am–2:30pm Mon & Wed–Sun. **◑** main public hols. 🎫

THIS COLOURFUL COLLECTION of ceramics was donated to the Greek Folk Art Museum in 1974 by Professor Vasíleios Kyriazópoulos. Now an annexe of the Folk Art Museum, the Kyriazópoulos Folk Ceramic Museum is housed in the imposing Tzistarákis Mosque (or the Mosque of the Lower Fountain). Of the hundreds of pieces on display, many are of the type still used today in a traditional Greek kitchen, such as terracotta water jugs from Aígina, earthenware oven dishes from Sífnos and storage jars from Thessaly and Chíos. There are also some ceramic figures and plates, based on mythological and folk stories, crafted by Minás Avramídis and Dimítrios Mygdalinós who came from Asia Minor in the 1920s.

The mosque itself is of as much interest as its contents. It was built in 1759 by the newly appointed Turkish *voivode* Tzistarákis. The *voivode* was the civil

Ceramic of a young girl from Asia Minor

governor who possessed complete powers over the law courts and the police. He collected taxes for his own account, but also had to pay for the sultan's harem and the treasury. His workmen dynamited the 17th column of the Temple of Olympian Zeus *(see p111)* in order to make lime to be used for the stucco work on the mosque. Destruction of ancient monuments was forbidden by Turkish law and this act of vandalism was the downfall of Tzistarákis. He was exiled the same year. The mosque has now been well restored after earthquake damage in 1981.

Tower of the Winds ❷

Αέρηδες

Within Roman Agora ruins, Pláka. **Map** 6 D1. **℡** 210 324 5220. **Ⓜ** Monastiráki. **◑** 8:30am–2:45pm Tue–Sun. **◑** main public hols. 🎫 ♿

THE REMARKABLE Tower of the Winds is set within the ruins of the Roman Agora. Constructed from marble in the 2nd century BC by the Syrian astronomer Andrónikos Kyrrestes, it was built as a combined weather vane and water clock. The name comes from the external friezes, personifying the eight winds. Sundials are etched into the walls beneath each relief.

The tower is well preserved, standing today at over 12 m (40 ft) high with a diameter of 8 m (26 ft). Still simply called Aérides ("the winds") by Greeks today, in the Middle Ages it was thought to be either the school or prison of Socrates, or even the tomb of Philip II of Macedon *(see p242)*. It was at last correctly identified as the Horologion (water clock) of Andronikos in the 17th century. All that remains today of its elaborate water clock are the origins of a complex system of water pipes and a circular channel cut into the floor which can be seen inside the tower.

The west and southwest faces of the Tower of the Winds

The west- and north-facing sides each contain a hole which lets light into the otherwise dark interior of the tower.

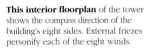

This interior floorplan of the tower shows the compass direction of the building's eight sides. External friezes personify each of the eight winds.

NORTH

Boreas blows the cold north wind through a large conch shell.

NORTHWEST

Skiron scatters glowing ashes from a bronze vessel.

WEST

Zephyros is a semi-naked youth scattering flowers.

Flea Market ❸
Παζάρι

From Plateía Monastirakíou to
Plateía Avyssinías, Pláka. **Map** 5 C1.
Ⓜ *Thiseío.* ◯ *8am–2pm Sun.*

Shoppers browsing in Athens' lively flea market

A BANNER WELCOMES visitors to Athens' famous flea market, past the ubiquitous tourist trinket shops of Adrianoú and Pandrósou streets. For the locals, the true heart of the market lies just west of Plateía Monastirakíou, in Plateía Avyssinías and its warren of surrounding streets.

On Sunday mornings when the shops are closed, the market itself bursts into action. Traders set out their bric-a-brac on stalls and the pavement and many bargains can be found, especially the colourful handwoven woollen cloths and the many bangles and beads sold by hippies. More expensive items are also on sale, including brassware, leatherware and silverware.

During the week the shops in the surrounding area are open and filled with much the same as the Sunday stalls. Individual shops each have their own specialities, so hunt around before making a purchase. You can buy almost anything, from antiques and old books to taverna chairs and army surplus gear.

***The southwest wind**, Lips, heralds a swift voyage. The reliefs show that each wind was given a personality according to its characteristics, and each promises different conditions. Gentle Zephyros and chilly Boreas, mentioned in Western literature and represented in art and sculpture, are the best known of these.*

Whirling dervishes used the tower as a monastery in the mid-18th century. The dervishes were a Muslim order of ascetics. The tower's occupants became a popular attraction for Grand Tour visitors who came to witness the weekly ritual of a frenzied dance, which is known as the sema.

| **SOUTHWEST** | **SOUTH** | **SOUTHEAST** | **EAST** | **NORTHEAST** |
| | | Relief carving of mythological figure | Metal rod casting shadow | Lines of sundial carved into wall of tower |

Lips holds the *aphlaston* (or stern ornament) of a ship as he steers.

Notos is the bearer of rain, emptying a pitcher of water.

Euros is a bearded old man, warmly wrapped in a cloak.

Apeliotes is a young man bringing fruits and corn.

Kaïkias empties a shield full of icy hailstones on those below.

Miss T K, by Giánnis Mitarákis, in the Municipal Art Gallery

Municipal Art Gallery ❹
Πινακοθήκη του Δήμου Αθηναίων

Plateía Koumoundoúrou, Omónoia. **Map** 1 C4. ☏ 210 324 3023. Ⓜ *Omónoia.* ⏰ *9am–1pm & 5–9pm Mon–Fri, 9am–1pm Sat & Sun.* ⏺ *3 Oct, main public hols.* 📷

THIS LITTLE-VISITED museum has one of the finest archive collections of modern Greek art. Designed by architect Panagiótis Kálkos in 1872, the home of the museum is the old Neo-Classical Foundling Hospital. It was built to cope with the city's population explosion towards the end of the 19th century; unwanted babies were left outside the main entrance to be cared for by hospital staff.

The Municipality of Athens has been amassing the collection since 1923. It now offers a fine introduction to the diverse styles of modern Greek artists. Many paintings are passionate reflections on the Greek landscape, such as Dímos Mpraésas's (1878–1967) landscapes of the Cyclades, or Konstantínos Parthénis's (1882–1964) paintings of olive and cypress trees.

There are also portraits by Giánnis Mitarákis and still lifes by Theófrastos Triantafyllídis. Paintings such as Nikólaos Kartsonákis's *Street Market* (1939) also reveal the folk roots that are at the heart of much modern Greek art.

Kerameikós ❺
Κεραμεικός

THIS ANCIENT CEMETERY has been a burial ground since the 12th century BC. The Sacred Way led from Eleusis *(see pp156–7)* to Kerameikós and the Panathenaic Way set out from the Dípylon Gate here to the Acropolis *(see pp94–7)*. Most of the graves remaining today are along the Street of the Tombs. The sculptures excavated in the early 1900s are in the National Archaeological Museum *(see pp68–71)* and the Oberlander Museum; however, plaster copies of the originals can be seen *in situ*.

Grave *Stele* of Hegeso
This is from the family burial plot belonging to Koroibos of Melite. It shows his wife, Hegeso, admiring her jewels with a servant and dates from the late 5th century BC.

Precinct of Aristion

STREET OF THE TOMBS

The Precinct of Lysimachides contains a marble dog, originally one of a pair.

The Sanctuary of Hekate was sacred to the ancient goddess of the underworld. It contained an altar and votive offerings.

South terrace

Oberlander Museum

★ **Tomb of Dionysios of Kollytos**
This fine tomb belongs to a rich treasurer. A bull often represents the god Dionysos.

STAR MONUMENTS

★ **Tomb of Dionysios of Kollytos**

★ ***Stele* of Demetria and Pamphile**

STREET OF THE TOMBS

Most of the monuments in the Street of the Tombs date from the 4th century BC. The different styles, from the lavish *stelae* (relief sculptures) to the simple *kioniskoi* (small columns), all reveal the dignity that is typical of Greek funerary art.

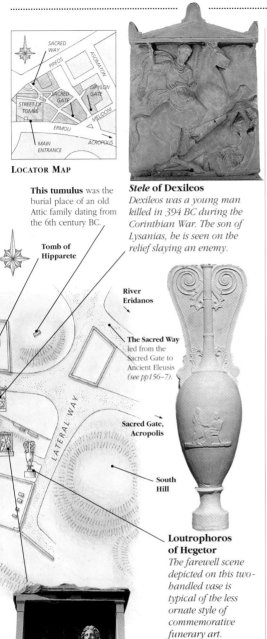

LOCATOR MAP

This tumulus was the burial place of an old Attic family dating from the 6th century BC.

Stele **of Dexileos**
Dexileos was a young man killed in 394 BC during the Corinthian War. The son of Lysanias, he is seen on the relief slaying an enemy.

VISITORS' CHECKLIST

Ermoú 148, Thiseío. **Map** 1 B5.
210 346 3552. Thiseío.
8:30am–3pm Tue–Sun.
1 Jan, 25 Mar, Easter Sun,
1 May, 25, 26 Dec.

Oberlander Museum
This museum is named after Gustav Oberlander (1867–1936), a German-American industrialist whose donations helped fund its construction in the 1930s. In Gallery 1, some large fragments from grave *stelae* found incorporated into the Dipylon and Sacred Gates are exhibited. These include a marble sphinx (c.550 BC) that once crowned a grave *stele*. Galleries 2 and 3 offer an array of huge Proto-geometric and Geometric amphorae and black-figure *lekythoi* (funerary vases). The most moving exhibits come from children's graves and include pottery toy horses and terracotta dolls. There are also examples of some of the 7,000 *ostraka* (voting tablets) *(see pp90–91)* found in the bed of the river Eridanos. Among the superb painted pottery, there is a red-figure *hydria* (water vase) of Helen of Troy and a *lekythos* of Dionysos with satyrs.

Winged sphinx from grave *stele*

Tomb of Hipparete

River Eridanos

The Sacred Way led from the Sacred Gate to Ancient Eleusis *(see pp156–7).*

Sacred Gate, Acropolis

South Hill

Loutrophoros of Hegetor
The farewell scene depicted on this two-handled vase is typical of the less ornate style of commemorative funerary art.

★ *Stele* of Demetria and Pamphile
This moving sculpture shows the seated Pamphile with her sister Demetria behind her. This was one of the last ornate stelae to be made in the late 4th century BC.

Geometric funerary amphora from the Oberlander Museum

Ancient Agora ⑥
Αρχαία Αγορά

Voting lot

Tʜᴇ ᴀɢᴏʀᴀ, or market-place, formed the political heart of ancient Athens from 600 BC. Democracy was practised in the *Bouleuterion* (Council) and the law courts, and in open meetings. Socrates was indicted and executed in the state prison here in 399 BC. The theatres, schools and stoas filled with shops also made this the centre of social and commercial life. Even the city mint that produced Athens' silver coins was here. The American School of Classical Studies began excavations of the Ancient Agora in the 1930s, and since then the vast remains of a complex array of public buildings have been revealed.

View across the Agora from the south showing the reconstructed Stoa of Attalos on the right

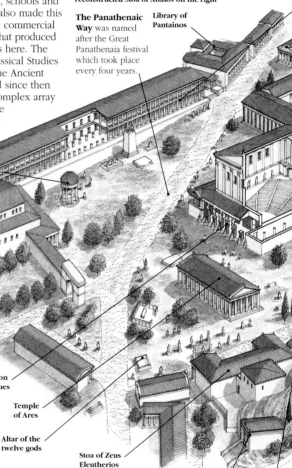

The Panathenaic Way was named after the Great Panathenaia festival which took place every four years.

Library of Pantainos

Monopteros temple

Triton statues

Temple of Ares

Altar of the twelve gods

Stoa of Zeus Eleutherios

Hellenistic temple

Temple of Apollo Patroös

Odeion of Agrippa
This statue of a triton (half-god, half-fish) once adorned the façade of the Odeion of Agrippa. It dates from AD 150 and is now in the Agora museum.

Rᴇᴄᴏɴꜱᴛʀᴜᴄᴛɪᴏɴ ᴏꜰ ᴛʜᴇ Aɴᴄɪᴇɴᴛ Aɢᴏʀᴀ
This shows the Agora as it was in c.AD 200, viewed from the northwest. The main entrance to the Agora at this time was via the Panathenaic Way, which ran across the site from the Acropolis in the southeast to the Kerameikós in the northwest.

0 metres   50
0 yards   50

Stoa of Attalos
This colonnaded building was reconstructed in the mid-20th century as a museum to house finds from the Ancient Agora site.

Statue of Hadrian
Hadrian was Emperor of Rome from AD 117–38. Athens was under his authority. The statue dates from the 2nd century AD.

Southeast temple

The middle stoa housed shops.

Altar of Zeus

Southwest temple

Heliaia

Southwest fountain

Latrines

The Tholos was the Council headquarters.

Bouleuterion or Council chamber

Monument of the Eponymous Heroes

Oil flask in the Archaic style

Metroön

Arsenal

Hephaisteion
This temple, also known as the Theseion, is the best-preserved building on the site. It was built c.449–440 BC.

VISITORS' CHECKLIST
Main entrance at Adriánou, Monastiráki. **Map** 5 C1.
📞 210 321 0185. Ⓜ *Thiseío, Monastiráki.* **Museum & site**
🕐 8:30am–3pm Tue–Sun.
⚫ 1 Jan, 25 Mar, Easter Sun, 1 May, 25, 26 Dec. 📷
♿ limited.

Ostrakon condemning a man named Hippokrates to exile

🏛 Stoa of Attalos
This fine building was rebuilt between 1953 and 1956, helped by a huge donation from John D Rockefeller, Jr. An impressive two-storey stoa, or roofed arcade, founded by King Attalos of Pergamon (ruled 159–138 BC), it dominated the eastern quarter of the Agora until it was burnt down by the Heruli tribe in AD 267. Reconstructed using the original foundations and ancient materials, it now contains a museum whose exhibits reveal the great diversity and sophistication of ancient life. Artifacts include rules from the 2nd-century AD Library of Pantainos, the text of a law against tyranny from 337 BC, bronze and stone lots used for voting and a *klepsýdra* (water clock) used for timing speeches. *Ostraka* (voting tablets on which names were inscribed) bear such famous names as Themistokles and Aristeides the Just, the latter banished, or "ostracized", in 482 BC. More everyday items, such as terracotta toys and portable ovens, and hobnails and sandals found in a shoemaker's shop, are equally fascinating. Also on display are some beautiful black-figure vases and an unusual oil flask moulded into the shape of a kneeling boy.

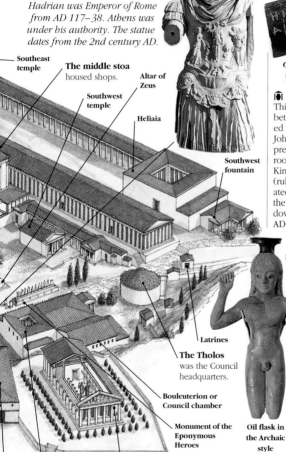

Acropolis
Ακρόπολη

IN THE MID-5TH CENTURY BC, Perikles persuaded the Athenians to begin a grand programme of new building work in Athens that has come to represent the political and cultural achievements of Greece. The work transformed the Acropolis with three contrasting temples and a monumental gateway. The Theatre of Dionysos on the south slope was developed further in the 4th century BC, and the Theatre of Herodes Atticus was added in the 2nd century AD.

LOCATOR MAP

★ Porch of the Caryatids
These statues of women were used in place of columns on the south porch of the Erechtheion. The originals, four of which can be seen in the Acropolis Museum, have been replaced by casts.

An olive tree now grows where Athena first planted her tree in a competition against Poseidon.

The Propylaia was built in 437–432 BC to form a new entrance to the Acropolis *(see p96).*

★ Temple of Athena Nike
This temple to Athena of Victory is on the west side of the Propylaia. It was built in 426–421 BC (see p96).

The Beulé Gate was the first entrance to the Acropolis *(see p96).*

Pathway to Acropolis from ticket office

STAR SIGHTS

★ Parthenon

★ Porch of the Caryatids

★ Temple of Athena Nike

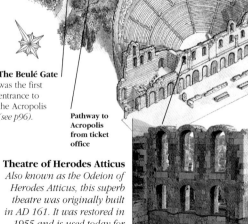

Theatre of Herodes Atticus
Also known as the Odeion of Herodes Atticus, this superb theatre was originally built in AD 161. It was restored in 1955 and is used today for outdoor concerts (see p100).

◁ **The Porch of the Caryatids on the Erechtheion**

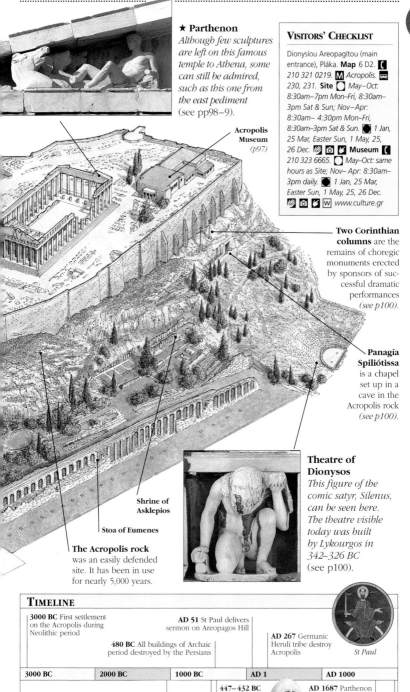

★ **Parthenon**
Although few sculptures are left on this famous temple to Athena, some can still be admired, such as this one from the east pediment (see pp98–9).

VISITORS' CHECKLIST

Dionysiou Areopagitou (main entrance), Pláka. **Map** 6 D2. 210 321 0219. **M** Acropolis. 230, 231. **Site** May–Oct: 8:30am–7pm Mon–Fri, 8:30am–3pm Sat & Sun; Nov–Apr: 8:30am– 4:30pm Mon–Fri, 8:30am–3pm Sat & Sun. 1 Jan, 25 Mar, Easter Sun, 1 May, 25, 26 Dec. **Museum** 210 323 6665. May–Oct: same hours as Site; Nov– Apr: 8:30am–3pm daily. 1 Jan, 25 Mar, Easter Sun, 1 May, 25, 26 Dec. **W** www.culture.gr

Acropolis Museum
(p97)

Two Corinthian columns are the remains of choregic monuments erected by sponsors of successful dramatic performances *(see p100)*.

Panagía Spiliótissa is a chapel set up in a cave in the Acropolis rock *(see p100)*.

Shrine of Asklepios

Stoa of Eumenes

The Acropolis rock was an easily defended site. It has been in use for nearly 5,000 years.

Theatre of Dionysos
This figure of the comic satyr, Silenus, can be seen here. The theatre visible today was built by Lykourgos in 342–326 BC (see p100).

TIMELINE

3000 BC First settlement on the Acropolis during Neolithic period

AD 51 St Paul delivers sermon on Areopagos Hill

480 BC All buildings of Archaic period destroyed by the Persians

AD 267 Germanic Heruli tribe destroy Acropolis

St Paul

3000 BC	2000 BC	1000 BC	AD 1	AD 1000

1200 BC Cyclopean wall built to replace original ramparts

510 BC Delphic Oracle declares Acropolis a holy place of the gods, banning habitation by mortals

447–432 BC Construction of the Parthenon under Perikles

Perikles (495–429 BC)

AD 1687 Parthenon damaged by Venetians

AD 1987 Restoration of the Erechtheion completed

Exploring the Acropolis

Relief of *Mourning* Athena

ONCE THROUGH the first entrance, the Beulé Gate, straight ahead is the Propylaia, the grand entrance to the temple complex. Before going through here, it is worth exploring the Temple of Athena Nike, on the right. Beyond the Propylaia are the Erechtheion and the Parthenon *(see pp98–9)* which dominate the top of the rock. There are also stunning views of Athens itself from the Acropolis. Since 1975, access to all the temple precincts has been banned to prevent further damage. Buildings located at the foot of the Acropolis and the hills immediately to the west are covered on pages 100–101.

View of the Acropolis from the southwest

⋔ Beulé Gate
The gate is named after the French archaeologist Ernest Beulé who discovered it in 1852. It was built in AD 267 after the raid of the Heruli, a Germanic people, as part of the Roman Acropolis fortifications. It incorporates stones from the *choregic* monument *(see p109)* of Nikias that was situated near the Stoa of Eumenes. Parts of the original monument's dedication are still visible over the architrave. There is also an inscription identifying a Roman, Flavius Septimius Marcellinus, as

donor of the gateway. In 1686, when the Turks destroyed the Temple of Athena Nike, they used the marble to build a bastion for artillery over the gate.

⋔ Temple of Athena Nike
This small temple was built in 426–421 BC to commemorate the Athenians' victories over the Persians. The temple frieze has representative scenes from the Battle of Plataiaí (479 BC). Designed by Kallikrates, the temple stands on a 9.5-m (31-ft) bastion. It has been used as both observation post and an ancient shrine to the goddess of Victory, Athena Nike, of whom there is a remarkable sculpture situated on the balustrade. Legend records the temple site as the place from which King Aegeus threw himself into the sea, believing that his son Theseus had been killed in Crete by the Minotaur. Built

The eastern end of the Erechtheion

of Pentelic marble, the temple has four Ionic columns 4 m (13 ft) high at each portico end. It was reconstructed in 1834–8, after being destroyed in 1686 by the Turks. On the point of collapse in 1935, it was again dismantled and reconstructed according to information resulting from more recent research.

⋔ Propylaia
Work began on this enormous entrance to the Acropolis in 437 BC. Although the outbreak of the Peloponnesian War in 432 BC curtailed its completion, its architect Mnesikles created a building admired throughout the ancient world. The Propylaia comprises a rectangular central building divided by a wall into two porticoes. These were punctuated by five entrance doors, rows of Ionic and Doric columns and a vestibule with a blue-coffered ceiling decorated with gold stars. Two wings flank the main building. The north wing was home to the *pinakothíki*, an art gallery.

During its chequered history – later as archbishop's residence, Frankish palace, and Turkish fortress and armoury – parts of the building have been accidentally destroyed; it even suffered the misfortune of being struck by lightning in 1645, and later the explosion of the Turkish gunpowder store *(see p98)*.

⋔ Erechtheion
Built between 421 and 406 BC, the Erechtheion is situated on the most sacred site of the Acropolis. It is said to be where Poseidon left his trident marks in a rock, and Athena's olive tree sprouted, in their battle for possession of the city. Named after Erechtheus, one of the mythical kings of Athens, the temple was a sanctuary to both Athena Polias and Erechtheus-Poseidon.

Famed for its elegant and extremely ornate Ionic architecture and caryatid columns in the shape of women, this extraordinary monument is built on different levels. The large rectangular cella was divided into three rooms. One contained the holy olive wood statue of Athena Polias. The cella was bounded by north, east and south porticoes. The south is the Porch of the Caryatids, the maiden statues which are now in the Acropolis Museum.

The Erechtheion complex has been used for a range of purposes, including a harem for the wives of the Turkish *disdar* (commander) in 1463. It was almost completely destroyed by a Turkish shell in 1827 during the War of Independence *(see pp40–41)*. Recent restoration has caused heated disputes: holes have been filled with new marble, and copies have been made to replace original features that have been removed to the safety of the museum.

A youth leading a cow to sacrifice, from the Parthenon's north frieze

Acropolis Museum
Built below the level of the Parthenon, this museum is located in the southeast corner of the site. Opened in 1878, it was reconstructed after World War II to accommodate a collection devoted

to finds from the Acropolis. Treasures include fine statues from the 5th century BC and well-preserved segments of the Parthenon frieze.

The collection begins chronologically in **Rooms I, II** and **III** with 6th-century BC works. Fragments of painted pedimental statues include mythological scenes of Herakles grappling with various monsters, ferocious lions devouring calves, and the more peaceful votive statue of the *Moschophoros*, or Calf-Bearer, portraying a young man carrying a calf on his shoulders (c.570 BC).

Room V houses a pediment from the old Temple of Athena showing part of a battle where the figures of Athena and Zeus against the giants represent the Greek triumph over primitive forces. **Room IV** has recently restored sculptures dating from c.550 BC and **Rooms IV** and **VI** also contain a unique collection of *korai* from c.550–500 BC. These were votive statues of maidens offered to Athena. They represent the development of ancient Greek art – moving from the formal bearing of the *Peplos Kore* to the more natural body movement of the *Kore of Euthydikos* and *Almond-Eyed Kore*. Other representative statues of this later period are the *Mourning Athena*, head of the *Blond Boy* and the *Kritios Boy*.

Rooms VII and **VIII** contain, among other exhibits, a well-preserved *metope* from the south side of the Parthenon

The *Moschophoros* (Calf-Bearer), a sculpture from the Archaic period

showing the battle between the Lapiths and centaurs. The remaining parts of the Parthenon frieze depict the Panathenaic procession, including the chariot and *apobates* (slaves riding the chariot horses), the *thallophoroi* (bearers of olive branches), and a sacrificial cow being led by youths.

Room IX ends the collection with four caryatids from the Erechtheion south porch. They are the only ones on display in Athens and are carefully kept in a temperature-controlled environment.

THE ELGIN MARBLES

These famous sculptures, also called the Parthenon Marbles, are held in the British Museum in London. They were acquired by Lord Elgin in 1801–3 from the occupying Turkish authorities. He sold them to the British nation for £35,000 in 1816. There is great controversy surrounding the Marbles. While some argue that they are more carefully preserved in the British Museum, the Greek government does not accept the legality of the sale and many believe they belong in Athens. A famous supporter of this cause was the Greek actress and politician, Melína Merkoúri, who died in 1994.

The newly arrived Elgin Marbles at the British Museum, in a painting by A Archer

The Parthenon
Ο Παρθενώνας

ONE OF THE WORLD'S most famous buildings, this temple was begun in 447 BC. It was designed by the architects Kallikrates and Iktinos, primarily to house the 12 m (40 ft) high statue of Athena Parthenos (Maiden), sculpted by Pheidias. Taking nine years to complete, the temple was dedicated to the goddess in 438 BC. Over the centuries, it has been used as a church, a mosque and an arsenal, and has suffered severe damage. Built as an expression of the glory of ancient Athens, it remains the city's emblem to this day.

View of the Parthenon today, from the west

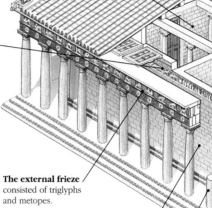

Akroterion

The west cella was used as a treasury.

The external frieze consisted of triglyphs and metopes.

Marble walls concealed the cellas, or inner rooms.

Each column was constructed from fluted drums of marble. The fluting was added once the columns were in place.

The Elgin Marbles (see p97) were taken largely from the internal frieze.

Parthenon Frieze
The frieze, designed by Pheidias, ran around the inner wall of the Parthenon. The metopes (sections of the frieze) depicted myths and the Great Panathenaia festival, honouring Athena.

RECONSTRUCTION OF THE PARTHENON

This reconstruction, from the southeast, shows the Parthenon as it was in the 5th century BC. It was 70 m (230 ft) long and 30 m (100 ft) wide. The entablature of this peripteral temple (with a single row of columns around the edge) was painted in blue, red and gold.

VEDUTA DEL CAST: D'ACROPOLIS DALLA-PARTE DI TRAMONTANA

Explosion of 1687
During the Venetian siege of the Acropolis, General Francesco Morosini bombarded the Parthenon with cannon-fire. The Turks were using the temple as an arsenal at the time and the ensuing explosion demolished much of it, including the roof, the inner structure and 14 of the outer columns.

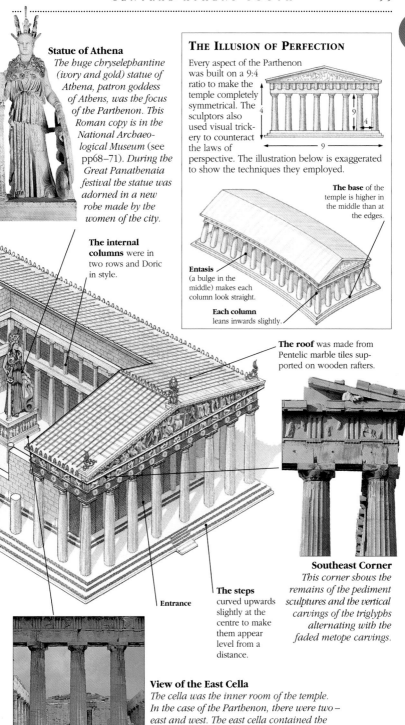

Statue of Athena
The huge chryselephantine (ivory and gold) statue of Athena, patron goddess of Athens, was the focus of the Parthenon. This Roman copy is in the National Archaeological Museum (see pp68–71). During the Great Panathenaia festival the statue was adorned in a new robe made by the women of the city.

THE ILLUSION OF PERFECTION

Every aspect of the Parthenon was built on a 9:4 ratio to make the temple completely symmetrical. The sculptors also used visual trickery to counteract the laws of perspective. The illustration below is exaggerated to show the techniques they employed.

The base of the temple is higher in the middle than at the edges.

Entasis (a bulge in the middle) makes each column look straight.

Each column leans inwards slightly.

The internal columns were in two rows and Doric in style.

The roof was made from Pentelic marble tiles supported on wooden rafters.

Southeast Corner
This corner shows the remains of the pediment sculptures and the vertical carvings of the triglyphs alternating with the faded metope carvings.

The steps curved upwards slightly at the centre to make them appear level from a distance.

Entrance

View of the East Cella
The cella was the inner room of the temple. In the case of the Parthenon, there were two – east and west. The east cella contained the enormous cult statue of Athena and the offerings bestowed upon it. The west cella was the back room, reserved for the priestess.

Around the Acropolis

Throne from the Theatre of Dionysos

THE AREA AROUND THE ACROPOLIS was the centre of public life in Athens. In addition to the Agora in the north *(see pp90–91)*, there were the two theatres on the south slope, used for drama festivals in honour of the god Dionysos. Political life was largely centred on the Pnyx and the Areopagos, the hills lying to the west of the Acropolis: the Assembly met on the former and murder trials were heard by a council of ex-magistrates on the latter. Other ancient remains and the Acropolis Study Centre provide a fascinating insight into daily life in ancient Athens.

The remains of the Theatre of Dionysos

⋔ Theatre of Herodes Atticus

This small Roman theatre seats 5,000 spectators and is still in use today. Built by the Roman consul Herodes Atticus between AD 161 and 174, in memory of his wife, the shape was hollowed out of the rocks on the southern slope of the Acropolis. The semicircular orchestra in front of the stage was repaved with alternating blue and white marble slabs in the 1950s. Behind the stage, its distinctive colonnade once contained statues of the nine Muses. The whole theatre was originally enclosed by a cedarwood roof that gave better acoustics and allowed for all-weather performances. Today it is used for a range of entertainment, including plays and concerts, both classical and popular *(see p119)*.

⋔ Theatre of Dionysos

Cut into the southern cliff face of the Acropolis, the Theatre of Dionysos is the birthplace of Greek tragedy, and was the first theatre built of stone. Aeschylus, Sophocles,

Euripides and Aristophanes all had their plays performed here, during the dramatic contests of the annual City Dionysia festival, when it was little more than a humble wood-and-earth affair. The theatre was rebuilt in stone by the Athenian statesman Lykourgos between 342–326 BC, but the ruins that can be seen today are in part those of a much bigger structure, built by the Romans, which could seat 17,000. They used it as a gladiatorial arena, and

added a marble balustrade with metal railings to protect spectators. In the 1st century AD, during Emperor Nero's reign, the orchestra was given its marble flooring, and in the 2nd century AD the front of the stage was decorated with reliefs showing Dionysos's life.

Above the theatre there is a cave sacred to the goddess Artemis. This was converted into a chapel in the Byzantine era, dedicated to **Panagía i Spiliótissa** (Our Lady of the Cave), and was the place where mothers brought their sick children. Two large Corinthian columns nearby are the remains of choregic monuments erected to celebrate the benefactor's team winning a drama festival. The Sanctuary of Asklepios to the west, founded in 420 BC, was dedicated to the god of healing. Worshippers seeking a cure had to take part in purification rites before they could enter the temple precincts.

⌾ Acropolis Study Centre

Makrygiánni 2–4, Makrygiánni. **☎** 210 923 9381. **●** *for restoration.*
Earthquake damage has forced this building to close for restoration. When it reopens, (scheduled for end-2003) this handsome Neo-Classical building will resume its function as a research centre and storehouse of historical information on the Acropolis. Displays will include a scale model of the Parthenon, a complete plaster-cast representation of its frieze and a fascinating account of the quarrying of the famous white Pentelic marble and of how it was brought to Athens.

Interior of the Panagía Spiliótissa chapel, above the Theatre of Dionysos

⛰ Areopagos Hill

There is little left to see on this low hill today, apart from the rough-hewn, slippery steps and what are thought to be seats on its summit. The Areopagos was used by the Persians and Turks during their attacks on the Acropolis citadel, and played an important role as the home of the Supreme Judicial Court in the Classical period. It takes its name, meaning the "Hill of Ares", from a mythological trial that took place here when the god Ares was acquitted of murdering the son of Poseidon. The nearby **Cave of the Furies** inspired the playwright Aeschylus *(see p57)* to set Orestes' trial here in his play *Eumenides* (The Furies). The hill also achieved renown in AD 51, when St Paul delivered his sermon "On an unknown God" and gained his first convert, Dionysios the Areopagite, who subsequently became the patron saint of Athens.

⛰ Pnyx Hill

Today's role for the Pnyx, as outdoor theatre for multilingual son et lumière performances, seems a sad fate for the home of 4th- and 5th-century BC democracy. This is where the *Ekklesia* (citizens' assembly) met to discuss and vote upon all but the most important matters of state, until it lost its powers during Roman rule. In its heyday, 6,000 Athenians gathered 40 times a year to listen to speeches and take vital political decisions. Themistokles, Perikles and Demosthenes all spoke from the *bema* (speaker's platform) that is still visible today. Carved out of the rock face, it formed the top step of a platform that doubled as a primitive altar to the god Zeus. There are also the remains of the huge retaining

wall which was built to support the semicircular terraces that placed citizens on a level with the speakers. It completely surrounded the auditorium which was 110 m (358 ft) high.

🔒 Agios Dimítrios

Dionysiou Areopagitou, south slope of Acropolis. ⬤ *daily.* 🄴 *except Sun.*

This Byzantine church is often called Agios Dimítrios Loumpardiáris, after an incident in 1656. The Turkish *disdar* (commander) at the time, Yusuf Aga, laid plans to fire a huge cannon called Loumpárda, situated by the Propylaia *(see p96)*, at worshippers in the church as they celebrated the feast day of Agios Dimítrios. However, the night before the feast, lightning struck the Propylaia, miraculously killing the commander and his family.

Cross from Agios Dimítrios church

⛰ Filopáppos Hill

The highest summit in the south of Athens, at 147 m (482 ft), offers spectacular views of the Acropolis. It has always played a decisive defensive role in Athens' history – the general Demetrios Poliorketes built an important fort here overlooking the strategic Piraeus road in 294 BC, and Francesco Morosini bombarded the Acropolis from here in 1687. Popularly called

The Monument of Philopappus AD 114–116

The Asteroskopeíon on the Hill of the Nymphs

Filopáppos Hill after a monument still on its summit, it was also known to the ancient Greeks as the Hill of Muses or the Mouseion, because the tomb of Musaeus, a disciple of Orpheus, was traditionally held to be located here.

Built between AD 114–16, the Monument of Philopappus was raised by the Athenians in honour of Caius Julius Antiochus Philopappus, a Roman consul and philhellene. Its unusual concave marble façade, 12 m (40 ft) high, contains niches with statues of Philopappus and his grandfather, Antiochus IV. A frieze around the monument depicts the arrival of Philopappus by chariot for his inauguration as Roman consul in AD 100.

🌲 Hill of the Nymphs

This 103-m (340-ft) high tree-clad hill takes its name from dedications found carved on rocks in today's Observatory Garden. The Asteroskopeíon (Observatory), built in 1842 by the Danish architect Theophil Hansen, with funds from philanthropist Baron Sína, occupies the site of a sanctuary to nymphs associated with childbirth. The modern church of Agía Marína nearby has similar associations of childbirth; pregnant women used to slide effortlessly down a smooth rock near the church, in the hope of an equally easy labour.

Street-by-Street: Central Pláka

PLAKA IS THE HISTORIC HEART of Athens. Even though only a few houses date back further than the Ottoman period, it remains the oldest continuously inhabited area of the city. One explanation of its name comes from the word *pliaka* (old), which was used to describe the area by Albanian soldiers in the service of the Turks who settled here in the 16th century. Despite the crowds of tourists and the many Athenians, who come to eat in the tavernas or browse in antique shops, it still retains the feel of a residential neighbourhood.

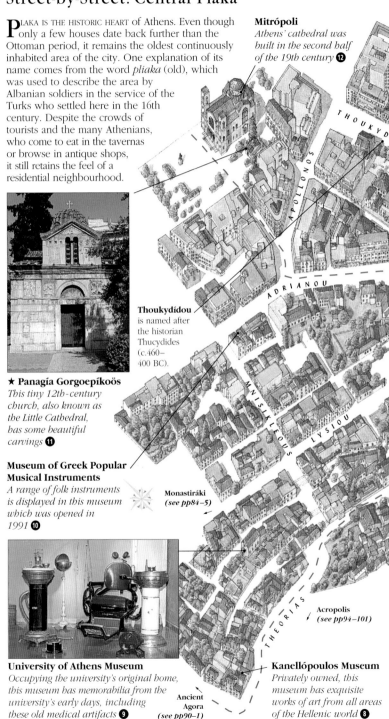

Mitrópoli
Athens' cathedral was built in the second half of the 19th century **12**

Thoukydídou
is named after the historian Thucydides (c.460–400 BC).

★ **Panagía Gorgoepíkoös**
This tiny 12th-century church, also known as the Little Cathedral, has some beautiful carvings **11**

Museum of Greek Popular Musical Instruments
A range of folk instruments is displayed in this museum which was opened in 1991 **10**

Monastiráki
(see pp84–5)

Acropolis
(see pp94–101)

University of Athens Museum
Occupying the university's original home, this museum has memorabilia from the university's early days, including these old medical artifacts **9**

Ancient Agora
(see pp90–1)

Kanellópoulos Museum
Privately owned, this museum has exquisite works of art from all areas of the Hellenic world **8**

Plateía Syntágmatos (see p112)

Greek Folk Art Museum
Offering the best of Greek folk art, this has everything from shadow puppets to terracotta ornaments **16**

LOCATOR MAP
See Street Finder maps 5–6

CENTRAL ATHENS NORTH

CENTRAL ATHENS SOUTH

0 metres   50
0 yards   50

Agios Nikólaos Ragavás
This 11th-century, Byzantine chapel is a popular location for weddings **13**

Plateía Lysikrátous
Named after the monument in its centre, this square was a favourite haunt of the poet Byron **15**

KEY
– – – Suggested route

STAR SIGHT
★ Panagía Gorgoepíkoös

Anafiótika
The whitewashed houses and winding streets resembling a Cycladic village were built in the 19th century by settlers from the island of Anáfi **14**

Rempétika musicians, Museum of Greek Popular Musical Instruments

Kanellópoulos Museum **8**
Μουσείο Κανελλοπούλου

Corner of Theorías & Pános, Pláka.
Map 6 D2. **[** 210 321 2313.
M *Monastiráki.* **○** *8:30am–3pm
Tue–Sun, noon–3pm Good Fri.*
● *1 Jan, 25 Mar, Easter Sun, 25,
26 Dec.* 🖼️ 📷

I N AN IMMACULATELY restored
Neo-Classical town house,
this museum contains what
was the private collection of
wealthy collectors Pávlos and
Alexándra Kanellópoulos. A
varied collection of artifacts
from all over the Hellenistic
world, the three floors of exhibits include a selection of
coins, 6th-century BC helmets,
5th-century BC gold Persian
jewellery and Attic vases. There
are also Cycladic
figurines, some

**Sculpture of a triton
from the Kanellópoulos Museum**

unusual terracotta figures of
actors in their theatrical masks
and a fine 2nd-century AD El
Faiyûm portrait of a woman.
   A huge block of stone that
fell from the walls of the
Acropolis, so heavy that the
museum was built around it,
can still be seen as an exhibit
on the ground floor.

University of Athens Museum **9**
Μουσείο Ιστορίας του
Πανεπιστημίου Αθηνών

Thólou 5, Pláka. **Map** 6 E2.
[210 324 0861. **M** *Monastiráki.*
○ *Oct–May: 2:30–7pm Mon & Thu,
9:30am–2:30pm Tue, Wed & Fri;
Jun–Sep: 9:30am–2:30pm Tue, Wed
& Fri.* **●** *Aug & main public hols.*

T HIS THREE-STOREY house
was the first home of the
University of Athens. It
opened on 3 May 1837 with
52 students and 33 professors
in its first year. In
November 1841
the University
moved to its
new quarters
and from 1922
the building was
home to many immigrant
families. While they were

there, a taverna known as the
"Old University" was opened
on the ground floor.
   In 1963 the building was
declared a National Monument.
Later reacquired by the university, the old building was
opened as a museum in 1974.
Today, the "Old University",
as it is still known, has an
eclectic collection of memorabilia such as corporeal body
maps, anatomical models,
scientific instruments and
medicine jars. There is also a
display about the university's
past professors and students.

Museum of Greek Popular Musical Instruments **10**
Μουσείο Ελληνικών
Λαϊκών Μουσικών
Οργάνων

Diogénous 1–3, Aérides Square.
Map 6 D1. **[** 210 325 0198.
M *Monastiráki.* **○** *10am–2pm
Tue–Sun, noon–7pm Wed (6pm in
winter).* **●** *17 Nov, main public hols.*

C RETAN MUSICOLOGIST Phoebus
Anogianákis donated over
1,200 musical instruments from
his impressive collection to the
Greek State in 1978. In 1991
this study centre and museum
was opened, devoted to the
history of popular Greek
music, including Anogianákis's
collection. The museum traces
the development of different
styles of island music and the
arrival of *rempétika* (Greek
"blues") from Smyrna in 1922.
   Instruments from all over
Greece are displayed on the
three floors, with recordings
and headphones available at
every exhibit. The basement
contains a selection of church
and livestock bells, as well
as water whistles, wooden
clappers and flutes, which
are sold during pre-Lenten
carnival celebrations. The
ground floor has wind instruments on display including
tsampoúna, bagpipes made
from goatskin. On the first
floor, there is a selection of
string instruments, such as the
bouzouki, the *santoúri* and
the Cretan *lýra*. There is also
a beautiful 19th-century ivory
and tortoiseshell lute.

Panagía Gorgoepíkoös ⓫
Παναγία η Γοργοεπήκοος

VISITORS' CHECKLIST

Plateia Mitropóleos, Pláka.
Map 6 E1. **M** Monastiráki.
🚪 7am–7pm daily. 🚻

Bas-relief from south façade

THIS DOMED CRUCIFORM CHURCH is built entirely from Pentelic marble, now weathered to a rich corn-coloured hue. Dating from the 12th century, it measures only 7.5 m (25 ft) long by 12 m (40 ft) wide. The size of the church is in scale with Athens when it was just a village in the 12th century. Adorned with friezes and bas-reliefs taken from earlier buildings, the exterior mixes the Classical and Byzantine styles. Although dedicated to Panagía Gorgoepíkoös (the Madonna who Swiftly Hears) and Agios Elefthérios (the saint who protects women in childbirth), it is often affectionately known as the Mikrí Mitrópoli (Little Cathedral).

The south façade of the church, dwarfed by the giant Mitrópoli

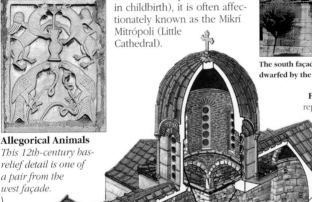

Allegorical Animals
This 12th-century bas-relief detail is one of a pair from the west façade.

Four brick pillars
replaced the original marble ones in 1834.

The floor
is lower than ground level by about 30 cm (12 in).

Fragments of Classical buildings made from Pentelic marble were combined with new Byzantine sections in the style of a Classical frieze.

Main entrance

Lintel Frieze
This relief depicting the months of the year dates from the 4th century BC. The central cross was added in the 12th century.

Modern mosaics above the main entrance to Athens' cathedral, Mitrópoli

Mitrópoli
Μητρόπολη

Plateía Mitropóleos, Pláka. **Map** 6 E1.
C 210 322 1308. **M** Monastiráki.
O 6:30am–7pm daily.

Work began in 1840 on this huge cathedral, using marble from 72 demolished churches for its walls. The cornerstone was laid in a ceremony by King Otto and Queen Amalía on Christmas Day 1842. It took another 20 years to finish the building, using three different architects (François Boulanger, Theophil Hansen and Dimítrios Zézos) which may account for its slightly ungainly appearance. On 21 May 1862, it was formally dedicated to Evangelismós Theotókou (the

Annunciation of the Virgin) by the king and queen. At 40 m (130 ft) long, 20 m (65 ft) wide and 24 m (80 ft) high, it is the largest church in Athens.

The cathedral is the official seat of the Bishop of Athens, and remains a popular city landmark that has been used for ceremonial events from the coronations of kings to the weddings and funerals of the rich and famous.

Inside, there are the tombs of two saints murdered by the Ottoman Turks: Agía Filothéi and Gregory V. The bones of Agía Filothéi, who died in 1589, are still visible in a silver reliquary. Her charitable works included the ransoming of Greek women enslaved in Turkish harems. Gregory V, Patriarch of Constantinople,

was hanged and thrown into the Bosphorus in 1821. His body was rescued by Greek sailors and taken to Odessa. It was eventually returned to Athens by Black Sea (Pontic) Greeks 50 years later.

Agios Nikólaos Ragavás
Άγιος Νικόλαος ο Ραγυαβάς

Corner of Prytaneíou & Epichármou, Pláka. **Map** 6 E2. **C** 210 322 8193.
M Monastiráki. **∎** 1, 2, 4, 5, 9, 10, 11, 12, 15, 18. **O** 8am–noon, 5–8pm daily. **&** limited.

This typical 11th-century Byzantine church, rebuilt in the 18th century and restored to some of its former glory in the late 1970s, incorporates marble columns and other remains of ancient buildings in its external walls. It is one of the favourite parish churches of Pláka, frequently used for colourful Greek weddings which spill out on to the street at weekends. It was the first church in Athens to have a bell after the War of Independence (1821), and the first to ring out after the city's liberation from the Germans on 12 October 1944.

Anafiótika
Αναφιώτικα

Map 6 D2. **M** Monastiráki.

Nestling beneath the northern slopes of the Acropolis, this area is one of the oldest settlements in Athens. Today, its whitewashed houses, cramped streets, lazy cats and pots of

Looking down on Agios Nikólaos Ragavás church from Anafiótika

◁ **View from Anafiótika towards the Ancient Agora**

basil on windowsills still give it the atmosphere of a typical Cycladic village. Its first residents were refugees from the Peloponnesian War *(see p30)*. By 1841, it had been colonized by workmen from Anáfi, in the Cyclades, who eventually gave the area its name. Part of the influx of island craftsmen, who helped to construct the new city following Independence, ignored an 1834 decree declaring the area an archaeological zone, and completed their houses overnight, installing their families by morning. By Ottoman law, this meant the authorities were powerless to knock the new houses down.

The area is bounded by two 17th-century churches: Agios Geórgios tou Vráchou to the east, which has a tiny courtyard filled with flowers, and Agios Symeón to the west, which contains a copy of a miraculous icon, originally brought from Anáfi.

Akrokérama, or terracotta sphinxes, on a roof in Anafiótika

Plateía Lysikrátous ⑮
Πλατεία Λυσικράτους

Lysikrátous, Sélley & Epimenídou, Pláka. **Map** 6 E2. 🚋 *1, 5, 9, 18.*

SITUATED IN THE EAST of the Pláka district, this square is named after the monument of Lysikrates that dominates it. Despite Lord Elgin's attempts to remove it to England, the elegant structure is the city's only intact choregic monument. These monuments were built to commemorate the victors at the annual choral and dramatic festival at the Theatre of Dionysos *(see p100)*. They take their name from the rich sponsor *(choregos)* who produced the winning team. Built in 334 BC, this is the earliest known example where Corinthian

capitals are used externally. Six columns rise in a circle to a marble dome, decorated with an elegant finial of acanthus leaves which supported the winner's bronze trophy. It bears the inscription "Lysikrates of Kikynna, son of Lysitheides, was choregos; the tribe of Akamantis won the victory with a chorus of boys; Theon played the flute; Lysiades, an Athenian, trained the chorus; Evainetos was archon". The Athenians elected nine magistrates known as archons each year, and referred to the year by the name of one of them, the "eponymous archon." A frieze above this inscription, probably the theme of the winners' performance, depicts a battle between Dionysos, the god of theatre, and Tyrrhenian pirates. Surrounded by satyrs, the god transforms them into dolphins and their ship's mast into a sea serpent.

Capuchin friars converted the monument into a library. Grand tour travellers, such as Chateaubriand (1768–1848) and Byron *(see p149)*, stayed at their convent, which was founded on the site in 1669.

The monument of Lysikrates, named after the *choregos* **of the winning team of actors**

Byron was inspired while staying there and wrote some of his poem, *Childe Harold*, sitting in the monument during his final visit to Athens in 1810.

Not far from the monument is the beautifully restored 11th-century Byzantine church of Agía Aikateríni (St Catherine). In 1767 it was given to the monastery of St Catherine of Mount Sinai. It was renovated but in 1882 the monastery was forced to exchange it for land elsewhere and it became a local parish church.

ICON PAINTERS IN PLAKA

Pláka is littered with small artists' studios where icons are still painted using traditional methods. The best are situated just south of Plateía Mitropóleos, among the ecclesiastical shops selling vestments and liturgical objects, on Agías

Filothéis and Apóllonos streets. In some workshops, painters still use the Byzantine method of painting in egg-based tempera on specially treated wood. Customers of all religions can order the saint of their choice in a variety of different sizes. A medium-sized icon depicting a single saint, 25 cm by 15 cm (10 in by 6 in) and copied from a photograph, takes about one day to complete.

Ornate embroidery from Ioánnina, Epirus, on display in the Greek Folk Art Museum

Greek Folk Art Museum ⓰

Μουσείο Ελληνικής Λαϊκής Τέχνης

Kydathinaíon 17, Pláka. **Map** 6 E2.
🄲 210 321 3018. 🚌 2, 4, 9, 10, 11, 12, 15. 🚋 1, 5. ◕ 10am–2pm Tue–Sun. ● main public hols. 🎫 ♿ limited. 📷

GREEK FOLK ART, including some unrivalled regional embroidery and costumes from the mainland and Aegean islands, fills five floors in this fascinating museum. The collection also covers the renaissance of decorative crafts in the 18th and 19th centuries, to reveal a rich heritage of traditional techniques in skills such as weaving, woodcarving and metalwork.

The ground floor has an extensive collection of fine embroidery work, showing a wide range of techniques.

Displays on the mezzanine floor include ceramics, metalwork and woodcarving. The ceramics range from architectural works, such as chimneys, to decorative or practical pieces such as household pots. Made from terracotta

Decorative plate from Rhodes

and faïence, they include both glazed and unglazed pieces. The metalwork on view includes examples made from copper, bronze, iron, steel and pewter. Many are covered with intricate decoration. The woodcarving products are equally impressive in their decoration, often being inlaid with mother-of-pearl, ivory or silver. The wood used varies widely, from walnut to fragrant cedar and wild olive. Also on the mezzanine are disguise costumes. Their origin is thought to be in the ancient Greek drama festivals in honour of Dionysos which made use of overtly expressive masks. The puppets from the Karagkiózis theatre *(see p151)* amused the audience by satirizing topical political and social life.

The first floor houses popular paintings, including works by Theófilos Chatzimichaïl *(see p218)*. There is an excellent collection of silverware on the second floor of the museum, with displays of various ecclesiastical items such as chalices and crosses, as well as secular pieces, such as ornate weaponry and delicate jewellery. Examples of traditional weaving and stonecarving can be found on the third floor. The range of materials used for weaving includes lamb's wool, goat's hair, silk and plant fibres. Traditional costumes are also on show on this floor. The decorations and design, which are frequently elaborate, vary according to the geographical region. Costumes from many different areas are on display.

Reconstruction of the ark from Pátra

Jewish Museum of Greece ⓱

Εβραϊκό Μουσείο της Ελλάδος

Níkis 39, Sýntagma. **Map** 6 F2.
🄲 210 322 5582. Ⓜ Sýntagma. 🚌 1, 2, 4, 5, 9, 10, 11, 12, 15, 18. ◕ 9am–2:30pm Mon–Fri, 10am–2pm Sun. ● Main public hols & Jewish festivals. ♿ 🎥 📷

THIS SMALL MUSEUM moved in 1996 to improved quarters. It traces the history of Greece's Jewish communities which date back to the 3rd century BC. The exhibits present a revealing portrait of the Sephardic Jews, who fled Spain and Portugal in the 15th century, to settle throughout Greece in the religiously tolerant years of the Ottoman Empire.

Among the examples of traditional costumes and religious ceremonial instruments, one item of particular interest is the reconstruction of the *ehal*. This is the ark containing the Torah from the Pátra synagogue, which dates from the 1920s. It was rescued by Nikólaos Stavroulákis, founder of the museum, who has also written several books about the Greek Jews, on sale in the museum bookshop.

Moving displays of documentation record the German occupation of Greece during World War II when 87 per cent of the Jewish population here was wiped out. Over 45,000 Greeks from Thessaloníki alone were sent to Auschwitz and other concentration camps during a period of five months in 1943.

Hadrian's Arch, next to the Temple of Olympian Zeus

Temple of Olympian Zeus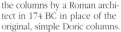
Ναός του Ολυμπίου Διός

Corner of Amalías & Vasilíssis Olgas, Pláka. **Map** 6 F3. 📞 210 922 6330. 🚊 2, 4, 11. 🕐 8:30am–3pm Tue–Sun. ● main public hols. 📷 ♿ limited.

THE TEMPLE of Olympian Zeus is the largest in Greece, exceeding even the Parthenon in size. Work began on this vast edifice in the 6th century BC, in the reign of the tyrant Peisistratos, who allegedly initiated the building work to gain public favour. Although there were several attempts over many years to finish the temple, it was not completed until 650 years later.

The Roman Emperor Hadrian dedicated the temple to Zeus Olympios during the Panhellenic festival of AD 132, on his second visit to Athens. He also set up a gold and ivory inlaid statue of the god inside the temple, a copy of the original by Pheidias at Olympia (*see pp170–72*). Next to it he placed a huge statue of himself. Both these statues have since been lost.

Only 15 of the original 104 Corinthian columns remain, each 17 m (56 ft) high – but enough to give a sense of the enormous size of this temple, which would have been approximately 96 m (315 ft) long and 40 m (130 ft) wide. Corinthian capitals were added to the columns by a Roman architect in 174 BC in place of the original, simple Doric columns.

The temple is situated next to Hadrian's Arch, built in AD 131. It was positioned deliberately to mark the boundary between the ancient city and the new Athens of Hadrian.

The Russian Church of the Holy Trinity

Russian Church of the Holy Trinity ⑲
Ρωσική εκκλησία Αγίας Τριάδας

Filellínon 21, Pláka. **Map** 6 F2. 📞 210 323 1090. 🚊 1, 2, 4, 5, 9, 10, 11, 12, 15, 18. 🕐 7:30–10am Mon–Fri, 7–11am Sat & Sun. ● main public hols. ♿ limited.

STILL IN USE BY the Russian community, this was once the largest church in the city. Built in 1031 by the Lykodímou family (also called Nikodímou), it was ruined by an earthquake in 1701. In 1780 the Turkish *voivode* (governor), Hadji Ali Haseki, partly demolished the church to use its materials for the defensive wall that he built around the city. During the siege of the city in 1827, it received more damage from Greek shells fired from the Acropolis.

The church remained derelict until the Russian government restored it 20 years later. It was then reconsecrated as the Church of the Holy Trinity.

A large cruciform building, its most unusual feature is a wide dome, 10 m (33 ft) in diameter. Its interior was decorated by the Bavarian painter Ludwig Thiersch. The separate belltower also dates from the 19th century, its bell a gift from Tsar Alexander II.

The remaining Corinthian columns of the Temple of Olympian Zeus

The Tomb of the Unknown Soldier in Plateía Syntágmatos

Plateía Syntágmatos ⑳
Πλατεία Σύνταγματος

Sýntagma. **Map** 6 F1. 🚌 *1, 5, 9, 10, 12, 15, 18.* Ⓜ *Sýntagma.*

THIS SQUARE (also known as Sýntagma Square) is home to the Greek parliament, in the Voulí building, and the Tomb of the Unknown Soldier, decorated with an evocative relief depicting a dying Greek hoplite warrior. Unveiled on 25 March 1932 (National Independence Day), the tomb is flanked by texts from Perikles's famous funeral oration. The other walls that enclose the square are covered in bronze shields celebrating military victories since 1821.

The National Guard *(évzones)* are on continuous patrol in front of the tomb, dressed in their famous uniform of kilt and pom-pom clogs. They are best seen at the changing of the guard, every Sunday at 11am.

National Gardens ㉑
Εθνικός Κήπος

Borders Vasilíssis Sofías, Iródou Attikoú, Vasilíssis Olgas & Vasilíssis Amalías, Sýntagma. **Map** 7 A1. Ⓜ *Sýntagma.* 🚌 *1, 3, 5, 7, 8, 10, 13, 18.* Ⓞ *dawn–dusk.* **Botanical Museum, zoo, cafés** Ⓞ *7:30am–3pm daily.*

BEHIND THE VOULÍ parliament building, this 16-ha (40-acre) park, cherished by all Athenians and formerly known as the "Royal Gardens", was renamed the National Gardens by decree in 1923. Queen Amalía ordered the creation of the park in the 1840s; she even used the fledgling Greek Navy to bring 15,000 seedlings from around the world. The gardens were landscaped by the Prussian horticulturalist Friedrich Schmidt, who travelled the world in search of rare plants.

Although the gardens have lost much of their original grandeur, they remain one of the most peaceful spots in the city. Shady paths meander past small squares, park benches and ponds filled with goldfish. A huge feral cat population is also resident in the park. Remains of Roman mosaics excavated in the park and an old aqueduct add atmosphere. Modern sculptures of writers, such as Dionýsios Solomós, Aristotélis Valaorítis and Jean Moreas, can be found throughout the park. There is also a small **Botanical Museum** to visit, a ramshackle zoo, and cafés.

South of the park lies the **Záppeion**

exhibition hall, an impressive building in use today as a conference centre. It was donated by Evángelos and Konstantínos Záppas, cousins who made their fortunes in Romania. Built by Theophil Hansen, architect of the Athens Academy *(see p81)*, between 1874 and 1888, it also has its own gardens. The elegant café next door to the Záppeion is a pleasant place to relax and refresh after a walk around these charming, peaceful gardens.

The tranquil National Gardens

Presidential Palace ㉒
Προεδρικό Μέγαρο

Iródou Attikoú, Sýntagma. **Map** 7 A2. Ⓜ *Sýntagma.* 🚌 *3, 7, 8, 13.* ⬤ *to the public.*

THIS FORMER royal palace was designed and built by Ernst Ziller *(see p81)* in c.1878. It was occupied by the Greek Royal Family from 1890 until the hasty departure of King Constantine in 1967. It is still guarded by the *évzones* whose barracks are at the top of the street. After the abolition of the monarchy, it became the official residence of the President of Greece and he still uses it today when hosting dignitaries. Its well-maintained gardens can just be seen through the iron railings.

Voulí parliament building in Plateía Sýntagmatos, guarded by *évzones*

Kallimármaro Stadium ㉓
Καλλιμάρμαρο Στάδιο

Archimídous 16, Pagkráti. **Map** 7 B3.
📞 210 752 6386. 🚌 3, 4, 11.
🕐 8am–sunset daily. ♿

THIS HUGE marble structure set in a small valley by Ardittós Hill occupies the exact site of the original Panathenaic Stadium built by Lykourgos in 330–329 BC. It was first reconstructed for gladiatorial contests during Hadrian's reign (AD 117–138), then rebuilt in white marble by the wealthy Roman bene- factor Herodes Atticus for the Panathenaic Games in AD 144. Neglected for many years, its marble was gradually quarried for use in new buildings or burnt down to make lime.

In 1895 Geórgios Avérof gave four million drachmas in gold for the restoration of the stadium in time for the start of the first modern Olympic Games on 5 April 1896. Des- igned by Anastásios Metaxás, the present structure is a faith- ful replica of Herodes Atticus's

Some of the ornate tombs in the First Cemetery of Athens

stadium, as described in the *Guide to Greece* by Pausanias *(see p56)*. Built in white Pen- telic marble, it is 204 m (669 ft) long and 83 m (272 ft) wide and can seat up to 60,000 spectators. Metaxás was also helped by the plans of archi- tect Ernst Ziller, who excava- ted the site between 1869 and 1879. Among his finds was a double-headed statue of Apollo and Dionysos, one of many that were used to divide the stadium's running track down its length. It is on show in the National Archaeological Museum *(see pp68–71)*.

First Cemetery of Athens ㉔
Πρώτο Νεκροταφείο Αθηνών

Entrance in Anapáfseos, Méts.
Map 7 A4 📞 210 923 6118. 🚌 2,
4. 🕐 5:30am–6pm daily. ♿ limited.

ATHENS' MUNICIPAL cemetery, which is not to be con- fused with the Kerameikós, the ancient cemetery *(see p88–9)*, is a peaceful place, filled with pine and olive trees and the scent of incense burn- ing at the well-kept tombs.

Fine examples of 19th- century funerary art range from the flamboyance of some of the marble mauso- leums to the simplicity of the *belle époque Kimoméni* or *Sleeping Maiden (see p42)*. Created by Giannoúlis Chalepás, this beautiful tomb is found to the right of the main cemetery avenue where many of Greece's foremost families are buried.

Among the notable 19th- and 20th-century figures with tombs here are Theódoros Kolokotrónis *(see p80)*, British philhellene historian George Finlay (1799–1875), German archaeologist Heinrich Schliemann *(see p180)*, the Nobel prize-winning poet Giórgos Seféris (1900–71) and the actress and politician Melína Merkoúri (1922–94).

In addition to the large number of tombs for famous people that are buried here, the cemetery contains a moving, single memorial to the 40,000 Athenians who perished through starvation during World War II.

A lone athlete exercising in the vast Kallimármaro Stadium

SHOPPING IN ATHENS

SHOPPING IN ATHENS offers many delights. There are open-air street markets, quiet arcades, traditional arts and crafts shops, and designer fashion boutiques to rival Paris and New York. Most Athenians go to the triangle which is formed by Omónoia, Sýntagma and Monastiráki squares to buy everyday household items, clothes and shoes. For leather goods, bargain hunters should head for Mitropóleos, Ermoú, Aiólou and nearby streets. Along the smarter Stadíou and Panepistimíou, there are world-class jewellers and large clothing stores. The maze of arcades in the

Colourful shadow puppet

centre also houses smart leather-goods shops, booksellers, cafés and *ouzerís*. The most stylish shopping is to be found in Kolonáki where some of the city's most expensive art galleries and antique shops are clustered among the foreign and Greek designer outlets selling the latest fashions. Around Athinás, Monastiráki and Pláka there is an eclectic mix of aromatic herb and spice stores, religious retailers selling icons and church candlesticks, second-hand bookshops with rare posters and prints, and catering stores packed with household goods such as pots and pans.

OPENING HOURS

SHOPS GENERALLY open from 8am–2pm or 9am–3pm, Monday to Saturday. On Tuesdays, Thursdays and Fridays there is late shopping from 5:30–8:30pm. The exceptions are department stores, tourist shops, supermarkets, florists and *zacharoplasteía* (cake shops) which often open for longer. Many shops also open every year throughout August, the time when many Greeks take their holidays.

DEPARTMENT STORES AND SUPERMARKETS

THE MAIN STORES are **Fokás** and **Lambrópoulos**. They stock a wide range of beauty

Lambrópoulous, one of the largest department stores in Athens

products, clothes, gifts, and electrical and household goods. Fokás is not as big as Lambrópoulos but it is more exclusive, with departments for clothes, cosmetics and gifts. **Marinópoulos**, **Carrefour** and **AB Vassilópoulos** are all supermarket chains in the city centre.

MARKETS

ATHENS IS FAMOUS FOR its flea markets. **Monastiráki** market starts early in the morning every Sunday, when dealers set out their wares along Adrianoú and neighbouring streets. Hawkers of *salépi* (a drink made from sesame seeds) and gypsy clarinet players weave through the crowds.

The commercial tourist and antique shops of Pandrósou and Ifaístou, which collec-

tively refer to themselves as "Monastiráki Flea Market", are open every day. Friday, Saturday and Sunday mornings are the best times to visit Plateía Avissynías, when dealers arrive with piles of bric-a-brac.

For food, the **Central Market** is excellent, as are the popular *laikés agorés* (street markets) selling fruit and vegetables, which occur daily in different areas. Centrally located *laikés agorés* include one on **Xenokrátous** in Kolonáki which takes place each Friday.

Greeks buy in bulk and stallholders will find it strange if you try to buy very small quantities of things. It is not really acceptable to buy less than half a kilo (1lb) of a fruit or vegetable. In most cases, you will be given a bag to serve yourself – do not be afraid to touch, smell and even taste.

ART AND ANTIQUES

AS AUTHENTIC GREEK antiques become increasingly hard to find, many shops are forced to import furniture, glassware and porcelain from

Shoppers in Adrianoú at the centre of Monastiráki flea market

around the globe. Fortunately, however, there are still reasonable buys in old Greek jewellery, brass and copperware, carpets and embroidery, engravings and prints. Some can be found at **Antiqua**, just off Plateía Syntágmatos. Kolonáki is a prime area for small, exclusive stores around Sólonos, Skoufá and their side streets. Try **Patrick François** for early Greek advertising posters and **Serafetinídis** for excellent antique kilims and carpets. They are both on Cháritos. Kolonáki is also the art centre with well-established galleries selling paintings and prints. The **Zoumpouláki Galleries** specialize in art and antiques.

Monastiráki also has many antique shops. Look out for **Giórgos Goútis** – these are two stores selling 19th-century jewellery and costumes. Try **Iákovos Serapian** for popular art and glassware and **Vergína** for copperware, particularly nautical items. **Martínos** has some beautiful, ornate icons and silverware.

Antique jewellery and ornaments in Giórgos Goútis

TRADITIONAL FOLK ART AND CRAFTS

AFFORDABLE POPULAR folk art, crafts and souvenirs are plentiful in Monastiráki and Pláka. There are innumerable stores filled with ecclesiastical ephemera and cramped icon painters' studios. In addition, there are more unusual shops offering a unique service. **Stávros Melissinós**, a self-styled poet sandal-maker, makes a wide

The famous shoemaker and poet Stávros Melissinós

variety of sturdy sandals and leather goods and is famous for handing out translations of his work as a parting gift. Many shops stock elegant wood carvings, rustic painted wooden trays and richly coloured *flokáti* rugs *(see p209)*. **Amorgós** is packed with fine wood carvings and puppets as seen in the Karagkiózis theatre in Maroúsi *(see p151)*.

The **National Welfare Organization** offers an excellent selection of different goods including tapestries, rugs and needlepoint cushions. Beautiful carved shepherds' crooks from Epirus as well as a large variety of finely crafted ceramics can be found at the fascinating **Centre of Hellenic Tradition**.

JEWELLERY

ATHENS IS JUSTLY FAMED for its jewellery stores. There is no shortage in Monastiráki and Pláka, which is full of small shops selling gold and silver. But the best known are to be found in Voukourestíou, which is packed with such exclusive jewellers as **Anagnostópoulos** and **Vourákis**. Window displays also dazzle at the designer of world class fame, **Zolótas**, whose own pieces copy museum treasures. Another famous name is that of the designer Ilías Lalaoúnis, whose collections, inspired by Classical and other

archaeological sources, such as the gold of Mycenae, are eagerly sought by the rich and famous. At the **Ilías Lalaoúnis Jewellery Museum** over 3,000 of his designs are exhibited, and there is also a workshop where you can watch the craftsmen demonstrate the skills of the goldsmith and buy some of the jewellery.

MUSEUM COPIES

MUSEUM SHOPS provide some of the better buys in the city. Well-crafted, mostly tasteful copies draw on the wide range of ancient and Byzantine Greek art. They come in all shapes and sizes, from a life-size Classical statue to a simple Cycladic marble bowl. Many fine reproductions of the exhibits in the **Benáki Museum** *(see pp78–9)* can be bought from a collection of silverware, ceramics, embroidery and jewellery in the museum shop.

The **Museum of Cycladic Art** *(see pp74–5)* has some fine Tanagran and Cycladic figurines, bowls and vases for sale. There is a large selection of reproduction statues and pottery at the **National Archaeological Museum** *(see pp68–71)* souvenir shop. Apart from the museums, the Monastiráki shop **Orféas** offers good quality marble and pottery copies of Classical Greek works as well as glittering Byzantine icons.

Display of red- and black-figure reproduction vases for sale

Períptero in Kolonáki selling English and Greek newspapers

BOOKS, NEWSPAPERS AND MAGAZINES

ALL THE PERIPTERA (kiosks) in the city centre sell foreign newspapers and magazines. English publications include the weekly *Athens News* and the monthly magazine *Odyssey*. Athens' wealth of bookshops includes many selling foreign language publications. **Raÿmóndos**, situated on Voukourestíou, offers the widest selection of foreign magazines, but for foreign books, go to the huge branch of **Eleftheroudákis** on Panepistimíou, with seven floors of English and Greek books, and a café. Try **Andro-méda Books** for Classical and archaeological subjects and **Ekdotikí Athinón** for history and guide books.

One of the many designer stores to be found in Kolonáki

CLOTHES

ALTHOUGH THERE are some famous Greek designers, such as **Askánis** who produces colourful party dresses, and **Parthénis** whose hallmark is black and white minimalism, most fashion stores concentrate on imported clothes. However, there are plenty of high-quality clothes: every designer label can be found in the city's main fashion centre, Kolonáki. There are branches of such internationally famous names as **Ralph Lauren** and **Max Mara**. Such upmarket stores as **Sótiris**, **Helen B** and **Mohnblumchen** typify the area's urban chic. For good-quality high-street fashion there is **Marks & Spencer**.

KITCHENWARE

CAVERNOUS CATERING stores in the side streets around the Central Market specialize in classic Greek kitchen- and tableware. There are tiny white cups and copper saucepans used to make Greek coffee, long rolling pins for making filo pastry, and metal olive oil pourers. **Kotsóvolos** in 3 Septemvriou has a huge range of cheap and cheerful equipment, including traditional *kantária* (wine-measuring jugs), used to serve retsina in restaurants, round *tapsiá* (metal roasting dishes), and *saganákia* (two-handled pans) used for frying cheese. More stylish products can be found at **Méli Interiors** in Kolonáki. A good selection of tinware is on display, as well as traditional Greek pottery and miniature taverna chairs.

FOOD AND DRINK

THERE ARE MYRIAD gourmet treats in Athens, including unusual *avgotáracho* (smoked cod roe preserved in beeswax), herbs and spices, cheeses and wines. The bakeries and *zacharoplasteía* (patisseries) are irresistible, brimming with delicious breads and biscuits, home-made ice cream and yoghurt. **Aristokratikón**, off Plateía Syntágmatos, sells luxurious chocolates and marzipan. One of Athens' best patisseries, **Asimakópoulos**, is crammed with decadent *mpaklavás* and crystallized fruits.

The Central Market on Athinás is one of the most enticing places for food shopping. It is surrounded by stores packed with cheeses, pistachio nuts, dried fruits and pulses such as *fáva* (yellow split peas) and *gígantes* (butter beans). You will find over 20 different types of olive and pickle at **Papa-lexandrís**, and a range of herbs and spices at **Bahar**, in particular dried savory and sage, lemon verbena and saffron. A new delight is **Green Farm**, part of a chain of organic supermarkets.

Two enterprising *cáves* (wine merchants), **Oino-Pnévmata** in Irakleítou and **Cellier** in Kriezótou, offer a broad range of wines and spirits from the new generation of small Greek wineries. **Vrettós** in Pláka has an attractive and varied display of own-label spirits and liqueurs.

A crammed Athenian kitchenware store

DIRECTORY

DEPARTMENT STORES AND SUPERMARKETS

AB Vassilópoulos
Stadíou 19, Sýntagma.
Map 2 F5.
[210 322 2405.
One of several branches.

Carrefour
Palaistínis 1, Alimos.
[210 985 1048.

Fokás
Ermou 11 & Voulis,
Sýntagma. **Map** 6 E1.
[210 285 5524.

Lambrópoulos
Aiólou 99 and Lykoúrgou
26, Omónoia. **Map** 2 E4.
[210 324 5811.

Marinópoulos
Kanári 9, Kolonáki.
Map 3 A5.
[210 362 4907.
One of several branches.

MARKETS

Central Market
Athinás, Omónoia.
Map 2 D4.

Monastiráki
Adrianoú & Pandrósou,
Pláka.
Map 6 E1.

Xenokrátous
Xenokrátous, Kolonáki.
Map 3 C5.

ART AND ANTIQUES

Antiquities
Pandrósou 58,
Monastiráki. **Map** 6 D1.
[210 325 0539.

Antiqua
Amaliás 2,
Sýntagma.
Map 4 F2.
[210 323 2220.

Giórgos Goútis
Dimokrítou 10,
Kolonáki. **Map** 3 A5.
[210 361 3557.

Iákovos Serapian
Ifaístou 6, Monastiráki.
Map 5 C1.
[210 321 0169.

Katerina Avdelopoulou-Vonta
Lykavittoú 8, Kolonáki.
Map 3 A5.
[210 361 6386.

Martínos
Pandrósou 50, Pláka.
Map 6 D1.
[210 321 3110.

Patrick François
Cháritos 27, Kolonáki.
Map 3 B5.
[210 725 7716.

Serafetinídis
Cháritos 29, Kolonáki.
Map 3 B5.
[210 721 4186.

Vergína
Adrianoú 37, Pláka.
Map 6 E1.
[210 321 7065.

Zoumpouláki Galleries
Kriezótou 7, Kolonáki.
Map 2 F5.
[210 363 4454.
One of three branches.

TRADITIONAL FOLK ART AND CRAFTS

Amorgós
Kódrou 3, Monastiráki.
Map 6 E1.
[210 324 3836.

Centre of Hellenic Tradition
Mitropóleos 59 (Arcade) –
Pandrósou 36,
Monastiráki. **Map** 6 D1.
[210 321 3023.

National Welfare Organization
Ypatías 6 and Apóllonos,
Monastiráki. **Map** 6 E1.
[210 325 0524.

Stávros Melissinós
Pandrósou 89,
Monastiráki. **Map** 6 D1.
[210 321 9247.

JEWELLERY

Anagnostópoulos
Voukourestíou 13,
Kolonáki. **Map** 2 F5.
[210 360 4426.

Ilías Lalaoúnis Jewellery Museum
Karyatidon 4a, Pláka.
Map 6 D3.
[210 922 1044.

Vourákis
Voukourestíou 8,
Kolonáki. **Map** 2 F5.
[210 331 1089.

Zolótas
Stadíou 9 & Kolokotroni,
Kolonáki. **Map** 2 F5.
[210 322 1222.

MUSEUM COPIES

Orféas
Pandrósou 28B, Pláka.
Map 6 D1.
[210 324 5034.

BOOKS, NEWSPAPERS AND MAGAZINES

Androméda Books
Mavromicháli 46–50,
Exárcheia. **Map** 2 F3.
[210 360 0825.

Ekdotikí Athinón
Akadímias 34, Kolonáki.
Map 2 F5.
[210 360 8911.

Eleftheroudákis
Panepistimíou 17,
Kolonáki. **Map** 2 F5.
[210 325 8440.

Raÿmóndos
Voukourestíou 18,
Kolonáki. **Map** 2 F5.
[210 364 8189.

CLOTHES

Askánis
Anagnostopoúlou 16,
Kolonáki. **Map** 3 A4.
[210 360 0049.

Helen B
Tsakálof & Dimokrítou 34,
Kolonáki. **Map** 3 A5.
[210 363 6188.

Marks & Spencer
Ermou 33–35, Sýntagma.
Map 6 E1.

Max Mara
Akadímias 14, Kolonáki.
Map 3 A5.
[210 360 2142.

Mohnblumchen
Plateía Dexamenís 7,
Dexaméni.
Map 3 B5.
[210 723 6960.

Parthénis
Dimokrítou 20, Kolonáki.
Map 3 A5.
[210 363 3158.

Ralph Lauren
Kassavéti 19, Kifisiá.
[210 808 5550.
One of two branches.

Sótiris
Anagnostopoúlou 30,
Kolonáki. **Map** 3 A4.
[210 363 9281.
One of two branches.

KITCHENWARE

Kotsóvolos
3 Septemvriou 10,
Omónoia.
Map 2 D4.
[210 289 1000.

Méli Interiors
Voukourestiou 41,
Kolonáki. **Map** 3 A5.
[210 360 9324.

FOOD AND DRINK

Aristokratikón
Karagiórgi Servías 9,
Sýntagma. **Map** 2 E5.
[210 322 0546.

Asimakópoulos
Charil1áou Trikoúpi 82,
Exárcheia. **Map** 3 A3.
[210 361 0092.

Bahar
Evripídou 31, Omónoia.
Map 2 D4.
[210 321 7225.

Cellier
Kriezótou 1, Kolonáki.
Map 3 A5.
[210 361 0040.

Green Farm
Dimokrítou 13, Kolonáki.
Map 3 A5.
[210 361 4001.

Oino-Pnévmata
Irakleítou 9A, Kolonáki.
Map 3 A5.
[210 360 2932.

Papalexandrís
Sokrátous 9, Omónoia.
Map 2 D4.
[210 321 1461.

Vrettós
Kydathinaíon 41, Pláka.
Map 6 E2.
[210 323 2110.

ENTERTAINMENT IN ATHENS

ATHENS EXCELS in the sheer variety of its open-air summer entertainment. Visitors can go to outdoor showings of the latest film releases, spend lazy evenings in garden bars with the heady aroma of jasmine, or try a concert in the atmospheric setting of the Herodes Atticus Theatre, which sits beneath the Acropolis.

The Mousikís Mégaron Concert Hall has given the city a first-class classical concert venue and draws some of the best names in the music world. For most Athenians,

Two Athens listings magazines

however, entertainment means late-night dining in tavernas, followed by bar- and club-hopping until the early hours. There is also an enormous number of large discotheques, music halls and intimate *rempétika* clubs, playing traditional Greek music, throughout Athens. Whatever your musical taste, there is something for everyone in this lively city. Sports and outdoor facilities are also widely available, in particular watersports, which are within easy reach of Athens along the Attic coast.

LISTINGS MAGAZINES

THE MOST comprehensive Greek weekly listings magazines are *Athinorama* and *Downtown*, both published on Fridays. Both list events and concerts, and the latest bars and clubs. The English language publications such as the weekly *Athens News*, the weekly (Thursday) *Hellenic Star* and the bimonthly *Odyssey* also have listings sections. All are generally available at kiosks.

BOOKING TICKETS

ALTHOUGH IT IS NECESSARY to book tickets in advance for the summer Athens Festival *(see p46)* and for concerts at the Mégaron Concert Hall, most theatres and music clubs sell tickets at the door on the day of the

performance. However, there is also a central ticket office, open daily from 10am to 4pm, located near Plateía Syntágmatos, where tickets can be purchased for concerts at both the Mégaron Concert Hall and for the various events of the summer Athens Festival *(see p46)*.

THEATRE AND DANCE

THERE ARE MANY FINE theatres scattered around the city centre, often hidden in converted Neo-Classical mansion houses or arcades. Numerous popular revues that combine an entertaining mixture of contemporary political satire and comedy are regularly performed in theatres such as the **Lampéti**.

Some excellent productions of 19th-century Greek and European plays are staged at

Ibsen at the Evros Theatre, Psyrrí

the **National Theatre**. Playhouses such as the Evros, **Athinón**, **Alfa** and **Vrettánia** also mount Greek-language productions of works by well-known 19th- and 20th-century playwrights such as Ibsen.

The major classical venues, including the National Theatre, put on contemporary dance and ballet as well as plays and operas. The **Dóra Strátou Dance Theatre** on Filopáppos Hill performs traditional regional Greek dancing nightly between May and September.

The Dóra Strátou Dance Theatre performing traditional Greek dancing outdoors

The doorway to the outdoor Refresh Dexamení cinema

CINEMA

ATHENIANS LOVE GOING to the cinema, especially from late May to September when the warm weather means that local open-air cinemas are open. All foreign-language films are subtitled, with the exception of children's films which are usually dubbed. The last showing is always at 11pm, which makes it possible to dine before seeing a movie.

The city centre has several excellent, large-screen cinemas showing the latest international releases. **Ideál**, **Elly** and **Astor Nescafé** are large, comfortable, indoor cinemas equipped with with Dolby Stereo sound systems. The **Alphaville-Highlights-Cinema** and **Aavóra** tend to show a comprehensive range of art-house and cult movies.

Athenians like to hang out at the bars and tavernas next to open-air cinemas, such as **Refresh Dexamení** and **Athinaía** in Kolonáki or the **Riviéra** in Exárcheia, before catching the last performance. The acoustics are not always perfect but the relaxed atmosphere, in the evening warmth, with street noises, typically cats and cars, permeating the soundtrack, is an unforgettable experience. These cinemas seem more like clubs, with tables beside the seats for drinks and snacks. The outdoor

Thiseíon cinema comes with the added attraction of a stunning view of the Acropolis.

CLASSICAL MUSIC

THE ANNUAL Athens Festival, held throughout the summer, attracts the major international ballet and opera companies, orchestras and theatrical troupes to the open-air **Herodes Atticus Theatre**, which seats 5,000 people, and to other venues around the city. This has always been the premier event of the classical music calendar. In 1991, the **Mousikís Mégaron Concert Hall** was inaugurated, providing a year-round venue for opera, ballet and classical music performances. This majestic marble building contains two recital halls with superlative acoustics, an exhibition space, a shop and a restaurant. The Olympia Theatre is home to the **Lyrikí Skiní** (National Opera), and stages excellent ballet productions as well as opera.

Details of concerts held at cultural centres such as the **French Institute** can be found in listings magazines and newspapers.

TRADITIONAL GREEK MUSIC

THE LIVELY GREEK music scene thrives in a variety of venues throughout central Athens. The large music halls of Syngróu advertise on omnipresent billboards around the city. **Diogénis Studio**, **Fever** and the **Tunnel Club** attract the top stars and their loyal fans. The more old-fashioned venues in Pláka, such as **Zoom** and **Mnisikléous**, offer more intimate surroundings for the haunting sounds of *rempétika* music, which draws its inspiration and defiant stance from the lives of the urban poor.

Rempétiki Istoría and **Taksími** are two of the places at which you can hear genuine bouzouki (Greek mandolin) music. Both

Accordionist
in Plateía
Kolonakíou

bars have well-known bouzouki players, and reasonable prices.

Mpoémissa attracts a much younger crowd, more concerned with dancing the night away than with the authenticity of the music.

A classical concert at the Herodes Atticus Theatre

ROCK AND JAZZ MUSIC

INTERNATIONAL ACTS usually perform at large stadiums or the open-air **Lykavittós Theatre** as part of the annual Athens Festival. The **Ródon**, a successfully converted cinema, also attracts the very cream of foreign and Greek rock bands. Greek bands can be enjoyed at the **An Club**, and at the **Decadence** club, which offers patrons the intriguing prospect of Greek rock-and-roll dinner dancing.

The city's premier jazz venue is the **Half Note Jazz Club**. Housed in a former stonemason's workshop, opposite the First Cemetery, this cosy club presents the best of foreign contemporary jazz. For blues, check out the aptly named **Blues** in Ambelokipi.

Alternatively, to hear Afro-Latin music, head for **Café Asante** or the **Cubanita Havana Club** which feature Cuban bands whose performances are often as lively as their music.

Live music in the Ródon, one of the city's popular rock clubs

NIGHTCLUBS

ATHENS IS A HIVE of bars and nightclubs that come and go at an alarming rate. Most offer special DJ nights that attract the paparazzi and the dedicated followers of fashion. Many large dance clubs, such as **Prime Vision**, **+Soda** and the **Camel Club**, offer a hedonistic atmosphere and dancing until the early hours. Also worth trying are the designer-sleek **Kalúa**, **Wild Rose** and **Exo**, all with a sophisticated crowd.

Marathon runner in Athens retracing the path of his ancestors

SPORT

MOST TAXI DRIVERS will reel off their favourite football team to passengers before they have had a chance to mention their destination. Such is the Athenian passion for football that the two main rival teams, Panathenaïkós and Olympia-kós, are always the subject of fervent debate. Each team is backed by a consortium of private companies, each of which also owns a basketball team of the same name. Football matches are played every Wednesday and Sunday during the September to May season. The basketball teams play weekly, in what is the latest popular national sport.

Lack of adequate parkland within the city means that joggers are a rare sight, despite the annual **Athens Open Marathon** every October. The athletes run from Marathon to the Kallimármaro Stadium in the centre of Athens *(see p113)*. The **Olympiakó Stadium** in Maroúsi seats 80,000 spectators and was built in 1982. The Panathen-aïkós football team are based here. It has ex-cellent facilities for all sports and includes an indoor sports hall and tennis courts in its 100 ha (250 acres) of grounds. The **Karaïskáki Stadium** in Piraeus is the home of the Olympiakós football team. There are also facil-ities there for many other sports including volley-ball and basketball.

Another famous event is the **Acropolis Rally**, a celebration of vintage cars, held around the Acropolis every spring. It attracts be-tween 50 and 100 cars.

Outside the city centre, there are more facilities on offer, including bowling at the **Bowling Centre of Piraeus** and golf at the fine 18-hole **Glyfáda Golf Course**, which is located close to the airport. Tennis courts are available for players to hire at various places, including the **Pefki Tennis Club**.

Proximity to the Attic coast means that a large variety of watersports is on offer. Wind-surfing and water-skiing are widely available on most beaches. Contact the **Hellenic Water-Ski Federation** for details of water-skiing schools offering tuition. There are several scuba-diving clubs, such as the **Piraeus Karteliás School**, which offers diving lessons to beginners as well as more advanced divers.

Basketball, an increasingly popular national sport among the Greeks

DIRECTORY

THEATRE AND DANCE

Alfa
Patisíon & Stournára 37,
Exárcheia. **Map** 2 E2.
[210 523 8742.

Athinón
Voukourestíou 10,
Kolonáki. **Map** 2 E5.
[210 331 2343.

Dóra Strátou Dance Theatre
Filopáppou Hill,
Filopáppou. **Map** 5 B4.
[210 921 4650.

Lampéti
Leof Alexándras 106,
Avérof. **Map** 4 D2.
[210 646 3685.

National Theatre
Agíou Konstantínou 22,
Omónoia. **Map** 1 D3.
[210 322 3242.

Vrettánia
Panepistimíou 7,
Sýntagma. **Map** 2 E4.
[210 322 1579.

CINEMA

Aavóra-Nescafé
Ippokrátous 180,
Neápolis. **Map** 2 E4.
[210 646 2253.

Alphaville-Highlights-Cinema
Mavromicháli 168,
Neápolis. **Map** 2 F4.
[210 646 0521.

Astor Nescafé
Stadiou 28,
Kolonáki. **Map** 2 E5.
[210 323 1297.

Athinaía
Cháritos 50, Kolonáki.
Map 3 B5.
[210 721 5717.

Elly
Akadimias 64,
Omónia. **Map** 2 E3.
[210 363 2789.

Ideál-Lux
Panepistimíou 46,
Omónoia. **Map** 2 E4.
[210 382 6720.

Refresh Dexamení
Plateía Dexamenís,
Dexamení. **Map** 3 B5.
[210 362 3942.

Riviéra
Valtetsioú 46,
Exárcheia. **Map** 2 F3.
[210 384 4827.

Thiseíon
Apostólou Pávlou 7,
Thiseío. **Map** 5 B2.
[210 347 0980.

CLASSICAL MUSIC

French Institute
Sína 29–31, Kolonáki.
Map 3 A4.
[210 339 8601.

Herodes Atticus Theatre
Dionysíou Areopagítou,
Acropolis. **Map** 6 C2.
[210 323 9132.

Lyrikí Skiní, Olympia Theatre
Akadimías 59,
Omónoia. **Map** 2 F4.
[210 361 2461.

Mousikís Mégaron Concert Hall
V Sofías & Kókkali,
Stégi Patrídos. **Map** 4 E4.
[210 728 2333.

TRADITIONAL GREEK MUSIC

Diogénis Studio
Leof A Syngroú 259,
N. Smyrni.
[210 942 5754.

Fever
Leof. A Syngrou &
Lagousitsi 25, Kallithéa.
[210 322 7418.

Mnisikléous
Mnisikleous 22,
Pláka. **Map** 6 D1.
[210 322 5558.

Mpoémissa
Solomoú 19,
Exárcheia. **Map** 2 D2.
[210 384 3836.

Rempétiki Istoría
Ippokrátous 181,
Neápoli. **Map** 3 C2.
[210 642 4937.

Taksími
C Trikoúpi & Isávron 29,
Neápoli. **Map** 3 A2.
[210 363 9919.

Tunnel Club
Leof Syngroú 123,
Nea Smyrni.
[210 935 5665.

Zoom
Kydathinaíon 39,
Pláka. **Map** 6 E2.
[210 322 5920.

ROCK, JAZZ AND ETHNIC MUSIC

An Club
Solomoú 13–15,
Exárcheia. **Map** 2 E2.
[210 330 5058.

Blues
Panórmou 20,
Ambelokipi. **Map** 4 F2.
[210 643 3372.

Café Asante
Damaréos 78,
Pangrati. **Map** 8 E3.
[210 756 0102.

Cubanita Havana Club
Karaïskáki 28, Psyrri.
Map 1 C5.
[210 331 4605.

Decadence
Voulgaroktónou 69 &
Poulcherias 2, Strefi Hill.
Map 3 A2.
[210 882 3544.

Half Note Jazz Club
Trivonianoú 17,
Stádio.
Map 6 F4.
[210 921 3310.

Lykavittós Theatre
Lykavittós Hill.
Map 3 B4.
[210 722 7209.

Ródon
Márni 24,
Váthis.
Map 1 C3.
[210 524 7427.

NIGHTCLUBS

Camel Club
Irakleidón 74, Thiselo.
Map 5 B1.
[210 347 6847.

Exo
Márkou Mousoúrou 1,
Mets. **Map** 7 A3.
[210 923 5818.

Kalúa
Amerikís 6,
Sýntagma. **Map** 2 F5.
[210 360 8304.

Prime
Vouliagménis 22,
N Kosmos. **Map** 6 F5.
[210 924 8705.

+Soda
Ermoú 161,
Thiseío. **Map** 1 A5.
[210 345 6187.

Wild Rose
Panepistimíou 10,
Sýntagma. **Map** 2 E4.
[210 364 2160.

SPORT

Bowling Centre of Piraeus
Profítis Ilías,
Kastélla.
[210 412 7077.

Glyfáda Golf Course
Glyfáda.
[210 894 2338.

Hellenic Water-Ski Federation
Leof Possidónos,
16777 Athens.
[210 894 7413.

Karaïskáki Stadium
Néo Fáliro.
[210 481 2902.

Olympiakó Stadium
Leof Kifisías 37, Maroúsi.
[210 683 4000.

Pefki Tennis Club
Peloponnissou 3,
Ano Pefki
[210 806 6162.

Piraeus Karteliás School
Mikrás Asías 3,
Néo Fáliro
[210 482 5887.

ATHENS STREET FINDER

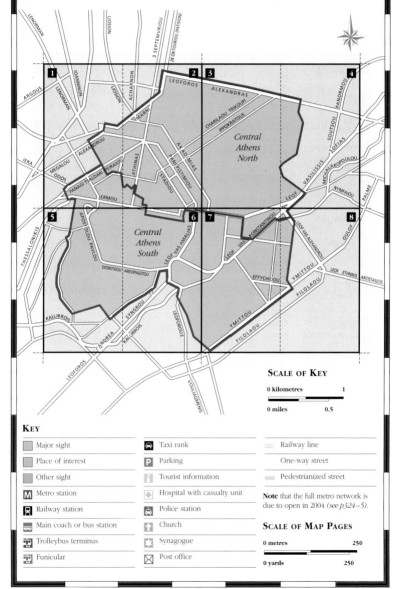

Mᴀᴘ ʀᴇꜰᴇʀᴇɴᴄᴇꜱ given for sights in Athens refer to the maps on the following pages. References are also given for Athens hotels *(see pp264–7)*, Athens restaurants *(see pp286–9)* and for useful addresses in the *Survival Guide* section *(see pp296–325)*. The first figure in the reference tells you which Street Finder map to turn to, and the letter and number refer to the grid reference. The map below shows the area of Athens covered by the eight Street Finder maps (the map numbers are shown in black). The symbols used for sights and features are listed in the key below.

SCALE OF KEY

0 kilometres   1

0 miles   0.5

KEY

▨ Major sight	🚕 Taxi rank	═ Railway line
▨ Place of interest	🅿 Parking	One-way street
▨ Other sight	ℹ Tourist information	▬ Pedestrianized street
Ⓜ Metro station	➕ Hospital with casualty unit	**Note** that the full metro network is due to open in 2004 *(see p324–5)*.
🚉 Railway station	🚓 Police station	
🚌 Main coach or bus station	🚔 Church	**SCALE OF MAP PAGES**
🚎 Trolleybus terminus	🔯 Synagogue	0 metres 250
🚟 Funicular	⊠ Post office	0 yards 250

Street Finder Index

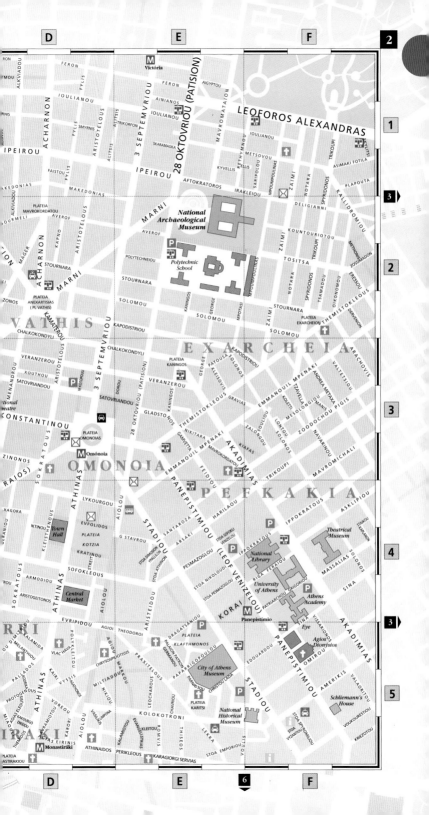

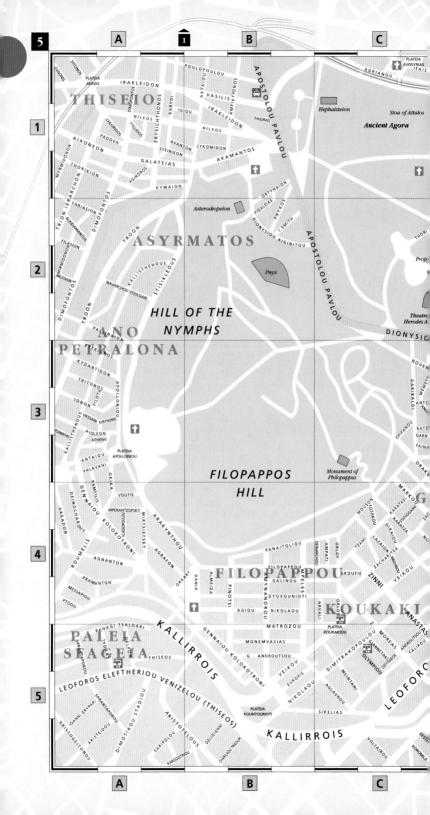

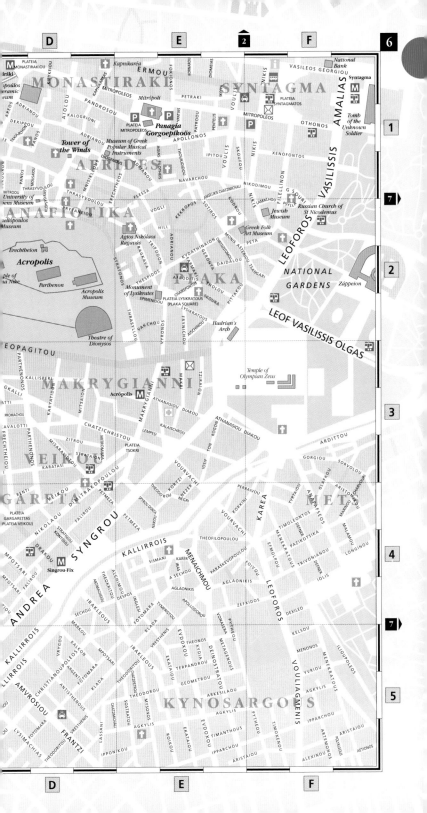

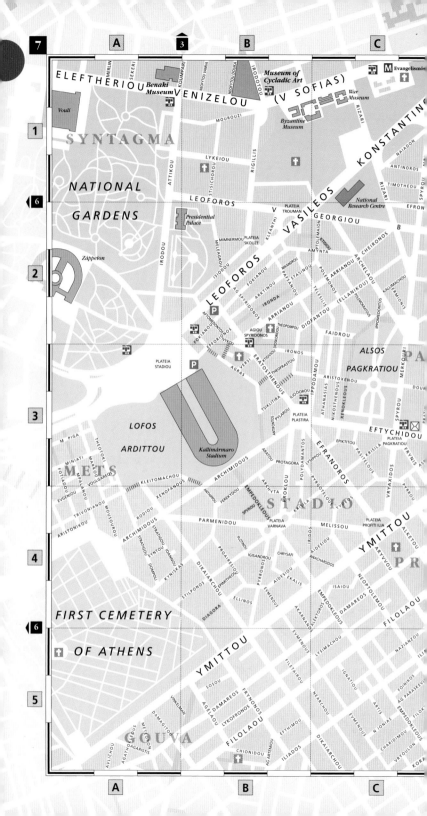

MAINLAND GREECE
AREA BY AREA

Mainland Greece at a Glance

T HE UNIQUE ATTRACTION of the mainland lies in the wealth of ancient remains, set in landscapes of great natural beauty. Classical sites are most notable in the south, around Athens, and the coasts of Attica and the Peloponnese, while Macedonian remains can be seen in the temperate northeast. Byzantine monasteries and churches are found all over the country, particularly on the holy peninsula of Mount Athos which is governed by its 20 monasteries.

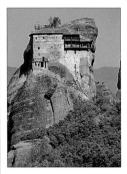

NORTHERN GREECE
(see pp232–57)

The Metéora area
(see pp216–17) combines extraordinary sandstone pinnacles with some of the first medieval monasteries in Greece, perched on the rocky peaks.

Delphi *(see pp228–31) is home to the evocative ruins of an ancient religious complex and theatre situated on Mount Parnassus.*

CENTRAL AND WESTERN GREECE
(see pp202–31)

Ancient Olympia *(see pp170–73) was, from the 8th century BC to the 4th century AD, the site of the Panhellenic Games, forerunner of today's Olympics. One of the best-preserved buildings is the Temple of Hera (left), dating from around the 6th century BC.*

THE PELOPONNESE
(see pp158–201)

Mystrás *(see pp192–3) is one of the best-preserved Byzantine complexes in Greece, exemplified in this church of Agía Sofía. It is a medieval city, and held out against the Ottomans until 1460.*

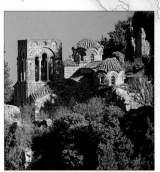

The Máni peninsula
(see pp194–9) is dotted with tower houses.

0 kilometres   50

0 miles   25

◁ **Moní Spiliótissa, near the Zagorian village of Arísti in Western Greece**

Thessaloníki's *Archaeological Museum (see pp246–7) has spectacular gold finds from the tombs of the Macedonian kings, and this bronze head from around AD 235 of Alexander Severus.*

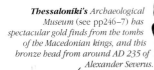

Osios Loúkas *monastery (see pp222–3) is beautifully set in a flowering orchard. The octagonal design of the 11th-century dome was widely copied. Its plain exterior conceals the gold-ground mosaics inside.*

Mount Athos has, since 1060, been entirely occupied by monks *(see pp252–5).*

Ancient Corinth (see pp162–6), *capital of the Roman province of Achaia, was renowned for its luxury and elegance, exemplified by this ornate capital.*

The Monastery of Dafní *(see pp152–3) is a famous work of Byzantine architecture with outstanding medieval mosaics decorating the interior of the church.*

AROUND ATHENS *(see pp140–57)*

Athens

Mycenae (see pp178–80), *one of Greece's oldest sites, dates back to 1550 BC; the Lion Gate was the entrance to the citadel. Mycenae was possibly ruled by Agamemnon.*

Epidaurus *(see pp184–5) has one of the best-preserved theatres in Greece.*

Monemvasía (see pp186–8) *means "one way in", a reference to the strategic advantage of this heavily fortified Byzantine seaport. Its former role as the main port of Byzantine Greece is reflected in the buildings of the old town.*

AROUND ATHENS

ATTICA

T HE AREA AROUND ATHENS, *known as Attica, is the spiritual heartland of ancient and modern Greece. Its archaeological sites have attracted generations of scholars and plunderers alike, and its mountains and coastline have provided important refuge in times of strife. Today the golden beaches along the eastern coast attract those simply wishing to escape the bustle of modern Athens.*

The land of Attica was the basis of Athenian wealth. The fine marble from the quarries on Mount Ymittós and Mount Pentéli was used for the temples and sculptures of ancient Athens. The silver from Lávrio financed their construction, and the produce from the local agricultural areas fed the population.

Waiting for a ferry in Piraeus

Attica has witnessed many significant historical events. The plain of Marathon was the site of one of the greatest battles in Greek history. Piraeus, now Greece's largest and busiest port, was also the port of ancient Athens. The Classical temples at lessknown archaeological sites around the countryside, such as Eleusis, Ramnoús and Brauron, offer a rural retreat from the overcrowding and pollution of the city. At Soúnio, the majestic, well-preserved Temple of Poseidon on the cape has been a beacon for mariners for centuries.

The Byzantine era also left a great legacy of fine architecture to the region. Two of the best examples of this are the imposing monasteries of Dafní and Kaisarianí, with their ornate mosaics and elegant stonework.

South of Athens, the summer heat of the Attic plain is ideal for growing crops. Grapes are a speciality in the Mesógeia (Midland) region, which produces some of the finest retsina in the country. North of Athens, the pine-forested Mount Párnitha provides interesting walks and offers superb views over the city from the summit.

The peaceful ruins of the Parthenon of the Bear Maidens at Ancient Brauron

◁ **The Christ Pantokrátor figure in the dome of the *katholikón* of the Monastery of Dafní**

Around Athens

BEYOND THE ENDLESS urban sprawl of Athens, the region around the city, known as Attica, offers the diversity of wild mountains, Byzantine monasteries and churches, evocative archaeological sites and sandy beaches. Not surprisingly, such easy accessibility to the coast and countryside has led to overcrowding in Athens' suburbs, and pollution around Piraeus and Ancient Eleusis. The hills of Mount Párnitha and Ymittós are rich in wildlife, with deserted trails, caves and icy spring water. In the summer months, Athenians move out to the Attic Coast, where the well-kept beaches have every kind of watersport facility, and there are bars and clubs. Towards the cape at Soúnio there are countless fish tavernas by the sea and quiet rocky coves ideal for snorkelling.

Lárisa, Ioánnina, Préveza, Vólos, Thessaloníki

Chalkída

ANCIENT OROPOS

↑ *Thebes*

3 (E962)

MOUNT PARNITHA

Boats moored in Mikrolímano harbour, Piraeus

ANCIENT ELEUSIS ⑯

8 (E94)

MEGARA

MONASTERY OF DAFNI ⑭ **ATHI**

ACHAR

8 (E94)

Corinth, Tripoli, Pátra, Kalamáta

⑮
PIRAEUS

PALAIO FA

SEE ALSO

- *Where to Stay* p268
- *Where to Eat* pp290–91

Key

▰▰▰	Dual-carriageway
▰▰▰	Major road
▰▰▰	Minor road
▰▰▰	Scenic route
~~	River
✳	Viewpoint

GETTING AROUND

Athens' international airport, Elefthérios, serves the region. There are two routes out of Athens to southeast Attica: the popular coastal road from Piraeus to Soúnio, and the inland road, via Korópi and Markópoulo, to the east coast towns of Pórto Ráfti and Lávrio. This is also the way for the turn-off to the port of Rafína, where there are ferry connections to Evvoia and the Cyclades. Frequent buses from Athens link all the towns in the area. Mount Párnitha and northern Attica are best reached by taking the 1 (E75) national road.

The Temple of Poseidon on the cape at Soúnio

LOCATOR MAP

SIGHTS AT A GLANCE

```
0 kilometres        10
0 miles         5
```

The *katholikón* of Moní Kaïsarianís

View of the Enkoimitírion at Oropós

Ancient Oropós ❶
Ωρωπός

Kálamos, Attica. **Road map** D4.
█ 22950 62144. ▦ Kálamos.
◯ daily. ● main public hols. ▨

THE PEACEFUL SANCTUARY of Oropós nestles on the left bank of the Cheímarros, a small river surrounded by pine trees and wild thyme bushes. It is dedicated to Amphiáraos, a hero credited with healing powers whom, according to mythology, Zeus rescued when he was wounded in battle. It is said that the earth swallowed up Amphiáraos while he was riding his chariot, and that he then miraculously reappeared through the sacred spring at this site. In ancient times visitors would throw coins into the spring in the hope of being granted good health.

The Amphiaraion sanctuary came to prominence as a healing centre in the 4th century BC, when its Doric temple and sacrificial altar were built, attracting the sick from all over Greece. Houses erected during the Roman period, when the area became a popular spa centre, are still visible on the right bank of the river. The Enkoimitírion was the site's most interesting building. It was a long stoa, the remains of which are still visible today, where the patients underwent treatment by *enkoimisis*. This gruesome ritual entailed the sacrifice of a goat in whose bloody hide the patient would then spend the night. The next morning, priests would prescribe medicines based on their interpretations of the dreams of the patient.

Above the Enkoimitírion are the remains of an impressive theatre, which has a well-preserved *proskenion* (stage) and five sculpted marble thrones, once reserved for the use of priests and guests of honour. On the right bank of the valley, opposite the altar, is a water clock dating from the 4th century BC.

Marble throne from the theatre at Oropós

Ramnoús ❷
Ραμνούς

Attica. **Road map** D4. █ 22940 63477. ▦ ◯ daily (Sanctuary of Nemesis only). ● main public hols. ▨ &

RAMNOUS is a remote but beautiful site, overlooking the gulf of Evvoia. It is home to the only Greek sanctuary dedicated to the goddess of vengeance, Nemesis. The sanctuary was demolished when the Byzantine Emperor Arcadius decreed in AD 399 that all temples left standing should be destroyed. Thus only the remains of this sanctuary can be seen today.

Within its compound, two temples are preserved side by side. The smaller and older Temple of Themis dates from the 6th century BC. Used as a treasury and storehouse in ancient times, its impressive polygonal walls are all that now survive. Within the cella, some important statues of the goddess and her priestess, Aristonoë, were uncovered. They can now be seen in the National Archaeological Museum (see pp68–71).

The larger Temple of Nemesis dates from the mid-5th century BC. It is very similar in design to the Hephaisteion in Athens' Agora (see pp90–91) and the Temple of Poseidon at Soúnio (see p148). Built in the Doric

The remains of the Temple of Nemesis at Ramnoús

style, the temple contained a statue of Nemesis by Agorakritos, a disciple of Pheidias (*see p98*). The statue has been partially reconstructed from fragments, and the head is now in the British Museum.

The quayside at the port of Rafína

Marathónas ❸
Μαραθώνας

Attica. **Road map** D4. 🕻 *22940 55155.* 🚌 **Site & Museum** ⭘ *Tue–Sun.* ⬤ *main public hols.* 📷

THE MARATHON PLAIN is the site of the great Battle of Marathon, where the Athenians defeated the Persians. The burial mound of the Athenians lies 4 km (2 miles) from the modern town of Marathónas. This tumulus is 180 m (590 ft) in circumference and 10 m (32 ft) high. It contains the ashes of the 192 Athenian warriors who died in the battle. The spot was marked by a simple *stele* of a fallen warrior, Aristion, by the sculptor Aristocles. The original is now in the National Archaeological Museum (*see pp68–71*) in Athens. There is a copy at the site, inscribed with an epigram by the ancient poet Simonides: "The Athenians fought at the front of the Greeks at Marathon, defeating the gold-bearing Persians and stealing their power."

In 1970 the burial mound of the Plataians and royal Mycenaean tombs were found nearby in the village of Vraná. The Plataians were the only other Greeks who sent warriors in time to assist the Athenians already at the battle. The **Marathon Museum** displays archaeological finds from these local sites. There are also some beautiful

Plate discovered in the tomb of Plataians

Egyptian-style statues from the 2nd century AD, found on the estate of Herodes Atticus, on the Marathon Plain. This wealthy benefactor was born and bred in this area. He is known for erecting many public buildings in Athens, including the famous theatre located on the southern slope of the Acropolis (*see p100*) that was named in his honour.

ENVIRONS: Just 8 km (5 miles) west of Marathónas is **Lake Marathónas**, which is crossed by a narrow causeway. This vast expanse of water is manmade. The impressive dam, made from white Pentelic marble, was built in 1926. It created an artificial lake that was Athens' sole source of water up until 1956. The lake is fed by the continuous streams of the Charádras and Varnávas which flow down from Mount Párnitha (*see p151*) and makes a good setting for a picnic.

Rafína ❹
Ραφήνα

Attica. **Road map** D4. 🏘 *8,600* 🚌 🚌

THE CHARM OF RAFINA is its lively fishing port, packed with caïques and ferries. After Piraeus it is the main port in Attica. Frequent buses from Athens bring passengers for the regular hydrofoil and ferry connections to the Cyclades and other Aegean islands.

One of the administrative *demes* (regions) of ancient Athens, Rafína is a long-established settlement. Although there is little of historical or archaeological interest, the town offers a selection of excellent fish restaurants and tavernas. Choose one by the waterside to sit and watch the hustle and bustle of this busy port.

ENVIRONS: North of Rafína, a winding road leads to the more picturesque resort of **Máti**. Once a quiet hamlet, it is packed today with trendy cafés and bars, apartment blocks and summer houses owned by Athenians.

THE BATTLE OF MARATHON

When Darius of Persia arrived at the Bay of Marathon with his warships in 490 BC, it seemed impossible that the Greeks could defeat him. Heavily outnumbered, the 10,000 Greek hoplites had to engage 25,000 Persian warriors. Victory was due to the tactics of the commander Miltiades, who altered the usual battle phalanx by strengthening the wings with more men. The Persians were enclosed on all sides and driven back to the sea. Around 6,000 Persians died and only 192 Athenians. The origins of the marathon run also date from this battle. News of the victory was relayed by a runner who covered the 41 km (26 miles) back to Athens in full armour before dying of exhaustion.

Vase showing Greek hoplites fighting a Persian on horseback

Ancient Brauron 5

Βραυρώνα

SITUATED NEAR MODERN VRAVRONA, Brauron is one of the most evocative sites near Athens. Although little remains of its former architectural glory, finds in the museum reveal its importance as the centre of worship of Artemis, goddess of childbirth and protectress of animals (see p53). Legend relates that it was founded by Orestes and Iphigéneia, the children of Agamemnon, who introduced the cult of Artemis into Greece. Evidence of Neolithic and Mycenaean remains have been found on the hill above the site, but the tyrant Peisistratos brought Brauron its fame in the 6th century BC when he made the worship of Artemis Athens' official state religion.

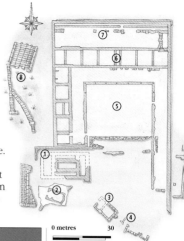

0 metres 30
0 yards 30

KEY TO THE SANCTUARY OF ARTEMIS

① Temple of Artemis
② Chapel of Agios Geórgios
③ Sacred House
④ Tomb of Iphigéneia
⑤ Parthenon of the Bear Maidens
⑥ Dormitories
⑦ Stoa
⑧ Stone Bridge

The Parthenon of the Bear Maidens at Brauron

Exploring Ancient Brauron
The centre of this compact site lies just north of the prehistoric acropolis. The 5th-century BC Doric **Temple of Artemis**, of which only the foundations remain, formed the focal point of the·sanctuary to the goddess. Beside the temple stands a late Byzantine chapel, dedicated to **Agios Geórgios**. From here a path leads southeast to the oldest cult site in the sanctuary. This is said to be the **Tomb of Iphigéneia**,

The small Byzantine chapel of Agios Geórgios

the high priestess of Artemis. Next to it are the foundations of the **Sacred House**, which was used as a home for the cult's priestesses. The most extensive remains at the site are to the northeast, at the **Parthenon of the Bear Maidens**. This courtyard may have been the place where young girls performed the

bear dance. Surrounded by a late 5th-century BC **stoa**, the courtyard had rooms behind that were used as dining areas and **dormitories**. Only the foundations remain, but the stone sleeping couches and bases of statues can still be seen. There is also a 5th-century BC **stone bridge** to the west.

BRAURONIA CEREMONY

Held every four years in the spring, the Brauronia festival was celebrated in atonement for the killing of one of Artemis's sacred pet bears. Although little is known about the mysterious rites today, Aristophanes mentions the "bear dance" that initiates had to perform in his play *Lysistrata*. Disguised as bears and adorned with saffron-coloured robes, young girls, aged between 5 and 10, performed a dance honouring this sacred animal.

Relief showing pilgrims approaching the altar of Artemis at the Brauronia ceremony

VISITORS' CHECKLIST

10 km (6 miles) NE of
Markópoulo, Attica. **Road map**
D4. ☎ 22990 27020. ▤
Site ○ 8:30am–3pm Thu–Sun.
Museum ○ 8:30am–3pm
Tue–Sun. ● 1, 6 Jan, 25 Mar,
Shrove Mon, Good Fri am,
Easter Sun, Mon, 1 May, 25,
26 Dec. ▨ ⓑ limited access
on site. ⓞ

**Mycenaean vase from the
Brauron Museum, 1200–1100 BC**

🏛 Brauron Museum

This fascinating museum has a wealth of finds from the site. In Room 1, there are cases filled with assorted votive offerings such as miniature vases and jewellery. In Room 2 are the serene statues of *árktoi* ("bear maidens"). Room 3 has a fine votive relief of the gods Zeus, Leto, Apollo and Artemis, and the remains of an altar. Rooms 4 and 5 offer a variety of prehistoric and Mycenaean finds, including some ornate Geometric vases.

Statue of a bear maiden

RETSINA

Although many Greeks prefer drinking whisky to wine these days, retsina is still favoured by millions of tourists. Around 16 million bottles were drunk in 1994, and 50 per cent of them were exported around the world. The unique, distinctive flavour comes from the Aleppo pine resin which is added in small quantities to the grape juice during fermentation. This method has been used since antiquity to preserve and flavour wine in Greece. Since entry into the EEC (now called the EU) in 1981, traditional production areas have had their own appellations. Aficionados agree that some of the best retsina comes from the Mesógeia appellation in Attica, where the Savatiano grape is cultivated. Kourtákis, the largest producers of retsina, have their vineyards in Markópoulo and Koropí.

Collection of pine resin

Pórto Ráfti ❻
Πόρτο Ράφτη

Attica. **Road map** D4. 🏠 3,300. ▤

PÓRTO RÁFTI takes its name from Ráfti island which is visible just off the headland. On the island is a colossal marble statue of a seated female, made in the Roman period, known as "the tailor" *(ráftis)*. It was most likely built to be used as a beacon for shipping and would have lit up the harbour. Pórto Ráfti has one of the best natural harbours in Greece, although the town itself has never developed into an important seafaring port. In April 1941, during World War II, 6,000 New Zealand troops were successfully evacuated from the beach. Today it is primarily a pleasant holiday resort, with tavernas and bars. The area is rich in archaeological history. Many Mycenaean tombs have been found south of the bay of Pórto Ráfti, at Peratí, a port that flourished in the 7th and 6th centuries BC.

ENVIRONS: The remains of a fortress that was built during the Chremonidean War (268–261 BC) between Egypt and Macedon can be seen on the southern **Koróni** headland. The northern coastline of **Peratí** is pockmarked with unexplored caves, and attracts many people who come to swim in the clear water and fish off the craggy rocks.

Markópoulo, a thriving market town and viticultural centre 8 km (5 miles) inland, is famous for its tavernas. Spicy sausages are for sale in the butchers' shops and the bakeries are fragrant with the smell of fresh bread.

Pórto Ráfti harbour with Ráfti island in the background

One of the many 19th-century Neo-Classical buildings in Lávrio

Lávrio **❼**
Λαύριο

Attica. **Road map** D4. **⚞** 8,800.
🚌 **⚓** **⛴** Thu.

Lávrio was famous for its silver mines in ancient times. They were used as a source of revenue for the Athenian state and financed Perikles's programme of grand public buildings in Athens in the 5th century BC *(see p30)*. They also enabled the general Themistokles to construct a fleet capable of beating the Persians at the Battle of Salamis in 480 BC. It was this excellent naval fleet which established Athens as a naval power. Before their final closure in the 20th century, the mines were also exploited by French and Greek companies for other minerals such as manganese and cadmium.

Originally worked by slaves, over 2,000 mine shafts have been discovered in the surrounding hills, and some are now open to visitors as the **Mineralogical Museum**. It is the only such museum in Greece. Traces of ore and minerals in the rock face can be seen on tours of the old mines. Since their closure the area has suffered high unemployment. The old Neo-Classical houses and empty harbourfront warehouses indicate the former prosperity of the town. Makrónisos, the narrow island opposite the port, was used as a prison for political detainees during the Civil War *(see p42)*.

🏛 Mineralogical Museum
Leof Andréa Kordelá. **☎** 22920 26270. **◷** 10am–noon Wed, Sat & Sun. **📷** **♿**

Soúnio **❽**
Σούνιο

9 km (5.5 miles) S of Lávrio, Attica.
Road map D4. **☎** 22920 39363. **🚌** to Lávrio. **◷** 10am–sunset daily. **📷** **▯**

THE TEMPLE OF POSEIDON, built on a site set back from sheer cliffs tumbling into the Aegean Sea at Soúnio (Cape Sounion), was ideally located for worship of the powerful god of the sea. Its brilliant white marble columns have been a landmark for ancient and modern mariners alike.

The present temple, built in 444 BC, stands on the site of older ruins. An Ionic frieze, made from 13 slabs of Parian marble, is located on the east

The Doric columns of the Temple of Poseidon

side of the temple's main approach path. It is very eroded but is known to have depicted scenes from the mythological battle of the Lapiths and centaurs, and also the adventures of the hero Theseus, who was thought to be the son of Poseidon, according to some legends.

Local marble, taken from quarries at nearby Agriléza, was used for the temple's 34 slender Doric columns, of which 15 survive today. The temple also possesses a

The ruins of the Temple of Poseidon on Soúnio

unique design feature which helps combat the effects of sea-spray erosion: the columns were cut with only 16 flutings instead of the usual 20, thus reducing the surface area exposed to the elements.

When Byron carved his name on one of the columns in 1810, he set a dangerous precedent of vandalism at the temple, which is now covered with scrawled signatures.

A waterside restaurant at Várkiza, along the Attic coast

Attic Coast 🄽
Παραλία Αττικύς

Attica. **Road map** D4. 🚌

THE COASTAL STRIP from Piraeus to Soúnio is often called the "Apollo Coast" after a small Temple of Apollo discovered at Vouliagméni. It is covered with beaches and resort towns that are always very busy at weekends, and particularly so in the summer holiday season.

One of the first places along the coast from Piraeus is the tiny seaside resort of **Palaió Fáliro** which is home to the Phaleron War Cemetery. In this quiet spot is the Athens Memorial, erected in May 1961 to 2,800 British soldiers who died in World War II.

Noisy suburbs near Athens airport, like **Glyfáda** and **Alimos** (famous as the birthplace of the ancient historian Thucydides), are very commercialized with a large number of marinas, hotels and shopping malls.

At chic **Vouliagméni**, with its large yacht marina, luxury

BYRON IN GREECE

The British Romantic poet Lord Byron (1788–1824) first arrived in Greece in 1809 at the tender age of 21, and travelled around Epirus and Attica with his friend John Cam Hobhouse. In Athens he wrote *The Maid of Athens*, inspired by his love for his landlady's daughter, and parts of *Childe Harold*. These publications made him an over-night sensation and, when back in London in 1812, he proclaimed: "If I am a poet it is the air of Greece which has made me one." He was received as a hero on his return to Greece in 1823, because of his desire to help fight the Turks in the War of Independence *(see pp40–41)*. However, on Easter Sunday 1824 in Mesolóngi, he died of a fever without seeing Greece liberated. Proving in his case that the pen is mightier than the sword, Byron is still venerated in Greece, where streets and babies are named after him.

Lord Byron, in traditional Greek costume, by T Phillips (1813)

---

hotels line the promontory. A short walk northwards away from the coast, beside the main road, is the enchanting Vouliagméni Lake. This unusual freshwater lake lies beneath low, limestone cliffs. The stunning stretch of warm, sulphurous water has been used for years to bring relief to sufferers of rheumatism. There are changing rooms and a café close by.

At **Várkiza**, the wide bay is filled with windsurfers. By the main road there are two massive gin-palace music halls, *On the Rocks* and *Riba's*, where popular Greek singers perform throughout the summer season. From Várkiza, a road snakes inland to **Vári**, renowned for its

restaurants serving meat dishes. The Vári cave is located about 2 km (1 mile) north of the village. Inside is a freshwater spring and some fine stalactites have developed. Some minor Classical ruins remain in the caves, although many have been removed. There is unrestricted access and no admission charge.

From Várkiza to Soúnio, the coastal road is lined with quiet bathing coves, fish tavernas and luxury villas. **Anávysos** is a thriving market town surrounded by vineyards and fields. In its harbour, caïques sell locally caught fish every day, and there is a small street market every Saturday, with stalls piled high with seasonal fruit and vegetables.

Colourful stall of local produce in Anávyssos

Sculpture in the gardens of the Vorrés Museum

Paianía ⑩
Παιανία

Attica. **Road map** D4. 🏛 *9,700.* 🚌
🚊 *Tue.*

JUST EAST OF ATHENS, Paianía
is a town of sleepy streets
and cafés. In the main square,
the church of **Zoödóchou
Pigís** has some fine modern
frescoes by the 20th-century
artist Fótis Kóntoglou. The
birthplace of the orator
Demosthenes (384–322 BC),
Paianía is more famous today
for the **Vorrés Museum**. Set
in beautiful gardens, this
features private collector
Ion Vorrés' eclectic array of
ancient and modern art. The
museum is divided into two
sections, encompassing 3,000
years of Greek history and
heritage. The first is housed

in what was the
collector's private
home: two tradi-
tional village
houses filled with
ancient sculptures,
folk artifacts, cera-
mics, Byzantine
icons, seascapes
and furniture. The
second section,
housed in a spec-
ially built modern
building, offers a
unique overview
of contemporary
Greek art since
the 1940s, with
many excellent
works by more
than 300 differ-
ent painters and
sculptors, encom-
passing every
major art movement from
Photo-Realism to Pop Art.

🖼 Vorrés Museum
Diadóchou Konstantínou 1. 📞 *210
664 4771.* 🕐 *Sat & Sun.* 🔴 *Aug &
main public hols.* 🈲 ♿

ENVIRONS: Above Paianía,
Koutoúki Cave is hidden in
the foothills of Mount Ymittós.
It was found in 1926 by a
shepherd looking for a goat
which had fallen into the
12,200 sq m (130,000 sq ft)
cave. There are tours every
half hour, with son et lumière
effects lighting up the stalagmites and stalactites. The temperature inside is 17˚C (62˚F).

🎇 Koutoúki Cave
4 km (2.5 miles) W of Paianía.
📞 *210 664 2108.* 🕐 *9am–4pm
daily.* 🈲

Moní Kaïsarianís ⑪
Μονή Καισαριανής

5 km (3 miles) E of Athens, Attica.
Road map D4. 📞 *210 723 6619.*
🚌 *to Kaisarianís.* 🕐 *8:30am–3pm
Tue–Sun.* 🔴 *main public hols.* 🈲

LOCATED IN A WOODED valley
of Mount Ymittós, Moní
Kaïsarianís was founded in
the 11th century. In 1458,
when Sultan Mehmet II
conquered Athens, the
monastery was exempted
from taxes in recognition of
the abbot's gift to the sultan
of the keys of the city. This
led to great prosperity until
1792, when it lost these
privileges and went into
decline. The complex was
used briefly as a convent after
the War of Inde-
pendence, until
1855. Its build-
ings were event-
ually restored
in 1956.

The small
katholikón is
dedicated to the
Presentation of
the Virgin. All
the frescoes
date from the
16th and 17th
centuries. The

**Decorative
stonework on
Moní Kaïsarianís**

finest are those in the narthex,
painted by the Peloponnesian
artist Ioánnis Ýpatos in 1682.

The large, peaceful gardens
in the monastery are owned
by the Athens Friends of the
Tree Society, who planted
them after all the trees were
cut down during World War II.
Just above the monastery, the
source of the River Ilissós has

Moní Kaïsarianís, hidden in the hills around Mount Ymittós

been visited since antiquity for its sacred Kylloú Péra spring whose water is reputed to cure sterility; water still gushes from an ancient marble ram's-head fountain on the eastern side of the monastery. Before the Marathon dam was built *(see p145)*, the spring was Athens' main source of water.

Kifisiá ⑫
Κηφισιά

12 km (7.5 miles) NE of Athens, Attica.
Road map D4. 🚌 40,000. 🚋
Ⓜ *Kifisiá.*

The tiny chapel of Agía Triáda on the hillside of Mount Párnitha

K IFISIÁ HAS BEEN a favourite summer retreat for many Athenians since Roman times. Once the exclusive domain of rich Greeks, it is congested today with apartment blocks and shopping malls. Traces of its former tranquillity can still be seen by taking a ride in a horse-drawn carriage. These wait by the metro station offering drives down shady streets lined with mansions and villas, built in a bizarre variety of hybrid styles such as Alpine chalet and Gothic Neo-Classicism.

The **Goulándris Natural History Museum**, which opened in 1974, is housed in one of these villas. Its large collection covers all aspects of Greece's varied wildlife and minerals. There are 200,000 varieties of plants in the herbarium, and over 1,300 examples of taxidermy; the stuffed creatures are carefully displayed in their natural habitats.

Clam shell outside the Goulándris Natural History Museum, Kifisiá

🏛 Goulándris Natural History Museum
Levídou 13. 📞 210 801 5870.
🕐 9am–2:30pm Sat–Thu.
⬤ main public hols. 🈲

ENVIRONS: In Kifisiá's suburb Maroúsi is the small **Spathári Museum of Shadow Theatre**. Opened in 1995, it is devoted to the fascinating history of the Karagkiózis puppet theatre. Shadow theatre originally came to Greece from the Far East, via players who used to travel throughout the Ottoman Empire performing for the aristocracy in the 18th century. It was soon transformed into a popular folk art by entertainers who would travel around Greece with their makeshift theatres. The name Karagkiózis refers to the indomitable and impoverished Greek character who is tormented by the other standard theatrical characters such as the rich Pasha and toughguy Stávrakas. The museum displays the history of two generations of the Spathári family, who were the leading exponents of this dying art, along with the colourful home-made sets and puppets that were used in their past performances.

Puppet from the Museum of Shadow Theatre

🏛 Spathári Museum of Shadow Theatre
Vas Sofias & D. Ralli, Maroussi. 📞 210 612 7245. 🕐 10:30am–1:30pm Sun–Fri. ⬤ main public hols.

Mount Párnitha ⑬
Όρος Πάρνηθα

Attica. **Road map** D4. 🚌 to Acharnés, Thrakomakedónes & Agía Triáda.

I N ANCIENT TIMES, Mount Párnitha sheltered wild animals. Today, this rugged range, which extends nearly 25 km (16 miles) from east to west, is rich in less dangerous fauna. Tortoises can be seen in the undergrowth and birds of prey circle the summit of Karampóla at 1,413 m (4,635 ft). Wild flowers are abundant, particularly in autumn and spring when cyclamen and crocus carpet the mountain. There are spectacular views of alpine scenery, all within an hour's drive of the city. At the small town of **Acharnés**, a cable car ascends to a casino perched at over 900 m (3,000 ft).

Still little used by hikers, the mountain has plenty of demanding trails. The most popular walk leads from Thrakomakedónes, in the foothills of the mountain, to the Báfi refuge. This uphill march takes about two hours, and offers superb views of the surrounding mountain scenery. Starting with thorny scrub typical of the Mediterranean *maquis*, it follows well-trodden paths to end among alpine firs and clear mountain air. Once at the Báfi refuge, it is worth walking on to the Flampoúri refuge which has some dramatic views.

Monastery of Dafní **⓮**
Μονή Δαφνίου

Fresco detail

THE MONASTERY OF DAFNI was founded in the 5th century AD. Named after the laurels *(dáfnes)* that used to grow here, it was built with the remains of an ancient sanctuary of Apollo, which had occupied this site until it was destroyed in AD 395. In the early 13th century, Otto de la Roche, the first Frankish Duke of Athens, bequeathed it to Cistercian monks in Burgundy. Greek Orthodox monks took the site in the 16th century, erecting the elegant cloisters just south of the church. An earthquake in 2000 means that the beautiful gold-leaf Byzantine mosaics in the *katholikón* (main church) cannot be seen until restoration is completed.

Aerial view of the monastery complex

The Gothic exonarthex was built almost 30 years after the main church.

Cloisters
This arcade was built in the 16th century. On the other side of the courtyard, above a similar arcade, are the monks' cells.

The symmetry of the design makes Dafní one of the most attractive examples of Byzantine architecture in Attica.

KEY TO MOSAICS IN THE KATHOLIKON

WALLS
1 Resurrection
2 Adoration of the Magi
4 Archangel Gabriel
5 Archangel Michael
6 Nativity of the Virgin
8 St John the Baptist
9 Entry into Jerusalem
12 Dormition of the Virgin
13 Last Supper
14 Washing of the Feet
15 Betrayal by Judas
16 Prayer of Sts Anne and Joachim
17 Blessing of the Priests
18 Presentation of the Virgin
20 St Thomas

CEILING AND DOME
3 Nativity
7 Annunciation
10 Christ Pantokrátor
11 Transfiguration
19 Baptism

Esonarthex

Exonarthex

Entrance

Entrance

★ Christ Pantokrátor

The Pantokrátor ("Almighty") gazes sternly down from the dome of the katholikón. Around the central figure are images of the 16 prophets.

The dome is 8 m (26 ft) in diameter and 16 m (52 ft) high at the centre.

Nave

The Transfiguration
This is in the northwest corner under the dome. Elijah and Moses are on either side of Christ and the apostles Peter, James and John are below.

The Windows
Elaborate three-tiered brickwork surrounds each of the windows.

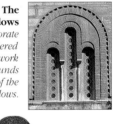

Ticket office and museum

★ Esonarthex Mosaics
These mosaics include depictions of the Last Supper *and the* Washing of the Feet. *The finest is the* Betrayal by Judas. *Christ stands unmoved as Judas kisses Him.*

Piraeus ⑮
Πειραιάς

Waiting for a ferry

O NE OF THE BIGGEST Mediterranean ports, Piraeus is also one of the largest cities in Greece. It has been the port of Athens since ancient times. The Long Walls between Piraeus and Athens were started in 480 BC by Themistokles. However, Sulla destroyed the walls in 86 BC and by the Middle Ages Piraeus was little more than a fishing village. When Athens became the Greek capital in 1834, Piraeus was once again revitalized, with Neo-Classical buildings and modern factories. In 1923, 100,000 refugees came here from Asia Minor, bringing their culture and contributing to the cosmopolitan feel of this port city.

Small boats moored in peaceful Tourkolímano harbour

View across Kentrikó Limáni with ferries in the foreground

Exploring Piraeus

After the Junta *(see p43)* razed many irreplaceable public buildings in the town centre in the early 1970s, civic pride re-emerged with a vengeance. Beside the Municipal Theatre, there are elegant open-air restaurants and fountains in the shade of Neo-Classical façades. On the streets behind the main banks and ticket offices that rim the **Kentrikó Limáni** (the main ferry port), there are smart restaurants and shops, as well as some fine examples of Neo-Classical architecture, such as the **Town Hall**. For information on ferry departures from Kentrikó Limáni, see page 321.

South of the railway station around Navarínou lies the lively market area, including fishmongers', fruit and vegetable stalls, ships' chandlers and hardware stores. On Sunday mornings there is also a bustling flea market, which

is centred on the antique shops around Plateía Ippodameías, and also on Alipédou and Skylítsi streets.

There are two harbours in Piraeus, situated east of Kentrikó Limáni. **Pasalimáni** (Pasha's Port, also known as Limáni Zéas) was once used to harbour the Ottoman fleet. Today it is filled with luxurious yachts. Once known simply as Zéa, Pasalimáni used to be one of Themistokles's major naval ports, with dry docks for 196 triremes. Marína Zéas, the mouth of Pasalimáni, is a jetty used as a dock for hydrofoils to the Argo-Saronic islands. The second harbour, **Tourkolímano**

(also known as Mikrolímano, or Little Harbour) houses many colourful fishing caïques. It is popular for its waterside fish restaurants and has a more relaxing ambience than the larger harbours.

On the coastal road between Pasalimáni and Tourkolímano, smart bars and clubs inhabit the renovated Neo-Classical mansions in the gentrified Kastélla neighbourhood. Even traditionally working-class areas, such as Drapetsóna (the most important manufacturing centre of the country) are now popular for their late-night restaurants.

🎭 Municipal Theatre

Agíou Konstantínou 2. 🔲 *210 412 0333.* ◯ *Tue–Sun.*
The Neo-Classical façade of this imposing building is one of the delights of Piraeus. Designed by Ioánnis Lazarímos (1849–1913), who based his plans on the Opéra Comique in Paris, it has seating for 800, making it one of the largest modern theatres in Greece. It took nearly ten years to complete and was finally

Façade of the Municipal Theatre

inaugurated on 9 April 1895. Today, it is the home of both the **Municipal Art Gallery** and also the **Pános Aravantinoú Museum of Stage Decor**. The Museum of Stage Decor has displays of set designs by the stage designer Pános Aravantinoú (who worked with the Berlin opera in the 1920s), as well as general ephemera from the Greek opera.

Archaeological Museum

Chariláou Trikoúpi 31.
210 452 1598. ○ Tue–Sun.
● main public hols.

This museum is home to some stunning bronzes. Found by workmen in 1959, these large statues of Artemis with her quiver, Athena with her helmet decorated with owls, and Apollo reveal the great expressiveness of Greek sculpture. The Piraeus *koúros* of Apollo, dating from 520 BC, is the earliest full-size bronze

Statue of Athena in the Archaeological Museum

to be discovered. There is also a seated cult statue of the earth goddess Cybele and a fine collection of Greek and Roman statues and grave stelae. Near the museum are the remains of the 2nd-century BC **Theatre of Zéa**; the remains include a well-preserved orchestra.

Hellenic Maritime Museum

Aktí Themistokléous, Freatýda. 210 451 6264.
○ Tue–Sat. ● main public hols, Aug.

On the quayside of Marína Zéas, an old submarine marks the entrance to this fascinating museum. Its first room is built around an original section of Themistokles's Long Walls. More than 2,000 exhibits, such as models of triremes, ephemera from naval battleships and paintings of Greek *trechantíri* (fishing caïques), explore the world of Greek seafaring. From early voyages around

VISITORS' CHECKLIST

10 km (6 miles) SW of Athens, Attica. **Road map** D4. 200,000. Kentrikó Limáni. Kékropos (for Peloponnese), Kanári (for Northern Greece). Piraeus. Plateía Koraï (for Athens), Plateía Karaiskáki (other destinations). Marína Zéas (210 413 5730). Sun (flea market). theatre & music festival: May–Jul.

the Black Sea by trireme, to 20th-century emigration to the New World by transatlantic liner, the museum unravels the complexities of Greek maritime history. Exhibits include models of ships, maps, flags, uniforms and pictures. The War of Independence is well documented with information and memorabilia about the generals who served in it. The old naval ship *Averof*, which was the flagship of the Greek fleet up until 1951, has been fully restored and is berthed nearby. As part of the museum, the ship is also open to visitors.

PIRAEUS CITY CENTRE

Archaeological Museum ④
Hellenic Maritime Museum ⑥
Municipal Theatre ②
Pasalimáni ③
Theatre of Zéa ⑤
Town Hall ①

0 metres   150
0 yards   150

KEY

Ferry service
Tourist information
Church

MARINA ZEAS

Ancient Eleusis ⑯
Αρχαία Ελευσίνα

Eleusis was an ancient centre of religious devotion that culminated in the annual Eleusinian Mysteries. These attracted thousands of people from around the Greek-speaking world, for whom the only initial requirement for becoming a *mystes* (or initiate) was to be neither a murderer nor a barbarian. Both men and women were freely admitted. Existing from Mycenaean times, the sanctuary was closed by the Roman Emperor Theodosius in AD 392, and was finally abandoned when Alaric, king of the Goths, invaded Greece in AD 396, bringing Christianity in his wake.

Anaktoron
This small rectangular stone edifice had a single entrance. It was considered the holiest part of the site. Meaning "palace", it existed long before the Telesterion, which was built around it.

Telesterion
Designed by Iktinos, this temple was built in the 5th century BC. It was constructed to hold several thousand people at a time.

4th-century BC shops and bouleuterion (council chamber)

Temple of Kore hewn out of rock

Roman houses

THE ELEUSINIAN MYSTERIES

Perhaps established by 1500 BC and continuing for almost 2,000 years, these rites centred on the myth of the grieving goddess Demeter, who lost her daughter Persephone (or Kore) to Hades, god of the Underworld, for nine months each year *(see p52)*. Participants were sworn to secrecy, but some evidence of the details of the ceremony does exist. Sacrifices were made before the procession from the Kerameikós *(see pp88–9)* to Eleusis. Here the priestesses would reveal the vision of the holy night, thought to have been a fire symbolizing life after death for the initiates.

A priestess with a *kiste mystika* (basket)

ANCIENT ELEUSIS

This reconstruction is of Eleusis as it was in Roman times (c.AD 150) when the Mysteries were still flourishing. The view is from the east. Although there is little left today, it is still possible to sense the awe and mystery that the rites of Eleusis inspired.

Ploutonion

This cave is said to be where Persephone was returned to earth. It was a sanctuary to Hades, god of the Underworld and the abductor of Persephone.

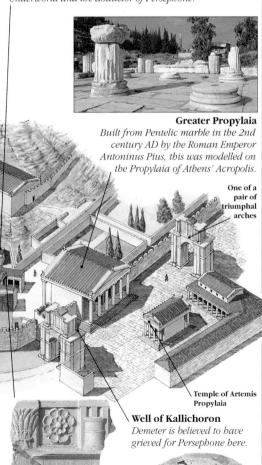

Greater Propylaia

Built from Pentelic marble in the 2nd century AD by the Roman Emperor Antoninus Pius, this was modelled on the Propylaia of Athens' Acropolis.

One of a pair of triumphal arches

Temple of Artemis Propylaia

Well of Kallichoron

Demeter is believed to have grieved for Persephone here.

Lesser Propylaia

This fragment shows sheaves of grain and poppies, which were used to make kykeon, *the drink of the initiates.*

VISITORS' CHECKLIST

Gioka 2, Eleusis, 22 km (14 miles) NW of Athens, Attica. **Road map** D2. **Site & Museum** [ ] 210 554 6019. [ ] [ ] summer: 8:30am–2:30pm Tue–Sun; winter: 8:30am–3pm. [ ] main public holidays. [ ] [ ] [ ]

Relief from the Telesterion, now in the museum

Eleusis Museum

This small museum, south of the Telesterion, has five rooms. The entrance hall contains a copy of the famous relief from the Telesterion showing Triptólemos receiving grain from Demeter. Also in this room are a large 7th-century BC amphora and a copy of the Ninnion votive painting, one of the few remaining representations of the Eleusinian Mysteries. The other rooms are arranged on the left of the hall. In the first of these there is an elegant 6th-century BC *koûros* and a 2nd-century BC Roman statue of Dionysos. In the second room there are two models of the site. The third room has a Classical period terracotta sarcophagus and a large caryatid from the Lesser Propylaia carrying a *kiste mystika* basket on her head. The last room has a variety of pottery fragments, including examples of unusual terracotta containers that were used to carry foodstuffs in the annual *kernoforía* procession.

Fleeing maiden

THE PELOPONNESE

PELOPONNESE

O NE OF THE PRIMARY *strongholds and battlefields of the 1821–31 Revolution, the Peloponnese is the kernel from which the modern Greek state grew. This enormous peninsula, which falls short of being an island by the mere 6-km (4-mile) width of the Corinth isthmus, also has some of the most spectacularly varied scenery and monuments on the mainland.*

The name "Peloponnese" means "island of Pelops", who in legend was fed to the gods by Tantalos, his father. Resurrected, he went on to sire the Atreid line of kings, whose semi-mythical misadventures and brooding citadels were given substance by the discovery of remains at Mycenae. Today the ancient and medieval sites of the Argolid region, to the south of Corinth, contrast with the elegantly Neo-Classical town of Náfplio.

Leonidas statue, Spárti town

In the west lies Ancient Olympia, the athletic and religious nexus of the ancient world and inspiration for the games' revival in modern times. The lush coastal plain of Ileía, heart of an early medieval Crusader principality, spawned Frankish-Byzantine architecture, most famously at Chlemoútsi.

More purely Byzantine art adorns the churches of Mystrás, Geráki and the remote Máni region, whose warlike medieval inhabitants claimed to be descended from the warriors of ancient Sparta. Imposing Venetian fortifications at the beach-fringed capes of Methóni, Koróni and Monemvasía allowed the Venetians to play a role here after most of their other Aegean possessions were lost to the Ottomans.

In Arcadia, at the centre of the Peloponnese, lushly cultivated valleys rise to conifer-draped mountains and deep gorges such as the Loúsios; cliff-side monasteries and sombre hilltowns, like Stemnítsa, are a world apart from the popular Mediterranean image of Greece.

Restaurant terrace overlooking the sea, Monemvasía

◁ Náfplio, seen from the stairs leading to the town's Venetian citadel, Palamídi

Exploring the Peloponnese

A NCIENT AND MEDIEVAL ruins are abundant on the Peloponnese, and provide the main focus of sightseeing. Though there are few highly developed resorts away from the Argolid, such areas as the Loúsios Gorge and Kalógria attract thousands of trekkers and naturalists. A rural economy is still paramount inland, with Pátra being the only large city. The land-scape is dominated by forested moun-tains and the west coast, between Pátra and Methóni, boasts some of the finest beaches in the Mediterranean.

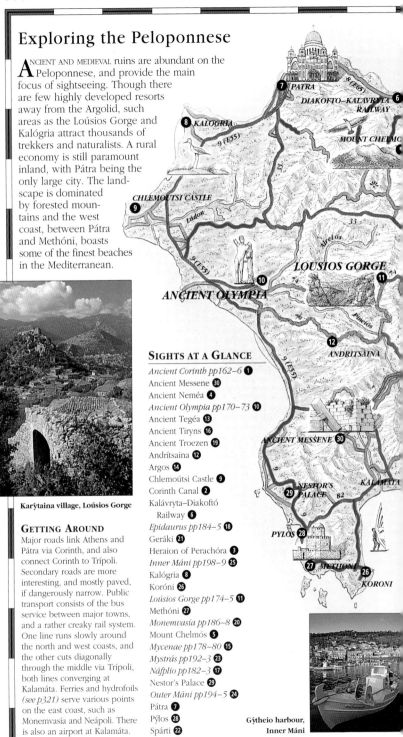

Karýtaina village, Loúsios Gorge

GETTING AROUND

Major roads link Athens and Pátra via Corinth, and also connect Corinth to Trípoli. Secondary roads are more interesting, and mostly paved, if dangerously narrow. Public transport consists of the bus service between major towns, and a rather creaky rail system. One line runs slowly around the north and west coasts, and the other cuts diagonally through the middle via Trípoli, both lines converging at Kalamáta. Ferries and hydrofoils (*see p321*) serve various points on the east coast, such as Monemvasía and Neápoli. There is also an airport at Kalamáta.

SIGHTS AT A GLANCE

Ancient Corinth pp162–6 **1**
Ancient Messene **30**
Ancient Neméa **4**
Ancient Olympia pp170–73 **10**
Ancient Tegéa **13**
Ancient Tiryns **16**
Ancient Troezen **19**
Andrítsaina **12**
Argos **14**
Chlemoútsi Castle **9**
Corinth Canal **2**
Kalávryta–Diakoftó
    Railway **6**
Epidaurus pp184–5 **18**
Geráki **21**
Heraion of Perachóra **3**
Inner Máni pp198–9 **25**
Kalógria **8**
Koróni **26**
Loúsios Gorge pp174–5 **11**
Methóni **27**
Monemvasía pp186–8 **20**
Mount Chelmós **5**
Mycenae pp178–80 **15**
Mystrás pp192–3 **23**
Náfplio pp182–3 **17**
Nestor's Palace **29**
Outer Máni pp194–5 **24**
Pátra **7**
Pýlos **28**
Spárti **22**

Places named on map:
PATRA **7**
DIAKOFTO–KALAVRYTA RAILWAY **6**
KALOGRIA **8**
MOUNT CHELMO(S) **5**
CHLEMOUTSI CASTLE **9**
LOUSIOS GORGE **11**
ANCIENT OLYMPIA **10**
ANDRITSAINA **12**
ANCIENT MESSENE **30**
KALAMATA
NESTOR'S PALACE **29**
PYLOS **28**
METHONI **27**
KORONI **26**

**Gýtheio harbour,
Inner Máni**

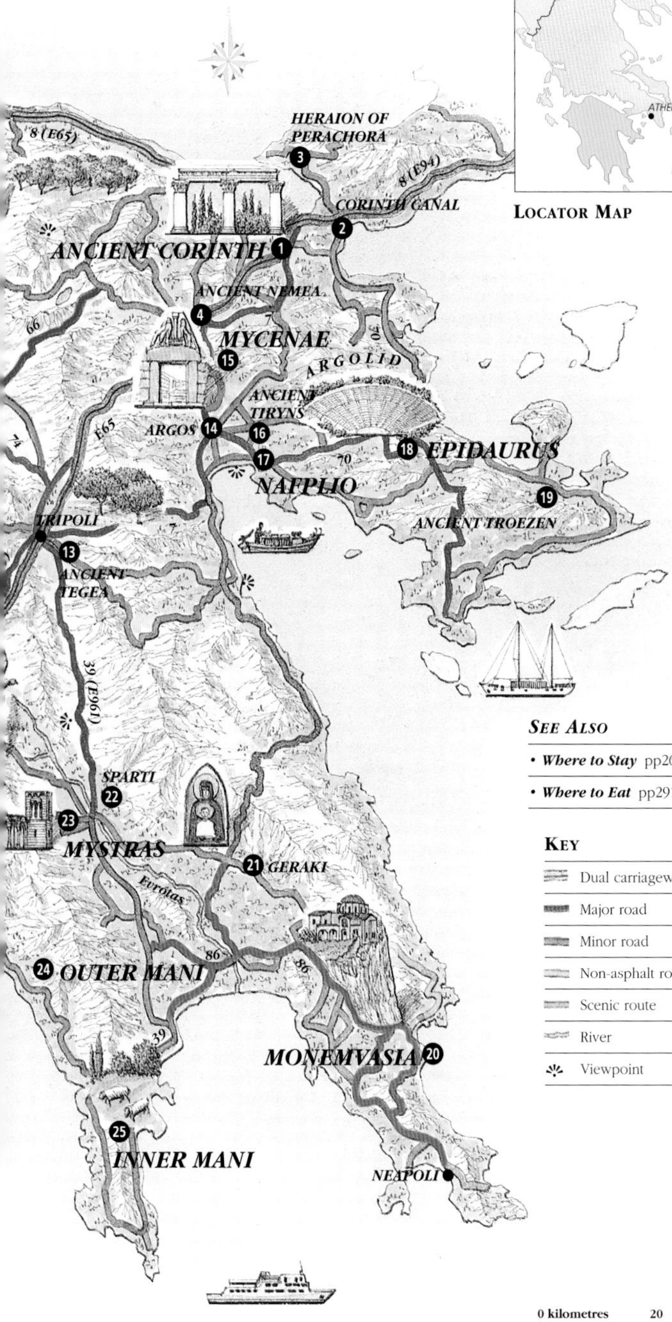
HERAION OF PERACHORA
3
8 (E65)
8 (E94)
CORINTH CANAL
2
ANCIENT CORINTH
1
ANCIENT NEMEA
4
66
MYCENAE
15
ARGOLID
70
ANCIENT TIRYNS
ARGOS
14
16
17
E65
74
18
EPIDAURUS
NAFPLIO
19
TRIPOLI
ANCIENT TROEZEN
13
ANCIENT TEGEA
39 (E961)
SPARTI
22
23
MYSTRAS
21
GERAKI
Eurotas
86
24
OUTER MANI
39
MONEMVASIA
20
25
INNER MANI
NEAPOLI

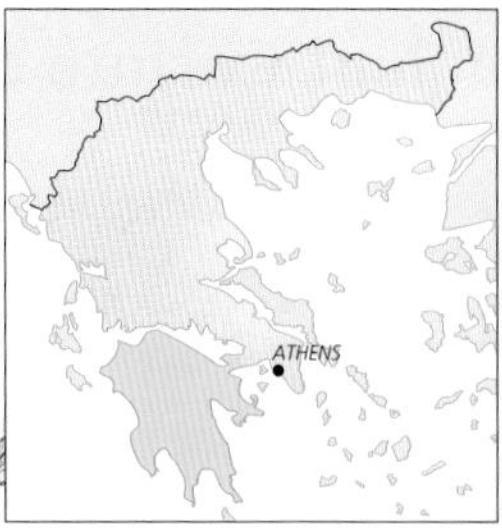
ATHENS

LOCATOR MAP

SEE ALSO

- ***Where to Stay*** pp269–71
- ***Where to Eat*** pp291–2

KEY

- Dual carriageway
- Major road
- Minor road
- Non-asphalt road
- Scenic route
- River
- Viewpoint

0 kilometres 20

0 miles 20

Ancient Corinth ●

Αρχαία Κόρινθος

ANCIENT CORINTH derived its prosperity from its position on a narow isthmus between the Saronic and Corinthian gulfs. Transporting goods across this isthmus, even before the canal *(see p167)* was built, provided the shortest route from the eastern Mediterranean to the Adriatic and Italy. Founded in Neolithic times, the town was razed in 146 BC by the Romans, who rebuilt it a century later. Attaining a population of 750,000 under the patronage of the emperors, the town gained a reputation for licentious living which St Paul attacked when he came here in AD 52. Excavations have revealed the vast extent of the city, destroyed by earthquakes in Byzantine times. The ruins constitute the largest Roman township in Greece.

LOCATOR MAP

The *bema* (platform), was where St Paul was accused of sacrilege by the Jews of Corinth.

Bouleuterion

The agora was the hub of Roman civic life.

South stoa

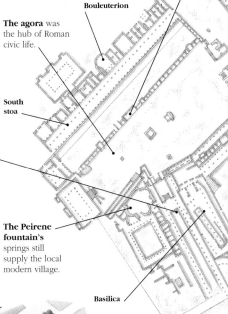

★ **Lechaion Way**
This marble-paved road linked the port of Lechaion with the city, ending at a still-surviving stairway and an imposing propylaion (entrance).

The Peirene fountain's springs still supply the local modern village.

Basilica

RECONSTRUCTION OF ANCIENT CORINTH (C.AD 100)

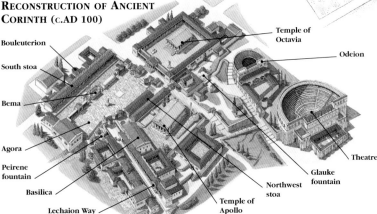

Bouleuterion

South stoa

Bema

Agora

Peirene fountain

Basilica

Lechaion Way

Temple of Octavia

Odeion

Temple of Apollo

Northwest stoa

Glauke fountain

Theatre

Temple of Octavia
These three ornate Corinthian columns, topped by a restored architrave, are all that remain of a temple, standing on a platform, dedicated to the sister of the Emperor Augustus.

VISITORS' CHECKLIST

7 km (4 miles) SW of modern Corinth, Peloponnese.
Road map C4. 27410 31207. **Site & Museum**
Apr–Oct: 8am–7pm daily; Nov–Mar: 8am–5pm daily.
1 Jan, 25 Mar, Good Fri am, Easter Sun, 1 May, 25, 26 Dec.
limited.
Acrocorinth: 4 km (2.5 miles) S of Ancient Corinth.
8:30am–3pm daily.

Acrocorinth
(see p166)

The museum contains artifacts from the site *(see p166).*

Odeion
This was one of several buildings endowed by Herodes Atticus, the wealthy Athenian and good friend of the Emperor Hadrian.

The theatre was modified in the 3rd century AD so water could be piped in and mock sea battles staged.

The Glauke fountain's four cisterns were hewn from a cubic monolith and filled by an aqueduct from the hills.

The northwest stoa had two series of columns, the outer being Doric and the inner being Ionic.

★ **Temple of Apollo**
The most striking structure of the lower city, this temple was one of the few buildings preserved by the Romans when they rebuilt the site in 46 BC. At the southeast corner an ingenious stepped ramp leads to the temple terrace.

STAR SIGHTS

★ Temple of Apollo

★ Lechaion Way

The surviving Doric columns of the Temple of Apollo, Ancient Corinth ▷

Pátra 🌑
Πάτρα

Peloponnese. **Road map** C4.
🏛 *231,000.* 🚢 🚌 🚏
ℹ *Filopiménos 26 (2610 620353).*

GREECE'S THIRD LARGEST city and second port is no beauty. Tower blocks dominate the few elegantly arcaded streets of this planned Neo-Classical town. Where Pátra excels is in its celebration of carnival – the best in Greece – for which the city's large gay community and student body both turn out in force.

On the ancient acropolis the originally Byzantine *kástro* bears marks of every subsequent era. The vast bailey, filled with gardens and orchards, often hosts public events, as does the nearby brick Roman odeion.

At the southwest edge of town, the mock-Byzantine basilica of **Agios Andréas** stands where St Andrew was supposedly martyred, and houses his skull and a fragment of his cross.

ENVIRONS: Founded in 1861, the **Achaïa Klauss Winery** was Greece's first commercial winery and is now one of the largest vintners in Greece. It produces 30 million litres (7 million gallons) a year, with grapes gathered from across the country. Tours include a visit to the Imperial Cellar, where Mavrodaphne, a fortified (15 per cent) dessert wine, can be tasted.

🍷 Achaïa Klauss Winery
6 km (4 miles) SE of Pátra.
🕻 *2610 325051.* 🕐 *11am–7pm daily.* ⬤ *main public hols.* ♿ ✔

Kalógria 🌑
Καλόγρια

Peloponnese. **Road map** B4.
🚌 *to Lápas.* ℹ *Lápas town hall (26930 31234).*

THE ENTIRE lagoon-speckled coast, from the Araxos river mouth to the Kotýchi lagoon, ranks as one of the largest wetlands in Europe. Incorporating the Strofiliá marsh and a 2,000-ha (5,000-acre) umbrella pine

Sandy beaches of Kalógria

dune-forest, the area enjoys limited protection as a reserve. Development is confined to a zone between the Prokópos lagoon and the excellent, 7-km (4-mile) beach of Kalogriá. The dunes also support Aleppo pines and valonea oaks, while bass, eels and water snakes swim in the marsh channels.

Migratory populations of ducks, including pintails and coots, live at Kotýchi, while marsh harriers, owls, kestrels and falcons can be seen all year round. A new **Visitor Centre** at Lápas runs nature trails through the dunes nearby.

🏠 Visitor Centre
Kotýchion Strofiliás, 🕻 *26930 27052.* 🕐 *Mon–Fri.* ⬤ *main public hols.* ♿ ✔

Chlemoútsi Castle 🌑
Χλεμούτσι

Kástro, Peloponnese. **Road map** B4.
🕐 *daily.*

THE MOST FAMOUS Frankish castle in Greece, known also as "Castel Tornesi" after the gold *tournois* coin minted here in medieval times, was erected between 1219 and 1223 to defend thriving Glaréntza port (Kyllíni) and the principality capital of Andreville (Andravída). To bolster the weak natural defences, exceptionally thick walls and a massive gate were built; much of the rampart catwalk can still be followed. The magnificent hexagonal keep has echoing, vaulted halls; a plaque by the entry commemorates the 1428–32 residence of Konstantínos Palaiológos, the last Byzantine emperor, while he was governor of Ileía.

Steps lead to a roof for views over the Ionian islands and the coastal plain. Chlemoútsi is now being reconstructed, with the enormous fan-shaped courtyard already used for summer concerts.

The modern Byzantine-style basilica of Agios Andréas, Pátra

Ancient Olympia ⑩

Ολυμπία

Aᴛ ᴛʜᴇ ᴄᴏɴꜰʟᴜᴇɴᴄᴇ of the rivers Alfeiós and Kládeos, the Sanctuary of Olympia enjoyed over 1,000 years of esteem as a religious and athletics centre. Though the sanctuary flourished in Mycenaean times *(see pp26–7)*, its historic importance dates to the coming of the Dorians and their worship of Zeus, after whose abode on Mount Olympos the site was named. More elaborate temples and secular buildings were erected as the sanctuary acquired a more Hellenic character, a process completed by 300 BC. By the end of the reign

Aerial view south over the Olympia site today

of Roman Emperor Hadrian (AD 117-38), the sanctuary had begun to have less religious and political significance.

The Temple of Hera, begun in the 7th century BC, is one of the oldest temples in Greece.

The Philippeion, commissioned by Philip II, honours the dynasty of Macedonian kings.

Olympia Museum *(see p172)*

Main entrance

Pheidias's Workshop
A huge statue of Zeus (see p241) *was made here. The ruins include those of a 5th-century AD basilica.*

The Heroön
housed an altar dedicated to an unknown hero.

0 metres		50
0 yards		50

Palaestra
This was a training centre for wrestlers, boxers and long-jumpers. Much of the colonnade which surrounded the central court has been reconstructed.

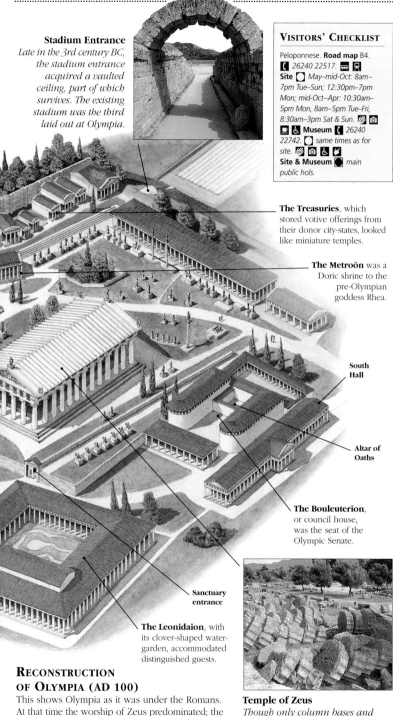

Stadium Entrance
*Late in the 3rd century BC,
the stadium entrance
acquired a vaulted
ceiling, part of which
survives. The existing
stadium was the third
laid out at Olympia.*

The Treasuries, which
stored votive offerings from
their donor city-states, looked
like miniature temples.

The Metroön was a
Doric shrine to the
pre-Olympian
goddess Rhea.

**South
Hall**

**Altar of
Oaths**

The Bouleuterion,
or council house,
was the seat of the
Olympic Senate.

**Sanctuary
entrance**

The Leonidaion, with
its clover-shaped water-
garden, accommodated
distinguished guests.

RECONSTRUCTION
OF OLYMPIA (AD 100)

This shows Olympia as it was under the Romans.
At that time the worship of Zeus predominated; the
games were dedicated to him, and his temple
(containing a huge statue of the god) was at
the heart of the Olympian enclosure.

Temple of Zeus
*Though only column bases and
tumbled sections remain, they
clearly indicate the grandeur of
this 5th-century BC Doric temple.*

Exploring the Olympia Archaeological Museum

Archaic clay head of Hera

THE OLYMPIA ARCHAEOLOGICAL MUSEUM, built opposite the excavation site to display its many treasures, officially opened in 1982 and is one of the richest museums in Greece. Except for the central hall, devoted solely to the pediment and metope sculptures from the Zeus temple, and the corner room dedicated to the games, the exhibit galleries are arranged chronologically, proceeding clockwise from the entrance hall from prehistory, through the Classical period, to the Romans.

Prehistoric, Geometric and Archaic Galleries

To the left of the entrance hall, the first of these rooms has as a centrepiece a 9th-century BC bronze horse; other contemporary finds include a bronze tripod cauldron and elongated male figures upholding cauldron handles. The second gallery contains an excellent exhibition of Asian-influenced bronze work moulded with imaginary beings. Griffin-headed cauldron ornaments were popular in the 7th century BC: a hammered-metal relief of a mother griffin nurses her young. Winged monsters serve as two shield devices, and a one-winged harpy retains eyes of inlaid bone.

Classical Galleries

Weapons, especially helmets, were a favourite offering to Zeus made by pilgrims and athletes at Olympia. Two famous ones used in the Persian Wars (see p29) are shown together in the Classical gallery: an Assyrian helmet, and that of Miltiades, victor at the Battle of Marathon (see p145). The same room contains a 5th-century BC Corinthian terracotta of Zeus and Ganymede, the most humanized of the portrayals of Zeus.

The central hall houses surviving relief statuary from the Temple of Zeus. Unusually, both pediments survive, their compositions carefully balanced though not precisely symmetrical. The more static east pediment tells of the chariot race between local king Oinomaos and Pelops, suitor for the hand of the king's daughter Hippodameia. Zeus stands between the two contestants; a soothsayer on his left foresees Oinomaos's defeat, and the two local rivers are personified in the corners. The western pediment, a metaphor of the tension between barbarism and civilization, portrays the mythological Battle of the Lapiths and the Centaurs. The centaurs, invited to the wedding of Lapith king Peirithous, attempt,

Zeus and Ganymede, in terracotta

while drunk, to abduct the Lapith women. Apollo, god of reason, is central, laying a reassuring hand on Peirithous's shoulder as the latter rescues his bride from the clutches of the centaur chief. Theseus is seen to the left of Apollo preparing to dispatch another centaur, while other women watch from the safety of the corners. The interior metopes, far less intact, depict the Twelve Labours of Herakles, a hero mythically associated with the sanctuary.

In its own niche, the fragmentary 5th-century BC Nike, by the sculptor Paionios, was a thanks-offering from Messene and Náfpaktos, following their victory over Sparta during the Peloponnesian War (see p30). A plaster reconstruction allows visualization of the winged goddess on the back of an eagle as she descends from heaven to proclaim victory.

The more complete Hermes, by Praxiteles, also has a room to itself, and shows the nude god carrying the infant Dionysos to safety, away from jealous Hera. The arm holding the newborn deity rests on a tree-trunk hung

Statue of Hermes by Praxiteles

with Hermes' cape; Dionysos reaches for a bunch of grapes in the elder god's now-vanished right hand.

Roman and Olympic Galleries

The penultimate room is devoted to a series of statues of Roman emperors and generals and a marble bull dedicated by Regilla, wife of Herodes Atticus.

The final gallery displays objects relating to the games. A 5th-century BC bronze statuette of a runner at the starting position is dedicated to Zeus by an athlete, as evidenced by an inscription on the runner's thigh. A set of halteres (jumping weights) are also on display, next to a bronze discus and part of a starting block.

The Origins of the Olympic Games

Title page of 1896 Games brochure

THE ESTABLISHMENT of the Olympic Games in 776 BC is traditionally treated as the first certain event in Greek history. Originally, men's sprinting was the only event and competitors were local; the first recorded victor was Koroivos, a cook from nearby Elis. During the 8th and 7th centuries BC, wrestling, boxing, equestrian events and boys' competitions were added. The elite of many cities came to compete and provided victory trophies although, until the Romans took charge in 146 BC, entry was restricted to Greeks. Local cities disputed control of the games, but a sacred truce guaranteed safe conduct to spectators and competitors. Part of a pagan festival, the Christians did not approve of the games and they were banned by Theodosius I in AD 393.

The ancient pentatblon *consisted of sprinting, wrestling, javelin- and discus-throwing, and the long jump (assisted by swinging weights). From 720 BC, athletes competed naked and women were excluded from spectating.*

Wrestling and boxing *are depicted on this 6th-century BC amphora. The boxers are shown wearing* himantes, *an early type of boxing glove made of leather straps wrapped around the hands and wrists.*

The Olympic revival *came in 1896, when the first modern games were held in Athens (see p113). They were organized by the Frenchman Baron Pierre de Coubertin.*

TIMELINE

Discus-thrower

470–456 BC Temple of Zeus constructed; Olympia at its zenith

AD 393 Games forbidden by Emperor Theodosius I

1896 Modern games revived

1875 Systematic German excavations begin, continuing to the present

3000 BC	2000 BC	1000 BC	AD 1	AD 1000

3rd millennium BC Site of Olympia first inhabited

776 BC First recorded games

AD 67 Nero competes, unfairly rescheduling the games, and "wins" most prizes

AD 600 Alfeiós River begins to bury the site in silt

AD 551 Earthquake destroys much of site

Loúsios Gorge ⓫

Φαράγγι του Λούσιου

Walkers in the gorge

Aᴌᴛʜᴏᴜɢʜ ᴍᴇʀᴇʟʏ ᴀ ᴛʀɪʙᴜᴛᴀʀʏ of the Alfeiós River, the Loúsios stream in its upper reaches boasts one of the most impressive canyons in Greece. Scarcely 5 km (3 miles) long, the Loúsios Gorge is nearly 300 m (985 ft) deep at the narrowest, most spectacular portion. Because of its remote mountain setting near the very centre of the Peloponnese, the Loúsios region was one of the strongholds of the revolutionaries during the Greek War of Independence (see pp40–41). Medieval monasteries and churches cling to the steep cliffs of the gorge, and hiking trails have recently been marked, connecting some of the area's highlights. The picturesque villages (see p176) of the canyon's east bank make suitable touring bases.

Dimitsána is the best place to join the path.

TRIPOLI

ZATUNA

Palaiochóri

LOÚSIOS GORGE

Loúsios

Néa Moní Filosófou

Situated on the west bank amid the narrows, this 17th-century monastery was recently renovated and restaffed by a caretaker monk. Frescoes in the church date from 1693 and illustrate many seldom-depicted biblical episodes, such as the Gadarene Swine.

★ Ancient Gortys

The Asklepieion, or therapeutic centre, of Ancient Gortys occupies a sunken excavation on the west bank. It includes the foundations of a 4th-century BC temple to Asklepios, the god of healing.

Agios Andréas, an 11th-century chapel, stands just below the Loúsios narrows.

Kókkoras Bridge

This restored medieval bridge once carried the age-old road linking the regions of Arcadia and Ileía. Anglers fish for trout here in the icy river water.

Sᴛᴀʀ Sɪɢʜᴛs
★ Moní Aimyalón
★ Ancient Gortys
★ Moní Agíou Ioánnou Prodrómou

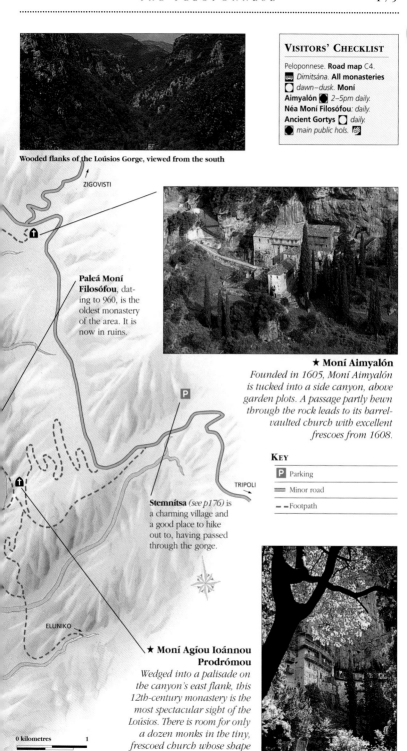

Wooded flanks of the Loúsios Gorge, viewed from the south

VISITORS' CHECKLIST

Peloponnese. **Road map** C4.
🚌 Dimitsána. **All monasteries**
🕐 dawn–dusk. **Moní
Aimyalón** 🕐 2–5pm daily.
Néa Moní Filosófou: daily.
Ancient Gortys 🕐 daily.
⬤ main public hols. 📷

ZIGOVISTI

Paleá Moní Filosófou, dating to 960, is the oldest monastery of the area. It is now in ruins.

★ Moní Aimyalón
Founded in 1605, Moní Aimyalón is tucked into a side canyon, above garden plots. A passage partly hewn through the rock leads to its barrel-vaulted church with excellent frescoes from 1608.

KEY

🅿	Parking
▬	Minor road
– –	Footpath

TRIPOLI

Stemnítsa *(see p176)* is a charming village and a good place to hike out to, having passed through the gorge.

ELLINIKO

★ Moní Agíou Ioánnou Prodrómou
Wedged into a palisade on the canyon's east flank, this 12th-century monastery is the most spectacular sight of the Loúsios. There is room for only a dozen monks in the tiny, frescoed church whose shape is dictated by the cliff face.

0 kilometres — 1

0 miles — 0.5

Exploring Around the Loúsios Gorge

OVERLOOKING THE GORGE are some of the most beautiful hill-towns in the Arcadia region, each making a good base from which to explore the area. Dimitsána has two bus services daily to Trípoli, one of these via Stemnítsa, while two weekday buses between Andrítsaina and Trípoli can be picked up just below Karýtaina. Getting around by car is best, though taxis are available in most towns. Winters can be chilly and wet, with snow chains often required.

Bridge over the Alfeiós river, below Karýtaina, complete with chapel

The narrow streets of Dimitsána

Dimitsána

Spread attractively along an airy ridge with the River Loúsios on three sides and glorious views down the valley, Dimitsána stands on the Classical site of Ancient Teuthis. The town boasts four belfries; that of **Agía Kyriakí** is illuminated at night, while the three-level **Pyrsogiannítiko** bell tower was erected by skilled Epirot masons in 1888.

Two clerics involved in the 1821 Revolution against Turkish rule *(see pp40–41)* were born here. The birthplace of Archbishop Germanós of Pátra, who helped instigate the Revolution, is marked by a plaque near the summit of westerly Kástro hill. A plaque dedicated to Patriarch Gregory V stands lower down in the market; he was hanged in Istanbul when news of the revolt reached the Sultan.

Dimitsána's three- and four-storey mansions date from its heyday as a trade centre in the 18th century. There were 14 powder factories here during the War of Independence.

Stemnítsa

Situated in a large hollow, the village of Stemnítsa forms a naturally hidden fortress. Like Dimitsána, it too has a venerable history, though the revival of its ancient name, Ýpsoús, has not been locally accepted. In medieval times, Stemnítsa was one of Greece's main metalworking centres, though today only one silversmith continues the tradition. A **Folk Museum** recreates workshops of indigenous craftsmen and local house interiors, and also hosts a top-floor gallery of weaponry, textiles and ceramics belonging to the Savvopoúlou family.

Among a number of magnificent medieval churches, those of **Treís Ierárches**, near the Folk Museum, and 10th-century **Profítis Ilías**, up on Kástro hill, have frescoes in excellent condition. Also at Kástro, the 12th-century **Panagía Mpaféro**, has an unusual portico, while the **Moní Zoödóchou Pigís**, on the northerly hillside, was where the revolutionary chieftains held their first convention during the War of Independence; it is for this reason that Stemnítsa was called the first capital of Greece.

🏠 Folk Museum
Stemnítsa. 📞 27950 81252.
🔘 *Wed – Mon.* 🔘 *main public hols.*

Karýtaina

In a strategic position on a bend of the Alfeiós, Karýtaina is now a virtual ghost town of less than 200 inhabitants. It has a 13th-century **Kástro**, dating to the time when the town was the seat of a Frankish barony. The castle was the hideout of Theódoros Kolokotrónis, who survived a long Turkish siege here in 1826. Nearby, the **Panagía tou Kástrou** boasts restored 11th-century column capitals with intricate reliefs.

ENVIRONS: East of Karýtaina, a bridge over the Alfeiós dates to 1439; four of six original arches survive, with a tiny chapel built into one pier. The bridge featured on one side of the old 5,000-drachma note.

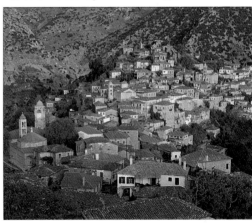
The town of Dimitsána, seen from the east

Andrítsaina 🕧
Ανδρίτσαινα

Peloponnese. **Road map** C4.
🚌 900. 🚌

DESPITE ITS CURRENT role
as the gateway to the
Temple of Bassae, the sleepy
town of Andrítsaina is hardly
touched by tourism. Tavernas
and shops around its central
square, home to a lively morning produce market, make
few concessions to modernity
in either their cuisine or their
vivid displays of merchandise.
These are echoes of the 18th
century, when this was a major
market centre. Downhill from
the 18th-century fountain of
Traní, a **Folk Museum** features
local rag-rugs, traditional
dress and metalware.

📷 Folk Museum
Andrítsaina. ⬜ daily. ⬤ main
public hols.

ENVIRONS: The 5th-century BC
Temple of Bassae graces a
commanding knoll, occupying
the most remote site of any
major ancient sanctuary. Today
it hides under an enormous
tent, until 50 million euros
(£33 million) can be raised to
re-install the architraves. Without them, winter frost damages
the temple's colonnades, now
reinforced by scaffolding.
Below Bassae lies the
modern village of Figaleía,
named after the ancient town
to the west. The citizens of
Ancient Figaleía built the
temple in thanks to Apollo
Epikourios for stopping a
plague. A path descends to
the gorge of the Néda river.

🏛 Temple of Bassae
14 km (9 miles) S of Andrítsaina.
📞 26260 23067. ⬜ daily. 🎫 ♿

Ancient Tegéa 🕭
Τεγέα

Peloponnese. **Road map** C4.
📞 27150 56540. 🚌 **Site** ⬜ daily.
Museum ⬜ Tue–Sun. ⬤ main
public hols. ♿

SOUTH OF modern Trípoli, the
remains of the ancient city
of Tegéa lie near the village
of Aléa. The most impressive

Typical street-café scene at the traditional town of Andrítsaina

ruin is the 4th-century BC
Doric temple of Athena Aléa,
with its massive column drums,
the second largest temple
in the Peloponnese after
Olympia's Temple of Zeus
(see p171). The site **museum**
has sculpture from the city,
including a number of fragments of the temple pediment.

Argos 🕮
Άργος

Peloponnese. **Road map** C4.
🚌 20,000. 🚌

ALTHOUGH ONE of the oldest
settlements in Greece,
modern Argos is a busy, rather
shabby market town, with its
open-air fairground next to a
restored Neo-Classical market-
place. To the east of the central
square, the **Archaeological
Museum** exhibits local finds
from all eras. Highlights include a bronze helmet and
breastplate, and an Archaic
pottery fragment showing
Odysseus blinding Polyphimos,
as well as a *krater* (bowl) from
the 7th century BC.
The most visible traces of
Ancient Argos lie on the way
to Trípoli, where Roman baths
and an amphitheatre are
dwarfed by the size of one of
the largest and most steeply
raked theatres in the Greek
world. From here a path climbs
Lárisa hill, one of Argos's two
ancient acropoleis.

📷 Archaeological Museum
E of Plateía Agíou Pétrou. 📞 27510
68819. ⬜ Tue–Sun. ⬤ main public
hols. 🎫 ♿

ENVIRONS: Heading south of
Ancient Argos, past the
theatre, a minor road leads to
the village of **Ellinikó** on the
outskirts of which stands an
intact pyramidal building.
Dating from the 4th century
BC, the structure is thought to
have been a fort guarding the
road to Arcadia.
Lérna, further south, is a
2200-BC palace dubbed the
"House of the Tiles" for its
original terracotta roofing. It
now shelters under a modern
protective canopy. Adjacent
Neolithic house foundations
and two Mycenaean graves,
inside the palace foundations,
suggest two millennia of habitation. Settlers were attracted
by springs which powered
watermills and still feed a
deep seaside pond. This was
the home of the legendary
nine-headed serpent Hydra,
which Herakles killed as one
of his Labours (see p53).

**Seating in the ancient theatre of
Argos, seen from the stage**

Mycenae ⓯

Μυκήναι

THE FORTIFIED PALACE complex of Mycenae, uncovered by the archaeologist Heinrich Schliemann *(see p180)* in 1874, is one of the earliest examples of sophisticated citadel architecture. The term "Mycenaean", more properly late Bronze Age, applies to an entire culture spanning the years 1700–1100 BC. Only the ruling class inhabited this hilltop palace, with artisans and merchants living just outside the city walls. It was abandoned in 1100 BC after a period of great disruption in the region.

Secret Stairway
A flight of 99 steps drops to a cistern deep beneath the citadel. Connected by pipes to a spring outside, the cistern was added to protect the water supply in times of siege.

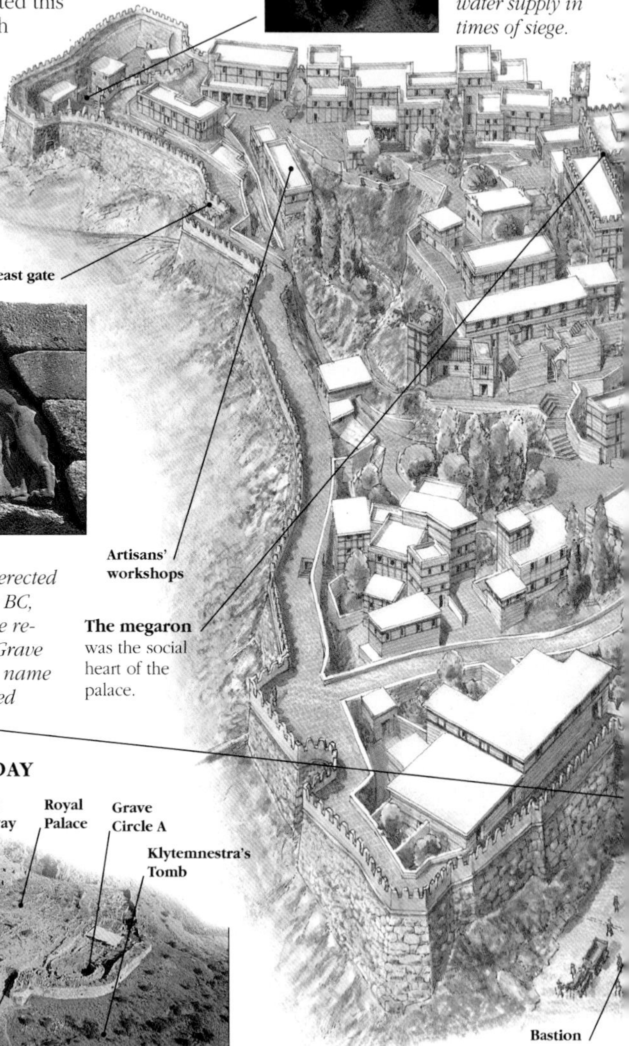

Northeast gate

Lion Gate
The Lion Gate was erected in the 13th century BC, when the walls were re-aligned to enclose Grave Circle A. It takes its name from the lions carved above the lintel.

Artisans' workshops

The megaron was the social heart of the palace.

MYCENAE TODAY

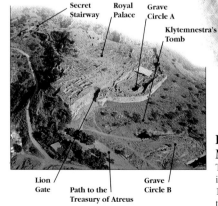

Secret Stairway   **Royal Palace**   **Grave Circle A**

Klytemnestra's Tomb

Lion Gate   **Path to the Treasury of Atreus**   **Grave Circle B**

Bastion

RECONSTRUCTION OF MYCENAE

This illustration shows Mycenae as it was in the time of the House of Atreus and the 1250 BC Trojan War *(see pp54–5)*. Most tombs lie outside the walls *(see p180)*.

Royal Palace
Situated at the acropolis summit, only the floors remain of this central structure. Burn-marks dating to its destruction in 1200 BC are still visible on the stone.

VISITORS' CHECKLIST

2 km (1 mile) N of Mykínes, Peloponnese. **Road map** C4.
🕿 27510 76585. 🚌 to Mykínes. ◻ Apr–Oct: 8am–7pm daily; Nov–Mar: 8am–5pm daily. ● 1 Jan, 25 Mar, Good Fri am, Easter Sun, 1 May, 25, 26 Dec. 🎫 📷 ♿ Treasury of Atreus only. ◻

The "Cyclopean" walls, up to 14 m (46 ft) wide, were unbreachable. Later Greeks imagined that they had been built by giants.

The houses of Mycenae yielded a number of tablets inscribed with an archaic script, known as Linear B, deciphered by Michaïl Ventrís in 1952.

The House of Tsoúntas, named after its discoverer, was a minor palace.

Great ramp

Klytemnestra, after murdering her husband, Agamemnon

THE CURSE OF THE HOUSE OF ATREUS

King Atreus slaughtered his brother Thyestes's children and fed them to him; for this outrage the gods laid a curse on Atreus and his descendants *(see p180)*. Thyestes's surviving daughter, Pelopia, bore her own father a son, Aigisthos, who murdered Atreus and restored Thyestes to the throne of Mycenae. But Atreus also had an heir, the energetic Agamemnon, who seized power.

Agamemnon raised a fleet to punish the Trojan Paris, who had stolen his brother's wife, Helen. He sacrificed his daughter to obtain a favourable wind. When he returned he was murdered by his wife, Klytemnestra, and her lover – none other than Aigisthos. The murderous pair were in turn disposed of by Agamemnon's children, Orestes and Elektra.

Grave Circle A
This contained six royal family shaft-graves containing 19 bodies. The 14 kg (31 lb) of gold funerary goods are on display in Athens (see p70).

Exploring the Tombs of Mycenae

MYCENAE'S NOBLES were entombed in shaft graves, such as Grave Circle A *(see p179)* or, later, in *tholos* ("beehive") tombs. The *tholos* tombs, found outside the palace walls, were built using successive circles of masonry, each level nudged steadily inward to narrow the diameter until the top could be closed with a single stone. The entire structure was then buried, save for an entrance approached by a *dromos* or open-air corridor.

The entrance to the Treasury of Atreus, with a gap over its lintel

Treasury of Atreus

The Treasury of Atreus *(see p179)* is the most outstanding of the *tholos* tombs. Situated at the southern end of the site, the tomb dates from the 14th century BC and is one of only two double-chambered tombs in Greece. It has a 36-m (120-ft) *dromos* flanked by dressed stone and a small ossuary (the second chamber) which held the bones from previous

burials. A 9-m (30-ft) long lintel stone stands over the entrance; weighing almost 120 tonnes (264,550 lb), it is still not known how it was hoisted into place, and is a tribute to Mycenaean building skills.

The treasury is also known as the Tomb of Agamemnon. However, the legendary king and commander of the Trojan expedition *(see pp54–5)* could not have been buried here, as the construction of the tomb predates the estimated period of the Trojan War by more than 100 years.

Tomb of Klytemnestra

Of the other *tholos* tombs only the so-called Tomb of Klytemnestra, which is situated just west of the Lion Gate, is as well preserved as that of Atreus. It is a small, single-chambered sepulchre with narrower and more steeply inclined walls, but the finely masoned *dromos* and similar triangular air hole over the entrance (which also relieved pressure on the lintel) date it to the same period.

HEINRICH SCHLIEMANN

Born in Mecklenburg, Germany, Heinrich Schliemann (1822–90) was self-educated and by the age of 47 had become a millionaire, expressly to fund his archaeological digs. Having discovered Troy and demonstrated the factual basis of Homer's epics, he came to Mycenae in 1874 and commenced digging in Grave Circle A. On discovering a gold death mask which had preserved the skin of a royal skull, he proclaimed: "I have gazed upon the face of Agamemnon!" Although archaeologists have since dated the mask to 300 years earlier than any historical Trojan warrior, the discovery corroborated Homer's description of "well-built Mycenae, rich in gold".

TREASURY OF ATREUS

Unlike their Greek contemporaries who would cremate their dead, the Mycenaeans buried their deceased in tombs. In the Treasury of Atreus, a Mycenaean king was buried with his weapons and enough food and drink for his journey through the Underworld.

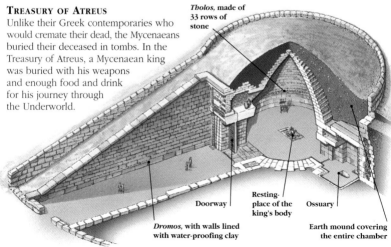

Tholos, made of 33 rows of stone

Doorway

Resting-place of the king's body

Ossuary

Dromos, with walls lined with water-proofing clay

Earth mound covering the entire chamber

Ancient Tiryns 🔟
Τίρυνθα

4 km (2 miles) NW of Náfplio,
Peloponnese. **Road map** C4.
📞 27520 22657. 🚌 🕐 8:30am–
3pm daily. 📷

T HE 13TH-CENTURY BC citadel
of Tiryns confirms Homer's
epithet "mighty-walled". A
700-m (2,300-ft) circuit of
Cyclopean walls (named
after the giants who could be
imagined manoeuvering the
huge blocks into place) attains
a thickness of 8 m (26 ft).
The fortifications, over double
their present height, were
necessarily stronger than those
of Mycenae since Tiryns was
not on a naturally strong site.

**Excavated ruins of the Cyclopean
walls, Tiryns**

The bluff on which it stood
was only 18 m (59 ft) higher
than the surrounding plain
which, in ancient times, was a
salt marsh.
    An inclined ramp to the east,
designed with sharp turns to
expose attackers' unshielded
sides, leads to the massive
middle gate, the lintel of which
has long been missing. At the
southern end of the complex,
beyond and beneath the
vanished inner gate, a gallery
with a pointed corbel ceiling
has had its walls polished by
the fleeces of sheep which
have sheltered here for centuries. On the west side, a
stone stairway between inner
and outer walls, leading to a
postern gate, has been completely preserved. The lower,
northern acropolis was the
last to be enclosed and was
used to protect commoners,
animals and (as at Mycenae)
a water supply.

ENVIRONS: The early
13th-century Byzantine
church of the Panagías
rears up startlingly in
the cemetery at **Agía
Triáda**, a village which
is 5 km (3 miles) north
of Tiryns. The walls
are constructed of
ancient masonry
to shoulder height;
above that, at the
southeast corner
of the building, the
builders have inserted
an entire Classical
grave *stele*.
    Further north, the
Argive Heraion was
the Archaic and Classical
religious centre of the Argolid.
The most impressive remains
are those of a late 5th-century
BC temple. Home to the priestesses of Hera, and a huge
ivory-and-gold cult statue of
the goddess, the temple was
flanked by stoas, identifiable
by remaining column stumps.
Above the temple is the ledge
where the Achaian leaders
swore loyalty to Agamemnon
before sailing for Troy. To
the west, complete with drain-
gutter, stands the "Peristyle
Building" where *symposia*
were hosted.

🏛 **Argive Heraion**
10 km (6 miles) N of Tiryns.
🕐 8:30am–3pm daily.

Náfplio 🔟

See pp182–3.

Epidaurus 🔟

See pp184–5.

Tower of Theseus, Ancient Troezen

Ancient Troezen 🔟
Τροιζήνα

60 km (37 miles) E of Náfplio,
Peloponnese. **Road map** D4.
🕐 unrestricted access.

N EAR THE MODERN village
of Troizína are the sparse
ruins of ancient Troezen, the
legendary birthplace of the
hero Theseus and the setting
for Euripides' incestuous tragedy *Hippolytus*. Remains from
many eras are scattered over a
wide area; most conspicuous
are three Byzantine chapels
known as *Episkopí*, from the
time when this was the seat
of the Bishops of Damála.
    The town was built on a
high bluff isolated by two
ravines; the westerly Damála
Gorge is sheer, and half an
hour's walk up it a natural
rock arch called the "Devil's
Bridge" spans the canyon.
Near the lower end of the
gorge stands the "Tower of
Theseus", Hellenistic at its
base, medieval higher up.

Foundations of the Argive Heraion, seen at dawn

Náfplio ⑰
Ναύπλιο

WITH ITS MARBLE PAVEMENTS, looming castles and remarkably homogenous architecture, Náfplio is the most elegant town in mainland Greece. It emerged from obscurity in the 13th century and endured many sieges during the struggles between Venice and Turkey for the ports of the Peloponnese. The medieval quarter, to the west, is mostly a product of the second Venetian occupation (1686–1715). From 1829 until 1834, the town was the first capital of liberated Greece.

View over Náfplio from the stairway to the Palamídi fortress

Exploring Náfplio

Defended to the south by the Akronafplía and Palamídi fortresses and to the north by Boúrtzi castle, Náfplio occupies the northern side of a peninsula at the head of the Argolic Gulf. Since the Venetian period, **Plateía Syntágmatos**

President Kapodístrias

has been the hub of public life, and still looks much as it did three centuries ago when a couple of mosques were erected by the victorious Ottomans. One stands at the east end of the square and now houses a cinema; Vouleftikó Mosque, to the south, was where the Greek parliament (*voulí*) first met. West of the bus station, **Agios Geórgios** cathedral was built as a mosque during the first Ottoman occupation (1540–1686). Also converted is the **Catholic church**, another early mosque near the top of Potamiánou, which contains a

monument honouring fallen philhellenes, including George Washington's nephew. Four Turkish fountains survive from the second Turkish occupation (1715–1822). The most famous are the scroll-arched one behind the "Cinema" Mosque and another opposite **Agios Spyrídon** on Kapodistríou; this is near where President Kapodístrias was assassinated on 9 October 1831. There are less elaborate Ottoman fountains up the steps at number 9 Tertsétou, and at the corner of Potamiánou and Kapodistríou.

Archaeological Museum

Plateía Syntágmatos. **[** 27520 27502. **○** 8:30am–3pm Tue–Sun. **●** main public hols.

Exhibits, housed in a Venetian warehouse, largely centre on pre-Mycenaean artifacts from various local sites, including Tiryns (*see p181*). Noteworthy are a Neolithic *thylastro* (baby-bottle), a late Helladic octopus vase and a full set of bronze Mycenaean armour. Strangest of all the exhibits are the female votive figurines from Mycenae (2300–2000 BC). Up to one-third life size, they could be hung on hooks like modern Orthodox *ex votos*.

Folk Art Museum

Ypsilántou 1. **[** 27520 28379. **○** 9am–3pm Wed–Mon. **✎**

This award-winning museum, established in a former mansion by the Peloponnesian Folklore Foundation, is devoted to textile crafts. The ground floor describes the cultivation and life cycle of fibre-bearing plants and animals, and then focuses on milling, spinning and loom-weaving, accompanied by examples of finished products. The upper floor displays numerous regional costumes, concluding with a high-quality gift shop. There is not enough space to show all the collection at once, so the exhibits change periodically.

Boúrtzi

NW of harbour. **ℹ** *Xenia Pallás Hotel, Akronafplia (0752 28981).*

This island fortress acquired its appearance during the second Venetian occupation, and until 1930 had the dubious distinction of being the local executioner's residence.

The fortified isle of Boúrtzi, north of Náfplio harbour

It defended the only navigable passage in the bay; the channel could be closed off by a chain extending from the fortress to the town.

♠ Akronafplía

W of Palamídi.

⬜ unrestricted access.

Akronafplía, also known as Its Kale ("Inner Castle" in Turkish), was the site of the Byzantine and early medieval town, and contains four Venetian castles built in sequence from west to east. The most interesting relic is the Venetian Lion of St Mark relief over the 15th-century gate just above the Catholic church. The westernmost "Castle of the Greeks" was Náfplio's ancient acropolis, now home to the clocktower, a major landmark.

♠ Palamídi

Polyzoïdou. **27520 28036.**

⬜ daily. ⬤ main public hols. 🅿

Palamídi, named after the Homeric hero Palamedes, the son of Náfplios and Kliméni, is a huge Venetian citadel built between 1711 and 1714. It was designed to withstand

Palamídi fortress seen from the isle of Boúrtzi

all contemporary artillery, though it fell to the Ottomans in 1715 after a mere one-week siege, and to the Greek rebels lead by Stáïkos Staïkópoulos on 30 November 1822, after an 18-month campaign.

The largest such complex in Greece, Palamídi consists of a single curtain wall enclosing seven self-suffcient forts, now named after Greek heroes; the gun slits are aimed at each other as well as outward, in case an enemy managed to penetrate the

Detail above fountain, Agía Moní

defences. Fort Andréas was the Venetian headquarters, with a Lion of St Mark in relief over its entrance. The Piazza d'Armi, from where Náfplio assumes toy-town dimensions below you, offers arguably the best views in the country. At the summit, an eighth fort, built by the Ottomans, looks south towards Karathóna beach.

ENVIRONS: The 12th-century convent of **Agía Moní** nestles 4 km (2 miles) outside Náfplio; the octagonal dome-drum rests on four columns with Corinthian capitals. Just outside the walls, in an orchard, the Kánathos fountain still springs from a niche decorated with animal reliefs; this was ancient Amymone, where the goddess Hera bathed each year to renew her virginity.

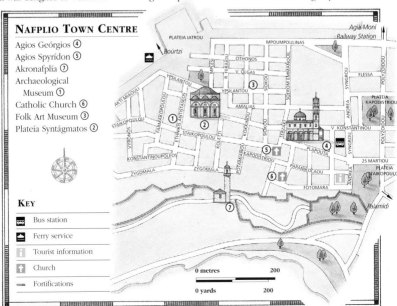

NÁFPLIO TOWN CENTRE

Agios Geórgios ④
Agios Spyrídon ⑤
Akronafplía ⑦
Archaeological Museum ①
Catholic Church ⑥
Folk Art Museum ③
Plateía Syntágmatos ②

KEY

🚌 Bus station
⚓ Ferry service
ℹ Tourist information
✝ Church
▬ Fortifications

0 metres 200
0 yards 200

Epidaurus
Επίδαυρος

THOUGH MOST RENOWNED for its magnificent theatre, the Sanctuary of Epidaurus was an extensive therapeutic and religious centre, dedicated to the healing god Asklepios. A mortal physician deified by Zeus after his death for retrieving a patient from the underworld, Asklepios was depicted in his temple here clutching a staff and flanked by a dog and a serpent – common symbols of natural wisdom. This sanctuary was active from the 6th century BC until at least the 2nd century AD, when the traveller-historian Pausanias recorded a visit.

Dusk over Epidaurus during a modern production at the theatre

The Theatre
Designed by Polykleitos the Younger late in the 4th century BC, the theatre is well known for its near-perfect acoustics which are endlessly demonstrated by tour group leaders. Owing to the sanctuary's relative remoteness, its masonry was never pilfered, remaining unrestored until only recently. It has the only circular *orchestra* (stage) to have survived from antiquity, though the altar that once stood in the centre has now gone. Two side corridors, or *paradoi*, gave the actors access to the stage; each had a monumental gateway whose pillars have

Foundations of the *tholos* building in the Asklepieion

now been re-erected. Behind the *orchestra* and facing the auditorium stand the remains of the *skene*, the main reception hall, and the *proskenion* which was used by performers as an extension of the stage. Today, the theatre is still the venue for a popular summer festival of ancient drama.

The Asklepieion
Most of the Asklepieion, or Sanctuary of Asklepios, is being re-excavated and many of its monuments are off-limits. One of the accessible sites is the *propylaia*, or monumental gateway, at the north edge of the sanctuary, its original entrance. Also preserved are a ramp and some buckled pavement from the Sacred Way which led north from the gateway to the coastal town of ancient Epidaurus. At the

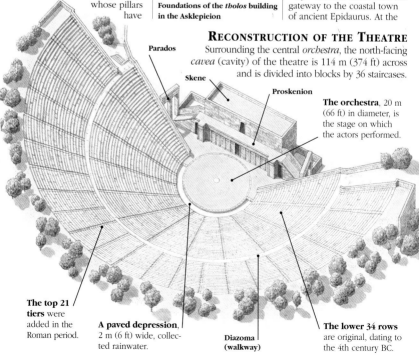

RECONSTRUCTION OF THE THEATRE
Surrounding the central *orchestra*, the north-facing *cavea* (cavity) of the theatre is 114 m (374 ft) across and is divided into blocks by 36 staircases.

Parados

Skene

Proskenion

The orchestra, 20 m (66 ft) in diameter, is the stage on which the actors performed.

The top 21 tiers were added in the Roman period.

A paved depression, 2 m (6 ft) wide, collected rainwater.

Diazoma (walkway)

The lower 34 rows are original, dating to the 4th century BC.

Overview of today's site showing the stadium at the bottom (west)

VISITORS' CHECKLIST

30 km (19 miles) E of Náfplio, Peloponnese. **Road map** C4. 27530 22009. **Site & Museum** ◑ May–Oct: 8am–7pm daily; Nov–Apr: 8am–5pm daily. ● 1 Jan, 25 Mar, Good Fri am, Easter Sun, 1 May, 25, 26 Dec. ◙ ◙ ⑮ limited. ◙ ▣

northwestern end of the sanctuary stand the remains of the *tholos* (a circular building of uncertain function, also designed by Polykleitos) whose concentric passages are thought to have been used either as a pit for sacred serpents, or possibly as the locale for rites by the cult's priests. Patients slept in the *enkoimitírion* – a hall north of the *tholos* where they would await a diagnostic dream or a visit from the harmless serpents. Therapeutic mineral springs, which are still on tap beside the museum, also played a part in the curing of patients who were brought here. Only the foundations of Asklepios's temple have survived, lying to the east of the *tholos*.

Another undisturbed point is the late Classical stadium south of the *tholos*. With intact rows of stone benches and a starting line still visible, this was used during the quadrennial festival in honour of Asklepios. The Romans built an odeion inside the Hellenistic gymnasium, to host the festival's musical contests.

ENVIRONS: The adjacent village of Lygourió reflects the importance of the region during Byzantine times. There are three Byzantine churches, the most distinguished being the 14th-century **Koímisis tis Theotókou**, which has superb early medieval frescoes.

THE ORIGINS OF GREEK DRAMA

Greek drama developed from ritual role-play at festivals of Dionysos *(see p52)*. First came group dancing – 6th-century BC Athenian vases show groups elaborately costumed, often as animals. In the late 6th century BC, the first Greek theatres appeared: rectangular (later round) spaces with seats on three sides. Singing and dancing choruses were joined by individual actors, whose masks made visible at a distance the various character roles, all played by just three male actors. The depiction of animal choruses on vases suggests humorous presentation, but the earliest plays in Athens were tragedies, staged in sets of three by a single writer *(see p57)*, in which episodes from epic poems and mythology were acted out. Historical events were rarely dramatized as they were politically sensitive. Comedy became part of the dramatic festival at Athens only in the 480s BC.

Theatre was mass entertainment and had to cater for large numbers – during the Roman period, the theatre at Epidaurus could hold 13,000 people – but it is uncertain whether women were permitted to attend the performances.

Masks were worn by actors to express the personality of the characters they played.

Souvenir statuettes, such as this terracotta figurine of a sinister character from one of the later comedies, could be bought as mementos after performances.

The chorus, though chiefly an impersonal commentator, often spoke directly to the characters, questioning them on the wisdom of their actions.

Monemvasía ⑳
Μονεμβασία

Mural above the main entrance to Agía Sofía

A FORTIFIED town built on two levels on a rock rearing 350 m (1,150 ft) above the sea, Monemvasía well deserves its nickname, "the Gibraltar of Greece". A town of 50,000 in its 15th-century prime, Monemvasía enjoyed centuries of existence as a semi-autonomous city-state, living off the commercial acumen (and occasional piracy) of its fleets and its strategic position astride the sea lanes from Italy to the Black Sea. Exceptionally well defended, it was never taken by force but fell only through protracted siege *(see p188)*. Though the upper town is in ruins, most of the lower town is restored.

Upper Town
A paved stair-street zigzags up the cliff face from the lower town to the tower gate of the upper town (see p188).

★ Agía Sofia
Standing at the summit of Monemvasía, this beautiful 13th-century church is the only intact remnant of the upper town (see p188).

Giánnis Rítsos's House
Immediately next to the gate, the birthplace of prominent poet and communist Giánnis Rítsos (1909–90) is marked by a plaque and a bust at the front.

Western gate

The mosque has been refurbished as a museum to display local finds, including some fine marble works.

Panagía Myrtidiótissa
The façade of this 18th-century church sports a Byzantine inscription and a double-headed eagle from an earlier Byzantine church.

STAR SIGHTS

★ Agía Sofia

★ Walls

VISITORS' CHECKLIST

Peloponnese. **Road map** C5.
800. Main square. Géfira.
27320 61210. **Mosque
Museum:** 27320 61403.
May–Oct:8:30am–7pm Tue–
Sun, noon–7pm Mon; Nov–Apr:
8:30am–3pm Tue–Sun. main
public hols.

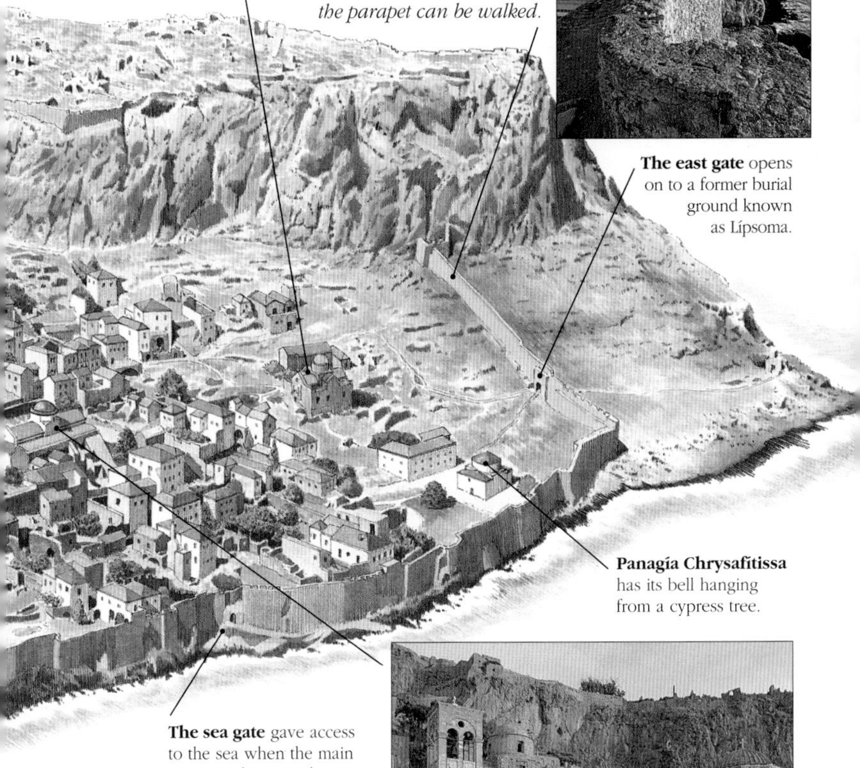

"The Gibraltar of Greece"
*Monemvasía was severed from the mainland by an
earthquake in AD 375, remaining an island until the
causeway was built in the 6th century.*

Agios Nikólaos, begun in
1703, resembles Myrtidiótissa
in its masonry, cruciform plan
and cement-covered dome.

★ **Walls**
*The 16th-century walls are
900 m (2,953 ft) long and up
to 30 m (98 ft) high. Much of
the parapet can be walked.*

The east gate opens
on to a former burial
ground known
as Lípsoma.

Panagía Chrysafítissa
has its bell hanging
from a cypress tree.

The sea gate gave access
to the sea when the main
port was threatened.

Christós Elkómenos
*Restored in 1697, this 13th-
century cathedral with its Venetian
belfry is stark inside; the only
decoration is the plaque of two
peacocks above the door.*

The cliff-top church of Agía Sofía, at dawn, Monemvasía upper town

THE SIEGE OF MONEMVASIA

The siege of Monemvasía by the Greeks, early in the War of Independence *(see pp40–41)*, began on 28 March 1821. Due to a Greek ruse, the town's Turkish garrison was badly supplied with food, and reinforcements failed to arrive. By late June, both Christians and Muslims were forced to eat weeds, cats and mice, some even resorting to cannibalism. Turkish civilians in the lower town urged surrender, but the garrison of the upper town refused. The besiegers also seemed set to give up, but one night, the Greek commander inside the town convinced three messengers to swim from the Portello Gate to the revolutionary forces on the mainland, giving them word to persevere. They did, and on 1 August the Turks surrendered, handing over the keys of the city to the Greek Prince Kantakouzinós.

The taking of Monemvasía by Prince Kantakouzinós

Exploring the Upper Town

First fortified in the 6th century as a refuge from raiding Avars, the upper town is the oldest part of Monemvasía. Largely in ruins, the area is now under the protection of the Greek archaeological service. Though in medieval times it was the most densely populated part of the peninsula,

Ruins of Monemvasía's 13th-century fortress

the upper town is deserted today, the last resident having departed in 1911.

A path climbs the cliff face above the town's north-western corner, leading to an entrance gate which still has its iron slats. Directly ahead a track leads to the summit's best-preserved building, the church of **Agía Sofia**. It was founded by Emperor Andronikos II (1282–1328) in emulation of Dafní monastery *(see pp152–3)* near Athens. With its 16-sided dome, the church perches on the brink of the northerly cliff and is visible from a considerable distance inland. The west portico is Venetian, while the niche on the south wall dates from its use as a mosque. A few frescoes surviving from the early 14th century are badly faded, but the *Ancient of Days* can be discerned in the sanctuary's vault, as can the *Birth of John the Baptist* in the north vault. Carved ornamentation has fared better, such as the

marble capitals flanking the south windows, depicting mythical monsters and a richly dressed woman.

To the west are the remains of a 13th-century **fortress**, amid the debris of former barracks, guardrooms and a gunpowder magazine from the Venetian period. A vast **cistern** recalls the times of siege when great quantities of water had to be stored. Food supplies, entirely imported, were more of a problem, as was demonstrated by the siege of 1821.

Agía Paraskeví, viewed from Byzantine Geráki

Geráki ㉑
Γεράκι

Peloponnese. **Road map** C5.
2,000. 🚌

OCCUPYING A SPUR of Mount Párnonas, Geráki is like a miniature Mystrás with its kástro overlooking the frescoed Byzantine churches on the slopes below. The polygonal **kástro** was built in 1254–5 by the Frank, Jean de Nivelet, though it was ceded in 1262 to the Byzantines, together with Monemvasía and Mystrás. Inside, 13th-century **Agios Geórgios** is a hybrid Franko-Byzantine church, the third

aisle and narthex added after 1262; a carved marble screen and varied frescoes decorate its interior.

Below the west gate, 13th-century **Zoödóchou Pigís** sports a complete Gothic door and south window, while inside later frescoes include *Christ on the Road to Calvary.*

At the base of the hill, the domeless, 14th-century church of **Agía Paraskeví** has a fine *Nativity* in its cross vault, plus a painting of the donor family on the west wall.

ENVIRONS: Four more churches stand a short drive to the west in **Geráki** village. Both 12th-century Agios Athanásios and 13th-century Agios Sózon share a cross-in-square plan, with a high dome on four piers. Market edicts of the Roman Emperor Diocletian, inscribed on stone, flank the doorway of barrel-vaulted, 14th-century Agios Ioánnis Chrysóstomos, covered inside with scenes from the life of Christ and the Virgin. Tiny Evangelístria has a Pantokrátor fresco in its dome.

7th-century BC clay head of a woman, from Spárti acropolis

Spárti ㉒
Σπάρτη

Peloponnese. **Road map** C5.
🏛 20,000. 🚌 ℹ *Town Hall, Plateia Kentriki (27310 26516).*

THOUGH ONE of the most powerful of the Greek city-states, Ancient Sparta was unfortified and has few ruins dating to its heyday. The acropolis lies 700 m (2,300 ft) northwest of the modern town centre which in itself has little of interest. On the western side of the acropolis is the cavity of the Roman theatre, its masonry largely pilfered to build Mystrás, while directly east stands the long, arcaded stoa which once held shops. Of the Artemis Orthia sanctuary just east of town, where Spartan youths were flogged to prove their manhood, only some Roman seating remains. The most interesting finds are on display in the museum.

The highlight of the rich **Archaeological Museum** is the fine collection of Roman mosaics, including two lions rampant over a vase, Arion riding his dolphin, Achilles disguised as a woman on Skýros, and a portrait of Alkibiades. A Classical marble head of a warrior, possibly Leonidas I *(see p224)*, was found on the acropolis, while bas-reliefs of Underworld serpent-deities hail from a sanctuary of Apollo at Amyklés, 8 km (5 miles) south of Spárti. Bizarre ceramic masks are smaller replicas of those used in dances at the Artemis Orthia sanctuary.

🏛 **Archaeological Museum**
Agiou Nikonos 71. 📞 27310 28575.
⬤ 8:30am–3pm Tue–Sun. ⬤ *main public hols.* 📷 ♿

LIFE IN ANCIENT SPARTA

Rising to prominence around 700 BC, Sparta became one of the most powerful city-states of ancient Greece. Its power was based on rigid social and military discipline, as well as hatred of foreigners, which eventually led to its downfall as it had no allies. The "city" was made up of five villages, where the male citizens lived communally in constant readiness for war. Warriors were selected at the age of seven and subjected to rigorous training – whipping contests, with young boys as the victims, were held in the sanctuary of Artemis Orthia. Sparta was able to support its citizens as professional soldiers because it had conquered neighbouring Messenia, and the enslaved population provided all the food required. Sparta led the Greek forces against the Persians, but ceased to be a major power after defeat by Thebes in 371 BC.

5th-century BC bronze figurine of a Spartan warrior

Mystrás ㉓
Μυστράς

Double-eagle marble plaque, Mitrópolis

MAJESTIC MYSTRAS occupies a panoramic site on a spur of the severe Taÿgetos range. Founded by the Franks in 1249 to replace medieval Spárti, it soon passed to the Byzantines, under whom it became a town of 20,000 and, after 1348, the seat of the Despots of Morea. The despotate acted semi-independently and had become the last major Byzantine cultural centre by the 15th century, attracting scholars and artists from Italy and Serbia as well as Constantinople. One result was the uniquely cosmopolitan decoration of the Mystrás churches – their pastel-coloured frescoes, crowded with detail, reflect Italian Renaissance influence.

VISITORS' CHECKLIST

5 km (3 miles) W of Spárti, Peloponnese. **Road map** C5.
27310 83377. to Néos Mystrás. May–Oct: 8:00am–7pm daily; Nov–Apr: 8:30am–3pm daily. 1 Jan, 25 Mar, Good Fri, Easter Sun, 1 May, 25, 26 Dec.

PLAN OF MYSTRAS

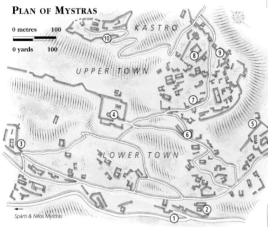

0 metres 100
0 yards 100

KASTRO
UPPER TOWN
LOWER TOWN
Spárti & Néos Mystrás

KEY TO PLAN

① Lower town entrance
② Mitrópolis
③ Moní Perivléptou
④ Moní Pantánassas
⑤ Vrontóchion
⑥ Monemvasía Gate
⑦ Despots' Palace
⑧ Agía Sofía
⑨ Upper town entrance
⑩ Kástro

Exploring Mystrás

Now in ruins, Mystrás consists of a lower and upper town, linked by the Monemvasía Gate. The site can be entered from the castle at the top of the upper town or from the base of the lower town. Allow half a day for exploring the monasteries, churches, palaces and houses which line the narrow, winding streets. An unusual northwest-to-southeast alignment of the churches is dictated by the site's steep topography.

⚑ Mitrópoli

The Mitrópoli, situated by the lower town entrance, is the oldest church in Mystrás. It is approached through a double

The 14th-century fresco of the *Nativity* in the south vault of Moní Perivléptou

courtyard. Like many Balkan cathedrals, it began life in 1291 as a barrel-vaulted nave flanked by two aisles. The domes were added early in the 1400s in a clumsy attempt to equal the architecture of the Pantánassas and Afentikó churches. Frescoes, mostly early 14th-century, show the martyrdom of the church's patron (Agios Dimítrios) in the northeast vaulting, while Christ's miracles begin next to these with the *Healing of the Lepers* and continue on the southwest aisle in such scenes as the *Wedding at Cana*. In the narthex is the *Preparation of the Throne of Judgment*, flanked by angels, a theme repeated in the southwest diaconicon (sacristy). The last Byzantine emperor, Konstantínos Palaio-lógos, was crowned here in 1449; a double-eagle plaque marks the spot.

⚑ Moní Perivléptou

Squeezed against the rock face, the 14th-century monastery of Perivléptou has a compact, three-aisled church. Its small dome retains a fresco of the Pantokrátor, flanked by the Virgin and prophets, arranged in diminishing order of importance. The 14th-century frescoes, the most refined in Mystrás, focus on the 12 major church feasts. They include a vivid *Nativity* and *Baptism* in the south vault, the *Transfiguration* and *Entry into Jerusalem*, complete with playing children, in the west aisle, and *Doubting Thomas* and the *Pentecost* in the north vault, decorating the wall over the entrance.

◁ **Healing of the Paralytic fresco, Moní Pantánassas, Mystrás**

The hillside with remains of Byzantine Mystrás, seen from the south

🔒 Moní Pantánassas

Dating to 1428, Pantánassas was the last church built at Mystrás. With its decorated apses and the brickwork of its arcaded belfry it imitates Afentikó in the Vrontóchion as an eclectic architectural experiment. The highest frescoes, from 1430, are of most merit, particularly a vivid *Raising of Lazarus* in the northeast vault. Both the *Nativity* and the *Annunciation* in the southwest vault feature animals. The southeast aisle displays the *Descent into Hell*, in which Christ raises Adam and Eve from their coffins, opposite a lively *Entry into Jerusalem.*

🔒 Vrontóchion

A 13th-century monastic complex built by Abbot Pachómios, the Vrontóchion was the cultural centre of medieval Mystrás – in the 15th century, the Neo-Platonist philosopher Geórgios Gemistós, or Plethon, (1355–1452) taught here. It has

two churches; the earliest, Agioi Theódoroi, dates from 1295 and has the largest dome at Mystrás, supported on eight arches. Few frescoes survive. The early 14th-century Afentikó (or Panagía Odigítria) is richly frescoed, with six domes. The galleries and two north-side chapels are shut, but in the west gallery dome a *Virgin Orans* (praying) and *Prophets* are visible; in the south vault, a crowded *Baptism* includes water monsters. Above the altar, apostles gesticulate towards the aura of the rising Christ in the *Ascension*. The best-preserved frescoes can be found in the north bay of the narthex.

🏛 Despots' Palace

The Despots' Palace consists of two wings which are now being reconstructed. The northeast wing was begun by the Franks; the northwest hall, erected after 1348 and a rare example of Byzantine civic

architecture, has the throne room of the rulers of the Cantacuzene and Palaiológos dynasties. The square was a venue for public events under the despots and a marketplace under the Ottomans.

The ruins of the Despots' Palace, viewed from the south

♣ Kástro

Flanked by sheer ravines to the south and west, and crowning the summit of the upper town, the kástro is reached by a path leading from the upper entrance which stands above the church of Agía Sofía. Built by Guillaume de Villehardouin in 1249, the kástro retains its original Frankish design, though it was greatly altered by the Byzantines and Turks. A double circuit of curtain walls encloses two baileys and a walkway can be taken around most of the structure, affording panoramic views over the lower town.

It was here that the German writer Goethe, in Part Two of *Faust*, set the meeting of Faust and Helen of Troy, revived after 3,000 years.

Afentikó church, part of the Vrontóchion complex

Outer Máni ㉔
Έξω Μάνη

A HARSH, REMOTE REGION, bounded by mountains to the north, the rocky Máni was the last part of Greece to embrace Christianity, doing so in the 9th century with an enthusiasm borne out by dozens of surviving Byzantine chapels. Though well defended against invaders, the area has a history of internal feuding which led to the building of its many tower houses. A ravine at Oítylo divides Inner Máni, to the south *(see pp198–9)*, from the more fertile Outer, or Messenian, Máni which boasts some of the finest country in the Mediterranean.

VISITORS' CHECKLIST

Peloponnese. **Road map** C5.
Kalamáta.

LOCATOR MAP

ANAVRYTI & PALAIOPANAGIA

Exochóri
Kardamýli
PIGADIA & KALAMÁTA • Stoúpa
Agios Nikólaos
Langáda

MOUNT TAYGETOS

OUTER MÁNI

GERAKI & MONEMVASIA

Gýtheio

Oítylo • Néo Oítylo

Oítylo

Though administratively within the region of Lakonía, by tradition the village of Oítylo (pronounced "Itilo") belongs to the Outer Máni. It affords superb panoramic views over Limeníou Bay and across a flanking ravine, traditionally the border betwen the Inner and Outer Máni, to Kelefá Castle *(see p198)*. Its relatively good water supply fosters a lush setting around and below the village, with cypresses and a variety of orchard trees. Unlike most Mániot villages, Oítylo is not in economic decline. Its many fine houses include graceful 19th-century mansions. The village was capital of the Máni between the 16th and 18th centuries, and was the area's most infamous slave-trading centre; both Venetians and Turks were sold to each other here. A plaque in the square, written in French and Greek, commemorates the flight, in 1675, of 730 Oítylots to Corsica – 430 of whom were from the Stefanópoulos clan. Seeking refuge from the Turks, the Oítylots were granted passage by the Genoese and, once in Corsica, founded the villages of Paomia and Cargèse. These towns account for the stories of Napoleon's part-Mániot origins.

ENVIRONS: From the southwestern corner of Oítylo, a broad path descends west to **Moní Dekoúlou**, nestled in its own little oasis. The 18th-century church features an ornate *témblon* (wooden altar screen) and vivid original frescoes; though they have been preserved in the darkness, a torch is required to see them now. The monastery is only open in the evenings or by prior arrangement with the resident caretakers.

The village of **Néo Oítylo** stands 4 km (2 miles) south of the monastery. Quietly secluded, the village has a pebble beach with fine views.

THE MANIOT FEUDS

By the 15th century, a number of refugee Byzantine families had settled in the Máni, the most powerful forming a local aristocracy known as the Nyklians. Feuding between clans over the inadequate land was rife, though only Nyklians had the right to construct stone towers *(see p20)*, which attained four or five storeys and came to dominate nearly every Mániot village.

Pétros Mavromichális

Once commenced, blood feuds could last months, even years, with periodic truces to tend to the crops. Clansmen fired at each other from facing towers, raising them in order to be able to catapult rocks on to opponents' roofs. The hostilities ended only with the total destruction or submission of the losing clan. Historically, the most important clans were those of Mavromichális at Areópoli, Grigorákis at Gýtheio and Troupákis at Kardamýli, whose members boasted of never having been completely subjugated by any foreign power. The Ottomans wisely refrained from ruling the Máni directly, but instead quietly encouraged the clans to feud in order to weaken potential rebellions, and appointed a Nyklian chieftain as *bey* (regional lord) to represent the sultan locally. Under the final *bey*, Pétros Mavromichális, the clans finally united, instigating the Greek Independence uprising on 17 March 1821 *(see pp40–41)*.

Oítylo viewed from the northwest, looking towards Kelefá Castle

Agios Spyrídon south window, framed with marble reliefs

Kardamýli

Kardamýli was the lair of the Troupákis family, important rivals of the Mavromichális clan. Nicknamed Moúrtzinos or "Bulldogs" for their tenacity in battle, they claimed to be descended from the Byzantine dynasty of Palaiológi. Olive oil *(see p283)* used to be the chief source of income for Kardamýli, but this has now been superseded by tourism.

Inland rises the ancient and medieval acropolis, represented by twin Mycenaean chamber tombs. Also on the site are Troupákis-built towers which stand alongside the 18th-century church of **Agios Spyrídon**. This building is made of Hellenistic masonry and graced by a pointed, four-storey belfry; the south window and doorway are framed by intricate marble reliefs.

ENVIRONS: Two paths lead from Kardamýli, one upstream along the **Vyrós Gorge** where two monasteries shelter beneath the cliffs; the other to the villages of Gourniés and Exochóri. A short drive to the south, **Stoúpa** is popular for its two sandy bays; novelist Níkos Kazantzákis (1883– 1957) lived here briefly and partly based his Zorba the Greek character on a foreman who worked nearby. The village of **Agios Nikólaos**, a short walk to the south, curls around Outer Máni's most photogenic harbour. It has four tavernas and the closest beach is at Agios Dimítrios, 3 km (2 miles) further south.

Mount Taÿgetos

The distinctive pyramidal summit and knife-edged ridge of Mount Taÿgetos, standing at 2,404 m (7,885 ft), divides the regions of Messinía and Lakonía. Formed of limestone and densely clad in black pine and fir, the range is the

Taÿgetos, seen through the Vyrós Gorge

watershed of the region and offers several days of wilderness trekking to experienced, well-equipped mountaineers.

Anavrytí and Palaiopanagiá, on the east, and Pigádia and Kardamýli on the west, are the usual trailhead villages. Various traverses can be made by using the Vyrós and Ríntomo gorges which drain west from the main ridge; an unstaffed alpine refuge at Varvára-Deréki, above Palaiopanagiá, is the best starting point for those wanting to head straight for the summit.

The ridge of Mount Taÿgetos with an olive grove in the foreground

Inner Máni ㉕
Μέσα Μάνη

INNER, OR LAKONIAN, MANI is divided into two regions – the "Shadowed", western flank and the "Sunward", eastern shore. The former is famous for its numerous caves and churches, the latter for its villages which perch dramatically on crags overlooking the sea. With its era of martial glory over *(see p194)*, Inner Máni is severely depopulated, its only future being as a holiday venue. Retired Athenians of Mániot descent have restored the famous towers *(see p20)* as hunting lodges for the brief autumn shoot of quail and turtle dove.

LOCATOR MAP

Gýtheio
Oítylo • Kelefá
Passavá
INNER
Areópoli• *MÁNI*
• Pýrgos Diroú
• Charoúda
• Vámvaka
Stavrí • Káto Gardenítsa
Gerolimenás • Áno Mpoulárioi
Váthela•

CAPE TAINARO

Gýtheio
The lively town of Gýtheio is the gateway to the Máni peninsula and one of the most attractive coastal towns in the southern Peloponnese. It was once the naval base of Ancient Sparta *(see p189)*, though the main ancient relic is a Roman theatre to the north. The town was wealthy in Roman times when it exported the purple molluscs used for colouring

imperial togas. Until World War II, Gýtheio exported acorns used in leather-tanning, gathered by women and children from nearby valleys.

The town's heart is Plateía Mavromicháli, with the quay extending to either side lined by tiled, 19th-century houses. The east-facing town enjoys sunrises over Cape Maléas and the Lakonian Gulf while snowy Mount Taÿgetos looms beyond a low ridge to the north.

In the bay, and linked to the waterfront by a causeway, lies the islet of Marathonísi, thought to be Homer's Kranaï islet. It was here that Paris of Troy and Helen spent their first night together *(see p52)*. It is dominated by the Tzanetbey Grigorákis tower, a crenellated 18th-century fortress which now houses the **Museum of the Máni**. The subject of the exploration of the Máni in medieval times is covered on the ground floor, while the exhibits of the upper storey place the tower houses in their social context.

VISITORS' CHECKLIST

Peloponnese. **Road map** C5.
🚉 Gýtheio. 🚌 Areópoli.
🛈 Vasíleos Pávlou 21, Areópoli
(27330 22100). **Museum of the
Máni** Marathonísi Islet.
📞 27330 51209. ◯ daily. 🖼
Pýrgos Diroú Caves & Museum
12 km (7 miles) S of Areópoli.
📞 & 📠 27330 52223.
◯ 8:30am–3pm Tue–Sun.

ENVIRONS: Standing 12 km (7 miles) to the southwest, the **Castle of Passavá** was built in 1254 by the Frankish de Neuilly clan to guard a defile between Kelefá and Oítylo. Its name stems from *passe-avant*, the clan's motto, though the present building is an 18th-century Turkish construction. The Turks left the castle in 1780 after Tzanetbey Grigorákis avenged the murder of his uncle by massacring 1,000 Muslim villagers inside. Today's overgrown ruins are best approached from the southwest.

Areópoli
The Mavromichális *(see p194)* stronghold of Tsímova was renamed Areópoli, "the city of Ares" (god of war), for its role in the War of Independence *(see p40)*; it was here that the Mániot uprising against the Turks was proclaimed by Pétros Mavromichális. Now the main town of the Máni, its central old quarter features two 18th-century churches: **Taxiarchón** boasts the highest belltower in the Máni, as well as zodiacal apse reliefs, while **Agios Ioánnis**, adorned with naive frescoes, was the chapel of the Mavromichális.

ENVIRONS: With Passavá to the east, Ottoman **Kelefá Castle**, standing 10 km (6 miles) north of Areópoli, is the second castle guarding the Máni. It was built in 1670 to command the bays of Oítylo and Liméni and counter the impending Venetian invasion

19th-century houses lining the harbour of Gýtheio

◁ **Semi-ruined tower houses of Vátheia village, the architectural jewel of the Máni**

(see p38). The bastions of the pentagonal curtain walls are preserved. The castle can be reached by paths from Areópoli and Oítylo *(see p194).*

Pýrgos Diroú Caves

The Pýrgos Diroú cave system is one of the largest and most colourful in Greece. During summer, crowds wait for the 30-minute punt ride along the underground stream which passes through Glyfáda cavern, reflecting the overhanging stalactites. A 15-minute walk then leads to the exit. A nearby chamber, called Alepótrypa cave, is drier and, though currently shut, is just as spectacular with waterfalls and a lake. Until an earthquake closed the entrance, the cave was home to Neolithic people, and a separate **museum** reveals their life and death.

The Shadowed Coast

Between Pýrgos Diroú and Geroliménas lies the 17-km (11-mile) shore of the Shadowed Coast. Once one of the most densely populated regions of the Máni, it is famous for its numerous Byzantine churches built between the 10th and 14th centuries. The ruins of many Mániot tower houses can also be found.

Among the finest churches is 11th-century **Taxiarchón**, at Charoúda, with its interior covered by vivid 18th-century frescoes. Heading south, the road continues to **Agios Theódoros**, at Vámvaka, where the dome is supported by

Corner turret of Ottoman Kelefá Castle, near Areópoli

carved beams; birds bearing grapes adorn its marble lintel.

Káto Gardenítsa boasts the 12th-century **Agía Soteíra**, with its frescoed iconostasis and domed narthex, while 12th-century **Episkopí**, near Stavrí, has a complete cycle of 18th-century frescoes.

Near Ano Mpoulárioi village, doorless **Agios Panteleímon** offers 10th-century frescoes (the earliest and the most primitive in the Máni), while in the village, the 11th-century **Agios Stratigós** bears a set of 12th- and 13th-century frescoes – the *Acts of Christ* is the most distinguished.

Vátheia, 10 km (6 miles) east of Geroliménas, is one of the most dramatically located of the villages; overlooking the sea and Cape Taínaro, its bristling tower houses constitute a showpiece of local architectural history.

Tower houses of Vátheia village, viewed from the southeast

Koróni **㉖**
Κορώνη

Peloponnese. **Road map** C5.
🚶 1,400. 🚌

ONE OF THE "eyes of Venice" (along with Methóni), Koróni surveys the shipping lanes between the Adriatic and Crete. It stands at the foot of a Venetian castle, begun in 1206, whose walls now shelter the huge **Timíou Prodrómou** convent. A Byzantine chapel and foundations of an Artemis temple stand by the gate of the convent whose cells and chapels command fine views.

The town, lying beneath the castle and divided by stepped streets, dates to 1830. It has changed little recently and many houses retain elaborate wrought-iron balconies, horizontal-slat shutters and tile "beaks" on the undulating roofs. A lively seafront is the sole concession to tourism.

Methóni **㉗**
Μεθώνη

Peloponnese. **Road map** B5.
🚶 1,300. 🚌

METHONI, a key Venetian port, controlled the lucrative pilgrim trade to Palestine after 1209. With the sea on three sides, its rambling **castle** is defended by its landward side by a Venetian moat, bridged by the French in 1828. The structure combines Venetian, Ottoman and even French military architecture. The remains within the walls include two ruined *hamam*s

(baths), a Venetian church, minaret bases and the main street. Boúrtzi, an islet fortified by the Turks, stands beyond the Venetian sea-gate.

⚓ Castle
🕐 9am–7pm daily (9am–3pm winter).

Pýlos **㉘**
Πύλος

Peloponnese. **Road map** C5.
🚶 2,500. 🚌

THE TOWN OF PYLOS, originally known as Avaríno, (later Navaríno) after the Avar tribes which invaded the area in the

---

6th century, is French in design, like Methóni. Life is confined to Plateía Trión Navárchon and the seafront on either side.

To the west, the castle of **Niókastro**, Ottoman and Venetian in origin, was extensively repaired by the French after 1828; their barracks are now a gallery of antiquarian engravings by the artist René Puaux (1878–1938). An institute of underwater archaeology is situated in the former dungeons of the hexagonal keep. The roof gives views over the outer bailey, immense Navaríno Bay and Sfaktiría island, site of a memorable Athenian victory over the Spartans.

The fortified islet of Boúrtzi, off the coast at Methóni, with its 16th-century octagonal tower

The arcaded former mosque, now Sotíros church, Pýlos

The perimeter walls are dilapidated, but it is possible to walk along the parapet, starting from the imposing west bastion overlooking the mouth of the bay, and finishing above the east gate. The domed and arcaded church of **Sotíras**, once a mosque, is the only medieval survival in the outer bailey.

♣ Niókastro
Town centre. 🅲 27230 22897.
🅾 Apr–Oct: daily;
Nov–Mar: Tue–Sun.
● main public hols.
🈲 🅶 limited.

ENVIRONS: Boat tours visit a number of memorials on and around **Sfaktiría**, which commemorate sailors lost in the Battle of Navaríno, foreign philhellenes and revolutionary heroes.

The north end of Navaríno Bay, 11 km (7 miles) north of Pýlos, has excellent beaches, especially **Voïdokoiliá** lagoon, where Telemachos, Odysseus's son, disembarked to seek news of his father from King Nestor. You can walk up the dunes to **Spiliá tou Néstora**, an impressively large cave, which may have been the inspiration for Homer's cave in which Nestor and Neleus kept their cows. A more strenuous path continues to Palaiókastro, the ancient acropolis and Franko-Venetian castle, built on Mycenaean foundations.

Nestor's Palace ㉙
Ανάκτορο του Νέστορα

16 km (10 miles) NE of Pýlos,
Peloponnese. **Road map** B5.
🅲 27630 31437. 🚌
Site 🅾 daily. **Museum** 🅾 Tue–Sun
● main public hols. 🈲 🅶 limited.

Discovered in 1939, the 13th-century BC Palace of Mycenaean King Nestor was excavated by Carl Blegen from 1952. Hundreds of tablets in the ancient Linear B script were found, as well as a bathtub and olive oil jugs (the contents of which fuelled the devastating fire of 1200 BC). Today, only waist-high walls and column bases under a protective roof suggest the typical Mycenaean plan of a two-storey complex around a central hall. The **museum**, 3 km (2 miles) away in Chóra, has frescoes from the palace.

13th-century BC bathtub
excavated from Nestor's Palace

Ancient Messene ㉚
Αρχαία Μεσσήνη

34 km (21 miles) NW of Kalamáta,
Peloponnese. **Road map** C5.
🅲 27240 51201. 🚌
Site 🅾 daily. ● main public hols.

Ancient messene is now confusingly known as Ithómi – named after the mountain that sits overhead.

It is an underrated, intriguing site, which is still undergoing excavation. The city walls are 9 km (6 miles) long and date from the 4th century BC. They enclose a vast area that incorporates the foundations of a Zeus temple, and the acropolis on Mount Ithómi to the northeast. The massive, double Arcadia Gate situated on the north side is flanked by square towers.

The archaeological zone includes the picturesque village of Mavrommáti, whose water is still supplied by the ancient Klepsýdra fountain at the heart of the site. Below the village you will find an odeion (amphitheatre), a *bouleuterion* (council hall), stoas and a monumental stairway, all of which surround the foundations of an Asklepios temple. Just a little way further down the hill from here lies a well-preserved stadium.

Remains of the Arcadia Gate, with its fallen lintel, Ancient Messene

CENTRAL AND WESTERN GREECE

EPIRUS · THESSALY · STEREA ELLADA

*C*ENTRAL AND WESTERN GREECE *encompass many of the lesser-known regions of mainland Greece and are, therefore, little touched by tourism. Though Epirus has produced a distinctive and largely autonomous culture, Stereá Elláda has always been of strategic importance, with the pass at Thermopylae and the Vale of Tempe providing invasion routes into the very heart of Greece.*

This region of Greece is dominated by the central plain of Thessaly (the former bed of an inland sea) and the sights of interest lie largely on the periphery. Isolated by the Píndos mountains, the Epirus region, to the west, has the strongest of regional identities, having played a minor role in ancient Greece and maintained a large degree of autonomy under the Turks. The regional capital, Ioánnina, is thus a fascinating mixture of Turkish architecture and the local traditions of silversmithing and wood carving.

To the east, the grand Katára Pass, guarded in Ottoman times by the town of Métsovo, cuts through the mountains, providing access to the Byzantine

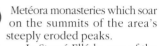

Woman from Métsovo, northern Píndos

Metéora monasteries which soar on the summits of the area's steeply eroded peaks.

In Stereá Elláda, one of the country's most important ancient sights, the ruins of the Delphic Oracle, stands only a short drive away from the Monastery of Osios Loúkas, perhaps the finest of late Byzantine buildings, decorated with some of the period's greatest mosaics.

While the Gulf of Corinth has many popular resorts, the towns of Lamía, Arta, Tríkala, and Mesolóngi (where the British poet Lord Byron died) make few concessions to tourism and so offer a more accurate picture of life in Greece today: its markets, tavernas, church-going and the evening *vólta*.

Megálo Pápigko, one of the many remote, once-isolated villages of Zagória in the Epirus region

◁ The Byzantine Monastery of Osios Loúkas, with the belltower in the foreground

Exploring Central and Western Greece

STRETCHING FROM ATTICA in the south to Macedonia in the north, the vast expanse of Central and Western Greece has a little of everything, from excellent beaches to the venerable towns of Ioánnina and Métsovo with their craftsmen's guilds and Ottoman heritage. The Pílio offers the best combination of scenery and coastal resorts, while no one should miss the two prime attractions of Ancient Delphi, site of the oracle of Apollo, and the Byzantine splendour of the monasteries of Metéora. Walkers should head north where, in addition to the Víkos Gorge, the Píndos Mountains have several of Greece's highest peaks. The flora and fauna are both splendid here, especially in spring, but wildlife enthusiasts should not miss the wonderful wetlands around Mesolóngi and the beautiful Amvrakikós Gulf, near Arta.

PINDOS MOUNTAINS ❶

Vlorë

VÍKOS GORGE ❸   ❷ ZAGÓRIA

22 (E853)   30 (E90)

15 Kozáni

❹ 6 (E92)
MÉTSOVO   METEO

IOÁNNINA ❺

6 (E90)

DODÓNI ❻

E (E951)

Arachthos

6 (E55)

19   ❼ PÁRGA

19

KASSÓPI ❽   21

ARTA ❿

❾ PRÉVEZA   3 (E951)

Lake Kremastón

42

5 (E55)

Achelóos   Lake Trichonída

MESOLÓNGI ㉑ 5 (E55)

Agíou Nikoláou, one of Metéora's soaring monasteries

SIGHTS AT A GLANCE

Doric columns of the Temple of Apollo, Delphi

LOCATOR MAP

GETTING AROUND

There are domestic airports at Préveza, which receives European charter flights in summer, Larisa and Ioánnina. Internal flights are fairly inexpensive if travelling from another part of Greece, but within the region a car is by far the best way to travel. Central Greece's main roads are generally good, though twisting mountain routes can make journeys longer than they seem on the map. The E55 is a good, fast road, as are the other major E roads which circle the region. Trains serve only a small part of the eastern side of the area, though bus connections are good between major towns, with services to smaller villages.

Terraced bar overlooking the west coast, Párga

SEE ALSO

- *Where to Stay* pp271–3
- *Where to Eat* pp293–4

0 kilometres 25

0 miles 25

Lake Drakolímni, behind the sheer cliffs of Astráka

Píndos Mountains ❶
Οροσειρά Πίνδου

Epirus. **Road map** B2. ✈ 🚌 *Ioánnina.*
ℹ *Napoléonta Zérva 2, Ioánnina
(26510 25086).*

THE PINDOS is a vast range
stretching from the Greek
border with Albania south
beyond Métsovo. It extends
east into Macedonia, and west
towards the Ionian Sea, incorporating two national parks,
Greece's second longest

gorge and its second highest
mountain, Oros Smólikas,
standing at 2,640 m (8,660 ft).
The Píndos National Park lies
just inside western Macedonia,
between Métsovo and Vovoúsa,
while the Víkos–Aóos National
Park is a boot-shaped area
encompassing the Víkos Gorge
(see p208) and the Aóos River.

The peaks are snow-covered
from October until May, when
the melting snows water the
ground, producing swathes
of lilac crocus, gentians,

grass-of-Parnassus and many
species of orchid *(see p23)*.
The protection offered by the
parks provides the visitor
with an increased chance of
seeing roe deer, wild boar and
the European wild cat, all of
which exist in small numbers.

Smólikas is accessible during
summertime for those who are
well equipped and prepared
for camping or staying in
mountain huts. Slightly easier
to reach from the fascinating
Zagorian villages by the Víkos
Gorge are Gamíla 2,500 m
(8,200 ft) and Astráka 2,440 m
(8,000 ft), while the two
mountain lakes both called
Drakolímni are each worth
the effort it takes to get to
them. One is below Gamíla,
near a sheer drop to the Aóos
River, while the other stands
beneath Smólikas.

Although there are good
walking guides and maps of
the area, with mountain huts
to stay in and accommodation
in some of the larger villages,
visitors should not venture into
the mountains unless they are
prepared for the terrain and
are experienced walkers. The
weather can change quickly,
and in many places you will be
a long way from any kind of
settlement – though this is
one of the main attractions
of the Píndos Mountains.
They show the rugged side
of Greece, offering remote
valleys and routes where
few visitors venture.

WILDLIFE OF THE PÍNDOS MOUNTAINS

Visitors to the coastal lowlands are often
sceptical when told that wolves and bears
still survive in Greece. However, despite the
severe erosion of their natural habitat over
the last 20 years, both European wolves and
European brown bears can be found. The
Píndos mountains, and particularly the
northern regions towards Albania, continue to harbour the greatest numbers of
these endangered and now protected
creatures. They are extremely
wary of man, having been
persecuted by farmers and
goatherds down the centuries.
Therefore, visitors should
consider themselves very
fortunate if they see a bear.
Wolves are just as hard to see
but more evident, as they can
often be heard howling at
dawn and dusk, and will
even respond to imitations
of their howls. They pose
no real threat to visitors.

**The silver European
wolf, a rare native
of the region**

**One of the 80 European brown
bears of the northern Píndos**

Zagória ❷
Ζαγόρια

Epirus. **Road map** B2.

SOME OF EUROPE'S most spectacular scenery can be found only 25 km (15 miles) north of Ioánnina (see p210), in the area known as Zagória. Though the soil is largely un-cultivable, on the forested hillsides some 45 traditional Epirot villages still survive; many of them boast imposing archontiká (see p21) dating to prosperous 18th- and 19th-century Ottoman times when Zagória was granted autonomy.

Vlach and Sarakatsan shep-herds (see p209) make up most of the settled population. Over the winter months, the shepherds used to turn to crafts, forming into guilds of itinerant masons and wood-carvers, who would travel the Balkans selling their trades. This hard and ancient way of life is under threat, as the villagers, and especially the younger generation, prefer to earn their living from tourism.

A series of arched packhorse bridges are among the most memorable monuments to the skills of the local people and are unique features of the region. Two especially fine examples can be seen at either end of the village of **Kípoi**.

Vítsa village, by the Víkos Gorge

Southwestern Zagória is the busiest area, with a bus from Ioánnina to Monodéndri bringing in walkers and climbers. Some of the villages in the east of the region, such as **Vrysochóri**, were refuges for guerrillas during World War II and therefore burnt by the Germans; they have recovered only slowly.

Near the almost-deserted village of **Vradéto**, a 15th-century muletrack zigzags its way up a steep rockface beyond which the path leads to a stunning view of the spectacular Víkos Gorge (see p208). **Monodéndri**, opposite Vradéto, is the usual startingpoint for the gorge trail, though another path can be taken from **Vítsa**. Nearby are the two villages of **Megálo Pápigko** and **Mikró Pápigko**. They are 4 km (2 miles) apart and their names reflect their sizes, but even "big" Pápigko is no more than a scattering of houses around cobbled streets, with a choice of restaurants, and rooms available in renovated mansions.

Further south, though still surrounded by mountains, is the relatively thriving village of **Tsepélovo**. It has a bus service to Ioánnina and a restored mansion which provides accommodation, as well as a number of pensions and tavernas. Its cobbled streets and slate-roofed houses provide a perfect portrait of a Zagorian village.

Packhorse bridge near the village of Kípoi

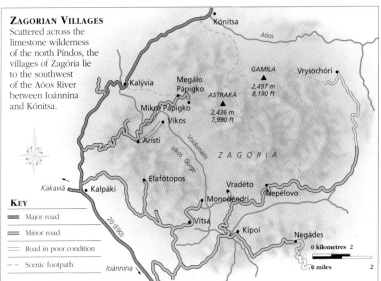

ZAGORIAN VILLAGES
Scattered across the limestone wilderness of the north Píndos, the villages of Zagória lie to the southwest of the Aóos River between Ioánnina and Kónitsa.

Kónitsa

Aóos

GAMILA ▲ 2,497 m 8,190 ft

Vrysochóri

Kalývia

Megálo Pápigko

ASTRAKA ▲ 2,436 m 7,990 ft

Mikró Pápigko

Víkos

Arísti

Víkos Gorge

Voïdomátis

Z A G O R I A

Elafótopos

Vradéto

Monodéndri

Tsepélovo

Kakaviá

Kalpáki

KEY

Vítsa

Kípoi

Negádes

Major road

Minor road

Road in poor condition

Scenic footpath

20 (E90)

Ioánnina

0 kilometres 2

0 miles 2

Víkos Gorge Walk ❸

To trek the length of the Víkos Gorge is to undertake what is arguably the greatest walk in Greece. Carved by the Voïdomátis River, the sheer, deeply eroded limestone walls rise to 915 m (3,000 ft). The gorge cuts through the Víkos-Aóos National Park, established in 1975. Cairns and waymarks define the route which snakes through the boulder-strewn ravine bed and continues up through stands

Greek tortoise

of beech, chestnut and maple to the higher ground. Several birds of prey, including the Egyptian vulture, are commonly seen circling in the thermals, and lizards and tortoises abound. Though the main route through the gorge begins at Monodéndri, a shorter 4-km (2-mile) walk can be made between the northern villages of Mikró Pápigko and Víkos.

IOANNINA

Mikró Pápigko ⑤

Víkos

④

Voïdomátis

Megálo Pápigko ⑤
One of the area's protected traditional villages, stone-built Megálo Pápigko stands at 950 m (3,117 ft), beneath the cliffs of Pýrgi.

Rock pinnacle ④
For the Pápigko villages, cross the Víkos here beneath a landmark pinnacle of rock. The path branches to the west for Vítsiko.

Z A G O R I A

③ 🏛

Agía Triáda ③
After three hours you pass the white shrine of Agía Triáda, standing opposite a well.

Oxiá Viewpoint ②
From Monodéndri, a road can be taken to the Oxiá site, one of the area's finest viewpoints, along with Mpelóï opposite.

② ⁂ ⁂ Mpelóï viewpoint

🏛

①

🅿

• Vítsa

Monodéndri ①
With its magnificent views over the gorge, this village is the most popular start for the walk. The path is signposted from the church in the lower square.

IOANNINA

KEY

– – Walk route	🏛 Monastery
═ Minor road	⁂ Viewpoint
═ Road in poor condition	🅿 Parking

0 kilometres — 5
0 miles — 2

TIPS FOR WALKERS

Starting point: Monodéndri.
Getting there: 40 km (25 miles) NW of Ioánnina, by car or bus.
Length: 14 km (8 miles) to Megálo Pápigko.
Difficulty: Straightforward, though hiking boots required.
Walking time: 6–7 hours.

Métsovo ❹
Μέτσοβο

Epirus. **Road map** B2. 🏠 *3,500.* 🚌
ℹ️ *0656 41233.*

Situated close by the Katára Pass (the route crossing the Píndos Mountains), Métsovo has a vitality unique among Greek mountain towns. It was originally a small village inhabited by Vlach shepherds, though it became one of the region's most important commercial centres after being granted tax privileges in return for guarding the pass during Ottoman times *(see pp38–9)*. Local merchant families invested their new wealth in the town and continue to do so today by providing endowments and grants to encourage industry among the local craftspeople.

One such family was the Tosítsas, and some idea of the size of their wealth can be gained by touring the rebuilt 18th-century **Archontikó Tosítsa**, preserved as a museum *(see pp20–21)*. Rising to three floors, the mansion contains an armoury and washroom on the ground floor, with huge wood-panelled reception rooms and

Shepherds' crooks, rugs and silverware in a souvenir shop in Métsovo

bedrooms upstairs, carpeted with beautiful, locally woven *kilim* rugs. Intricate gold- and silverware are on display, as well as collections of Epirot costumes and embroidery. Would-be visitors must wait outside for the half-hourly guided tour.

Another of Métsovo's benefactors was the writer and politician Evángelos Avérof (1910–90) who founded the **Avérof Gallery**. The core of

Interior of the Archontikó Tosítsa, Métsovo

the gallery is Avérof's own collection of some 200 paintings and sculptures he acquired over the years, always with the ambition of opening a museum of modern Greek art in his home town. His collection has been expanded to show the work of several dozen Greek artists from the 19th and 20th centuries.

Ancient traditions have survived in the area, from the simple craft of carving shepherds' crooks (handed down since Métsovo first made its money through sheep farming in the rich pastures around) to embroidery and wine- and cheese-making. Some of the older men (and a few women) still wear traditional costumes; you can see them, dressed in black, sitting in the shelters and cafés around the town square. The shelters are needed during winter when the town, at 1,156 m (3,793 ft) becomes a popular ski resort. The rugs on sale in the souvenir shops also reflect this alpine character.

🏛️ **Archontikó Tosítsa**
Off main thoroughfare. 📞 *26560 41204.* ☐ *Mon–Wed, Fri–Sun.* 🖼️
🏛️ **Avérof Gallery**
Off central square. 📞 *26560 41210.* ☐ *Mon, Wed–Sun.* 🖼️

Environs: Fifteen minutes' walk south, signposted from the centre of town, stands the small and charming 14th-century **Moní Agíou Nikoláou**. Now it is inhabited only by caretakers who are more than happy to show visitors the church's vivid post-Byzantine frescoes, the monks' living quarters and their own supplies of flowers, fruit and vegetables.

Vlach Shepherds

Of unknown origin, the nomadic Vlach shepherds are today centred in the Píndos Mountains, particularly in and around Métsovo. Their language, which has no written form, is a dialect of Latin origin, and it is thought that they might be descended from Roman settlers who moved through Illyria into the northern Balkans. Traditionally, their way of life has been transhumant – spending summers in the mountains before moving down to the plains of Thessaly with their sheep for six months to avoid the worst of the winter snows. It is a hard way of life which is gradually disappearing, and the shepherds who remain can be found in such villages as Métsovo and Vovoúsa in Epirus, or Avdélla, Samarína and Smíxi in western Macedonia – their traditional summer settlements. Their winter homes lie mainly around Kastoriá *(see p240)*.

Zagorian Vlach shepherd

Ioánnina 5

Ιωάννινα

Chalice made of Ioánninan silver

THE CAPITAL of the Epirus region, Ioánnina prospered during Ottoman times (see pp38–9) when its famous craftsmen's guilds, including the silversmiths', were formed. The Turkish influence is most visible in the fortress area which extends on a small headland into Lake Pamvótis (it was once moated on its landward side). Though dating to the 13th century, the area was rebuilt in 1815 by Ali Pasha, the Turkish tyrant most closely associated with it. Inside the fortress precinct a village-like peace reigns, though the bustle of the bazaar and the modern area is a reminder that this is still the region's busiest city.

Ioánnina and the isle of Nisí, seen from the north

Aslan Pasha Mosque, housing the Popular Art Museum

Popular Art Museum

Aslan Pasha Mosque. **(** 26510 26356. **○** daily. **●** main public hols.

Situated in the northern corner of the fortress, this small museum is housed within the Aslan Pasha Mosque, built by Aslan Pasha in 1618. While the interior of the mosque itself, which retains the original decoration on its dome, makes a visit worthwhile, the weapons and costumes on display tell something of Ioánnina's recent past. Turkish furniture inlaid with mother-of-pearl can also be found, alongside Jewish rugs and tapestries.

Byzantine Museum

Inner Fortress. **(** 26510 25989. **○** 8am–5pm daily (12:30–3pm Mon). **●** main public hols.

This modern museum, situated in the inner fortress, contains a few items from local archaeological excavations, but the core is an imaginative display of icons from the 16th to the 19th centuries. Silverware, for which the town is renowned, is displayed in a separate annexe, once the treasury, with a reconstruction of a typical silversmith's workshop.

Archaeological Museum

Plateía 25 Martíou 6. **(** 26510 33357. **○** 8am–6pm Tue–Fri; 8:30am–3pm Sat, Sun; noon–6pm Mon. **●** main public hols.

Set in a small park south of the fortress, the Archaeological Museum has a small collection of artifacts, including items from Dodóni such as a bronze eagle from the 5th century BC and some statuettes of young children. Lead tablets inscribed with questions for the oracle can also be found.

Folk Museum

Michaíl Angélou 42. **(** 26510 20515. **○** Tue–Sun. **●** main public hols.

At the far end of a side street, almost opposite the Archaeological Museum is the mansion containing a collection of local crafts. As well as silver-work and traditional costumes, there are woven textiles made by the nomadic, tent-dwelling Sarakatsans who number less than the Vlach tribe (see p209).

ALI PASHA

Ali Pasha was born in Albania in 1741 and, in 1788, was installed at Ioánnina by the Turks as Pasha of Epirus. Though a murderer, he was a great administrator who made the town one of the wealthiest in Greece. His aim was to gain independence from his overlords and by 1820 he had an empire stretching from Albania to the Peloponnese. When news spread of his intention to create a Greco-Albanian state, Sultan Mahmud II of Turkey dispatched troops to put him to death. After a long siege within the fortress at Ioánnina, Ali Pasha agreed to meet the Turkish commander on the island of Nisí where, on 24 January 1822, he was hunted down, trapped and killed.

Tapestry of Ali Pasha (centre), Moní Agíou Panteleímonos, Nisí

🎭 Nisí

15 minutes by boat NE from fortress.
Though its first inhabitants
were the monks who came
here in the early years of the
13th century, the single village
on the isle of Nisí owes its
existence to 17th-century refugees from Mániot feuds *(see
p194).* Its main building is
Moní Agíou Panteleímonos,
where the reconstructed room
in which Ali Pasha was shot
can be visited, the bullet holes
still visible in the floor. Other
rooms contain a few of his
possessions, some costumes
and period prints.

Stalactites in the Pérama Caves

ENVIRONS: Greece's largest
cave network, the **Pérama
Caves**, can be found near
the village of Pérama, 4 km
(2 miles) north of Ioánnina.
They were discovered in 1940
by a shepherd hiding from the
Germans, but only fully explored years later. Now there
are regular guided tours taking visitors along the 1,700 m
(5,600 ft) of passages, where
multicoloured lights pick out
the stalactites and stalagmites.

🎭 Pérama Caves

Pérama. 📞 *26510 81521.*
🕐 *daily.* 💰

The theatre of Dodóni, one of the largest in Greece

Dodóni ❻
Δωδώνη

Epirus. **Road map** B3. 📞 *26510
82287.* 🚌 🕐 *daily.* ● *main public
hols.* 💰 ♿

DATING to at least 1000 BC,
the Oracle of Zeus at
Dodóni is the oldest in Greece
and was second in status
only to the one at Delphi *(see
pp228–9).* The site is located
22 km (14 miles) southwest
of Ioánnina in a placid green
valley on the eastern slopes
of Mount Tómaros.

The oracle focused on a
sacred oak tree ringed with
tripods which held a number
of bronze cauldrons placed so
that they touched each other.
Prophecies were divined from
the sound these made, in
harmony with the rustling
of the oak leaves, when one
of the cauldrons was struck.
Petitioners would inscribe
their questions on lead tablets
for the priestess to read
to Zeus; some of
these have been
found on the
site and can
be seen in the
Archaeological
Museum in
Ioánnina. The
reputed power
of the oak tree
was such that
Jason, on his
quest for the
Golden Fleece *(see
p220),* travelled across from
the Pílio to acquire one of its
branches to attach to his ship,
the Argo. By the 3rd century
BC a colonnaded courtyard
was built around the tree for

**Justinian, the last Roman
Emperor to visit Dodóni**

protection; it contained a small
temple of which only foundations remain. The tree was
uprooted in AD 393 on the
orders of the Roman Emperor
Theodosios (ruled 379–395)
in accordance with his policy
of stamping out pagan prac-
tices. He also believed that
buried treasure might be found
beneath the site.

The main feature of Dodóni
today is the theatre which,
with its capacity for 17,000
spectators, is one of the largest in Greece. Its huge walls
rise to 21 m (69 ft) and are
supported by solid towers
where kestrels now nest. Used
by the ancient Greeks for drama
performances, the Romans
later converted it to an arena
for animal fights; bulls and
big cats would have been
kept in the two triangular pens
on either side of the stage.
The whole structure of the
theatre was restored in the
early 1960s and is now used
for performances dur-
ing the summer.

Dodóni also in-
cludes the ruins
of a stadium,
acropolis and
Byzantine
basilica – all
reminders of
the time when
this empty
valley was the
location of a
flourishing
market town.

Dodóni fell into ruin in the
6th century AD when the
Roman Emperor Justinian
decided to found the new
and more easily defendable
city of Ioánnina.

The tiered, amphitheatre-shaped town of Párga, seen across Párga Bay

Párga ❼
Πάργα

Epirus. **Road map** B3. 🏛 2,000. 🚌
🛈 Alexandrou Pága 18 (26840
31222). 🚢 Tue.

Párga, the main beach resort of Epirus, is a busy holiday town whose charms are often overwhelmed by the number of summer visitors. The Venetian fortress dominating the west side of the harbour was built in the late 16th century on the site of a building destroyed in 1537 during a brief period of Turkish rule. The Ottomans later returned under the command of Ali Pasha (see p210), who bought the town from the British in 1819. After this, many of Párga's inhabitants left for Corfu, though it was regained by the Greeks in 1913.

There are two small beaches within walking distance of the town centre and two larger ones about 2 km (1 mile) away: Váltos, the biggest, is to the north and Lychnos to the southwest. Fish restaurants line Párga's waterfront, affording fine views across the harbour to a group of small islands.

Environs: 37 km (23 miles) south of Párga stands the **Necromanteion of Efyra** (Oracle of the Dead) – the mythological gateway to Hades. Steps descend to the vaults where, in the 4th century BC, drugs and mechanisms may have heightened the sensation of entering the Underworld for visitors who came to ask the advice of the dead.

Kassópi ❽
Κασσώπη

Zálongo, Epirus. **Road map** B3. 🚌 🚫 daily.

The kassopians were a tribe which lived in this region in the 4th century BC. The remains of their capital city stand on a hillside plateau overlooking the Ionian Sea, from where the shadowy island of Paxoí is plainly visible. Kassópi is reached by a pleasant walk through pine groves from the village of Kamarína and, though the ruins are scarcely visible, a site

Greek Orthodox priests in Párga

plan illustrates the layout of the once-great city, now the home of birds and lizards.

Just to the southeast is **Moní Zalóngou**, with its monument commemorating the women of Soúli who threw themselves from the cliffs in 1806 rather than be captured by Turkish-Albanian troops.

The remains of the city of Kassópi

Préveza ❾
Πρέβεζα

Epirus. **Road map** B3. 🏛 13,000.
✈ 🚌 🛈 Eleftheriou Venizélou
(26820 21078). 🚢 daily (fish).

Often seen as a transit point, the charming town of Préveza repays a longer visit, particularly for the lively atmosphere among its waterfront cafés and tavernas. It is picturesquely situated on the northern shore of the narrow "Channel of Cleopatra", at the mouth of the Amvrakikós Gulf. It was here that the naval Battle of Actium was fought in 31 BC (see p34).

Two ruined forts, on either side of the straits, recall the town's Venetian occupation in 1499, though in 1798 it passed, via the French, into the hands of Ali Pasha *(see p210).*

ENVIRONS: Seven km (4 miles) north of Préveza stand the ruins of **Nikópoli** ("Victory City"), built by the Roman Emperor Octavian to celebrate his victory at Actium. The city was founded on the site where the emperor's army was camped. Later sacked by the Goths, it was finally destroyed by the Bulgars in 1034. The remains are dominated by the city walls and the theatre. A museum displays artifacts from the site which is now overgrown.

Nikópoli
26820 41336. daily.
main public hols.

Arta ➓
`Άρτα

Epirus. **Road map** B3. *33,000.*
 26810 78551. *Mon–Sat (veg).*

THOUGH IT is the second largest town in Epirus, after Ioánnina, Arta remains largely untouched by tourism and offers a chance to see a traditional Greek market town. It has a lively, bazaar-like market area, established by the Turks who occupied Arta from 1449 to 1881. The **fortress**, which is now closed to the public, dates from the 13th century when the city was the capital of the despotate of Epirus. The despotate, which stretched from Thessaloníki to Corfu, was an independent Byzantine state set up after the fall of Constantinople in 1204 *(see p37).* It lasted until the start of the Turkish occupation. Some

Timber-framed houses in the Old Quarter of Tríkala

of the town's many 13th- and 14th-century Byzantine churches can be found in the streets leading up to the fortress, the most striking being the **Panagía Parigorítissa.** Built between 1283 and 1296, it is a three-tier building topped with towers and domes. **Agía Theódora**, on Pýrrou, contains the marble tomb of the saintly wife of 13th-century Epirot ruler Michael II.

Approaching from the west, the main road into town crosses the river Arachthos by a 17th-century stone **bridge**. According to local folklore, the builder of the bridge, frustrated by each day's work being ruined by the river at night, was advised by a bird that the problem could be solved by putting his wife in the bridge's foundations. This he did, burying her alive, after which the bridge was successfully completed.

Metéora ⓫

See pp216–17.

Tríkala ⓬
Τρίκαλα

Thessaly. **Road map** C2. *68,000.*
   24310 27401.
 Mon–Sat.

TRIKALA WAS THE HOME of Asklepios, the god of healing, and today is the market centre for the very fertile plain of Thessaly. As such it is a thriving town with a number of remains from its Turkish past. One is the **market** near the main square, another the **Koursoúm Tzamí**, a graceful mosque built in 1550 on the south side of the River Lithaíos. Surrounding the **fortress** is the Old Quarter of Varósi, with a number of Byzantine churches *(see pp18–19).* The fortress is built on the site of the ancient acropolis, which was built in the 4th century BC. It is situated in beautiful grounds overlooking the river.

Vale of Tempe ⓭
Κοιλάδα των Τεμπών

Thessaly. **Road map** C2.

AS THE E75 approaches Macedonia, it follows the river Pineiós through the Vale of Tempe – the fertile valley where Apollo was said to have purified himself after slaying the serpent Python. Close to the **Wolf's Jaws** or **Lykostómio** (the narrowest point of the gorge) is the **Spring of Daphne**, where a bridge leads to the chapel of **Agía Paraskeví**, carved out of the rock. The **Kástro Gónnon** at the northern end of the Vale was built by Perséas, leader of the Macedonians during the war with Rome *(see pp32–33),* to control what has long been a vital route between Central and Northern Greece.

The arched packhorse bridge of Arta, leading into town from the west

Metéora ⓫

Μετέωρα

Icon of Our
Lord, Varlaám

Τ HE NATURAL sandstone towers of Metéora (or
"suspended rocks") were first used as a religious retreat when, in AD 985, a hermit named
Barnabas occupied a cave here. In the mid-
14th century Neílos, the Prior of Stagai convent,
built a small church. Then in 1382 the monk
Athanásios, from Mount Athos, founded the huge
monastery of Megálo Metéoro on one of the many
pinnacles. Twenty-three monasteries followed,
though most had fallen into ruin by the 19th
century. In the 1920s stairs were cut to make the remaining
six monasteries more accessible, and today a religious
revival has seen the return of many monks and nuns.

**Monastic
cells**

LOCATION OF MONASTERIES OF METEORA

**Outer
walls**

Rousánou

*Moní Rousánou,
perched precariously
on the very tip of a
narrow spire of rock, is
the most spectacularly
located of all the
monasteries. Its church
of the Metamórfosis
(1545) is renowned for
its harrowing frescoes,
painted in 1560 by
the iconographers
of the Cretan school.*

VARLAAM

Founded in
1518, the monas-
tery of Varlaám is
named after the first
hermit to live on this rock
in 1350. The *katholikón* was
built in 1542 and contains some
frescoes by the Theban icono-
grapher Frágkos Katelános.

Megálo Metéoro

*Also known as the Great Meteoron,
this was the first and, at 623 m
(2,045 ft), highest monastery to be
founded. By the entrance is a cave in
which Athanásios first lived. His body
is buried in the main church.*

◁ **Moní Rousánou on the left in the foreground, with Moní Varlaám towering behind**

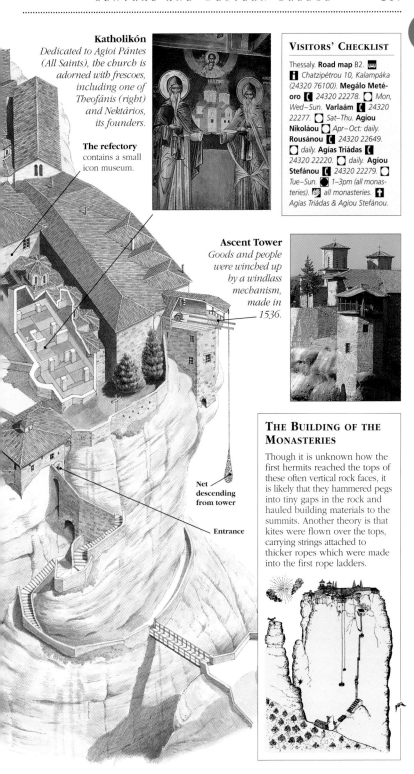

Katholikón
Dedicated to Agioi Pántes (All Saints), the church is adorned with frescoes, including one of Theofánis (right) and Nektários, its founders.

The refectory contains a small icon museum.

VISITORS' CHECKLIST

Thessaly. **Road map** B2. ⌷ Chatzipétrou 10, Kalampáka (24320 76100). **Megálo Metéoro** ☎ 24320 22278. ○ Mon, Wed–Sun. **Varlaám** ☎ 24320 22277. ○ Sat–Thu. **Agíou Nikoláou** ○ Apr–Oct: daily. **Rousánou** ☎ 24320 22649. ○ daily. **Agías Triádas** ☎ 24320 22220. ○ daily. **Agíou Stefánou** ☎ 24320 22279. ○ Tue–Sun. ● 1–3pm (all monasteries). 🎫 all monasteries. 🕆 Agías Triádas & Agíou Stefánou.

Ascent Tower
Goods and people were winched up by a windlass mechanism, made in 1536.

Net descending from tower

Entrance

THE BUILDING OF THE MONASTERIES

Though it is unknown how the first hermits reached the tops of these often vertical rock faces, it is likely that they hammered pegs into tiny gaps in the rock and hauled building materials to the summits. Another theory is that kites were flown over the tops, carrying strings attached to thicker ropes which were made into the first rope ladders.

Pílio ⑭
Πήλιο

Taxiárchis church fresco, Miliés

THE MYTHOLOGICAL HOME of the forest-loving centaurs, the Pílio peninsula, with its woods of chestnut, oak and beech, is one of the most beautiful regions of the mainland. The mountain air is sweet with the scent of herbs which, in ancient times, were renowned for their healing powers. The area became populated in the 13th century by Greeks retreating from the Ottomans *(see pp38–9)*, under whose rule they were taxed onerously. Most villages were built close to mountain monasteries, though the thick stone walls and narrow windows of a typical Pílio house indicate how uncertain their freedom really was. After centuries of protecting their culture, this is now one of the few areas of Greece to have a strong local cuisine.

Makrinítsa
Cars are banned from the steep cobbled streets of this traditional village (see p220).

Agía Kyriakí
Overlooked by the isolated hilltop village of Tríkeri, this small fishing port lacks a beach and hotels but has a working boatyard and good, simple fish tavernas for those very few visitors who take the trouble to travel here.

Anakasiá, now little more than a suburb of Vólos, has a museum to the Greek painter Theófilos Chatzimichaïl.

Vólos is the capital of the region, straddling the only route into the peninsula. It has an excellent Archaeological Museum *(see p220).*

THEOFILOS CHATZIMICHAIL

Born on Lésvos in 1873, Theófilos came to the Pílio in 1894 after reportedly killing a Turk in Smyrna. His favoured medium was the mural, though he also painted ceramics and the sides of fishing boats, *kafeneío* counters or horse carts when the mood struck him. He executed numerous mural com-missions in the Pílio, notably at the Kontós mansion in Anakasiá.

Konstantínos Palaiológos mural (1899) by Theófilos

Though unhappily isolated, and mocked by the locals for his strange habits (he dressed in the costumes of his heroes, including Alexander the Great), he had a passion for all things Greek. After Lésvos's unification with Greece in 1912, he returned home destitute and ill. His fortunes changed after meeting his future patron Stratís Eleftheriádis who provided for the painter's needs until Theófilos's death in 1934.

KEY

▭	Major road
▭	Minor road
▭	Non-asphalt road
---	Ferry route
ⓘ	Tourist information
⚹	Viewpoint

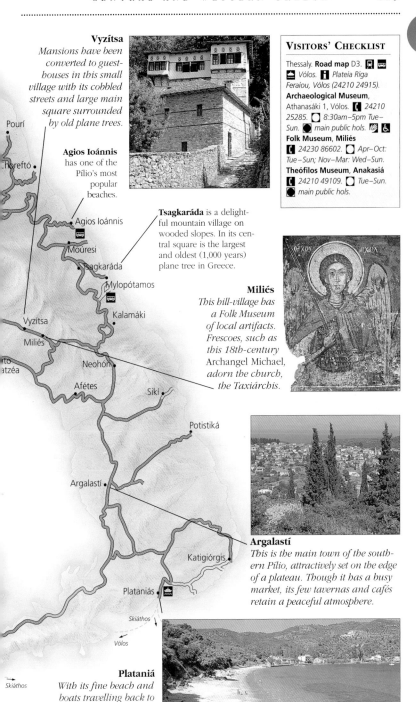

Vyzítsa
Mansions have been converted to guesthouses in this small village with its cobbled streets and large main square surrounded by old plane trees.

Agios Ioánnis
has one of the Pílio's most popular beaches.

Tsagkaráda is a delightful mountain village on wooded slopes. In its central square is the largest and oldest (1,000 years) plane tree in Greece.

Miliés
This hill-village has a Folk Museum of local artifacts. Frescoes, such as this 18th-century Archangel Michael, adorn the church, the Taxiárchis.

Pourí
Choreftó
Agios Ioánnis
Moúresi
Tsagkaráda
Mylopótamos
Kalamáki
Vyzítsa
Miliés
rto
atzéa
Neohóri
Afétes
Sikí
Potistiká
Argalastí
Katigiórgis
Plataniás
Skiáthos
Vólos
Skiáthos

VISITORS' CHECKLIST

Thessaly. **Road map** D3. 🚌 🚐
🚢 *Vólos*. 🛈 *Plateía Riga
Feraíou, Vólos (24210 24915).*
Archaeological Museum,
Athanasáki 1, Vólos. 📞 *24210
25285.* ⏰ *8:30am–5pm Tue–
Sun.* ⬤ *main public hols.* 🏛 ♿
Folk Museum, Miliés
📞 *24230 86602.* ⏰ *Apr–Oct:
Tue–Sun; Nov–Mar: Wed–Sun.*
Theófilos Museum, Anakasiá
📞 *24210 49109.* ⏰ *Tue–Sun.*
⬤ *main public hols.*

Argalastí
This is the main town of the southern Pílio, attractively set on the edge of a plateau. Though it has a busy market, its few tavernas and cafés retain a peaceful atmosphere.

Plataniá
With its fine beach and boats travelling back to Vólos and to Skiáthos island, Plataniá is popular with Greek tourists. A number of fish tavernas provide excellent seafood.

Exploring the Pílio

TRAVELLING BY CAR, a circular tour of the northern villages can be made in a day following the road southeast from Vólos to Afétes, via Tsagkaráda. The hills in this region rise to 1,650 m (5,415 ft) at the summit of Mount Pílio, and in addition to dense woodlands, the area produces a large number of apples, pears, peaches and olives. While less dramatic, the southern Pílio is still hilly enough to ensure that many villages are at the end of single "dead end" roads, making travel here time consuming.

Restored traditional mansions on the hillside of Makrinítsa

Vólos

Vólos is one of Greece's fastest-growing industrial centres and, since it was devastated by earthquakes in the 1950s, it is difficult to imagine its mythological past. Once the site of ancient Iolkós, the home of Jason, who went in search of the Golden Fleece, Vólos's history is illustrated by what can be found in the excellent **Archaeological Museum**. The museum, situated in a flowered garden, contains an extensive collection of painted funerary stelae from the 3rd

century BC, found at Dimitriás on the far side of the Gulf of Vólos. Important collections of Neolithic pottery from the nearby sites of Sésklo and Dimíni can also be found.

Northern Villages

From Vólos the road leads southeast, past Ano Lechónia, through the "Vólos Riviera", providing a circular route of the mountainous northern Pílio. From the popular inland resorts of **Miliés** and **Vyzítsa** (the latter preserved as a "traditional settlement" by the government), the road turns north past Tsagkaráda to **Agios Ioánnis**. This is the main resort of the east coast and, though the village beach itself is often crowded, the beaches of Papá Neró and Pláka are particularly fine and are both within easy walking distance. Some of the Pílio's best restaurants can be found in nearby **Moúresi**.

Returning towards Vólos, take the turning to **Makrinítsa** – a traditional mountain village, widely regarded as the most important destination for any traveller of the area. Founded in the 13th century by refugees from the first sacking of Constantinople *(see p37)*, the village has several beautiful churches, the most impressive being Agios Ioánnis, and the Moní Theotókou. A number of traditional mansions also survive, some functioning as guest houses. Close to Agios Ioánnis, there is a café with an interior decorated with frescoes painted by the artist Theófilos *(see p218)*.

Anakasiá is the last village before Vólos. Though few people stop for long here, the delightful Theófilos Museum is well worth a visit.

Fisherman with his nets at the waterfront, Vólos

JASON AND THE ARGONAUTS

According to legend, the Golden Fleece came from a winged ram sent by Hermes, the gods' messenger, to protect two children, Helle and Phrixus, from their evil stepmother. Though Helle drowned, Phrixus was reared in Kolchis, in present-day Georgia, where the ram was sacrificed and its fleece given to the king, Aeëtes. Years later, Jason, Phrixus's cousin, set sail from the kingdom of Iolkós (now Vólos) after his half-brother usurped the throne. Jason was in search of the Fleece, which made its wearer invincible. With a crew of 50, Jason came to Kolchis where King Aeëtes set several tasks before relinquishing the Fleece. After falling in love with the king's daughter, Medea, Jason achieved his tasks and the Argonauts carried the Fleece back to Iolkós in triumph.

Detail from *The Golden Fleece* (c.1905) by Herbert Draper (1864–1920)

Sarcophagus detail outside the Thebes Archaeological Museum

Thebes ⑮
Θήβα

Stereá Elláda. **Road map** D4.
🏛 20,000. 🚉 🚌 ℹ *main square (22620 22621).*

ALTHOUGH it was briefly the most powerful city of Greece, in the 4th century BC, the Thebes of today is little more than a quiet provincial town. It played an important role in the power struggles of Classical Greece, until defeated by Philip II of Macedon. Thebes' original acropolis has been built over through the years, but excavations have unearthed Mycenaean walls as well as jewellery, pottery and important tablets of Linear B script which are now in the **Archaeological Museum**. One of the highlights of the museum is the collection of Mycenaean sarcophagi, similar to those found on Crete. The museum's courtyard and well-tended garden stand alongside a 13th-century Frankish tower, all that remains of a castle ruined in 1311 by the Catalans.

A bridge over the river bed, a short walk eastwards from the museum, marks the traditional site of the Fountain of Oedipus, where the legendary King Oedipus is said to have

THE LEGEND OF OEDIPUS

According to legend, Oedipus was the ill-fated son of Laius and Jocasta, the king and queen of Thebes. Even before his birth, the Delphic Oracle *(see p228)* had foretold that he would kill his father and become his mother's husband. To defy the prophecy, Laius abandoned Oedipus, though the child was rescued and reared by the king and queen of Corinth whom Oedipus believed to be his real parents. Years later, when he heard of the prophecy, Oedipus fled to Thebes, killing a man on his way. On reaching Thebes, he found the city gates barred by the Sphinx which he vanquished by solving one of its riddles. The Thebans made him their king and he married the widowed Jocasta. When the truth about his past was revealed, Oedipus blinded himself and spent his final days as an outcast.

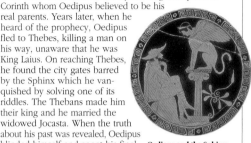

Oedipus and the Sphinx, from a 5th-century BC cup

washed blood from his hands after unwittingly killing his father on his way to the city.

🏛 Archaeological Museum
Plateía Threpsiádou 1. 📞 22620 27913. ☐ *May–Oct: Mon, Thu, Fri 8am–7pm, Sat, Sun 8:30am–3pm; Nov–Apr: 8:30am–3pm.* 🅿 ♿

ENVIRONS: 10 km (6 miles) north lie the ruins of **Gla**, once a Mycenaean stronghold *(see pp178–80)*. Its walls are 3 km (2 miles) long and up to 5 m (16 ft) high, surrounding a hill where the ruins of a palace and agora can be found.

Monastery of Osios Loúkas ⑯

See pp222–3.

Mount Parnassus ⑰
Όρος Παρνασσός

Stereá Elláda. **Road map** C3.
🚌 *Delfoí.* ℹ *Vasiléon Pávlou & Freiderikis 44, Delfoí (22650 82900).*

RISING to a height of 2,457 m (8,061 ft), the limestone mass of Mount Parnassus dominates the eastern region of Stereá Elláda. The lower slopes are covered with Cephalonian fir, and beneath them, in summer, the wild-flower meadows burst into colour. Vultures and golden eagles are common, as are wolves which come down from the Píndos Mountains *(see p206)* in winter.

The village of **Aráchova** is the best base for exploring the area and is renowned for its wine, cheese and sheep-skin rugs. There are many mountain trails for summer hikes, though a detailed walking map is recommended. Reaching the top of Liákoura, the highest peak, involves a long hike and camping over-night on the mountain.

From Aráchova, the ski centre at **Fterólaka** is only a 26-km (16-mile) drive away. Open from December to April, it provides a chair lift to 1,900 m (6,250 ft); from here a ski lift can be taken up to the ski slopes. In summer, Fterólaka functions as an excursion centre for the area.

Fir-covered foothills beneath the ridge of Mount Parnassus

Monastery of Osios Loúkas ⓰
Μονή Οσίου Λουκά

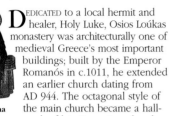

DEDICATED to a local hermit and healer, Holy Luke, Osios Loúkas monastery was architecturally one of medieval Greece's most important buildings; built by the Emperor Romanós in c.1011, he extended an earlier church dating from AD 944. The octagonal style of the main church became a hall-mark of late Byzantine church design *(see pp18–19)*, while the mosaics inside lifted Byzantine art into its final great period. During the time of the Ottoman Empire *(see pp38–9)*, Osios Loúkas witnessed a great deal of fighting, as the cannons in the courtyard testify. Here in 1821, Bishop Isaias declared his support for the Greek freedom fighters.

Madonna mosaic

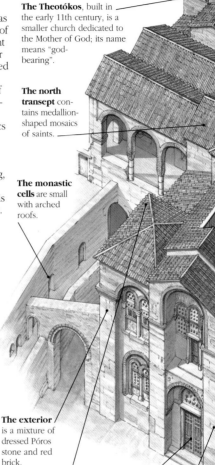

The Theotókos, built in the early 11th century, is a smaller church dedicated to the Mother of God; its name means "god-bearing".

The north transept contains medallion-shaped mosaics of saints.

The monastic cells are small with arched roofs.

The exterior is a mixture of dressed Póros stone and red brick.

West portal

The narthex is the western entrance hall; it contains a number of mosaics of Christ's Passion.

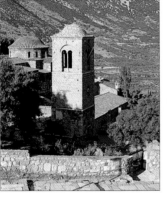

The monastery seen from the west with the slopes of Mount Elikónas in the background

★ **Washing of the Apostles' Feet**
Based on a style dating to the 6th century, this 11th-century work is the finest of the narthex mosaics. Set on a gold back-ground, it depicts Christ teaching his apostles humility.

STAR FEATURES

★ **Washing of the Apostles' Feet**

★ **Crypt**

Dome
*The main dome is decorated
with an imposing mural of Christ
surrounded by saints and angels,
painted in the 16th century to replace
fallen mosaics.*

The apse has a
mosaic of the
Virgin and Child
predating a devas-
tating earthquake
in 1659.

The katholikón,
or main church,
dates to 1011 and
is built in the
octagonal style.

★ Crypt
*This 10th-century shrine,
from the original site, contains the sarcophagus of Holy
Luke, and such frescoes as
this Descent from the Cross.*

**The southwest
chapel** has early
11th-century
frescoes.

The refectory was
used as a workshop as
well as for meals; it now
contains a museum of
Byzantine sculpture.

HOLY LUKE

Born in Aegina in 906, Osios Loúkas ("Holy
Luke") is known to have been a spiritual child
who, in his early teens, left home to seek
isolation in central Greece and developed a
reputation as a healer. In around 940 he arrived
at this spot on the western slopes of Mount
Elikónas, with its glorious view over a peaceful
valley of cornfields and groves of almond and
olive trees. Here he settled with some disciples,
adding the gift of prophecy to his healing
powers. He died in 953, by which time the first
monastic cells and the site's first small church
had been constructed.

The waterfront houses of Galaxídi in the Gulf of Corinth

Lamía and Thermopylae ⓲
Λαμία καί Θερμοπύλαι

Stereá Elláda. **Road map** C3.
🏛 68,000. 🚉 🚌 **ᵢ** Plateía Laoú 3
(22310 30065). 🚌 Sat.

SET IN THE VALLEY between two wooded hills, Lamía is typical of many medium-sized Greek towns; though it is little known, it has much to offer, with a lively Saturday market. A 14th-century Catalan **kástro**, built on the site of the town's ancient acropolis, provides excellent views over the roofs to the surrounding countryside.

Lamía is chiefly associated with the Lamian War (323–322 BC) when Athens tried to throw off Macedonian rule after the death of Alexander the Great (see pp32–3). This is recalled at the **Lamía Museum**, which also has displays of architectural remains from Delphi (see pp228–31).

A short drive east of Lamía, the Athens road crosses the **Pass of Thermopylae**. It was

here, in 480 BC, that an army of some 7,000 soldiers, under the command of Leonidas I of Sparta, met an overwhelming force from Persia whose numbers Herodotus (see p56) cites as 2,641,610. Though Leonidas held the pass for a number of days, the Persians forced a path through and attacked the Greeks from the rear. Only two Greek soldiers survived the ordeal after which all of central Greece, including Athens, fell to the Persians. The Persian land forces were eventually defeated by Athens and her allies at the Battle of Plataiai in 479 BC (see p29).

An impressive bronze statue of King Leonidas, cast in 1955, stands at the roadside opposite the burial mound of the soldiers who died here. Just to the left of the mound

Statue of King Leonidas at the Pass of Thermopylae

are the famous sulphur springs from which Thermopylae was given its name, which means the "Hot Gates".

The present landscape has changed considerably from the narrow gorge of old; the coastline to the north has been extended by the silt brought down by the River Spercheiós, pushing the sea back over 5 km (3 miles).

🏛 **Lamía Museum**
Kástro. **[** 22310 46106. **]** Tue–Sun. **●** main public hols. 🎫 &

Ancient Delphi ⓳

See pp228–31.

Gulf of Corinth ⓴
Κορινθιακός Κόλπος

Stereá Elláda. 🚌 to Náfpaktos.

THE NORTHERN COAST of the Gulf of Corinth contains several well-known resorts as well as many tiny coastal villages far removed from the usual tourist route. All are served by major roads which, like the resorts, offer fine views across the gulf to the mountains of the Peloponnese.

From Delphi the main road leads southwards through the largest olive grove in Greece, passing **Itéa**, a busy port. The church of Agios Nikólaos, 17 km (11 miles) west, stands prominently on a hill surrounded by the old stone buildings of **Galaxídi**. The history of the town is told in the Nautical Museum while the 19th-century mansions at the waterfront are reminders of the great wealth brought by the town's shipbuilding industry. Though the industry cleared the region of trees, a reforestation scheme begun early in the 20th century has successfully restored the area to its former beauty. The next major town is **Náfpaktos**. Though perhaps less attractive than Galaxídi, it still possesses plenty of charm and character.

A Venetian fortress stands above the town, its ramparts running down as far as the beach, almost enclosing the harbour. The Venetian name for the town was Lepanto. In 1571, the famous naval Battle of Lepanto (see p38), in which the Venetians, Spanish and Genoese defeated the Ottomans, was fought here. A popular story to emerge from the battle purports that the Spanish author Miguel de Cervantes (1547–1616) lost an arm in the conflict, though in fact only his left hand was maimed.

At **Antírrio** the coast comes closest to the Peloponnese, and from here a regular car ferry sails across the stretch of water known as the "little Dardanelles" to Río, on the southern shore. In addition, a new suspension bridge is being built. Beside the harbour stands the originally Frankish and Venetian Kástro Roúmelis. Another castle can be seen across the water on the Peloponnese.

Nautical Museum
Mouseíou 4, Galaxídi. 22650 41795. daily. main public hols.

Mesolóngi 21
Μεσολόγγι

Stereá Elláda. **Road map** B3.
12,000. Spyridonos Trikoupí 29 (26310 27220). Tue & Sat.

MEANING "amid the lagoons", Mesolóngi is a town perfectly located for fishing, though the industry is now in decline. In 1821 the town became a centre of resistance to the Turks during the War of Independence (see pp40–41), when a leader, Aléxandros Mavrokordátos, set up his headquarters here. In January 1824 Lord Byron (see p149) came to fight for the liberation of Greece, but died of a fever in April. His heart lies beneath his statue in the Garden of Heroes. Nearby, the Gate of the Exodus is a tribute to those who fought the Turks in 1826. After 12 months, 9,000 battled their way through the blockade; those left behind detonated their explosives just as they were taken by the enemy. This self-sacrifice led to the Turks surrendering Mesolóngi in 1828 without firing a shot.

Statue of Lord Byron at Mesolóngi

SALTPAN BIRDLIFE

With its importance for food preservation, the production of salt is a major enterprise in the Mediterranean, the most extensive areas in Greece being around Mesolóngi and the Amvrakikós Gulf. Seawater is channelled into large artificial lakes, or saltpans, which, with their high concentrations of salt, attract a large amount of wildlife. Brine shrimps thrive, providing food for a wide variety of birds. Two of the most striking waders are the avocet and the great egret, though also common is the black-winged stilt with its long red legs. The area is also home to Kentish plovers, stone curlews, and the short-toed lark.

Avocet

Great egret

The fortified harbour of Náfpaktos in the Gulf of Corinth

Ancient Delphi ⑲

Δελφοί

**Siphnian
Treasury
caryatid**

ACCORDING TO LEGEND, when Zeus released two eagles from opposite ends of the world their paths crossed in the sky above Delphi, establishing the site as the centre of the earth. Renowned as a dwelling place of Apollo, from the end of the 8th century BC individuals from all over the ancient world visited Delphi to consult the god on what course of action to take, in both public and private life. With the political rise of Delphi in the 6th century BC and the reorganization of the Pythian Games *(see p230)*, the sanctuary entered a golden age which lasted until the Romans came in 191 BC. The oracle was abolished in AD 393 with the Christianization of the Byzantine Empire under Theodosius.

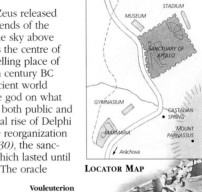

LOCATOR MAP

Modern
Delfoí

STADIUM

MUSEUM

SANCTUARY OF
APOLLO

GYMNASIUM

CASTALIAN
SPRING

MARMARIA

MOUNT
PARNASSUS

Aráchova

**Vouleuterion
(Delphic Council
House)**

**To museum
(see p231)**

The Athenian Treasury was built after the Battle of Marathon *(see p145)* and reconstructed in 1906.

**Siphnian
Treasury**

SACRED WAY

SACRED WAY

THE ORACLE OF DELPHI

The Delphic Oracle was the means through which worshippers could hear the words of the god Apollo, spoken through a priestess, or *Pythia*, over the age of 50. Questioners paid a levy called a *pelanos* and sacrificed an animal on the altar. The question was then put to the *Pythia* by a male priest. The *Pythia* would answer in a trance, perhaps induced by vapours from a crack in the ground over which she sat on a tripod. Her incantations were interpreted by the priest, though the answers were often ambiguous. King Croesus of Lydia (reigned 560–546 BC) came to ask if he should make war against Cyrus the Great of Persia and was told that if he crossed a river then he would destroy a great empire. In marching on Cyrus his troops crossed the River Halys and he did destroy an empire, though it turned out to be his own.

The main entrance was once a market place (agora) where religious objects could be bought.

The Rock of the Sibyl marks the place where, according to legend, Delphi's first prophetess pronounced her oracles.

★ **Sacred Way**
Leading to the Temple of Apollo, this path was lined with up to 3,000 statues and treasuries, built by city-states to house their people's offerings.

◁ **Dramatic view over the theatre at Delphi**

THE SANCTUARY OF APOLLO

Also known as the Sacred Precinct, this is at the
heart of a complex that also included a stadium and
a sacred spring *(see pp230–31)*. It is entered through
an agora from which the Sacred Way winds through
the ruins of memorials and treasuries.

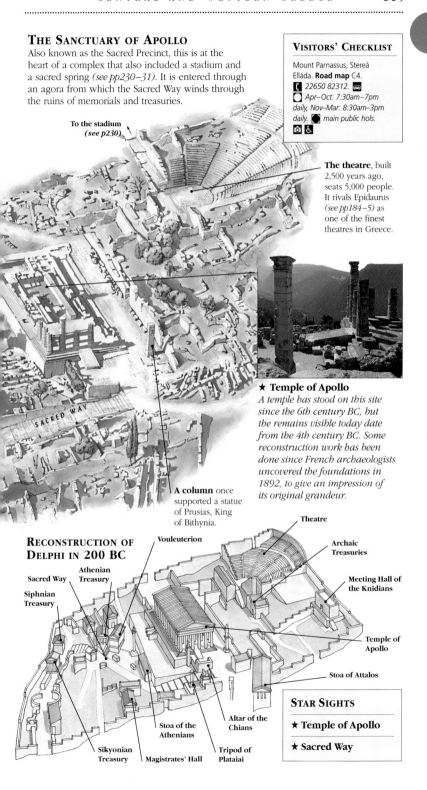

To the stadium
(see p230)

VISITORS' CHECKLIST

Mount Parnassus, Stereá
Elláda. **Road map** C4.
📞 22650 82312. 📠
🕒 Apr–Oct: 7:30am–7pm
daily, Nov–Mar: 8:30am–3pm
daily. ● main public hols.
📷 ♿

The theatre, built
2,500 years ago,
seats 5,000 people.
It rivals Epidaurus
(see pp184–5) as
one of the finest
theatres in Greece.

★ Temple of Apollo
*A temple has stood on this site
since the 6th century BC, but
the remains visible today date
from the 4th century BC. Some
reconstruction work has been
done since French archaeologists
uncovered the foundations in
1892, to give an impression of
its original grandeur.*

A column once
supported a statue
of Prusias, King
of Bithynia.

SACRED WAY

**RECONSTRUCTION OF
DELPHI IN 200 BC**

Vouleuterion

Theatre

Athenian
Treasury

Archaic
Treasuries

Sacred Way

Meeting Hall of
the Knidians

Siphnian
Treasury

Temple of
Apollo

Stoa of Attalos

Sikyonian
Treasury

Magistrates' Hall

Stoa of the
Athenians

Altar of the
Chians

Tripod of
Plataiai

STAR SIGHTS

★ Temple of Apollo

★ Sacred Way

Exploring Delphi

THE FIRST EXCAVATIONS at Delphi began in 1892, uncovering a much larger area than is apparent now. Though it is most famous for the Sanctuary of Apollo, Delphi also had a sanctuary dedicated to the goddess Athena, whose temple, along with a structure known as the *tholos*, can be seen in a second enclosure to the south. North of the theatre is the stadium where the Pythian Games were held. These, after the Olympic Games *(see p173)*, were the most important sporting event in the Greek calendar, providing an opportunity for strengthening the ethnic bond of the Greek nation which was otherwise divided into predominantly rival city-states.

Caryatid from the Siphnian Treasury

The Stadium, viewed from the remains of the entrance archway

Marmaria Precinct

Southeast of the Temple of Apollo, a path leads to the Marmaria Precinct, or "marble quarry", where the Sanctuary of Athena Pronaia can be found. At the sanctuary's entrance stand the ruins of a 4th-century BC temple dedicated to Athena. At the far end of the sanctuary are the remains of an earlier temple

to the goddess, which was built around 510 BC. Between the two temples stands the Marmaria's most remarkable, and most photographed, monument: the circular *tholos*. The purpose of this structure is still unknown. The rotunda dates from the start of the 4th century BC, and was originally surrounded by 20 columns. Three of

these columns were re-erected in 1938. They stand to provide some hint of the building's former beauty.

Stadium

This is one of the very best-preserved stadia in the country. Almost 200 m (655 ft) long and partly hewn out of the rocks above the main sanctuary, it held 7,000 spectators who gathered for the field and track events every four years during the Pythian Games. The games grew out of a musical festival, held in the theatre every eight years, to celebrate Apollo's mythical slaying of the serpent Python *(see p228)*. Though poetry and musical recitals remained central to the occasion, from 582 BC athletic events in the stadium were added and the festival became known as the Pythian Games. All prizes in these tournaments were purely honorary; each winner was awarded the traditional laurel wreath and the right to have his statue in the sanctuary.

Made entirely of limestone from Mount Parnassus, the present structure dates from Roman times and most of the seating is still intact. The best-preserved seats are the backed benches on the north side, made for the presidents of the games and honoured guests.

Castalian Spring

Before entering the Sacred Precinct, it is believed that everyone visiting Delphi for religious purposes, including

The *tholos* beside the Sanctuary of Athena Pronaia, Marmaria Precinct

athletes, was required to purify themselves in the clear but icy waters of the Castalian Spring – this process principally involved the washing of their hair. The Oracle *Pythia* *(see p228)* would also wash here before making her pronouncements. The visible remains of the fountain date either from the late Hellenistic or the early Roman period. A number of niches in the surrounding rock once held the votive offerings left for the nymph Castalia, to whom the spring was dedicated.

It is said that the British romantic poet Lord Byron *(see p149)* once plunged into the spring, inspired by the belief that the waters would enhance the poetic spirit.

The niches of the Castalian Spring

⋔ Gymnasium
Water from the Castalian Spring ran down to this area to provide cold baths (until the Romans added hot baths in the 2nd century AD) for athletes training for the Pythian Games. The original cold baths, which can be seen in a square courtyard, are some 9 m (30 ft) in diameter. East of the baths lies the Palaestra, or training area, surrounded by the remains of what once were changing rooms and training quarters. As well as an outdoor running track, a covered track 180 m (590 ft) in length provided a venue for the games in bad weather. The gymnasium was also used for intellectual pursuits – Delphi's poets and philosophers taught here – and built on many levels due to the sloping terrain.

🏛 Delphi Museum
The museum at Delphi contains a collection of sculptures and architectural remains of an importance second only to those of the Athenian Acropolis *(see pp94–101)*. Just inside the entrance stands the Omphalos, or "navel" stone. This is a Hellenistic or Roman copy of the stone that was believed to have marked the place above which Zeus's eagles met, establishing the sanctuary of Delphi as the centre of the earth *(see p228)*.

There are 13 rooms of exhibits, all on the ground floor. In one of the rooms there is a scale model that reconstructs the Sanctuary of Apollo in a triumph of limestone whites, blue marble, gold and terracotta. Surrounded by friezes and statues, the extent of Delphi's size and its former beauty is represented vividly.

Votive chapels, or "treasuries", lined the Sacred Way *(see p228)* and contained offerings of thanks, in the form of money or works of art, from towns grateful for good fortune following a favourable prophecy from the Oracle. The Theban Treasury, for example, was established after the victory of Thebes at the Battle of Leuktra in 371 BC. There are two rooms

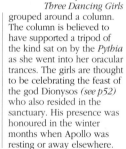

The bronze Charioteer

dedicated to the surviving sculpture from the Siphnian and Athenian treasuries, the wealth of the former illustrated by an outstanding frieze depicting the Greek heroes waging war on the giants.

The colossal Naxian Sphinx was presented by the wealthy citizens of Náxos in 560 BC; it stands 2.3 m (7.5 ft) high and once had its place atop a column reaching over 10 m (33 ft) in height.

The most famous of the museum's exhibits is a life-size bronze statue, the *Charioteer*. The statue was commissioned by a Sicilian tyrant named Polyzalos to commemorate a chariot victory in the Pythian Games in 478 BC. Another notable exhibit is the sculpture of *Three Dancing Girls* grouped around a column. The column is believed to have supported a tripod of the kind sat on by the *Pythia* as she went into her oracular trances. The girls are thought to be celebrating the feast of the god Dionysos *(see p52)* who also resided in the sanctuary. His presence was honoured in the winter months when Apollo was resting or away elsewhere.

Detail from the frieze of the Siphnian Treasury on display in the museum

NORTHERN GREECE

MACEDONIA · THRACE

ACEDONIA IS GREECE'S largest prefecture and contains the country's second city, Thessaloníki. It is the homeland of Alexander the Great, and the heart of the ancient Hellenistic empire. In contrast, Thrace has been largely influenced by Turkish culture but, like Macedonia, it is an area of comparatively unexplored natural beauty, with many mountain ranges and rivers.

The name Macedonia derives from the Makednoi, one of the tribes who first inhabited the region in the late 4th century BC. The legacy of the Macedonian Empire is evident in the many ancient sites, including Vergína, the location of Philip's tomb; Pélla, the birthplace of Alexander; and Díon, Philip's city in the foothills of Mount Olympos. During the reign of the Roman Emperor Galerius in the 3rd century AD, many fine monuments were built, including the landmark arch in Thessaloníki. The Byzantine era also left an outstanding legacy of architecture, seen in the many churches that abound throughout Northern Greece. Muslim influences remain strong, particularly

Head of Serapis in the Thessaloníki Archaeological Museum

in Thrace, where eastern-style bazaars and minarets can still be seen today. Macedonia and Thrace have a cooler, damper climate than much of Greece and hence a flourishing flora. Bordering Central Greece is the country's highest mountain, Olympos, and in the northwest lie the Préspa Lakes, part of a wildlife reserve. Local produce includes tobacco from Thrace, and wine from Náousa.

In contrast to the busy beaches on its western side, the Chalkidikí peninsula in Macedonia has the holy Mount Athos to the east. After a purported visit from the Virgin Mary, the Byzantine Emperor Monomáchos banished women and children from the site. This decree is still valid today.

Villagers at a taverna in the Néstos Valley

◁ Moní Grigoríou on the holy peninsula of Mount Athos

Exploring Northern Greece

NORTHERN GREECE OFFERS varied pleasures. The bustle of modern Thessaloníki can be combined with a beach holiday in Chalkidikí, or with an exploration of some of the ancient Macedonian sites. Lovers of natural history will appreciate the National Park around the Préspa Lakes on the border with Albania, and the Dadiá Forest and Evros River Delta to the east near Turkey. Walkers will want to explore the paths of Mount Olympos. Kastoriá and Kavála, two relatively little-known Greek towns, both reward a lengthy visit as well as making excellent bases for travelling further afield. Kavála offers access to the fascinating but little-visited region of Thrace. This region's three main towns – Xánthi, Komotiní and Alexandroúpoli – all offer the attractive combination of Greek and Turkish influence. Alexandroúpoli is also ideal as a family holiday resort with its beaches and seafront cafés.

A typical stall at the fruit and vegetable market in Xánthi, selling local produce

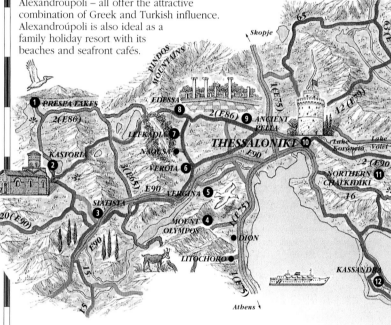

Reedbeds by the Mikrí Préspa lake

SIGHTS AT A GLANCE

GETTING AROUND

Thessaloníki's airport serves both international and domestic routes. Airports at Kastoriá, Kozáni and Alexandroúpoli are for domestic flights only. Ferry connections link Thessaloníki with the Sporades, and Kavála and Alexandroúpoli with the northern Aegean islands. Fast trains travel south from Thessaloníki to Athens, and east into Thrace and beyond to Istanbul. The main E75 highway runs south to Athens while the E90 highway joins Thessaloníki to Thrace. Buses go from Thessaloníki to Alexandroúpoli and Kastoriá.

LOCATOR MAP

| 0 kilometres | | 50 |
| 0 miles | 20 | |

NESTOS VALLEY 16
XANTHI 17
KOMOTINI 19
Lake Vistonída
DADIA FOREST 22
PHILIPPI
2 (E90)
2 (E90)
KAVALA 15
AVDIRA 18
MARONEIA 20
Istanbul
ALEXANDROUPOLI 21

SEE ALSO

• *Where to Stay* pp273–5

• *Where to Eat* pp294–5

MOUNT ATHOS 14

SITHONIA 13

KEY

≈≈≈	Dual-carriageway
▬▬▬	Major road
▬▬▬	Minor road
≈≈≈	Scenic route
≈≈	River
⁂	Viewpoint

The harbour of Kavála, in eastern Macedonia

Beautiful landscape of the Préspa Lakes

Préspa Lakes ❶
Εθνικός Δρυμός Πρεσπών

Macedonia. **Road map** B1.
🚌 to Flórina. 🛈 Agios Germanós
(23850 51452); Psarádes (23850
46316).

THIS IS THE ONLY national
park in Greece which is
made up largely of water. It
is one of the mainland's most
beautiful and unspoilt places

and was little visited until recently because of its rather
inaccessible location. The
border with Albania runs
through the southwest corner
of the Megáli Préspa lake,
joining the border of the
Former Yugoslav Republic of
Macedonia. The Greek area of
the lake, together with the
smaller Mikrí Préspa lake and
surrounding countryside, make
up the 255 sq km (100 sq

miles) of national park,
established in 1974. The area
is so important for wildlife
that Mikrí Préspa and the
reed beds that fringe it form
a park within a park, a core
of some 49 sq km (19 sq
miles) regarded as a com-
plete protection area. The
boundary of the core area is
clearly indicated by signs to
prevent accidental trespass.

Over 1,300 species of plant
can be found here, including
the endemic *Centaurea
prespana*, which has small
daisy-like flowers. There are
over 40 species of mammal,
such as bears, wolves, otters,
roe deer, wild boar and wild
cats. The area is also one of
the last remaining breeding
refuges in Europe for the
Dalmatian pelican, whose
numbers are down to less
than 1,000 pairs worldwide,
with about 150 of those
nesting in the Préspa Lakes.

Wetland Wildlife

IN CONTRAST TO THE DRY AND STONY terrain found
in much of Greece, the north has some
outstanding wetlands with a range of different
habitats. Reed-fringed lake margins hold large
colonies of breeding birds and amphibians,
while the open water is home to numerous
fish and aquatic insects. The marshes are rich
in flowers and full of songbirds; the manmade habitats such as saltpans and lagoons
offer sanctuary to nesting waders.

*Lake Korónia is easy to view from nearby
villages, most of which have their own
colonies of white storks. In spring, terrapins
and frogs gather in the shallow
margins of the lake.*

Kentish plovers nest on
the margins of wetlands,
such as the Préspa Lakes.

Kastoriá

Macedonia

Thessaloníki

The Préspa Lakes *support
colonies of rare Dalmatian
pelicans. When nesting they
need the peace and quiet
this protected area provides.*

The Axiós Delta is home
to dragonflies and, on the
margins, a wealth of spring
flowers and bee orchids.

Whipsnakes are common in
northern Greece, particularly
around Lake Korónia.

Other birds more frequently seen include herons, cormorants, egrets, storks, golden eagles and goosanders.

Scattered around the lakes are several small villages. One of these, on the shore of Megáli Préspa, is **Psarádes**, a pretty, traditional village where fishermen provide a boat service on to the lake.

Psarádes village on the banks of Megáli Préspa

From the boat you can see hermitages, icons painted on the rocks by the shore, and two churches: the 15th-century **Panagía Eleoúsa** and the 13th-century **Metamórfosi**. To the east of Mikrí Préspa is **Mikrolímni**. The village has wet meadows to the north that are rich in birdlife. Southwest of Mikrolímni a path leads to the Ellinikí Etaireía Biological Station, used as a base by research scientists who want to stay in the area while studying.

In summer, the beaches of fine, pale sand that stretch alongside Megáli Préspa can be enjoyed along with a dip in the blue, but rather cold, waters of the lake.

Fresco from Metamórfosi church

ENVIRONS: Northeast of the park lies the village of **Agios Germanós**, which has an 11th-century Byzantine church and a number of pretty, traditional houses, built in the local architectural style. The village is also home to the **Préspa Information Centre** which has a permanent exhibition explaining the ecological importance of the Préspa National Park. Guides are available to show visitors around the park, but this must be arranged in advance with the centre.

Just out of the village, a road leads up to the summits of Kaló Neró, at 2,160 m (7,090 ft) and Mázi, at 2,060 m (6,760 ft), which give superb views across the lakes below.

The Evros Delta *lies close to the border with Turkey and access to many of the best areas can be difficult. Numerous water birds, including little egrets, nest and feed in easily viewed locations.*

Glossy ibises *have one of their last remaining European strongholds in the wetlands of northern Greece. Seen in good light, their feathers have a metallic sheen.*

Purple herons nest in the reedbeds of the Evros Delta.

Pórto Lágos's lagoons, pools and marshes are a haven for ruddy shelducks.

Xánthi

Kavála

Thrace

Alexandroúpoli

The Néstos Delta *is one of the finest wetlands in Greece. Many species of birds inhabit the extensive reedbanks and clumps of trees, in particular large breeding colonies of herons and egrets.*

KEY

☐	Préspa Lakes
☐	Axiós Delta
☐	Lake Korónia
☐	Néstos Delta
☐	Pórto Lágos
☐	Evros Delta
—	National boundary

0 kilometres 50

0 miles 50

Fishing on the Préspa Lakes in the early morning ▷

Kastoriá
Καστοριά

Macedonia. **Road map** B2. 🏛 17,000.
✈ 10 km (6 miles) S of Kastoriá. 🚌
🛈 24670 26777. 🕐 Wed.

KASTORIA IS THE GREEK for "place of beavers". These animals used to live in Lake Kastoriá (also known as Lake Orestiáda) by which the town stands, one of the loveliest settings in Greece. Evidence of a prehistoric settlement was unearthed here in 1940. In 200 BC the Romans captured the town, then known as Keletron. The beavers first brought the furriers here in the 17th century and, despite the fact that the animals were extinct in the area by the 19th century, trading continued. By then the furriers were also importing unwanted fur scraps, including mink castoffs, and making desirable garments out of them. The fur trade exists today, with the craftsmen still making the fur coats that can be bought in shops here, in Thessaloníki and Athens.

The town prospered as a result of the fur trade, as its several remaining 17th- and 18th-century mansions testify *(see p20)*. Most of these are found in the southeast quarter of the town. The elegant Skoutári and Nanzí mansions have interior courtyards and three floors. The ground floor in each case is built of stone; the upper two are made of wood. They have fine timbered rooms fitted with cupboards, hearths and raised platforms. The lower stone floor is used for storage, while the living quarters are in the wooden upper floor which juts out over the street.

The town's **Folk Museum** is housed in the Aïvazí mansion. Built in the 15th century, it was lived in until as recently as 1972. It now has an eloquent display of the lifestyle of the wealthy fur traders. There is typically elaborate

The Skoutári mansion in Kastoriá, built in the 18th century

woodwork in the salon on the upper floor. The kitchens beneath and the wine cellar have also been restored.

Another notable feature of the town are its many Byzantine churches. Fifty-four survive, and most are listed as ancient monuments, including the 11th-century **Panagía Koumbelídiki**, situated towards the south end of Mitropóleos. The church is named after its unusually tall dome (or *kubbe*, in Turkish). Some of the churches are tiny and hidden away in Kastoriá's labyrinth of streets, as they were originally private chapels. Many are closed to the public, with some of their icons removed, most of which are now on display in the **Byzantine Museum**, which is also confusingly referred to as the Archaeological Museum. The collection is small, with the

Apse and cupola of Panagía Koumbelídiki

exhibit labels only in Greek, but there are some exquisite pieces on display, including some fine icons.

📷 **Folk Museum**
Kapetán Lázou. 📞 24670 28603.
🕐 daily. 🚫 🌑 main public hols.

📷 **Byzantine Museum**
Plateía Dexamenís. 📞 24670 26781.
🕐 Tue–Sun. 🌑 main public hols.

Siátista ❸
Σιάτιστα

Macedonia. **Road map** B2. 🏛 5,000.
🛈 Plateía Tsistopoúlou (24650 21280).

SIATISTA WAS FOUNDED in the 1430s, after the Turkish conquest of Thessaloníki. Like Kastoriá, the town flourished as a result of the fur trade despite the lack of local fur. Sable and martin remnants were brought in, mainly from Russia, made up into garments in Siátista, and then traded or sold in Western Europe.

The wealth that this created in the 18th century went into the building of many fine mansion houses *(see p20)*, very similar to those in Kastoriá. The Ottoman influence in their decoration is strong. The **Nerantzopoúlou** mansion is one of several in the town that can be visited. Keys and directions to the other mansions, including the **Manoúsi** and **Poulkídou**, can also be obtained here.

🏛 **Nerantzopoúlou Mansion**
Plateía Chorí. 🕐 Tue–Sun.
🌑 main public hols.

View across Siátista, in the Mount Askion range, western Macedonia

The impressive peaks of the Mount Olympos range rising above the village of Litóchoro

Mount Olympos ❹
Όλυμπος

17 km (10 miles) W of Litóchoro,
Macedonia. **Road map** C2. 🚌 Litóchoro. 🚹 EOS: Evángelou Karavákou
20, Litóchoro (23520 81111).

THE NAME Mount Olympos
refers to the whole range
of mountains, 20 km (12 miles)
across. The highest
peak in the range,
at 2,917 m (9,571
ft), is Mýtikas. The
whole area consti-
tutes the Olympos
National Park.

An estimated
1,700 plant species
are to be found
here, many of them
endemic to the park.
Chamois, boars and roe deer
also live within this area.

The base for walkers is the
village of **Litóchoro**, a lively
place with several hotels and
tavernas from which to choose.
Walking maps are available
here and a marked trail leads
up into the national park.
Mýtikas can be reached in a
demanding walk of at least
six hours. It is imperative to
camp out overnight or stay
in one of the two mountain
refuges, rather than attempt
to get up and down in a day.

ENVIRONS: About 10 km
(6 miles) north of Litóchoro
is the village of Díon, which
has an excellent museum
showing finds from **Ancient
Díon**. This site is near the

**Roman mosaic from
Ancient Díon**

modern village and splendidly
set between the coast and the
Olympian peaks, its very name
deriving from *Díos*, or "of
Zeus". To the Macedonians
it was a holy city and in the
4th century BC some 15,000
people lived here. The flat
plains were used as a military
camp and rallying point by
King Philip II of Macedon (see
pp32–3). Although
Díon was primarily
a military camp,
rather than a civil-
ian city, there was
a temple to Zeus,
a theatre and a sta-
dium at the site.
Later, the Romans
built a city here.
The ruins that can
be seen today date
mainly from that era, and include fine mosaics from the
2nd century AD and some
well-preserved Roman baths.

The remains also include a
theatre and the remnants of
a sanctuary dedicated to the
Egyptian goddess Isis. She was
worshipped by the Romans
as a foreign deity, along with
many others that were similarly
"adopted" into the pantheon.

The bright and modern
Díon Museum in the village
shows films of the excavations in several languages,
and it is worth seeing before
visiting the site. Also on display are toys, kitchen utensils
and jewellery, all finds from
the sanctuary of Isis. Together
they give a vivid picture of
life in Ancient Díon.

⋔ Ancient Díon
E of Díon. ◯ daily. ● main
public hols. ✎ except Sun.
⋔ Díon Museum
Díon. 🕻 23510 53206. ◯ daily.
● main public hols.
✎ except Sun.

THE HOME OF ZEUS

Zeus, chief and most powerful
of the ancient Greek gods, lived
on Mount Olympos along with
the other immortals and was
thought to be responsible for the
destinies of men. He was also god
of weather and thunderstorms.
Many of the myths tell of Zeus's
amorous liaisons and his numerous
children, some of whom were
gods or goddesses and some
heroes (see pp52–3). He was
worshipped at Olympia and
at Dodóni in Epirus, site of
the oldest oracle in Greece.

Vergína **5**
Βεργίνα

12 km (7 miles) SE of Véroia, Macedonia. **Road map** C2. 🚌 🏨 *at archaeological site (23310 92394).*

Outside the village of Vergína, during excavations in 1977, archaeologist Professor Manólis Andrónikos found an entrance to a tomb. The bones inside included a skull with one eye socket damaged, evidence that the tomb belonged to King Philip II of Macedon, who received such a wound in the siege of Methóni. The bones were discovered in a stunning gold funerary box, embellished with the symbol of the Macedonian Sun. The discovery confirmed that this area was the site of Aigai, the first capital of Macedon. The finds from this tomb, as well as several other **Royal Tombs** nearby, included many more gold objects as well as other items. They are now on display here and are considered the most important in Greece since Schliemann's discoveries at Mycenae *(see pp178–80).*

A short walk further along the road from Philip's tomb are some earlier discoveries, known as the **Macedonian**

Terracotta head of a young man, from the Museum at Véroia

Tombs. The dark interior hides splendid solid marble doors, as well as a beautiful marble throne.

The **Palace of Palatítsia** stands beyond on a mound. It is thought to have been first occupied in about 1000 BC, though the building itself dates from the 3rd century BC. Today only low foundations remain, along with the ruins of a theatre 100 m (330 ft) below, thought to be the site of Philip II's assassination.

⋔ Royal Tombs, Macedonian Tombs, Palace of Palatítsia
📞 23310 92347. ⏰ Jan–May: Tue–Sun; Jun–Dec: daily. ● main public hols. 📷

The Macedonian Royal Family

The gold burial casket found at Vergína is emblazoned with the Macedonian Sun, the symbol of the king. Philip II was from a long line of Macedonian kings, that began in about 640 BC with Perdiccas I. Philip was the first ruler to unite the whole of Greece as it existed at that time. Also incorrectly known as the Macedonian Star, the Sun is often seen on flags within the region. Much of Greece's pride in the symbol lies in the fact that Alexander the Great used it throughout his empire *(see pp32–3).* He was just 20 when his father was assassinated at Aigai in 336 BC. He inherited his father's already large empire and also his ambition to conquer the Persians.

In 334 BC Alexander crossed the Dardanelles with 40,000 men and defeated the Persians in three different battles, advancing as far as the Indus Valley before he died at the age of 33. With his death the Macedonian Empire divided.

Burial casket featuring the Macedonian Sun

Véroia **6**
Βέροια

Macedonia. **Road map** C2.
🚶 48,000. 🚌 🚉 🏨 *Mitropóleos 47 (23310 23977).* 🛒 Tue.

The largest town in the region, Véroia is interesting mainly for its 50 or so barnlike churches, which have survived from the 17th and 18th centuries.

The town's **Archaeological Museum** has a selection of interesting exhibits, discovered locally, and the bazaar area bustles on market days, as Véroia is the centre of the local peach-growing industry.

🏛 Archaeological Museum
Anoixéos 47. 📞 23310 24972.
⏰ Tue–Sun. ● main public hols. 📷

Chília Déndra park at Náousa, near Lefkádia

Lefkádia **7**
Λευκάδια

Macedonia. **Road map** C2.
📞 23320 41121. 🚌 ⏰ Tue–Sun. ● main public hols.

The four Macedonian Tombs of Lefkádia are set in a quiet agricultural area. The caretaker is usually at one of the two tombs that are signposted. The first of these is the **Tomb of the Judges**, or Great Tomb. This, the largest tomb, with a chamber 9 m (30 ft) square and a frescoed façade portraying Aiakos and Rhadamanthys, the Judges of Hades, has been recently restored. Beyond is the **Anthemíon Tomb**, or Tomb

Pebble mosaic of the Lion Hunt from the House of the Lion Hunt at Ancient Pélla

of the Flowers, with well-preserved flower paintings on the roof. The key to the **Tomb of Lyson and Kallikles** is sometimes available from the caretaker. The entrance is through a metal grate in the roof. The fourth tomb, called the **Tomb of Kinch** after its Danish discoverer, or the **Tomb of Niafsta** after its one-time occupant, is closed to visitors.

ENVIRONS: Renowned for the large park of Agios Nikólaos, also known as Chília Déndra (1,000 trees), **Náousa** is the home of the Boutari wine-making family. It is situated on the edge of the hills above the plain that extends east to Thessaloníki. Like Edessa, Náousa has waters flowing through it. Riverside tavernas in the park offer fresh trout as well as the good local wine.

Edessa ❽
Έδεσσα

Macedonia. **Road map** C1.
🏛 *16,000*. 🚌 🚊 🛈 *Plateía Egon 1 (23810 23444)*. 🛒 *Thu*.

Edessa is the capital of the modern Pélla region and a popular summer resort. It is renowned for its waterfalls, which plunge down a ravine from the town to the valley floor below. The largest fall is the **Káranos**, at 24 m (79 ft), which has a cave behind it. The surrounding gardens and park are pleasant, with cafés and restaurants.

Ancient Pélla ❾
Πέλλα

38 km (24 miles) NW of Thessaloníki, Macedonia. **Road map** C1. 🚌
📞 *23820 31278*. 🕐 *Tue–Sun*.
🌐 *main public hols*. 🅿 ♿

This small site, which straddles the main road, was once the flourishing capital of Macedon. The court was moved here from

Káranos waterfall at Edessa

Aigai (near modern Vergína) in 410 BC by King Archelaos, who ruled from 413 to 399 BC. It is here that Alexander the Great was born in 356 BC, and later tutored by the philosopher Aristotle. Some sense of the existence of a city can be gained from a plan of the site, which shows where the main street and shops were located. The palace is believed to have been north of the main site, but is still being excavated.

At the site, and in the museum, are some of the best-preserved and most beautiful pebble mosaics in Greece. The stones are uncut and have been carefully picked not only for their size, but also for their warm, subtle colouring. Dating from about 300 BC, the mosaics include vivid hunting scenes. One of the most famous is of Dionysos riding a panther, which is protected from the weather in the now-covered House of the Lion Hunt. This was built at the end of the 4th century BC and originally comprised 12 rooms around three open court-yards, the whole structure being 90 m (295 ft) long by 50 m (165 ft) wide.

Thessaloníki ⑩

Θεσσαλονίκη

THESSALONIKI, ALSO KNOWN AS Salonica, is Greece's second city, founded by King Kassandros in 315 BC. The Romans made it capital of their province of Macedonia Prima in 146 BC, and in AD 395 it became part of the Byzantine Empire. In 1430 it was captured by the Turks who held it until 1912. Today Thessaloníki is a bustling cosmopolitan city. It has a flourishing cultural life and is a major religious centre, with an array of splendid churches *(see p248)*, such as Agía Sofía and Agios Dimítrios, which is the largest church in Greece.

Lion from the Archaeological Museum

Exploring Thessaloníki

Greece's second city is also a very busy port, which adds to the bustle and the wealth of this fascinating metropolis. Situated on the Thermaic Gulf, it has an attractive waterfront promenade, known as the *paralía*, and a pleasant leafy park. It also boasts a large number of beautiful Byzantine churches *(see p248)*. In recent years Thessaloníki has developed its international exhibition facilities and become a major trade fair centre. The city has many museums, including the Archaeological Museum *(see pp246–7)*.

The Great Fire of August in 1917 destroyed nearly half the buildings within the medieval walls, including the entire Jewish quarter. Some, however, survived, and many from the

Furniture shop in the back streets

original Ottoman bazaar have been recently restored. One such building is the **Bezestèni**, once a hall for valuables and now home to plush shops. The **Modiáno**, a covered meat and produce hall, is named after the Jewish family who once owned it. West of Modiano are some of the best *ouzerí* bars, and **Plateía Aristotélous** is home to many posh cafés.

⋔ Arch of Galerius

Egnatía.

The principal architectural legacy of Roman rule is found at the eastern end of the long main street, Egnatía, which was itself a Roman construction, known as Via Egnatia. Here stands the Arch of Galerius, built in AD 303 by Galerius (then Caesar of the East, or deputy emperor) to celebrate his victory over the Persians in AD 297. Its carvings show scenes from the battle.

Section of carving from the Arch of Galerius

Cafés and fountains in the park near Plateía Chánth

There was once a double arch here, with a palace to the south. Some of its remains can be seen in Plateía Navarínou.

▦ White Tower

On the waterfront. 📞 2310 267832. ○ 8am–7pm Tue– Fri, 8:30am–3pm Sat, Sun. 🎫

Probably Thessaloníki's most famous sight is the White Tower on the *paralía*. Built in 1430, the Turks added three such towers to the 8-km (5-mile) city walls. Today it holds a collection of Byzantine icons and historical displays on several floors of small circular rooms. The original stone steps climb up to a roof with lovely views of the *paralía*.

▦ Rotónda

Filíppou.

Standing north of the Arch of Galerius is the Rotónda. It is thought that this impressive building was constructed as a Mausoleum for Galerius, emperor of the eastern Roman Empire AD 305–311. Today it is closed, but it has been used in the past both as a church – it is also known as Agios Geórgios – and as a mosque. The minaret nearby is now the only one in Thessaloníki.

▣ Museum of Byzantine Culture

Leofórou Stratoú 2. 📞 2310 868570. ○ 10:30–3pm Mon, 8:30am–3pm Tue–Sun. ● main public hols. 🎫 ♿

Situated behind the Archaeological Museum *(see pp246–7)*, this small, modern museum was opened in 1995. On display are Byzantine icons that date from the 15th to the 19th centuries, and also some fine jewellery. All of the items are beautifully displayed and lit, and there are plans to expand the collection.

White Tower on the seafront

was under Turkish rule. Photographs, newspapers, weapons, documents and personal items tell the story well. Vivid tableaux depict the struggle and its effect on ordinary people. In one, a Turk with a rifle bursts violently into a schoolroom while a Greek freedom fighter hides under the floorboards. This was the celebrated Pávlos Melás, who fought to free Macedonia from the Turks. Also on display in the museum, are his gun and dagger.

VISITORS' CHECKLIST

Macedonia. **Road map** C2.
🏙 1,000,000. ✈ 25 km (15 miles) SE of Thessaloníki. 🚢 off Koundouriótou. 🚉 Monastiríou. 🚌 Plateía Dikastírion (local buses) 28 Octovríou (long distance). ℹ Mitropóleus 34 & Aristotélous (2310 271888). 🎬 Thessaloniki Cultural Festival (cinema): Oct.

🔟 Museum of the Macedonian Struggle

Proxénou Koromilá 23. 🕻 2310 229778. ⭕ Tue–Sun. ⚫ main public hols.

This is situated in a late 19th-century mansion which originally housed the Greek Consulate when Thessaloníki

🔟 Folklife and Ethnological Museum

Vasilíssis Olgas 68. 🕻 2310 812343. ⭕ 9am–2pm Fri–Wed.

This museum, which recently underwent major renovation, is a 20-minute walk from the Archaeological Museum

directly along Vasilíssis Olgas. There are displays of folk costumes, and detailed small models showing rural activities such as breadmaking, ploughing, winnowing, threshing, and children playing. The gruelling life of the nomadic Sarakatsan shepherds is well documented, and a vivid display shows the incredible events at the annual fire-walking ceremony in Lagkadás, a village 20 km (12 miles) northeast of Thessaloníki. The museum also has an extensive archive of fascinating period photography showing the reality of life during the early 20th century.

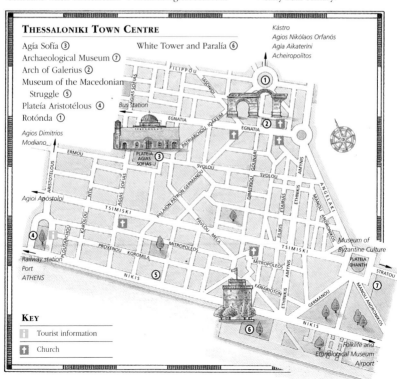

THESSALONIKI TOWN CENTRE

Agía Sofía ③
Archaeological Museum ⑦
Arch of Galerius ②
Museum of the Macedonian Struggle ⑤
Plateía Aristotélous ④
Rotónda ①

White Tower and Paralía ⑥

Kástro
Agios Nikólaos Orfanós
Agía Aikateríni
Acheiropoíitos

Agios Dimítrios
Modiano
Agioi Apóstoloi
Railway station
Port
ATHENS

Bus Station

Museum of Byzantine Culture

Folklife and Ethnological Museum
Airport

KEY

ℹ Tourist information

✝ Church

Thessaloníki Archaeological Museum
Αρχαιολογικό Μουσείο Θεσσαλονίκης

THIS MODERN MUSEUM, opened in 1963, contains a host of treasures. It concentrates on the finds made within the city and at the many sites in Macedonia. The displays progress chronologically through the ages, giving a clear picture of the area's history. A further annexe was added in 1980, and this contains a number of fabulous gold items from ancient Macedon, including the treasures discovered during excavations at Macedonian cemeteries. The annexe also contains a small exhibition on the prehistory of Thessaloníki.

Glass Vase
During the Roman period, the art of colouring glass came into use, as in this pink vase. Craftsmen experimented with shapes and colours, and a wide variety of glass items have been recovered from Roman tombs in Thessaloníki.

Faïence Vase
Found in a 2nd-century BC grave in Thessaloníki, this ornate vase is from Ptolemaic Egypt and is the only such faïence vase in Greece. Depicted on the bas-relief, among other subjects, is a detail of the goddess Artemis in a forest.

GALLERY GUIDE
An outer circle of rooms surrounds a block of inner rooms which houses the finds from Síndos. The outer rooms progress from Neolithic, through Classical, to Roman and Hellenistic artifacts and mosaics. An annexe contains Macedonian gold, and in a room below them are prehistoric exhibits.

Main entrance

Outdoor courtyard with Roman floor mosaic

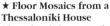

★ Floor Mosaics from a Thessaloníki House
These detailed mosaics depicting marine-world mythology are Roman. This mosaic shows a nereid (sea nymph) and a dolphin.

Marble Sarcophagus
This 2nd- or 3rd-century Roman sarcophagus is decorated with a vivid relief depicting an Amazon battle. The Amazons, a mythical warrior tribe of women, were a favourite subject for artists (see p55).

Statue of Harpokrates
The marble statue of Harpokrates, the son of Isis and Osiris, was found in Thessaloníki at the site of a sanctuary devoted to Serapis and other Egyptian gods. It has been dated to the end of the 2nd century.

VISITORS' CHECKLIST

Manóli Andrónikou & Leof Stratoú.
📞 2310 830538. 🚌 3. 🕐 8am–7pm Tue–Fri, 12:30–7pm Mon, 8:30am–3pm Sat, 8am–7pm Sun. ⬤ 1 Jan, 25 Mar, Easter, 1 May, 25, 26 Dec. 🖼 ♿

Head of Serapis
This fine marble head was discovered in the same sanctuary as the statue of Harpokrates and dates from the Roman period. Originally an Egyptian deity, Serapis was adopted by the Romans as a foreign cult.

★ Gold Bracelet from Europos
This gold bracelet is one of the highlights of the collection of Macedonian gold. It dates from the 3rd century BC and is accompanied in the exhibition by other gold finds of the 6th–2nd centuries BC.

KEY TO FLOORPLAN

- ☐ Prehistoric collection
- ☐ 2,300 years of Thessaloníki
- ☐ Finds from Síndos
- ☐ Macedonian Gold
- ☐ Roman collection
- ☐ Hellenistic collection
- ☐ Temporary exhibition space
- ☐ Non-exhibition space

★ Dervéni Krater
Dating from 300 BC, this bronze wine-mixing vase stands 1 m (3 ft) high. The detailed figures of maenads are exquisite; one is shown dancing with a satyr. The volutes at the top are decorated with the head of Herakles.

STAR EXHIBITS

★ Gold Bracelet from Europos

★ Floor Mosaics from a Thessaloníki House

★ Dervéni Krater

Exploring Thessaloníki's Churches

THESSALONIKI HAS THE RICHEST COLLECTION of Byzantine churches in Greece. Of the hundreds of 5th-century basilicas that once stood across the country, only two remain. Both of these, Agios Dimítrios and Acheiropoíïtos, are in Thessaloníki. The 8th-century Agía Sofía is a very significant Byzantine building, both for its mosaics and its role in influencing future architectural development. Three different 14th-century churches – Agios Nikólaos Orfanós, Agioi Apóstoloi and Agía Aikateríni – give an insight into what was a period of architectural innovation.

Agía Sofía church

The mosaic of Ezekiel's vision in Osios Davíd

🛈 Agios Dimítrios

Agiou Dimitríou. ◔ *Thu–Tue.* ♿

This, the largest church in Greece, was entirely rebuilt after the fire of 1917, which destroyed the 7th- and 13th-century fabric of the basilica. The oldest, 3rd-century AD portion is the crypt. Originally a Roman bath, this, according to legend, is the site of the imprisonment, torture and murder in 305 AD of the city's patron saint Dimítrios – a Roman soldier converted to Christianity and martyred on the orders of Emperor Galerius. Six small 5th–7th-century mosaics which survived the fire are found both on the piers flanking the altar and high up on the west side of the church. These mosaics rank among the finest in Greece and include depictions of Dimitrios with young children, or in the company of the church's builders.

🛈 Osios Davíd

Kástro. ◔ *daily.*

This delightful small chapel was founded some time in the late 5th century. Behind the altar is an original vivid mosaic of the *Vision of Ezekiel*, rare in that it depicts Christ without a beard. In marvellous condition, it owes its freshness to having been concealed beneath plaster and only discovered in 1921. There are also some frescoes from the 12th century, including a fine *Baptism* and *Nativity*. Although the church is usually locked, there is a caretaker who greets visitors and will unbolt the doors.

🛈 Agía Sofía

Plateia Agías Sofías. ◔ *daily.*

The church of Agía Sofía is dedicated to the Holy Wisdom (Sofiá) of God, just like the mosque of the same name in Istanbul. It was built in the mid-8th century. In 1585 it became a mosque, but was reconsecrated as a church in 1912. It contains many mosaics and frescoes dating back to the 9th and 10th centuries, including a fine *Ascension* scene in the 30-m (100-ft) high dome, which is 10 m (33 ft) in diameter. The entrance formerly had a portico, which was obliterated during an Italian air raid in 1941. The imposing nature of the building is emphasized by its location in a partially sunken garden.

🛈 Agios Nikólaos Orfanós

Kástro. ◔ *Tue–Sun; key available from warden at Irodhotou 17, opposite the church.* ♿

Situated in a garden plot amongst the lanes of the ancient Kástra district, or upper town, this small, triple-apsed 14th-century church began life as a dependency of the larger Moni Vlatádon, further up the hill. Today, Agios Nikólaos Orfanós retains the richest and best-preserved collection of late Byzantine frescoes in the city. Distributed over the central cella and both aisles, they show rare scenes from the Passion, including Christ mounting the Cross, and Pilate seated in judgement.

Agios Dimítrios, the largest church in Greece

The stretch of sandy beach at Kallithéa on Kassándra

Northern Chalkidikí ⓫
Βόρεια Χαλκιδική

Macedonia. **Road map** D2. ⬛ to Polýgyros.

THE NORTH OF CHALKIDIKI is a quiet and delightful hilly region, often overlooked by those whose main interests are the beaches to the south. A glimpse of the hidden interior is given when visiting the **Petrálona Caves**, situated on the edge of Mount Katsíka, 55 km (34 miles) southeast of Thessaloníki. It was in these red-rock caverns in 1960, the year after the caves were discovered by local villagers, that a skull was found. It was believed to be that of a young woman, aged about 25 when she died. A complete skeleton was subsequently discovered, and these are the oldest bones yet to be found in Greece, dating back at least 250,000 years, and possibly even 700,000. Amid the stalactites and stalagmites, reconstructions of the cave dwellers have been arranged in the caves, along with the bones, teeth and tools that were also found here.

In the northeast of the area is the small village of **Stágeira**, the birthplace of Aristotle (384–322 BC). On a hilltop, just outside the village, is a huge white marble statue of the philosopher, and there are sweeping views over the surrounding countryside.

Statue of Aristotle, Stágeira

🄽 **Petrálona Caves**
Mount Katsíka, 55 km (34 miles) SE of Thessaloníki. ◯ daily. ● main public hols. 🖼

Kassándra ⓬
Κασσάνδρα

Southern Chalkidikí, Macedonia. **Road map** D2. ⬛ to Kassándreia.

MUCH OF THIS area's population was killed in the War of Independence in 1821, and the numbers never really recovered. Little was left on the promontory of Kassándra other than a few fishing villages. However, over the last 30 years, many resorts have sprung up in this area.

Néa Poteídaia marks the start of Kassándra proper and straddles the narrow neck of the peninsula, with a good sandy beach, a marina and an attractive town square. On the west coast, **Sáni** has excellent beaches and a luxury resort complex. There are quiet bays around the village of **Possídi**, on a promontory halfway down the west coast. On the east coast, **Néa Fókaia** still functions as a fishing village in spite of the steady invasion of tourism, whereas **Kallithéa**, to the south, is the largest resort on Kassándra.

Sithonía ⓭
Σιθωνία

Southern Chalkidikí, Macedonia. **Road map** D2. ⬛ to Agios Nikólaos.

WHILE THE PENINSULA of Sithonía is only marginally larger than Kassándra, it has fewer resorts and a thickly wooded interior. The peninsula begins at **Metamórfosi** which has a sandy beach shaded by pine trees. **Vourvouroú** is one of the first villages you come to on the north side. A collection of villas spreads along the coast, with a few hotels and a selection of eating places.

To the south of this area is a long undeveloped stretch of coast, with several unspoilt beaches, until you reach the large resort of **Sárti**. At the tip of Sithonía is **Kalamítsi**, little more than a sandy beach and a few bars, while **Pórto Koufó** at the end of the west coast is still a pleasant fishing village set on a bay amid wooded hills. The **Pórto Karrás** resort complex, halfway down the west coast, was set up by the Karrás wine family. It has three hotels, a marina, a shopping centre, watersports, horseriding, a golf course and tennis.

Boats docked at Pórto Koufó on Sithonía

Mount Athos ⑭
Άγιον Όρος

To the Greeks, this is the Holy Mountain, which at 2,030 m (6,660 ft) is the highest point of Chalkidikí's most easterly peninsula. Unique in Greece, Athos is an autonomous republic ruled by the 1,700 monks who live

Mount Athos monk in its 20 monasteries. Only adult males may visit the peninsula, but it is possible to see many of the monasteries from a boat trip along the coast. Together, they include some fine examples of Byzantine architecture and provide an insight into monastic life.

THE MONASTERIES OF ATHOS

- - - Ferry route

Ouranoúpoli
The main town on Athos is where boat trips around the peninsula start.

Zográfou was founded around AD 971, but the present buildings are 18th- and 19th-century.

MOUNT ATHOS FROM THE WEST
This illustration shows the view seen when travelling by boat along the west of Athos. The most northerly monastery is Zográfou and the most southerly is Agíou Pávlou. The eastern monasteries are covered on p254.

Xiropotámou was founded in the 10th century, but the present buildings date from the 18th century.

← To Ouranoúpoli

Kastamonítou was founded in the 11th century by a hermit from Asia Minor.

Xenofóntos was founded in the late 10th century. A second chapel was built in 1837, incorporating some 14th-century mosaic panels.

0 kilometres   15

0 miles   10

Docheiaríou
This 10th-century monastery houses a fragment of the True Cross and an icon of the Virgin with healing powers.

Agíou Panteleímonos
Also known as Rousikón (of the Russians), this 12th-century monastery's imposing walls hide many colourful onion-domed churches, evidence of the Russian Orthodox influence on Athos.

◁ **The monastery of Agíou Panteleímonos, Mount Athos**

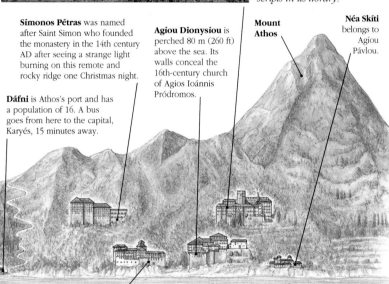

VISITORS' CHECKLIST

Athos Peninsula, Macedonia.
Road map D2 🚢 *Dáfni (boat
trips from Ouranoúpoli & Thessa-
loníki for the west coast, or from
Ierissós for the east coast).* 🚌 *to
Karyés.* 🎁 *donation.*

Agíou Pávlou
*This monastery houses 90
monks, many from Zákynthos
and Kefalloniá, and has some
13,000 books and manu-
scripts in its library.*

Néa Skíti
belongs to
Agíou
Pávlou.

**Mount
Athos**

Símonos Pétras was named
after Saint Simon who founded
the monastery in the 14th century
AD after seeing a strange light
burning on this remote and
rocky ridge one Christmas night.

Agíou Dionysíou is
perched 80 m (260 ft)
above the sea. Its
walls conceal the
16th-century church
of Agios Ioánnis
Pródromos.

Dáfni is Athos's port and has
a population of 16. A bus
goes from here to the capital,
Karyés, 15 minutes away.

Grigoríou
*Founded in the 14th century,
this monastery was totally
rebuilt after a disastrous fire
in 1761 which destroyed all
but a few holy relics. About
40 monks live here today.*

VISITING MOUNT ATHOS

Foreign visitors first need a letter
of recommendation from the
Greek consul in their country for
which a small charge will be
made. The Ministry of Foreign
Affairs in Athens, or Ministry of
Macedonia and Thrace in Thessaloníki, will then issue a permit to
visit Athos (to males only). Only
four permits are issued each day
in Athens, ten in Thessaloníki,
so the start date of your visit is
unpredictable and may be days
or weeks ahead. Permits allow a
stay of four nights, which may be extended by two nights.
Accommodation and meals are provided, with no payment
expected, although donations in the chapels will be appreciated. Visitors may be allowed into the services, and meals
are generally taken in communal refectories with the monks.

Vatopedíou refectory

Exploring Mount Athos

NOT ALL OF THE 20 MONASTERIES on Athos can be seen from the popular boat trips from Ouranoúpoli, although some boats do go round the whole peninsula. A few are hidden in the mountains and others cling to the eastern coast of the peninsula. In addition to the Greek Orthodox monasteries on Mount Athos, there is one Russian (Agíou Panteleímonos), one Bulgarian (Zográfou) and one Serbian (Chilandaríou). Remote hermitages and monastic villages in the hills of the peninsula are preferred by some monks, as a quieter alternative to the relatively busy monastery life.

The East Coast Monasteries

The first monastery to be founded on Athos was the **Megístis Lávras** (Great Lavra). It is situated at the southeastern end of the peninsula, on a rocky outcrop *(see pp36–7)*. It was founded in AD 963 by Athanásios the Athonite, and is the only one of the monasteries never to have suffered from fire. It also has the largest font of all the monasteries, which is outside, shaded by a cypress tree said to have been planted over 1,000 years ago by Athanásios himself.

Painting in Megístis Lávras

Halfway along the eastern coast stand the monasteries of Ivíron and Stavronikíta. **Moní Ivíron** was founded in the late 10th century by a monk from Iberia (modern Georgia), hence its name. Its church was built in the early 11th century and restored in 1513. The monastery's main courtyard contains another 16 chapels, one housing a miraculous icon of the Virgin Mary.

Stavronikíta, to the north, stands on top of a rocky headland. It was first mentioned in a document dated AD 1012.

Moní Vatopedíou, one of the largest monasteries on Athos, is sited on a small promontory at the northern end of the east coast. It was founded in the latter half of the 10th century, and a notable feature is its *katholikón*, or main church, also built in the 10th century. It contains icons dating from the 14th century, though they have been retouched over the years. A wealthy monastery, it is among the best preserved on Mount Athos.

ORTHODOX LIFE ON MOUNT ATHOS

Monks growing their own fruit and vegetables

Under the Byzantine time system operating on Athos, midnight is at dawn, and morning services begin about an hour before – around 3 or 4am, Greek time. A monk walks around striking a small wooden *símandro* (a carved plank) with a mallet to wake the other monks and call them to prayer. The monks eat two meals a day, consisting mostly of food they grow themselves. There are 159 fasting days in the year when only one meal is allowed which must contain no fish, eggs, cheese, milk or even oil. Meals are eaten after the morning and evening services, and the time in between is spent working, resting and praying.

The Megístis Lávras monastery, with its red *katholikón* in the centre

Kavála **⓯**
Καβάλα

Macedonia. **Road map** D1. 🏛
56,000. ✈ 35 km (22 miles) SE of
Kavála. 🚢 🚌 ℹ Dragoúmi (2510
222425). 🖀 daily.

KAVALA'S HISTORY goes back
to its foundation in the
6th century BC by settlers from
Thásos and Erétria. It became
part of the Roman Empire in
168 BC, and is where St Paul
first set foot on European soil
in AD 50 or 51 on his way to
Philippi. The biggest impact,
however, was the Turkish
occupation from 1371 to 1912.
It was the Turks who built the
16th-century aqueduct here.
Mehmet Ali (1769–1849), the
Pasha of Egypt, was born in
Kavála. His **birthplace**, a well-
preserved house, set in gardens
and marked by a bronze
statue of Ali on horseback, is
open to visitors.

Kavála is a busy
city, with an indus-
trial port that also
has a ferry service
to the northeast
Aegean islands.
Life centres around
the harbour be-
low the castle,
which is flood-
lit at night. At
its eastern end
there is a busy
fish, fruit and vegetable market.
To the west is the **Archaeological Museum**, which has
finds from Avdíra (see p256),
including a dolphin mosaic
and a painted sarcophagus.
There are also some delicate
3rd-century BC gold laurel
wreaths found at Amphipolis,
west of Kavála, and clay masks
and a 4th-century BC bust of
an unknown goddess.

The **Municipal Museum** is
housed in a late 19th-century
Neo-Classical building to the
west of the town hall. It has
a collection of costumes and
household items, and a good
display of work by local
artists, in particular Thasiot
sculptor Polýgnotos Vágis
(1894–1965).

**Sculpture by
Polýgnotos Vágis**

⌂ Mehmet Ali's Birthplace
Theodórou Poulídou 63. ▐ 2510
220061. ⃝ Apr–Oct: daily; Oct–Mar:
Sun only. ● main public hols.

The town and harbour of Kavála

⌂ Archaeological Museum
Erythroú Stavroú 17. ▐ 2510
222335. ⃝ Tue–Sun. ● main
public hols. 🎫 ♿
⌂ Muncipal Museum
Filíppou 4. ▐ 2510 222706.
⃝ Mon–Sat. ● main public hols.

Néstos Valley **⓰**
Κοιλάδα του Νέστου

Macedonia/Thrace border. **Road
map** D1. 🚉 🚌 Xánthi (liable to be
cancelled Nov–Apr).

THE NESTOS RIVER rises high
in the Rodópi mountains
in Bulgaria and its meandering
course down to the Aegean
near the island of Thásos
marks the boundary between
Macedonia and Thrace. On its
way it threads through remote
and inaccessible gorges, fed
by other rivers and streams,
until it passes under the
scenic mountain road which
links Xánthi in
Thrace with the
town of Dráma
in Macedonia.
This road, some-
times closed by
snowdrifts in
winter, makes for
a spectacular
scenic drive
through the
wooded gorge,
past the valley's
heavy beech
forests and
scattering of
small villages.
Stavroúpoli is
the largest of
these villages,
and has a good
café in its quiet
village square.

Xánthi **⓱**
Ξάνθη

Thrace. **Road map** E1. 🏛 25,000.
🚉 🚌 🖀 Sat.

FOUNDED in the 11th century,
it was not until the 1800s
that Xánthi flourished with the
development of the tobacco
industry. Displays on tobacco
are included in the **Folk
Museum**, which is housed
in two old mansions. The
museum's collection includes
embroidery, jewellery and
costumes. Xánthi's main
square has cafés and fountains, and east of the square
is the bazaar. This is over-
flowing on Saturdays when
people of all nationalities and
religions visit the busiest
market in the area.

⌂ Folk Museum
Antiká 7. ▐ 25410 25421. ⃝ daily.
● for repair. 🎫

The lush landscape of the Néstos Valley

The monastery of Agios Nikólaos on the banks of Lake Vistonída

Avdira ⑱
`Άβδηρα`

6 km (4 miles) S of modern Avdira,
Thrace. **Road map** E1. 🚌
🔵 daily. ⚫ main public hols.

THE ANCIENT CITY of Avdira
was founded in the mid-
7th century BC by refugees
from Klazomenae in Asia
Minor. The site is quite dispersed and overgrown. Most
of what can be seen today
dates from the Roman period.
Some Archaic and Classical
ruins are also evident, including the acropolis. The remains
of its walls stand on a small
headland, and ancient graves
have been discovered and
excavated just outside the
walls. Part of the original city
wall can also be seen.

ENVIRONS: Along the road
from Avdira to Maróneia is
Lake Vistonída, a haven for
wildlife. At one end is Pórto
Lágos (see pp236–7), an old
harbour with the white
monastery of Agios Nikólaos.

Komotiní ⑲
Κομοτηνή

Thrace. **Road map** E1. 🚹 38,000.
🚉 🚌 🚏 Tue.

ONLY 25 km (16 miles)
from the Bulgarian
border to the north, and less
than 100 km (62 miles) from
Turkey to the east, Komotiní
is a fascinating mix of Greek
and Turkish influence. First
founded in the late 4th
century AD, it was taken by

the Turks in 1363, and remained part of the Ottoman
Empire until 1920. Over 500
years of Turkish rule have left
their mark on the town,
especially since the area's
Muslims were excluded
from the population
exchange following
the Greek defeat in
Asia Minor in 1922.
There is a thriving
market with fish,
cattle and tobacco
for sale, along with a
good selection of
fresh produce grown
in fertile land. The
many old wooden
shops sell everything from
bric-a-brac to genuine,
valuable antiques.
A feel of the town's recent
past is given in the well-
cared-for **Museum of Folk
Life and History**. Its few

**Finial from a
gravestone,
Archaeological
Museum, Komotiní**

The domed roof and tall minaret
of a Turkish mosque, Komotiní

rooms, in an 18th-century
mansion, are crammed with
costumes, local copperware
and domestic items. There
is also a particularly good
collection of embroidery,
including examples of a
type known as Tsevrés,
used in Thracian wedding
ceremonies. The town's
**Archaeological
Museum** displays
the best of the finds
from the sites at
ancient Avdira and
Maróneia, including
gold jewellery found
in 4th-century BC
graves at Avdira. A
4th-century BC clay mask of
Dionysos is on display, found
at the god's sanctuary at
Maróneia. The museum also
has an extensive coin collection, painted sarcophagi,
votive reliefs and maps.

🏛 **Museum of Folk Life
and History**
Agíou Georgíou. 🔵 daily.
⚫ main public hols. 🎫 🛗 limited.
🏛 **Archaeological Museum**
Symeonídi. 📞 25310 22411.
🔵 daily. ⚫ main public hols. 🎫

Maróneia ⑳
Μαρώνεια

5 km (3 miles) SE of modern Maróneia,
Thrace. **Road map** E1. 🚌 to modern
Maróneia. 🔵 daily. ⚫ main public
hols. 🎫 🛗

THE ROAD to ancient
Maróneia leads through
tobacco and cotton fields,
past woodland and small
rural communities. A signpost

to the harbour of Agios Charálampos shows the way down a track to the remains of the site that are in a scenic position overlooking the sea. The city flourished from the 8th century BC until AD 1400. Olive groves now cover the area, which sits between Mount Ismaros and the sea, but a small theatre has been discovered and renovated. Further down the track are the remnants of a sanctuary, thought to have been dedicated to Dionysos, whose son, Maron, is credited with founding Maróneia.

Beyond the city of ancient Maróneia is the small but developing harbour of **Agios Charálampos**, surrounded by red cliffs, topped by a large hotel, a taverna and a scattering of houses.

ENVIRONS: Medieval **Maróneia** is a tiny but attractive place, mainly a farming community but with some larger mansions that provide evidence of a more prosperous past.

Alexandroúpoli ㉑
Αλεξανδρούπολη

Thrace. **Road map** E1. 36,000. ✈ 🚌 🚊 🚍 🚏 Tue.

ALEXANDROÚPOLI lacks the cultural mix and history of other large Thracian towns. It was only built up in 1878, under the Turkish name of Dedeagaç (meaning "Tree of the Holy Man"), derived from a group of hermits who first settled here in the 15th century.

The landmark lighthouse in Alexandroúpoli

Prior to that, it was simply an unremarkable fishing village. Alexandroúpoli was renamed in 1919 after the Greek king at the time, Aléxandros.

Today the town is a thriving holiday resort with a port, its own domestic airport, and train connections east to Istanbul, north into Bulgaria and west to Thessaloníki.

In the evening the promenade by the long stretch of beach is thronged with people, both visitors and locals. The lighthouse, built in 1800, is situated along the seafront. It is the town's most famous feature and is lit up at night.

Inland from the promenade, is a warren of narrow streets with junk shops, grocers, cobblers, goldsmiths and fish restaurants. The best eating

places are around tiny Plateía Polytechneíou. North from the square, beyond the main road, is the modern cathedral of Agios Nikólaos, notable for the **Ecclesiastical Art Museum** contained in its grounds. This fine collection of icons and other religious items is unfortunately seldom open, but those with a particular interest in seeing it may ask for access at the cathedral.

🏛 **Ecclesiastical Art Museum**
Palaiológou. ◻ variable. ● main public hols.

Dadiá Forest ㉒
Δάσος Δαδιάς

27km (17 miles) N of Féres, Thrace. **Road map** F1. 🚌 🚍 Féres. 🛈 1 km (0.5 miles) N of Dadiá village (25540 32209).

NORTH OF THE SMALL town of Féres in the Evros valley is the lovely Dadiá pine forest. Covering a series of hills known as the Evros mountains, it is considered to be one of the best places in Europe for observing rare birds. Of special interest is the presence of birds of prey, an indication of the remote location of the forest. There are 39 known species of birds of prey in Europe, 26 of which live and nest in this region.

Rare black vulture

There is an information centre in the heart of the forest, and observation huts have been placed near feeding stations, built to help preserve the rarer species that nest here. This is one of the black vulture's last refuges in eastern Europe. The forest is home to a huge number of protected and endangered species, including imperial eagles, golden eagles, griffon vultures, sparrowhawks and peregrines. Early morning is the best time to watch the different birds as they fly on the first thermals of the day.

Old mansion in modern Maróneia

TRAVELLERS' NEEDS

WHERE TO STAY

ACCOMMODATION IN GREECE is best described as functional in most cases, and only occasionally inspired. However, it is nearly always abundant in a country so heavily dependent on the tourist industry and, as a consequence, is good value compared with most other European destinations. Despite inroads of commercialization in the busier resorts, hospitality off the beaten

Doorman at the Grande Bretagne hotel, Athens

track can still be warm and heartfelt. Various types of accommodation are described over the next four pages. Information is included for the network of campsites and the more limited facilities for hostelling and alpine refuge stays. The listings section *(see pp264–75)* includes over 150 places to stay, ranging from informal *domátia* (rooms) to luxurious hotels and accommodation in restored buildings.

Malvásia Hotel *(see p270)* at Monemvasía, restored by the EOT during the 1970s

HOTELS

MOST GREEK HOTELS are of standard Mediterranean concrete architecture, though in coastal resorts height limits restrict towering structures. Many surviving hotels date from the 1967–74 Junta era, when massive investment in "modern" tourism was encouraged. A very few Neo-Classical, or older, hotels remain, now benefiting from government preservation orders. Hotels built since the 1980s are generally designed with more imagination and sensitivity to the environment. The more expensive hotels will have a correspondingly higher level of service, offered by trained personnel.

CHAIN HOTELS

GREECE, with its tradition of family business ownership, has not taken to the idea of chain hotels. Among the few that operate on the mainland, the oldest is the formerly state-run Xenía chain, founded during the 1950s. Most of their hotels, with well-worn facilities and indifferent service, are worth avoiding, though a few, like those at Andrítsaina and Kastoriá, are the best, or only, hotels available. Newer chains, such as **Chandrís** and **Diváni**, are a better bet. They both offer accommodation in the Athens area, and Diváni also has hotels in central Greece.

RESTORED SETTLEMENTS AND BUILDINGS

DURING THE 1970s, the EOT (Greek Tourist Office) began sponsoring the restoration of derelict buildings in vernacular style, located in isolated parts of the country. The completed units usually offer good value for money and an exceptionally atmospheric environment, though preservation considerations often mean that bathrooms are shared rather than *en suite*. Such properties are found at Areópoli and Vátheia

in the Máni, at Makrinítsa on the Pílio, at Megálo Pápigko in Epirus, and at Monemvasía. Some, such as the complex at Megálo Pápigko, have recently been privatized, with variable effects on efficiency.

In recent years, private entrepreneurs have seized the initiative in such renovation projects, installing small and medium-sized hotels in centuries-old buildings. Particularly successful ventures can be found at Stemnítsa, Galaxídi, Náfplio, and in several villages of the Zagória region and the Pílio.

DOMATIA

A LARGE PROPORTION of Greek accommodation is in *domátia*, or rented rooms. In the past, these often used to be in the home of the managing family, but nowadays they are far more likely to be within a separate, modern, purpose-built structure. They tend to be good value compared with hotels of a similar standard. Increasingly they have *en suite* bathrooms, are well appointed with neutral pine furniture, and often have a kitchen for

Front exterior of the King Othon Hotel, Náfplio *(see p270)*

◁ **Seafront café at Koróni in the Peloponnese**

Lobby at Grande Bretagne hotel, Athens *(see p267)*

the use of guests. There is usually no communal area, however, and hot water is provided either by an electric immersion heater or by a solar heating device.

GRADING

THE EOT grade Greece's hotels and *domátia*. Hotel categories range from E-class up to A-class, plus deluxe. *Domátia* range from C-class to A-class. There is supposed to be a direct correlation between amenities and the classification, but there are many local deviations – usually the result of a dispute with local authorities.

E-class hotels, with the most basic facilities and narrow profit margins, are almost extinct. D- class still survive, and these should have at least some rooms *en suite*. In a C-class hotel, all rooms must have *en suite* baths, and the hotel must have some sort of common area, if only a small combination bar and breakfast area where a basic continental breakfast can be served.

B-class hotels have extra amenities such as a full-service restaurant, a more substantial breakfast, and at least one sports facility, such as a pool or tennis court. A-class hotels are usually at seafront locations, and offer all conceivable diversions, as well as aids for the business traveller, such as conference halls and telecommunications facilities. Deluxe category hotels are effectively self-contained resort complexes. C-class *domátia*, with baths

A sign for rooms to rent

down the hall and "jail-like" decor, are on the way out, now supplanted by modern B-class blocks that guarantee bathrooms *en suite* and often have the benefit of a shared kitchen for the use of visitors. A-class *domátia* are nearly synonymous with apartments. The furnishings are superior and there is generally landscaping outside the building. A well-equipped kitchen is fitted into each unit.

PRICES

THE PRICE of hotel rooms and *domátia* should correspond to their official category, though this depends on the season and their location. For 18 euros or under, it is possible to find a C-class *domátio* for two without *en suite* bathroom, or an E/D-class hotel; 24 euros should cover a B-class double *domátio*, while A-class *domátia* and C-class

hotels charge between 26 and 32 euros. B-class hotels ask 32 to 44 euros per double room; A-class hotels typically cost 44 to 65 euros. Deluxe resorts are exempt from the EOT price control scheme and can easily run in excess of 88 euros per night.

All of these rate approximations are for high season, including VAT and taxes; prices can drop by almost 50 per cent in early spring or late autumn. Hotel rates include breakfast. Stays of less than three nights can carry a surcharge in high season. In mainland skiing resorts there is often a vast difference in weekend and mid-week rates.

OPENING SEASONS

MAINLAND HOTELS stay open year-round, except those at seafront resorts, which operate only from May to October. Hotels in skiing areas, conversely, may open only during the winter period.

BOOKING

THE MOST COMMON and cost-effective way of booking accommodation is through a package holiday agency. If you contact a hotel direct, do so by fax so that the transaction is recorded in writing. You may need to provide a credit card number or send travellers' cheques to the value of the first night's stay. It is also possible to book a hotel via the internet. A useful address to try is www.united-hellas.com.

The pool at the Aphrodite Astir Palace Hotel *(see p268)*

Monastery on Mount Athos *(see p252)*, **Northern Greece**

YOUTH HOSTELS

THE GREEK MAINLAND has
eight IYHF-recognized
youth hostels *(xenón neótitos)*.
They are found in Athens,
Náfplio, Mycenae, Olympia,
Pátra, Delphi, Thessaloníki
and Litóchoro. In addition,
there are a handful of un-
official hostels, which can
be just as good, if not better.

Greek hostels are not nearly
as regimented as their northern
European equivalents. Even
without an IYHF (International
Youth Hostel Federation) card
you can usually stay if a
vacancy is available, upon
payment of a small sup-
plementary charge. However,
the cost of a dormitory bunk
is such that, if travelling as
two, you will generally find
that a less expensive *domátio*
is better value.

ALPINE REFUGES

MOUNTAINS OF THE Greek
mainland are dotted with
over 40 alpine refuges
(katafýgia). Very few
are continuously staffed
– two on Mount
Olympos *(see p241)*
and one on Mount
Gamíla, in the Píndos
range, being notable
exceptions – so you
must contact the
relevant branch of the
EOS (Greek Alpine
Club) to rent keys. This
is expensive and not
worthwhile unless you
muster a large group.

Some of the mountain
huts make wonderful
base camps, fully

equipped with kitchens, bed
linen, and well-designed
common areas; others are
little more than shacks
originally built for shepherds
or fire-control personnel.
Another complication is that,
as many were built at a time
when approaches to the
mountain ranges were quite
different, today they are often
located well away from the
preferred hiking routes.

RURAL TOURISM

CONCEIVED DURING the 1980s
to give women in the
Greek provinces a measure of
financial independence, rural
tourism allows foreigners to
stay on a bed-and-breakfast
basis in a village house, but
also provides the opportunity
to participate, if desired, in
the daily life of a farming
community. There are four
such programmes: Agios
Germanós (Préspa Lakes),
Ampelákia (Thessaly),
Maróneia (Thrace) and

Aráchova in central Greece.
They are all managed by a
**Women's Rural Tourism
Cooperative**, and also usually
run a good-value restaurant
in the centre of the village,
featuring regional cuisine.

MONASTERIES

THE LESS-TOURISTED monas-
teries and convents in
Greece operate *xenónes* or
hostels, intended primarily for
Greek Orthodox pilgrims on
weekend visits. Pilgrims will
always have priority, but it is
often possible to find a
vacancy at short notice.

Accommodation is of the
spartan-dormitory variety,
with a frugal evening meal
and morning coffee also
provided; it is customary to
leave a donation in the
katholikón (main church).

The monasteries on Mount
Athos are the most accustomed
to non-Orthodox visitors,
though these are open to
men only. Visits – especially
in high season – need to be
carefully planned, as the
procedure for reserving space
and obtaining an entry permit
to this semi-autonomous
monastic republic is suitably
Byzantine *(see p253)*.

CAMPING

THE GREEK MAINLAND has
nearly 150 campsites
that are officially recognized.
Most of them are in attractive
seafront settings, and usually
cater to caravanners as well.
The last few still owned by
the EOT, or by the local municipality, are being sold
off; most are privately
run. All but the most
primitive sites have hot
showers heated by
solar power, shady
landscaping and a
snack bar or café.
Power hookups are
generally available
for an extra fee.

The most luxurious
campsites are miniature
holiday villages, with
swimming pool, tennis
courts, laundry rooms,
banking and postal
facilities, and bunga-
lows for the tentless.

Mountain refuge, Kóziakas mountain, Tríkala

Established sites usually have the advantage of mature shady trees. The ground is often sun-baked and very hard, so short pegs that can be banged in with a mallet are best. For a regularly updated booklet covering campsites and their amenities, contact the **Greek Camping Association**.

DISABLED TRAVELLERS

THE GUIDE *Holidays and Travel Abroad*, published by **RADAR** (Royal Association for Disability and Rehabilita-tion) – see page 299 for their address – provides details on wheelchair access to the more established hotels in Greece. Write to the **Holiday Care**

Service for an information sheet with hotels and useful contact numbers in Greece. In the hotel listings of this guide *(see pp264–75)* we have indicated which estab-lishments have suitable facilities, such as lifts and ramps, for the disabled.

Greek information sources for disabled travellers tend to be rudimentary; the EOT only publishes a questionnaire, which can be sent to specific accommodation establishments to assess their suitability.

FURTHER INFORMATION

AN INVALUABLE BOOKLET is pub-lished yearly by the EOT *(see p299)*. It is called *Guide to Hotels*, and a current copy can be obtained from any EOT office. The booklet covers all offi-cially registered hotels, indicating prices, facilities and their opera-ting season. The guide does not, however, offer information on *domátia* or villas.

Camping in one of the valleys of the Píndos mountain range

The EOT also periodically publishes an informative leaflet entitled *Rural Tourism*. Two other hotel manuals, which are both issued by private organizations, are the *Greek Travel Pages* (GTP) and the *Tourist Guide of Greece*. They are not as complete or authoritative as the EOT guides, but are published more frequently. The GTP is monthly, offering only skeletal information unless the hotel concerned has purchased advertising space; this is also true of the quarterly publica-tion *Tourist Guide of Greece*.

Níkos Saxónis *(see p272)* at Mégalo Pápigko

DIRECTORY

CHAIN HOTELS

Chandrís Hotels
Syngroú 385, 17564 Paleó Fáliron, Athens.
℡ 210 947 1000.
ⓦ www.chandris.gr

Club Mediterranée Hellas SA
Omírou 8, 10564 Athens.
℡ 210 937 0341.

Diváni Hotels
Parthenónos 19/25, 11742 Athens.
℡ 210 922 9650.

Stathópoulos Hotels
Filellínon 4, 10557 Athens.
℡ 210 323 5606.

Xenotel Hotels
Akadimías 35, 10672 Athens.
℡ 210 362 0662.

HOSTELS

IYHA (UK)
First Floor, Fountain House, Parkway, Welwyn Garden City, Hertfordshire AL8 6JH, England.
℡ 01707 324 170.

YHA (Greece)
Viktoros Ougó 16, 10438 Athens.
℡ 210 523 4170.

ALPINE REFUGES

EOHO (Ellinikí Omospondía Chionodromías kai Oreivasías)
(Hellenic Federation of Mountaineering Clubs)
Milióni 5, 10673 Athens.
℡ 210 363 6950.

EOS (Ellinikós Oreivatikós Sýndes-mos) (Greek Alpine Club)
Filadelfías 126,

13671 Acharnés, Attica.
℡ 210 246 1528.

SEO (Sýllogos Ellínon Oreivatón)
(Association of Greek Climbers) Plateía Aristoté-lous 5, Thessaloníki.
℡ 2310 224710.

WOMEN'S RURAL TOURISM COOPERATIVES

Agios Germanós
℡ 23850 51320.

Ampelákia
℡ 24950 93495.

Aráchova
℡ 22670 31519.

Maróneia
℡ 25330 41394.

CAMPING

Greek Camping Association

Sólonos 102, 10680 Athens.
℡ 210 362 1560.

DISABLED TRAVELLERS

Holiday Care Service
2nd Floor, Imperial Buildings, Victoria Road, Horley, Surrey RH6 7PZ, England.
℡ 01293-774 535.
ⓦ www.gtpweb.com

FURTHER INFORMATION

Greek Travel Pages
Psýlla 6, corner Filellínon, 10557 Athens.
℡ 210 324 7511.

Tourist Guide of Greece
Patission 137, 11251 Athens.
℡ 210 864 1688.

Choosing a Hotel

THESE HOTELS have been selected across a wide price range for their good value, facilities and location; they are listed by region, starting with Athens. Use the colour-coded thumb tabs, which indicate the areas covered on each page, to guide you to the relevant section of the chart. For Athens map references see pages *128–35*; for road map references see the inside back cover.

ATHENS

Hotel		NUMBER OF ROOMS	RESTAURANT	GARDEN OR TERRACE	SWIMMING POOL	AIR-CONDITIONING
AMPELOKIPOI: *Androméda* €€€€€		30	●			■
AREOS: *Park Hotel Athens* w www.park.hotel.gr €€€€€		143	●	■	●	■
EXARCHEIA: *Exarcheíon* €€€		58				
EXARCHEIA: *Museum* €€€		58				■
ILISIA: *Hilton* €€€€€		453	●	■	●	■
ILISIA: *Holiday Inn* €€€€€		191	●	■	●	■
KAISARIANI: *Divani Caravel* €€€€€		470	●	■	●	■
KOLONAKI: *Athenian Inn* €€€€€		25				■
KOLONAKI: *St George Lycabettus* €€€€€		167	●		●	■
KOUKAKI: *Marble House* €€€		16		■		
KOUKAKI: *Fíllipos* €€€€€		48				■
MAKRYGIANNI: *Ira* €€€€€		49		■		■

AMPELOKIPOI: *Androméda* €€€€€ 30
Timoléontos Vásou 22, 11521. **Map** 6 F4. **(** *210 646 6362.* **FAX** *210 646 6361.*
A deluxe hotel with immaculate attention to detail in all the rooms and a reception area featuring work by contemporary designers.

AREOS: *Park Hotel Athens* w www.park.hotel.gr €€€€€ 143
Leofóros Alexándras 10, 10682. **Map** 3 A1. **(** *210 883 2711.* **FAX** *210 823 8420.*
Situated opposite the relaxing Areos Park, this hotel has spacious rooms. There is also a good rooftop bar and a 24-hour coffee shop.

EXARCHEIA: *Exarcheíon* €€€ 58
Themistokléous 55, 10683. **Map** 2 F3. **(** *210 360 0731.* **FAX** *210 360 3296.*
This hotel is close to the late-night action of Plateía Exarcheíon. Rooms are basic, but there is a roof garden and a good pavement café.

EXARCHEIA: *Museum* €€€ 58
Mpoumpoulínas 16, 10682. **Map** 2 F2. **(** *210 380 5611.* **FAX** *210 380 0507.*
The modern façade of this building hides a genteel interior. Situated opposite the National Archaeological Museum, it is frequented by academics. The rooms are clean and quiet.

ILISIA: *Hilton* €€€€€ 453
Leofóros Vasilíssis Sofías 46, 11528. **Map** 4 D5. **(** *210 728 1000.* **FAX** *210 725 3110.*
Athens' best-known modern hotel. All the rooms have large balconies, providing stunning views across the city.

ILISIA: *Holiday Inn* €€€€€ 191
Michalakopoúlou 50, 11528. **Map** 8 E1. **(** *210 727 8000.* **FAX** *210 724 8187.*
This efficiently run hotel is popular with business travellers. It has large rooms, good restaurants and a rooftop swimming pool.

KAISARIANI: *Divani Caravel* €€€€€ 470
Leofóros Vasiléos Alexándrou 2, 16121. **Map** 8 D1. **(** *210 720 7000.* **FAX** *210 723 6683.* Popular for conferences, the Caravel has spacious rooms and several eating and drinking areas, including the Lord Byron piano bar.

KOLONAKI: *Athenian Inn* €€€€€ 25
Cháritos 22, 10675. **Map** 3 B5. **(** *210 723 9552.* **FAX** *210 724 2268.*
This hotel offers clean, basic rooms and friendly management. Situated in the heart of Kolonáki, among a choice of shops, restaurants and cafés.

KOLONAKI: *St George Lycabettus* €€€€€ 167
Kleoménous 2, 10675. **Map** 3 B4. **(** *210 729 0711.* **FAX** *210 729 0439.*
Situated beneath Lykavittós Hill, this small, luxury hotel offers large rooms with good views. The rooftop restaurant is excellent.

KOUKAKI: *Marble House* €€€ 16
Anastasíou Zínni 35, 11741. **Map** 5 C4. **(** *210 923 4058.* **FAX** *210 922 6461.*
At the end of a quiet cul-de-sac, this is a firm favourite among mid-range *pensions* for its cleanliness and helpful management. Most rooms are *en suite* and many have vine-covered balconies. Breakfast not included.

KOUKAKI: *Fíllipos* €€€€€ 48
Mitsaíon 3, 11742. **Map** 6 D3. **(** *210 922 3611.* **FAX** *210 922 3615.*
Sister property to the Iródeion, this modern hotel offers basic but clean accommodation. Some rooms have balconies.

MAKRYGIANNI: *Ira* €€€€€ 49
Falírou 9, 11742. **Map** 6 D4. **(** *210 923 5618.* **FAX** *210 924 7334.*
The rooms and public areas in this modern hotel are spotless. The hotel also has a coffee shop and a rooftop terrace.

<table>
<tr><td colspan="2">

Price categories are for a standard double room for one night in peak season, including tax, service charges and breakfast:
€ under 25 euros
€€ 25–35 euros
€€€ 35–45 euros
€€€€ 45–60 euros
€€€€€ over 60 euros.

</td></tr>
</table>

RESTAURANT
Restaurant within the hotel sometimes reserved for residents only.

GARDEN OR TERRACE
Hotel with garden, courtyard or terrace, often providing tables for eating outside.

SWIMMING POOL
Hotel swimming pools are usually quite small and are outdoors unless otherwise stated.

AIR-CONDITIONING
Hotel with air-conditioning in all the rooms.

	NUMBER OF ROOMS	RESTAURANT	GARDEN OR TERRACE	SWIMMING POOL	AIR-CONDITIONING
MAKRYGIANNI: *Best Western Athens Gate* €€€€€ Leofóros A Syngroú 10, 11742. **Map** 6 E3. **☎** 210 923 8302. **FAX** 210 923 7493. This centrally located, modern hotel offers comfortable rooms and a rooftop garden with views of the Acropolis and Hadrian's Arch.	100	●	▪		▪
MAKRIGIANNI: *Divani Palace Acropolis* €€€€€ Parthenónos 19–25, 11742. **Map** 6 D3. **☎** 210 928 0100. **FAX** 210 921 4993. Beautifully upgraded to deluxe standard, this hotel is just a short stroll from the Acropolis. An original section of the Themistoklean Long Walls is on view in the hotel lobby.	251	●	▪	●	▪
MAKRYGIANNI: *Iródeion* €€€€€ Rovértou Gkálli 4, 11742. **Map** 5 C3. **☎** 210 923 6832. **FAX** 210 921 1650. This hotel has large modern rooms, a patio shaded by pistachio trees and a roof terrace with views of the Acropolis.	90	●	▪		▪
MAKRYGIANNI: *Royal Olympic* €€€€€ Athanasíou Diákou 28–32, 11743. **Map** 6 E3. **☎** 210 922 6411. **FAX** 210 923 5851. The Royal Olympic has wonderful large rooms, all with superb views of the Temple of Olympian Zeus. Good grill restaurant.	304	●	▪	●	▪
METAXOURGEIO: *Stanley* €€€€€ Odysséos 1, Plateía Karaïskáki, 10437. **Map** 1 B3. **☎** 210 524 1611. **FAX** 210 524 4611. The Stanley hotel has large fully equipped rooms with balconies, a rooftop garden and pool and a busy bar and restaurant.	395	●	▪	●	▪
MONASTIRAKI: *Attalos* €€€€€ Athinás 29, 19554. **Map** 2 D5. **☎** 210 321 2801. **FAX** 210 324 3124. Ideally situated for shopping, near Monastiráki and Athinás, the Attalos offers adequate rooms, some with balconies. The hotel also has a roof garden with good views of the Acropolis.	80		▪		▪
MONASTIRAKI: *Hotel Carolina* €€€€€ Kolokotróni 55, 10560. **Map** 2 E5. **☎** 210 324 3551. **FAX** 210 324 3550. This delightful, newly renovated hotel offers clean rooms, some with ensuite bathrooms. There are views of the Acropolis from the terrace.	34		▪		▪
NEOS KOSMOS: *Christína* €€€€ Petmezá 15, 11743. **Map** 6 D4. **☎** 210 921 5353. **FAX** 210 921 5569. This is a fairly standard businessman's hotel just a short walk from the Acropolis. The rooms are clean and homely.	93	●			▪
NEOS KOSMOS: *Athenaeum Inter-Continental* €€€€€ Leofóros Andrea Syngroú 89–93, 11745. **Map** 6 E4. **☎** 210 920 6000. **FAX** 210 920 6500. **W** www.interconti.com Decorated with modern Greek art, this luxurious hotel offers a choice of restaurants, bars and shops. Facilities include a gym.	520	●		●	▪
NEOS KOSMOS: *Ledra Marriot* €€€€€ Leofóros Andrea Syngroú 115, 11745. **Map** 6 D4. **☎** 210 930 0000. **FAX** 210 935 8603. As well as all the amenities expected from a luxury hotel, the Marriot's rooms are large and spacious and the hotel boasts superb restaurants, particularly the trendy Polynesian Kona Kai.	259	●		●	▪
OMONOIA: *La Mirage* €€€ Maríkas Kotopoúli 3, 10431. **Map** 2 D3. **☎** 210 523 4071. **FAX** 210 523 3992. A favourite for those who want to be close to the 24-hour hustle and bustle of Plateía Omonoías. All rooms are double glazed.	208	●			▪
OMONOIA: *Dorian Inn* €€€€€ Peiraiós 17, 10552. **Map** 2 D3. **☎** 210 523 9782. **FAX** 210 522 6196. Situated in the heart of the city centre, the roof garden of this smart hotel offers spectacular views over Athens and the Acropolis.	146	●	▪	●	▪

Price categories are for a standard double room for one night in peak season, including tax, service charges and breakfast:
€ under 25 euros
€€ 25–35 euros
€€€ 35–45 euros
€€€€ 45–60 euros
€€€€€ over 60 euros.

RESTAURANT
Restaurant within the hotel sometimes reserved for residents only.

GARDEN OR TERRACE
Hotel with garden, courtyard or terrace, often providing tables for eating outside.

SWIMMING POOL
Hotel swimming pools are usually quite small and are outdoors unless otherwise stated.

AIR-CONDITIONING
Hotel with air-conditioning in all the rooms.

	NUMBER OF ROOMS	RESTAURANT	GARDEN OR TERRACE	SWIMMING POOL	AIR-CONDITIONING
OMONOIA: *Athens Acropolis* €€€€€ Peiraiós 1, 10552. **Map** 2 D3. ☎ 210 523 1111. **FAX** 210 523 1361. This hotel has large and comfortable public lounge areas, including a restaurant and bar, where you can relax and enjoy the ambience. All the rooms are quiet. 🖶 P ♿	167	●	■		■
OMONOIA: *Titánia* €€€€€ Panepistimiou 52, 10678. **Map** 2 E4. ☎ 210 330 0111. **FAX** 210 330 0700. The entrance to this well-appointed hotel is through a shopping arcade close to Plateía Omonoías. Rooms are well equipped and the rooftop terrace bar and ground-floor café are always busy. 🖶 P ♿ 🖝	396	●	■		■
PLAKA: *John's Place* €€ Patróou 5, 10557. **Map** 6 E1. ☎ 210 322 9719. One of the better bargain backpacking hotels. The rooms are small but very clean, and bathrooms are shared.	15				
PLAKA: *Faídra* €€€ Chairefóntos 16, 10558. **Map** 6 E2. ☎ 210 323 8461. **FAX** 210 322 795. The hotel's location next to the Lysikrates monument more than makes up for the slightly tacky quality of its rooms and public areas.	21				
PLAKA: *Koúros* €€€ Kódrou 11, 10557. **Map** 6 E2. ☎ 210 322 7431. Situated in the heart of Pláka, this cheap and cheerful small *pension* is housed in a converted Neo-Classical mansion house. Rooms are basic but clean and have balconies – some with a view of the Acropolis.	10				
PLAKA: *Acropolis House Pension* €€€€€ Kódrou 6–8, 10557. **Map** 6 E1. ☎ 210 322 2344. **FAX** 210 324 4143 Housed in a converted 19th-century building, the rooms in this *pension* are large and airy. All rooms have private balconies. 🖶 🖝	19				■
PLAKA: *Neféli* €€€€€ Angelikís Chatzimicháli 2, 10558. **Map** 6 E1. ☎ 210 322 8044. **FAX** 210 322 5800. A modern hotel, hidden away in a peaceful backwater in Pláka. The rooms are clean and of a good, basic standard. 🖶 ♿ 🖝	18				■
PLAKA: *Aphrodite* €€€€€ Apóllonos 21, 10557. **Map** 6 E1. ☎ 210 323 4357. **FAX** 210 322 5244. This hotel is well located and offers clean, good-value rooms, some of which enjoy wonderful views of the Acropolis. 🖶 P ♿ 🖝	84	●	■		■
PLAKA: *Byron* €€€€€ Výronos 19, 10558. **Map** 6 E2. ☎ 210 323 0327. **FAX** 210 322 0276. Situated on the southern fringe of Pláka, this small and basic hotel is close to the Acropolis. Some rooms have balconies. 🖶	20		■		■
PLAKA: *Myrtó* €€€€€ Níkis 40, 10558. **Map** 6 F1. ☎ 210 322 7237. **FAX** 210 323 4560. Close to the central areas of Plateía Syntágmatos and Pláka, this small hotel is ideal for short stays and is popular with young couples. 🖶	12				■
PLAKA: *Omiros* €€€€€ Apóllonos 15, 10557. **Map** 6 E1. ☎ 210 323 5486. **FAX** 210 322 8059. A lovely roof garden distinguishes this otherwise basic hotel which is located in a quiet area of Pláka. 🖶 ♿ 🖝	37		■		■
PLAKA: *Adrian* €€€€€ Adrianoú 74, 10556. **Map** 6 E2. ☎ 210 322 1553. **FAX** 210 523 4786. Situated in central Pláka, this hotel has simple, comfortable rooms as well as a quiet terrace to escape the bustle of the city. 🖶 ♿ 🖝	22		■		■

PLAKA: *Pláka* €€€€€ | 67
Mitropoleos & Kapnikareas 7, 10556. **Map 6 D1.** 210 322 2096. FAX 210 322 2412.
Set in the heart of Pláka, with a superb view of the Acropolis, this is a comfortable hotel with a friendly atmosphere.

PLAKA: *Ermís* €€€€€ | 45
Apóllonos 19, 10557. **Map 6 E1.** 210 323 5514. FAX 210 323 2073.
Despite a rather drab lobby, the rooms of this hotel are large, some having balconies overlooking a playground.

STATHMOS LARISSIS: *Oscar* €€€€€ | 164
Filadelfeías 25, 10439. **Map 1 C1.** 210 883 4215. FAX 210 821 6368.
Close to Laríssis railway station, this excellent modern hotel has large rooms, a rooftop pool and a good restaurant.

STATHMOS LARISSIS: *Novotel Athens* €€€€€ | 195
Michaíl Vóda 4–6, 10439. **Map 1 D1.** 210 820 0700. FAX 210 820 0777.
Run by the French group, Novotel, this smart, centrally located hotel has modern, well-equipped rooms and a stunning rooftop garden and swimming pool.

STREFI HILL: *Oríon* €€€ | 38
Anexartisías 5 & E Mpenáki 105, 11473. **Map 3 A2.** 210 382 7362. FAX 210 380 5193. Beside Stréfi Hill, just above the bustling Exárcheia area, this quiet hotel is popular with students looking for short-term accommodation.

SYNTAGMA: *Metropolis* €€€ | 25
Mitropóleos 46, 10563. **Map 6 D1.** & FAX 210 321 7469.
This five-storey hotel enjoys views over Athens' Mitrópoli (cathedral). Rooms are large and clean and the staff friendly. No breakfasts provided.

SYNTAGMA: *Amalía* €€€€€ | 98
Leofóros Vasilissis Amalías 10, 10557. **Map 6 F1.** 210 323 7301. FAX 210 322 3872.
Although the rooms are fairly small, all the bathrooms are marble. The hotel is centrally located and has good views of both the Parliament building and the National Gardens.

SYNTAGMA: *Aretoúsa* €€€€€ | 87
Mitropóleos 6–8 & Níkis 12, 10563. **Map 6 F1.** 210 322 9431. FAX 210 322 9439.
Decent value characterizes this centrally located hotel. The rooms are modern and there is a roof garden as well as a lively bar.

SYNTAGMA: *Astor* €€€€€ | 130
Karageórgi Servías 16, 10562. **Map 6 F1.** 210 335 1000. FAX 210 325 5115.
The popular all-year-round rooftop restaurant of this hotel boasts stunning views over Athens. The double rooms from the sixth floor upwards share this impressive view of the city.

SYNTAGMA: *Athens Cypria* €€€€€ | 71
Diomeias 5, 10557. **Map 6 E1.** 210 323 8034. FAX 210 324 8792.
Located in a quiet street, a few minutes from Plateía Syntágmatos, this hotel offers good value for money. Acropolis views from top floor rooms.

SYNTAGMA: *Electra* €€€€€ | 110
Ermoú 5, 10557. **Map 6 F1.** 210 322 3223. FAX 210 322 0310.
This centrally located hotel is ideally situated for shopping expeditions to Monastiráki. All the rooms are clean and pleasant.

SYNTAGMA: *Esperia Palace* €€€€€ | 184
Stadíou 22, 10564. **Map 2 E4.** 210 323 8001. FAX 210 323 8100.
A smart city hotel with marble lobbies and tastefully decorated rooms. Its restaurant and bar are popular with Athenians.

SYNTAGMA: *Grande Bretagne* €€€€€ | 450
Plateía Syntágmatos, 10563. **Map 6 F1.** 210 333 0000. FAX 210 322 8034.
This luxurious hotel was built in 1852 and is the landmark of Plateía Syntágmatos, the most desirable hotel location in Athens. The lobby and rooms are beautiful and the service is excellent.

SYNTAGMA: *Athens Plaza* €€€€€ | 177
Vasiléos Georgíou, 10564. **Map 6 F1.** 210 325 5301. FAX 210 323 5856.
This grand hotel offers luxurious blue and white rooms, all of which are soundproofed. There are good facilities and its Explorers' Lounge and Marco Polo restaurant are always busy.

For key to symbols see back flap

Price categories are for a standard double room for one night in peak season, including tax, service charges and breakfast:
€ under 25 euros
€€ 25–35 euros
€€€ 35–45 euros
€€€€ 45–60 euros
€€€€€ over 60 euros.

RESTAURANT
Restaurant within the hotel sometimes reserved for residents only.
GARDEN OR TERRACE
Hotel with garden, courtyard or terrace, often providing tables for eating outside.
SWIMMING POOL
Hotel swimming pools are usually quite small and are outdoors unless otherwise stated.
AIR-CONDITIONING
Hotel with air-conditioning in all the rooms.

AROUND ATHENS

	NUMBER OF ROOMS	RESTAURANT	GARDEN OR TERRACE	SWIMMING POOL	AIR-CONDITIONING
ANAVYSOS: *Xenía Ilios* €€€€€ 3 km (2 miles) N of Anávysos, 19013. **Road map** D4. 22910 37024. FAX 22910 36998. On a hillside overlooking the sea, this hotel has adequate rooms and is next to a beach. It is a training school for hotel staff in winter, and students work here in the summer. ● *Oct–May.*	103	●			■
GLYFADA: *Hotel Ilion* €€ Kondylii 4, 16675. **Road map** D4. 210 894 6011. Situated in Glyfáda, 2 km (1 mile) north of Vouliágmeni, this is ideally located near the town's chic shops. Rooms are plainly decorated, but some have views of the sea. No breakfast supplied.	34				
KIFISIA: *Hotel Grand Chalet* €€€€€ Kokkinara 38, 14562. **Road map** D4. 210 623 3120. FAX 210 808 5426. In an up-market northern suburb, this is a pleasant place to stay away from the bustle of the city centre. It has a restaurant serving international cuisine and an outdoor swimming pool in an attractive garden.	44	●	■	●	■
KIFISIA: *Pentelikón* €€€€€ Deligiánni 66, 14562. **Road map** D4. 210 623 0650-6. FAX 210 801 0314. Set within landscaped gardens, this Neo-Classical deluxe hotel offers beautiful, spacious rooms and discreet service.	44	●	■	●	■
MARATHONAS: *Golden Coast* €€€€€ Marathónas beach, 19005. **Road map** D4. 22940 57100. FAX 22940 57300. This luxury hotel is situated near the ancient site of Marathon. Amenities include a night club, restaurants, four swimming pools (one for children) and other sports facilities and shops. ● *Oct–Mar.*	541	●	■	●	■
MOUNT PARNITHA: *Casino Mont Parnes* €€€€€ 4 km (2 miles) N of Acharnaí, 13571. **Road map** D4. 210 246 9111. FAX 210 246 0768. Overlooking the plain of Attica, this hotel is known primarily for its casino. Whether you gamble or not, the fresh air and pine trees around the hotel are a wonderful relief from the Athens summer heat.	108	●	■	●	■
PIRAEUS: *Cava D'Oro* €€€€€ Vasiléos Pávlou 19, 18533. **Road map** D4. 210 412 2210. FAX 210 412 2210. Overlooking Mikrolímano harbour, this smart hotel boasts a popular disco and bar. The rooms are cool and airy.	74	●			■
PIRAEUS: *Kastélla* €€€€€ Vasiléos Pávlou 75, 18533. **Road map** D4. 210 411 4735 FAX 210 417 5716. Situated in the smart area of Kastélla, the modern rooms in this hotel have views of the yacht marina below.	32	●	■		■
PIRAEUS: *Park* €€€€€ Kolokotróni 103, 18535. **Road map** D4. 210 452 4611. FAX 210 452 4615. The central location of the Park hotel makes it ideal for exploring Piraeus. There is a breakfast terrace and the rooms are large.	80		■		■
SOUNIO: *Agaíon* €€€€€ Waterfront, 19500. **Road map** D4. 22920 39200. FAX 22920 39234. Overlooking a picturesque bay, this long-running hotel provides easy access to the Temple of Poseidon. All rooms have balconies and a wonderful sunset can be enjoyed from the large restaurant.	45	●	■		●
VOULIAGMENI: *Aphrodite Astir Palace* €€€€€ Apóllonos 40, 16671. **Road map** D4. 210 896 0211. FAX 210 896 2582. A luxury hotel in a resort development, 23 km (14 miles) south of Athens, by the sea. The plushest place to stay for combining the sites of Athens with the pleasures of the beach. ● *Oct–Apr.*	570	●	■	●	■

THE PELOPONNESE

ANCIENT CORINTH: *Shadow* €€ — 12
On access road to village, 20007. **Road map** C4. 27410 31481. FAX 27410 31481.
The rear rooms of this simple family hotel overlook Acrocorinth and the lush Kórinthos plain. The affiliated restaurant has live music. 🛌 P

AREOPOLI: *Pyrgos Kapetanákou* €€€ — 6
Off Plateía Areopóleos, 23062. **Road map** C5. 27330 51233. FAX 27330 51401.
In a three-storey tower dating from 1865, the rooms here vary sharply in price and range from a lone single to a family quintuple loft. Some have air-conditioning. There are mature gardens and a lovely breakfast salon. P

AREOPOLI: *Xenónas Lontas* €€€€ — 4
Off Plateía Taxiarchón, 23062. **Road map** C5. 27330 51360. FAX 27330 51012.
This recently restored tower house hotel has *en suite* rooms with good, arty decor. It is, however, slightly overpriced. 🛌 P

CHLEMOUTSI: *Chryssí Avgí* €€ — 10
Loutropóleos 9, 27050. **Road map** B4. 26230 95224.
Conveniently situated near the centre of the village, this hotel has spacious rooms, the rear six with magnificent views north over the countryside and east to the castle. ● *Nov–Apr.* 🛌 P

DIAKOFTO: *Chris-Paul* €€€€ — 25
Next to railway station, 25003. **Road map** C4. 26910 41715. FAX 26910 42128.
Still close to the town centre, this modern hotel is set in a peaceful location hidden by trees. All the rooms have private balconies with fine views, and a cosy fireplace greets guests in winter. 🛌 P 🖐

DIMITSANA: *Dimitsána* €€€€ — 27
Off Dimitsána–Stemnítsa road, 22100. **Road map** C4. 27950 31518.
A recently modernized hotel which is not extraordinary architecturally, but is situated in a lush and leafy setting overlooking the Loúsios Gorge. Most of the rooms have balconies. 🛌 P

FOINIKOUNTA: *Pórto Finíssia* €€€€ — 27
Foinikoúnta beach, 24006. **Road map** C5. 27230 71458. FAX 27230 71457.
Situated in a quiet resort, 14 km (9 miles) southeast of Methóni, the Foinikoúnta offers clean, well-equipped rooms, most of which overlook a beach. All rooms have balconies and telephones. ● *Nov–Apr.* 🛌 P 🖐

GYTHEIO: *Aktaíon* €€€€ — 22
Vasiléos Pávlou 39, 23200. **Road map** C5. 27330 23500. FAX 27330 22294.
Housed in a restored Neo-Classical building on the quayside, the Aktaíon offers clean rooms and balconies with sea views. 🛌

INNER MANI: *Tsitsiris Castle* €€€€€ — 20
Stavri, 230 71. **Road map** C5. 27330 56297. FAX 27330 56296.
Situated in Stavri, 5 km (3 miles) northwest of Geroliménas, this beautifully restored 18th-century tower has traditionally furnished rooms. There is a restaurant and a large terrace with superb mountain views. 🛌

KALAVRYTA: *María* €€€€ — 18
Syngroú 10, 25001. **Road map** C4. 26920 22296. FAX 26920 22686.
Well-decorated rooms are available at this small, quiet hotel overlooking a pedestrian street at the western edge of the town. 🛌 P

KALÒGRIA: *Kalògria Beach* €€€€€ — 220
Kalògria beach, 27052. **Road map** B4. 26930 31380. FAX 26930 31381.
This hotel comprises a main building and individual bungalows. All the rooms have verandas with views of the sea or nearby forest. A frequent bus service runs from Pátra to the hotel. ● *Nov–Mar.* 🛌 P

KARDAMYLI: *Kardamýli Beach* €€€€€ — 30
Kardamýli beach, 24022. **Road map** C5. 27210 73180. FAX 27210 73184.
Situated in Kardamýli, 34 km (21 miles) south of Kalamáta, this hotel sits at the foot of the Taÿgettos range and affords good views. 🛌 P

KORINTHOS: *Efyra* €€€ — 45
Ethnikís Antístasis 52, 20100. **Road map** C4. 27410 22434. FAX 27410 24514.
Situated in Kórinthos, 6 km (4 miles) northeast of Ancient Corinth, the Efyra is one of only a few hotels in the town from which to choose. Affordable accommodation is on offer, and the rooms are basic but clean. 🛌 🖐

Price categories are for a standard double room for one night in peak season, including tax, service charges and breakfast:
€ under 25 euros
€€ 25–35 euros
€€€ 35–45 euros
€€€€ 45–60 euros
€€€€€ over 60 euros.

RESTAURANT
Restaurant within the hotel sometimes reserved for residents only.

GARDEN OR TERRACE
Hotel with garden, courtyard or terrace, often providing tables for eating outside.

SWIMMING POOL
Hotel swimming pools are usually quite small and are outdoors unless otherwise stated.

AIR-CONDITIONING
Hotel with air-conditioning in all the rooms.

	NUMBER OF ROOMS	RESTAURANT	GARDEN OR TERRACE	SWIMMING POOL	AIR-CONDITIONING
KORONI: *Auberge de la Plage* €€€€	49	●	▪		▪
KYLLINI: *Robinson Club Kyllíni Beach* €€€€€	304	●	▪	●	▪
METHONI: *Odysséas* €€€€€	9		▪		▪
MONEMVASIA: *Malvásia* €€€€	28				
MYCENAE: *Belle Hélène* €€	8	●	▪		
NAFPLIO: *Epídavros* €€€	25		▪		
NAFPLIO: *Byron* €€€€	18		▪		▪
NAFPLIO: *King Othon* €€€€€	12				
NEOS MYSTRAS: *Byzántion* €€€	22	●			
OLYMPIA: *Pelops* €€	25	●	▪	●	
OLYMPIA: *Europa* €€€€€	42	●	▪	●	▪

KORONI: *Auberge de la Plage* €€€€   49
Zánga beach, 24004. **Road map** C5. **℡** 27250 22401. **FAX** 27250 22508.
This hotel overlooks the castle of Koróni and one of the best beaches in the Peloponnese. All rooms have balconies with good views. ● *Nov–Mar.*

KYLLINI: *Robinson Club Kyllíni Beach* €€€€€   304
Kyllíni beach, 27050. **Road map** B4. **℡** 26230 95205. **FAX** 26230 95206.
This large-scale complex is set in beautiful grounds next to a sandy beach. Organized sports for adults and children are on offer, as well as health facilities such as massage treatments. ● *Nov–Mar.*

METHONI: *Odysséas* €€€€€   9
Plateía Syngroú, 24006. **Road map** B5. **℡** 27230 31600. **FAX** 27230 31646.
This traditional-style hotel, with terracotta roof tiling and white walls, overlooks the castle of Methóni. The hotel has a television room and a large garden area. All rooms have balconies. ● *Nov–Mar.*

MONEMVASIA: *Malvásia* €€€€   28
Kástro, 23070. **Road map** C5. **℡** 27320 61323. **FAX** 27320 61722.
This restoration complex is scattered about the old town on three different sites that vary in price. Each room, furnished in wood, marble and bright textiles, has its own individual charm.

MYCENAE: *Belle Hélène* €€   8
Chrístou loúda, 21200. **Road map** C4. **℡** 27510 76225. **FAX** 27510 76179.
Dating from 1862, this simple but atmospheric building housed the archaeologist Schliemann during his excavations here. The ground-floor restaurant features an impressive guest register. ● *Jan–Feb.*

NAFPLIO: *Epídavros* €€€   25
Kokkínou 2, 21100. **Road map** C4. **℡** 27520 27541. **FAX** 27520 27541.
Every room of this tastefully renovated hotel is different, though all have pine floors and coffered ceilings. Some rooms have balconies. There are eight more rooms in an affiliated *pension* nearby. No breakfasts provided.

NAFPLIO: *Byron* €€€€   18
Plátonos 2, 21100. **Road map** C4. **℡** 27520 22351. **FAX** 27520 26338.
A beautifully restored hotel situated near the top of the old town. Some of the upper-floor rooms have views of the sea.

NAFPLIO: *King Othon* €€€€€   12
Farmakopoúlou 3, 21100. **Road map** C4. **℡** 27520 27585. **FAX** 27520 27595.
Housed in a Neo-Classical building, the King Othon has high ceilings and windows which contribute to its atmosphere. ● *Nov–Mar.*

NEOS MYSTRAS: *Byzántion* €€€   22
Main square, 23100. **Road map** C5. **℡** 27310 83309. **FAX** 27310 20019.
Situated in Néos Mystrás, 1 km (0.5 miles) east of Byzantine Mystrás, this recently restored hotel has individually decorated rooms with vaulted ceilings and wooden furniture. Prices vary depending on the view. ● *Nov–Feb.*

OLYMPIA: *Pelops* €€   25
Varelá 2, 27065. **Road map** B4. **℡** 26240 22543. **FAX** 26240 22213.
Situated in Olympía, 500 m (1,600 ft) east of Ancient Olympia, this hotel is run by an Australian-Greek team. The family atmosphere and vine-covered bar area make for a pleasant stay. ● *mid-Nov–mid-Feb.*

OLYMPIA: *Europa* €€€€€   42
Droúva 1, 27065. **Road map** B4. **℡** 26240 22650. **FAX** 26240 23166.
This welcoming, family-run hotel (a member of the Best Western chain) enjoys a superb hillside site in Olympía, 500 m (1,600 ft) east of Ancient Olympia. Facilities include a tennis court and riding stable.

PATRA: *Ránnia* €€€€ — 30
Ríga Feraíou 53, 26221. **Road map** C4. **℡** 2610 220114. **FAX** 2610 220537.
This is a reasonably priced hotel in a quiet location. The rooms have wooden furniture and balconies, and some overlook a pretty square.

PORTOCHELI: *Ververónda* €€ — 246
Sea front, 21300. **Road map** C4. **℡ FAX** 27540 51342.
A 10-minute walk from the town, this hotel overlooks a picturesque bay and comprises a complex of traditionally styled villas and bungalows. 🚌 🅿

PYLOS: *Káralis Beach* €€€€€ — 14
Kalamátas 26, 24001. **Road map** C5. **℡** 27230 23021. **FAX** 27230 22970.
Set at the end of the harbour, this hotel is far away from noisy traffic. Rooms are not huge, but some have sea views. ● *Nov–Mar.* 🚌 🅿 ♿ 🍽

SPARTI: *Maniátis* €€€€ — 80
Palaiológou 72, 23100. **Road map** C5. **℡** 27310 22665. **FAX** 27310 29994.
Situated in the centre of Spárti, this modern, efficiently run hotel lacks atmosphere, but is excellent value for money. 🚌 🍽

SPARTI: *Spárta Inn* €€€€ — 147
Thermopylón 109, 23100. **Road map** C5. **℡** 27310 25021. **FAX** 27310 24855.
One of the smarter hotels in this area, the Spárta Inn is situated in a tranquil spot and has a roof garden. 🚌 ♿ 🍽

STEMNITSA: *Trikolóneio* €€€€ — 20
Off main square, 22024. **Road map** C4. **℡** 27950 81297. **FAX** 27950 81483.
Situated in Stemnítsa, 8 km (5 miles) south of Dimitsána, the traditional-style Trikolóneio is housed in two 19th-century mansions with an annexe. There is an excellent restaurant attached. 🚌 🅿

ZACHLOROU: *Romántzo* €€€ — 10
Next to railway station, 25001. **Road map** C4. **℡** 26920 22758.
Situated in Zachloroú, 14 km (9 miles) west of Diakoftó, this is a rambling structure with verandas overlooking the Vouraïkós river. 🚌

CENTRAL AND WESTERN GREECE

AGIOS IOANNIS: *Eftychía* €€€€ — 17
Main road into village, 37012. **Road map** C3. **℡** 24260 31150.
Situated in Agios Ioánnis, 25 km (16 miles) north of Miliés, the Eftychía, with stone roof-tiles and a whitewashed exterior, is a typical Pílio-style hotel. There are sea views but no rooms with balconies. ● *Sep–May.* 🚌 🅿

ARACHOVA: *Apollon Inn* €€€ — 20
Delfón 20, 32004. **Road map** C3. **℡ & FAX** 22670 31057.
This excellent family-run hotel in Aráchova, 11 km (8 miles) east of Ancient Delphi, has a friendly atmosphere. There are no *en suite* rooms. 🚌 🅿 🍽

DELFOI: *Ermís* €€€€ — 40
Freideríkis 27, 33054. **Road map** C3. **℡** 22650 82318. **FAX** 22650 82639.
The Ermís is situated in Delfoí, 600 m (1,900 ft) east of Ancient Delphi. Rooms have fine views over olive groves to the Gulf of Corinth. 🚌 🍽

DELFOI: *Olympic* €€€€ — 20
Freideríkis 53B, 33054. **Road map** C3. **℡** 22650 82163. **FAX** 22650 82639.
Situated in Delfoí, 600 m (1,900 ft) east of Ancient Delphi, this luxurious hotel offers *en suite* rooms with fine views over an olive-filled valley. 🚌 🍽

DELFOI: *Varónos* €€€€ — 10
Vasiléon Pávlou & Freideríkis 25, 33054. **Road map** C3. **℡ & FAX** 22650 82345.
Set in a Neo-Classical-style building in Delfoí, 600 m (1,900 ft) east of Ancient Delphi, this hotel has spacious rooms and large balconies. 🚌 🍽

DELFOI: *Xenía* €€€€€ — 45
Apóllonos 69, 33054. **Road map** C3. **℡** 22650 82151. **FAX** 22650 82764.
Situated in Delfoí, 600 m (1,900 ft) east of Ancient Delphi, the rooms of this chain hotel are spacious with private balconies. 🚌 🅿 🍽

GALAXIDI: *Ganyméde* €€€€ — 8
Níkou Gourgourí 20, 33052. **Road map** C3. **℡** 22650 41328. **FAX** 22650 42160.
This atmospheric, Italian-run hotel has rooms overlooking a beautiful garden. Home-made jam is on offer at breakfast. ● *Nov–20 Dec.* 🚌 🍽

Price categories are for a standard double room for one night in peak season, including tax, service charges and breakfast:
€ under 25 euros
€€ 25–35 euros
€€€ 35–45 euros
€€€€ 45–60 euros
€€€€€ over 60 euros.

RESTAURANT
Restaurant within the hotel sometimes reserved for residents only.

GARDEN OR TERRACE
Hotel with garden, courtyard or terrace, often providing tables for eating outside.

SWIMMING POOL
Hotel swimming pools are usually quite small and are outdoors unless otherwise stated.

AIR-CONDITIONING
Hotel with air-conditioning in all the rooms.

	Number of Rooms	Restaurant	Garden or Terrace	Swimming Pool	Air-Conditioning
IGOUMENITSA: *Savoy* €€€€	12				
IOANNINA: *Olympic* €€€€€	55	●			▪
IOANNINA: *Xenía* €€€€€	60	●	▪		
KALAMPAKA: *Rex* €€	34	●			
KALAMPAKA: *Antoniádi* €€€€	59	●	▪	●	
KALAMPAKA: *Diváni* €€€€€	164	●	▪	●	▪
KARDITSA: *N Plastiras Hotel* €€€€€	14				
MAKRINITSA: *Archontikó Mouslí* €€€€€	8		▪		
MAKRINITSA: *Archontikó Xiradáki* €€€€€	12		▪		
MEGALO PAPIGKO: *Níkos Saxónis* €€€€€	8		▪		
METSOVO: *Apóllon* €€€€	40		▪		
METSOVO: *Egnatía* €€€€	37				

IGOUMENITSA: *Savoy* €€€€ — 12
Voreíou Ipeírou 3, 46100. **Road map** B2. ☎ 26650 23957. **FAX** 26650 23781.
Accommodation here consists of 12 traditional-style, furnished apartments. Units have wooden interiors and shutters and are equipped with a television. The children's playground makes it an ideal choice for families.

IOANNINA: *Olympic* €€€€€ — 55
Melanídi 2, 45332. **Road map** B2. ☎ 26510 25888. **FAX** 26510 22041.
A long-established, friendly hotel near the town centre, offering some of the best reasonably priced accommodation in Ioánnina.

IOANNINA: *Xenía* €€€€€ — 60
Leofóros Dodónis 33, 45221. **Road map** B2. ☎ 26510 47301. **FAX** 26510 47189.
This modern hotel offers comfortable, well equipped rooms. It is surrounded by gardens and there is a conference room available.

KALAMPAKA: *Rex* €€ — 34
Kastrakíou 11A, 42200. **Road map** B2. ☎ 24320 22042. **FAX** 24320 22372.
A simpler and cheaper hotel than many near Metéora. The Rex is in a peaceful location, with sizeable well-furnished rooms.

KALAMPAKA: *Antoniádi* €€€€ — 59
Trikálon 148, 42200. **Road map** B2. ☎ 24320 24387. **FAX** 24320 24319.
A new, but homely, small hotel which lacks views of Metéora but has a very friendly atmosphere and a first-class restaurant.

KALAMPAKA: *Diváni* €€€€€ — 164
At entrance to village, 42200. **Road map** B2. ☎ 24320 23330. **FAX** 24320 23638.
This smart hotel in the Diváni chain has close-up views of the Metéora rocks. All rooms have balconies and there is an open-air bar.

KARDITSA: *N Plastiras Hotel* €€€€€ — 14
Neraida Karditsas, Nikolau Plastira Lake. **Road map** C3.
☎ 24410 92460. **FAX** 24410 92461.
Set in the mountains with wonderful views, this hotel is popular with skiers in winter, but a picturesque place to stay in summer, too.

MAKRINITSA: *Archontikó Mouslí* €€€€€ — 8
Pílio, 37011. **Road map** D3. ☎ 24280 90151. **FAX** 24280 99140.
This restored traditional Pílio mansion in Makrinitsa, 14 km (9 miles) north of Vólos, has a tree-shaded patio and is an ideal place to relax.

MAKRINITSA: *Archontikó Xiradáki* €€€€€ — 12
Near main square, 37011. **Road map** D3. ☎ 24280 99250. **FAX** 24280 90151.
Situated in a peaceful part of Makrinitsa, 14 km (9 miles) north of Vólos, this 19th-century building has spacious verandas with good views.

MEGALO PAPIGKO: *Níkos Saxónis* €€€€€ — 8
Off main square, 44016. **Road map** D3. ☎ 26530 41615. **FAX** 26530 41891
Situated in Megálo Pápigko, 40 km (25 miles) south of Kónitsa, this smart hotel is made up of a cluster of tastefully restored 18th-century buildings. Rooms have original fireplaces and there is a delightful rose garden.

METSOVO: *Apóllon* €€€€ — 40
Main square, 44200. **Road map** B2. ☎ 26560 41844. **FAX** 26560 42110.
Situated in the heart of the town, the Apóllon is a chalet-style hotel with a wooden exterior and cosy wooden interior.

METSOVO: *Egnatía* €€€€ — 37
Tositsa 19, 44200. **Road map** B2. ☎ 26560 41900. **FAX** 26560 41485.
A mountain hotel with stone and woodwork decor. All the rooms are *en suite* and many have private balconies commanding fine views out across the Píndos mountains.

METSOVO: *Victória* €€€€€ | 37
Near Agios Geórgios Park, 44200. **Road map** B2. ☎ 26560 41761. FAX 26560 41454.
Situated a short distance from the village, this traditional-style hotel offers rooms with good views of the Píndos mountains. 🛌 🕭 🞂

MIKRO PAPIGKO: *Días* €€€ | 10
Mikró Pápigko, 47016. **Road map** D3. ☎ 26530 41257. FAX 26530 41892.
This traditional-style hotel in Mikró Pápigko, 38 km (24 miles) south of Kónitsa, has been modernized. It is within easy reach of the Víkos Gorge, and overlooks the famous limestone rock towers of the village. 🛌

MPOURAZANI: *Mpourazáni* €€€€€ | 20
SE of Melissópetra, 44100. **Road map** C3. ☎ 26550 61283. FAX 26550 61321.
Set in a wonderful wildlife park, 3 km (2 miles) southeast of the village of Melissópetra and 12 km (7 miles) west of Kónitsa, this hotel and wildlife research centre has rooms with balconies and mountain views. 🛌 P 🞂

NAFPAKTOS: *Náfpaktos* €€€€€ | 50
Korydalloú 4, 30300. **Road map** C3. ☎ 26340 29551. FAX 26340 29553
Well situated near the harbour, this hotel has a whitewashed interior and marble floors. All rooms have balconies, some offering sea views. 🛌 🕭 P 🞂

PARGA: *Galini* €€€ | 25
Agion Saránta 6, 48060. **Road map** B3. ☎ 26840 31581. FAX 26840 32221.
Although very close to the town centre, this simple hotel is situated in a quiet and leafy spot and has a friendly, family-like atmosphere. 🛌 P

PREVEZA: *Mínos* €€€ | 23
21 Oktovríou, 48100. **Road map** B3. ☎ 26820 28424. FAX 26820 24644.
This is one of the best of Préveza's limited choice of hotels. It has a friendly family atmosphere and clean, comfortable rooms. No breakfasts provided. 🛌

TRIKALA: *Achílleion* €€€€€ | 60
Asklipioú 2, 42100. **Road map** C2. ☎ 24310 28291. FAX 24310 74858.
A modern hotel, right by the main square in the town centre. Rooms are *en suite* with balconies that look out on to the old town. 🛌 🕭 🞂

VOLOS: *Fílippos* €€€€ | 39
Sólonos 9, 39001. **Road map** C3. ☎ 24210 37607. FAX 24210 39550.
A new and simple hotel, set one block back from the waterfront, on the edge of the main square. The upper rooms all have sea views. 🛌 🕭

VOLOS: *Park* €€€€€ | 119
Deligiórgi 2, 38221. **Road map** C3. ☎ 24210 36511. FAX 24210 28645.
This is one of the best hotels in Vólos. The rooms are modern, stylishly decorated and have balconies that overlook the sea or park. 🛌 P 🕭 🞂

VYZITSA: *Karagiannopoulos Mansion* €€€€ | 6
Off main road, 37010. **Road map** D3. ☎ 24230 86717.
Situated in Vyzítsa, 2 km (1 mile) north of Miliés, this hotel is housed in a traditional mansion, with woodcut ceilings and a garden terrace. 🛌

NORTHERN GREECE

ALEXANDROUPOLI: *Alkyón* €€€€ | 30
Moudaníon 1, 68100. **Road map** E1. ☎ 25510 27465. FAX 25510 27465.
A modern but traditional-style whitewashed hotel with rustic furnishings and a friendly atmosphere. The rooms have fine sea views. 🛌 P 🞂

ALEXANDROUPOLI: *Egnatía* €€€ | 96
Leofóros Mákris, 68100. **Road map** E1. ☎ 25510 83000. FAX 25510 37634.
Set in peaceful grounds on the seafront, the Egnatía is a short walk from the town centre. The rooms are simply decorated, but pleasant. 🛌 P 🕭 🞂

FANARI: *Vósporos* €€€€€ | 20
2 km (1 mile) SE of Fanári, 67063. **Road map** E1. ☎ 25350 31216. FAX 25350 31212
This modern hotel has pleasant, good-sized rooms, all with balconies overlooking the sea. Beaches are a short walk away. 🛌 P

FANARI: *Fanári* €€€ | 32
Next to campsite, 67063. **Road map** E1. ☎ 25350 31300. FAX 25350 31388.
All rooms in this clean, modern hotel boast good sea views. The Fanári also has its own bar and pastry shop. 🛌

For key to symbols see back flap

Price categories are for a standard double room for one night in peak season, including tax, service charges and breakfast:
€ under 25 euros
€€ 25–35 euros
€€€ 35–45 euros
€€€€ 45–60 euros
€€€€€ over 60 euros.

RESTAURANT
Restaurant within the hotel sometimes reserved for residents only.
GARDEN OR TERRACE
Hotel with garden, courtyard or terrace, often providing tables for eating outside.
SWIMMING POOL
Hotel swimming pools are usually quite small and are outdoors unless otherwise stated.
AIR-CONDITIONING
Hotel with air-conditioning in all the rooms.

	NUMBER OF ROOMS	RESTAURANT	GARDEN OR TERRACE	SWIMMING POOL	AIR-CONDITIONING
FLORINA: *Língos* €€€€€ Tagmatárchou Naoúm 3, 53100. **Road map** B1. **(** 23850 28322. **FAX** 23850 29643. This modern hotel, situated close to all amenities, offers an Italian-style roof garden and rooms with mountain views. 🖥 🕭 ✎	40	●	▪		
GERAKINI: *Gerakiní Beach Hotel* €€€€€ Gerakiní beach, 36100. **Road map** D2. **(** 23710 52302. **FAX** 23710 52118. A modern complex in Gerakiní, 17 km (11 miles) south of Néa Moudaniá, comprising a hotel and bungalows. Rooms are spacious, with balconies overlooking the sea. ● *Nov–Apr.* 🖥 P 🕭 ✎	503	●	▪	●	
KASTORIA: *Tsámis* €€€€€ Koromilá 3, Dispílio, 52100. **Road map** B2. **(** 24670 85334. **FAX** 24670 85777. Quietly situated on the far side of the lake from the town centre, this modern but traditional-style hotel has its own gymnasium and bar. Activities on the lake make the Tsámis an ideal choice for watersports enthusiasts. 🖥	78	●	▪		
KASTORIA: *Kastoriá* €€€€€ Leof. Nikis 122, 52100. **Road map** B2. **(** 24670 22565. **FAX** 24670 26391. This hotel, built in the traditional local style, has wonderful views over the town. Small and peaceful, it is suitable for families. 🖥 P ✎	37	●	▪		
KAVALA: *Blue Bay Beach Hotel* €€€€ Nea Iraklitsa, Blue Bay, 65500. **Road map** D1. **(** 25940 21800. **FAX** 25940 21555. Located 9 km (6 miles) outside Kavála, this hotel is situated right on the beach. Rooms are light and airy and there is also a roof garden. 🖥 P ✎	32	●	▪	●	▪
KAVALA: *Galaxy* €€€€ Venizélou 27, 65302. **Road map** D1. **(** 2510 224811. **FAX** 2510 226754. Situated in the heart of the town centre, this large, modern hotel is close to archaeological sites of interest and beaches. 🖥 P 🕭 ✎	150	●	▪		▪
KAVALA: *Lucy* €€€€ Kalamítsa beach, 65404. **Road map** D1. **(** 2510 242830. **FAX** 2510 242501. Set on the best beach outside Kavála, this comfortable hotel is suitable for those wanting to avoid the bustle of the town. ● *Nov–Mar.* 🖥 🕭 ✎	210	●	▪	●	▪
KOMOTINI: *Rodópi* €€€€ Ethnárchou Makaríou 3, 69100. **Road map** E1. **(** 25310 35988. **FAX** 25310 35991. The Rodópi is housed in a traditional-style wooden building with spacious rooms and balconies overlooking Mount Rodópi. 🖥 P	20	●	▪		
KOMOTINI: *Anatólia* €€€€€ Anchiálou 53, 69100. **Road map** E1. **(** 25310 36242. **FAX** 25310 23170. This friendly, family-run hotel is set in a peaceful location not far from the main park. Rooms are basic but clean. 🖥 P ✎	56	●			▪
KRYOPIGI: *Forest Park* €€€€ Kryopigí beach, 63077. **Road map** D2. **(** 23740 23771. **FAX** 23740 23772. Situated in Kryopigí, 25 km (16 miles) northeast of Néa Moudaniá, this hotel is surrounded on three sides by the beautiful Kassándra pinewoods. Rooms have modern facilities and spacious verandas. ● *Nov–Apr.* 🖥 P 🕭 ✎	50	●	▪	●	▪
LITOCHORO: *Myrtó* €€€ Agíou Nikoláou 5, 60200. **Road map** C2. **(** 23520 81398. **FAX** 23520 82298. Situated in Litóchoro, 21 km (13 miles) south of Katerína, this hotel has large, *en suite* rooms and a friendly atmosphere. 🖥 P 🕭	32		▪		
NEOS MARMARAS: *Sithonía Beach Hotel* €€€€€ 3 km (2 miles) E of village, 63081. **Road map** D2. **(** 23750 71221. **FAX** 23750 72130. Situated in Néos Marmarás, 52 km (32 miles) southeast of Néa Moudaniá, this modern hotel lies in a bay at the foot of the Melítonas mountains. All rooms have verandas with fine views over the Aegean. ● *Nov–Apr.* 🖥 P ✎	442	●	▪	●	▪

NYMFAIA: *La Moára* €€€€€ 8
At entrance to village, 53078. **Road map** E1. 2310 287626. FAX 2310 71502.
This traditional old building offers spacious accommodation in beautiful grounds. Facilities include billiards, a library and a wine bar, and the hotel provides easy access to the Vítsi mountain ski resort. ● *Jul.* ⌂ P ⌂

OURANOUPOLI: *Skítes* €€€€€ 15
Road to Mount Athos, 63075. **Road map** D2. 23770 71140. FAX 23770 71322.
A family-run hotel set in a peaceful spot, surrounded by pine woods, with whitewashed bungalows that are decorated in a rustic style. The veranda restaurant has spectacular views of the sea. ● *Nov–Apr.* ⌂ P ⌂ ⌂

PRESPA LAKES: *Agios Germanos Hostel* €€ 15
Main road, Agios Germanós village, 53077. **Road map** B1. 23850 51320.
This hostel, offering excellent views of the lake and the village, is run by the local women's association who create a very warm environment. ⌂ P

THESSALONIKI: *Vergína* €€€€€ 133
Monastiríou 19, 54627. **Road map** C2. 2310 516021. FAX 2310 529308.
One of the better hotels near the train and bus stations, this is a large and efficiently run establishment with spacious rooms. ⌂ ⌂

THESSALONIKI: *Anatolia* €€€€€ 68
Langadá 13, 54629. **Road map** C2. 2310 522421. FAX 2310 512892.
A Neo-Classical-style hotel within walking distance of the central square and port, and close to the bazaar. The rooms have balconies. ⌂ P ⌂

THESSALONIKI: *Electra Palace* €€€€€ 135
Plateía Aristotélous 9, 54624. **Road map** C2. 2310 232221. FAX 2310 235947.
An up-market central hotel, ideally situated just off the waterfront, with a style that mixes the modern and the traditional. All rooms are fully equipped with a telephone, television and minibar. ⌂ ⌂ ⌂

THESSALONIKI: *Macedonia Palace* €€€€€ 288
Megálou Alexándrou 2, 54640. **Road map** C2. 2310 861400. FAX 2310 897211.
This is a smart hotel situated within walking distance of the city centre. It boasts an unrivalled seafront setting and a cool, modern marbled interior. ⌂ ⌂ ⌂

THESSALONIKI: *Olympía* €€€€€ 110
Olýmpou 65, 54631. **Road map** C2. 2310 235421. FAX 2310 276133.
This is a well-kept hotel with good facilities. It is situated in the quieter back streets, but is just a short stroll from the city centre. ⌂ P ⌂

THESSALONIKI: *Panórama* €€€€€ 50
Analípseos 26, Panórama, 55236. **Road map** C2. 2310 344871. FAX 2310 344871.
Situated in the eastern hill-top suburb of Panórama, this comfortable hotel has a wonderful view of the city. Car or taxi is needed to reach the city centre, but the superior rooms compensate. ⌂

THESSALONIKI: *Park* €€€€€ 56
᾽Ionos Dragoúmi 81, 54630. **Road map** C2. 2310 524122. FAX 2310 524193.
Situated in a modern block close to the city centre, the hotel offers simply but comfortably furnished *en suite* rooms with balconies. ⌂ ⌂ ⌂

THESSALONIKI: *Queen Olga* €€€€€ 148
Vasilíssis Olgas 44, 54641. **Road map** C2. 2310 824621. FAX 2310 868581.
A modern and comfortable hotel, the Queen Olga is close to the city centre and has some rooms that overlook the sea. ⌂

VERGINA: *Pension Vergina* €€€ 10
Vergina Imagias 59031. **Road map** C2. 23310 92510. FAX 23310 92511.
Situated 200m (650 ft) from the tomb of King Philip II of Macedon, this hotel offers clean, well-kept rooms, some with balconies. ⌂

XANTHI: *Néstos* €€€€ 74
On Xánthi–Kaválan road, 67100. **Road map** E1. 25410 27531. FAX 25410 27535.
A large and modern, business-like hotel with good facilities. It is located outside the town centre, and near the railway station. ⌂ P ⌂ ⌂

XANTHI: *Orfeas* €€€ 34
Michaïl Karaolí 40, 67100. **Road map** E1. 25410 20121. FAX 25410 20998.
This friendly hotel offers simple, clean rooms. It is well situated near the market, shops and restaurants and has views over Xánthi. ⌂ P ⌂

For key to symbols see back flap

WHERE TO EAT

To eat out in Greece is to experience the democratic tradition at work. Rich and poor, young and old, all enjoy their favourite local restaurant, taverna or café. Greeks consider the best places to be where the food is fresh, plentiful and well-cooked, not necessarily where the setting or the cuisine is the fanciest. Visitors too have come to appreciate the simplicity and health of the traditional Greek kitchen – olive

A local cheese from Métsovo

oil, yoghurt, vegetables, a little meat and some wine, always shared with friends. The traditional three-hour lunch and siesta – still the daily rhythm of the countryside – is now only a fading memory for most city Greeks, who have adapted to a more Western European routine. But the combination of traditional cooking and outside influences has produced a vast range of eating places in Greece, with somewhere to suit almost everyone.

The Néon restaurant in the centre of Athens *(see p287)*

TYPES OF RESTAURANT

Often difficult to find in more developed tourist resorts, the *estiatórion*, or traditional Greek restaurant, is one of Europe's most enjoyable places to eat. Friendly, noisy and sometimes in lovely surroundings, *estiatória* are reliable purveyors of local recipes and wines, particularly if they have been owned by the same family for decades. Foreigners unfamiliar with Greek dishes may be invited into the kitchen to choose their fare. In Greece, the entire family dines together and takes plenty of time over the meal, especially at weekends.

Estiatória range from the very expensive in Athens, Thessaloníki and wealthier

suburbs, to the incredibly inexpensive *mageirió* or *koutoúki*, popular with students and workers. Here there is little choice in either wines or dishes, all of which will be *mageireftá* (ready-cooked). The food, however, is homemade and tasty and the barrel wine is at the very least drinkable, often good, and sometimes comes from the owner's home village.

Some restaurants may specialize in a particular type of cuisine. In Thessaloníki, for example, and in the suburbs of Athens, where Asia Minor refugees settled after 1923, you may find food to be spicier than the Greek norm, with lots of red peppers and such dishes as *giogurtlú* (kebabs drenched in yoghurt and served on pitta bread) or lamb-brain salad.

The menu *(see pp280– 81)* in a traditional restaurant tends to be short, comprising

A sign for a taverna in Párga

at most a dozen *mezédes* (starters or snacks), perhaps eight main dishes, four or five cooked vegetable dishes or salads, plus a dessert of fresh or cooked fruit, and a selection of local and national wines.

Many hotels have restaurants open to non-residents. Smaller country hotels occasionally have excellent kitchens, and serve good local wines, so check on any that are close to where you are staying.

In the last few years a new breed of young Greek chefs has emerged in *kultúra* restaurants, developing a style of cooking that encompasses Greece's magnificent raw materials, flavours and colours. These dishes are served with the exciting new Greek wines.

The Ostriá restaurant *(see p293)* **at Agios Ioánnis, on the Pílio peninsula**

Waiter outside a restaurant in Pláka, Athens

TAVERNAS

O NE OF THE GREAT pleasures for the traveller in Greece is the tradition of the taverna, a place to eat and drink, even if you simply snack on *mezédes* (Greeks rarely drink without eating). Traditional tavernas are open from mid-evening and stay open late; occasionally they are open for lunch as well. Menus are short and seasonal – perhaps six or eight *mezédes* and four main courses comprising casseroles and dishes cooked *tis óras* (to order), along with the usual accompaniments of vegetables, salads, fruit and wine.

Like traditional restaurants, some tavernas specialize in the foods and wines of the owner's home region, some in a particular cooking style and others in certain foods.

A *psarotavérna* is the place to find good fish dishes but, because fish is expensive, these tavernas often resemble restaurants and are patronized mainly by wealthy Greeks and tourists. In small fishing villages it is quite different and you may find the rickety tables of a *psarotavérna* literally on the beach. Close to the lapping waves the owner may serve fish that he himself caught that morning.

For delicious grills try a *psistariá*, a taverna that specializes in spit-roasts and char-grilling *(sta kárvouna)*. In countryside *psistariés* lamb, kid, pork, chicken, game,

offal, lambs' heads and even testicles are char-grilled, and whole lamb is roasted on the spit. At the harbourside, fish and shellfish are grilled and served with fresh lemon juice and olive oil. Country, family-run tavernas and cafés will invariably provide simple meals, such as omelettes and salads throughout the day, but many of these places close quite early in the evening. After your meal in the taverna, follow the Greeks and enjoy a visit to the local *zacharoplasteío (see p278)* for sweets and pastries.

CAFÉS AND BARS

C AFÉS, KNOWN AS *kafeneía*, are the pulse of Greek life, and even the tiniest hamlet has a place to drink coffee or wine. Equally important is the function it performs as the centre of communication – mail is collected here, telephone calls made, and newspapers read, dissected and discussed. *Kafeneía* serve Greek coffee, sometimes *frappé* (instant coffee served cold, in a tall glass), soft drinks, beer, ouzo and wine. Most also serve some kind of snack to order. All open early and remain open until late at night.

As the social hub of their communities, country *kafeneía*, as well as many in the city, open seven days a week.

A *galaktopoleío*, or "milk shop", has a seating area where you can enjoy fine yoghurt and honey; those around Plateía Omonoías in Athens remain open for most of the night.

A *kapileío* (wine shop with a café-bar attached) is the place to try local wines from the cask, and you may find a few bottled wines as well. The owner is invariably from a wine village or family and will often cook some simple regional specialities to accompany the wine.

In a *mezedopoleío*, or *mezés* shop, the owner will not only serve the local wine and the *mezédes* that go with it, but also ouzo and the infamous spirit, raki, both distilled from the remnants of the grape harvest. Their accompanying *mezédes* are less salty than those served with wine.

No holiday in Greece is complete without a visit to an *ouzerí*. Some of the best of these are to be found in Thessaloníki and in Athens' central arcades. You can order a dozen or more little plates of savoury meats, fish and vegetables and try the many varieties of ouzo that are served in small jugs. A jug or glass of water accompanies the ouzo to wash it down. These are traditionally inexpensive, noisy and fun places to eat and drink.

Bottle of ouzo

O Vláchos taverna *(see p290)* at Mount Párnitha, north of Athens

Waitress at To Geráni restaurant in Pláka, Athens (see p288)

FAST FOOD AND SNACKS

VISITORS can be forgiven for thinking Greeks never stop eating, for there seem to be snack bars on every street and vendors selling sweets, nuts, rolls, and seasonal corn and chestnuts at every turn.

Although American-style fast-food outlets dominate city streets, it is easy to avoid them by trying the traditional Greek eateries. The extremely cheap *souvlatzídiko* offers chunks of meat, fish or vegetables roasted on a skewer and served with bread, while an *ovelistírio* serves *gýros* – meat from a revolving spit in a pitta bread pocket. The food is sold *sto chéri* (in the hand).

Many bakeries serve savoury pies and a variety of tasty bread rolls, and in busy city neighbourhoods you can always find a *kafeneío* serving substantial snacks and salads. Street vendors sell *koulourákia* (rolls), small pies, corn on the cob, roast chestnuts, nut brittle and candies. Snacks are often local specialities: tiny open pizza-like pies in Thessaloníki; pies of wild greens or cheese *(see p284)* in Métsovo, and small flavourful sausages in Ioánnina.

If you have a sweet tooth you will love the *zacharoplasteío* (literally, "shop of the sugar sculptor"). The baker there makes traditional sweet breads *(see p282)*, tiny sweet pastries and a whole variety of fragrant honey cakes.

BREAKFAST

FOR GREEKS, this is the least important meal of the day. In traditional homes and cafés a small cup of Greek coffee accompanies *paximádia* (slices of rusk-like bread) or *koulourákia* (firm, sesame-covered or slightly sweet rolls in rings or s-shapes) or pound cakes with home-made jam. Elsewhere, and in many city *kafeneía*, this has been replaced by a large cup of brewed coffee and French-style croissants or delicious brioche-style rolls, also called *koulourákia*. In the summer, some *kafeneía* will still serve fresh figs, thick yoghurt, pungent honey and slightly sweet currant bread.

RESERVATIONS

THE MORE expensive the restaurant, the more advisable it is to make a reservation, and it is always worth doing so at the weekend. In country areas, and in the suburbs, it is the practice to visit the restaurant or taverna earlier in the day, or the day before, and check on the dishes to be served. The proprietor will take your order and reserve any special dish that you request.

Serving *gýros* on an Athens street

WINE

RESTAURATEURS IN Greece are only now learning to look after bottled wines. If the wine list contains the better bottles, such as Ktíma

Merkoúri, Seméli or Strofiliá, the proprietor probably knows how to look after the wine and it will be safe to order a more expensive bottle. For a good-value bottle there are the nationally known Cambás or Boutári wines.

Traditional restaurants and tavernas may only stock carafe wine, which is served straight from the barrel and is always inexpensive. Carafe wines are often of the region and, among Greek wines, the rosé in particular is noted for having an unusual but pleasing flavour.

HOW TO PAY

GREECE IS STILL largely a cash society. If you need to pay by credit card, check first that the restaurant takes credit cards, and if so, that they take the card you intend to use – many proprietors accept some but not others. *Kafeneía* almost never take credit cards, and café-bars rarely, but many will be happy to take travellers' cheques. In rural areas, country tavernas, restaurants and *kafeneía* will only accept cash.

The listings in this guide indicate whether or not credit cards are accepted at each establishment.

SERVICE AND TIPPING

GREEKS TAKE PLENTY of time when they eat out and expect a high level of attention. This means a great deal of running around on the part of

Patrons outside Thanásis kebab restaurant, Athens (see p287)

Interior patio of Ouzerí Aristotélous in Thessaloníki *(see p295)*

the waiter, but in return they receive generous tips – as much as 20 per cent if the service is good, though more often a tip is 10–15 per cent. Prices in traditional establishments do include service, but the waiters still expect a tip so always have coins ready to hand.

Western-style restaurants and tourist tavernas sometimes add a service charge to the bill; their prices can be much higher because of trimmings, such as telephones and air-conditioning.

Bread ring seller, Athens

DRESS CODE

THE GREEKS dress quite formally when dining out. Visitors should wear whatever is comfortable, but skimpy tops and shorts and active sportswear are not acceptable, except near the beach, although it is unlikely that tourist establishments would turn custom away. Some of the most expensive city restaurants, especially those attached to hotels, request formal dress; the listings indicate which places fall into this category.

In summer, if you intend dining outside, take a jacket or sweater for the evening.

CHILDREN

GREEK CHILDREN become restaurant and taverna habitués at a very early age – it is an essential part of their education. Consequently, children are welcome everywhere in Greece except in

the bars. In formal restaurants children are expected to be well behaved, but in summer, when Greeks enjoy eating outside, it is perfectly acceptable for children to play and enjoy themselves too. Facilities such as highchairs are unknown except in the most considerate hotel dining rooms, but more casual restaurants and tavernas are fine for dining with children of any age.

SMOKING

SMOKING is commonplace in Greece and, with the exception of the most expensive dining rooms, you will have difficulty finding anywhere that maintains a no-smoking policy. However, most restaurants are airy, and for at least half the year it is generally possible to enjoy your meal outside in the open air.

Drying octopus at a restaurant in Geroliménas, on the Máni peninsula *(see p199)*

WHEELCHAIR ACCESS

IN COUNTRY AREAS, where room is plentiful, there are few problems for wheelchair users. In city restaurants, however, it is a different matter, and access is often restricted. The streets themselves have uneven pavements and many restaurants have narrow doorways and possibly steps. Restaurants that do have wheelchair access are indicated in the listings pages of this guide. Also, the organizations that are listed on page 299 provide information for disabled travellers in Greece.

VEGETARIAN FOOD

GREEK CUISINE provides plenty of choice for vegetarians. Greeks enjoy such a variety of dishes for each course that it is easy to order just vegetable dishes for first and main courses in traditional restaurants, tavernas or *kafeneía*. Vegetable dishes are substantial, inexpensive, imaginatively prepared and satisfying.

Vegans may have more of a problem, for there are few places in Greece catering for special diets. However, as Greek cooking relies little on dairy products, it is possible to follow a vegan diet almost anywhere in Greece.

PICNICS

THE BEST TIME to picnic in Greece is in spring, when the countryside is at its most beautiful and the weather is not too hot. The traditional seasonal foods, such as Lenten olive oil bread, sweet Easter bread, pies filled with wild greens, fresh cheese and new retsina wine, all make perfect fare for picnics. Summer is the ideal time for eating on the beach. The best foods for summer snacks are peaches and figs, yoghurt and cheese, and tomatoes, various breads and olives.

The Classic Greek Menu

THE TRADITIONAL FIRST COURSE is a selection of
mezédes, or snacks; these can also be eaten in
ouzerís, or bars, throughout the day. Meat or fish
dishes follow next, usually served with a salad. The
wine list tends to be simple and coffee and cakes
are generally consumed after the meal in a nearby
pastry shop. In rural areas traditional dishes can be
chosen straight from the kitchen.

Mezédes are both a first course and a snack with wine or other drinks.

Taramosaláta *is a purée of salted mullet roe and breadcrumbs or potato. Traditionally a dish for Lent, it is now on every taverna menu.*

Souvlákia *are tiny chunks of pork, flavoured with lemon, herbs and olive oil, grilled on skewers. Here they are served with* **tzatzíki**, *a refreshing mixture of creamy yoghurt, cucumber, garlic and mint.*

Olives

Melitzanosaláta and revythosaláta *are both purées. Melitzanosaláta,* left, *is grilled aubergines and herbs; and revythosaláta, right, is chick peas, coriander and garlic.*

Fish are at their best around the coast and on the islands.

Melitzánes imám baïldí
are aubergines filled with a ragoût of onions, tomatoes and herbs. **Ntolmádes** *(bottom) are parcels of vine leaves tightly stuffed with currants, pine nuts and rice.*

Fried squid

ΜΕΖΕΣ
Mezés

Ελιές
Eliés

Ταραμοσαλάτα
Taramosaláta

Τζατζίκι
Tzatzíki

Σουβλάκια
Souvlákia

Ρεβυθοσαλάτα
Revythosaláta

Μελιτζανοσαλάτα
Melitzanosaláta

Ντολμάδες
Ntolmádes

Μελιτζάνες ιμάμ μπαϊλντί
Melitzánes imám baïldí

Χωριάτικη σαλάτα
Choriátiki saláta

ΨΑΡΙΑ
Psária

Πλακί
Plakí

Σχάρας
Scháras

Τηγανιτά καλαμάρια
Tiganitá kalamária

Choriátiki saláta, *Greek salad, combines tomatoes, cucumber, onions, herbs, capers and feta cheese.*

Scháras *means "from the grill". This summer dish of grilled swordfish is served with a salad of bitter greens.*

Psária plakí *is a whole fish baked in an open dish with carrots, leeks and potatoes in a tomato, fennel and olive oil sauce.*

BREAD IN GREECE

Bread is considered by Greeks to be the staff of life and is served at every meal. Village bakers vary the bread each day with flavourings of currants, herbs, wild greens or cheese. The many Orthodox festivals are celebrated with special breads.

Olive rolls with herbs **Pitta bread, unleavened**

Paximádia (twice-baked bread)

Koulourákia (sweet or plain rolls)

Tsouréki (festival bread loaf)

ΚΡΕΑΣ
Kréas

Μουσακάς
Mousakás

Κεφτέδες
Keftédes

Χοιρινό σουβλάκι
Choirinó souvláki

Κλέφτικο
Kléftiko

ΛΑΧΑΝΙΚΑ ΚΑΙ ΣΑΛΑΤΙΚΑ
Lachaniká kai salatiká

Μελιτζάνες και κολοκυθάκια τηγανιτά
Melitzánes kai kolokythákia tiganitá

Αγκινάρες α λα πολίτα
Agkináres a la políta

Σπαράγγια σαλάτα
Sparángia saláta

ΓΛΥΚΑ
Glyká

Φρέσκα φρούτα
Fréska froúta

Σύκα στο φούρνο με μαυροδάφνη
Sýka sto foúrno me mavrodáfni

Γιαούρτι και μέλι
Giaoúrti kai méli

Meat is more readily available on the mainland than the islands.

Kebabs of grilled pork

Vegetables and salads often use wild produce.

Fried aubergines and courgettes

Artichokes with potatoes, dill, lemon and oil

Asparagus in olive oil and lemon

Desserts are simple affairs of pastry, fruit or yoghurt.

Fresh fruit varies according to what is in season.

Mousakás *is made of layers of fried aubergine and potato slices, spicy minced meat and savoury béchamel sauce, topped with cheese.*

Keftédes *are pork mince with egg and breadcrumbs, flavoured with herbs, mint and cumin and fried in olive oil. They are served here with saffron rice.*

Sýka sto foúrno me Mavrodáfni *are fresh figs baked in Mavrodaphne wine sauce, served as a dessert or sweet treat. The sauce, of wine, spices and honey, is flavoured with orange-flower water.*

Giaoúrti kai méli *(yoghurt with honey) is the most wonderful snack in Greece, served in speciality "milk shops", to be eaten there or taken home.*

Kléftiko *is usually goat meat wrapped in parchment paper and cooked so that the juices and flavours are sealed in.*

What to Eat in Athens and the Peloponnese

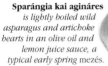

Slices of melon

ANCIENT GREECE regarded cooking as both a science and an art. In Athens, and through Attica and the Peloponnese, you still find the ingredients that inspired the chefs of antiquity and, later, the cuisine of the Ottoman Empire with its highly flavoured meat dishes. The simplicity of Greek cooking and its reliance on fresh raw materials are what make it distinctive.

Fresh fruit and vegetable market in Argos

ATHENS

The capital is a city of immigrants from the countryside, the islands and the shores of the eastern Mediterranean. Its diversity is reflected in the markets and the cuisine.

Sparángia kai agináres *is lightly boiled wild asparagus and artichoke hearts in an olive oil and lemon juice sauce, a typical early spring mezés.*

Avgotarácho *is the smoked and salted roe of the grey mullet. It is a rare and expensive treat.*

Souvlákia *are chunks of pork or lamb, marinated in lemon juice and herbs, then grilled on a skewer. Here it is served with a yellow saffron pilaf.*

Kotópoulo riganáto *is chicken slowly roasted on a spit or grill, glistening with olive oil and pungent with oregano, accompanied here by okra.*

Mprizóles *is a thin beef or pork steak basted with olive oil and lemon juice. Here it is served with a chopped salad.*

Ravaní

Pistachios in filo pastry

Sweet pastries *filled with nuts and honey, syrup-drenched cakes, pies, doughnuts and glyká (candied fruits) are mainly eaten in cafés.*

Loukoumádes

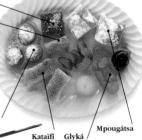

Mpougátsa

Kataïfi   **Glyká**

Sweets *such as nougat, pastéli (honey-sesame candy), loukoúmia (yeast doughnuts in syrup) and chalvás (halva, or sweetmeats) have been a part of Athens street life since the days of Aristotle. They are sold in small shops or stalls.*

Coffee *in Greece is traditionally made from very finely ground beans boiled up with water in a long handled mpríki (coffee pot) and drunk from a tiny cup. It is served in cafés rather than tavernas.*

THE PELOPONNESE

Ingredients here are as varied as the terrain: fish from the sea and, from the mountains, sheep, goat and game. From the hills come several varieties of cheese, olives and honey.

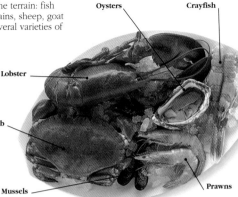

Oysters · Crayfish · Lobster · Crab · Mussels · Prawns

Fakés *is a warm or cold vegetable side dish of green lentils, black olives, lemon juice, fresh herbs and olive oil. It is also served as a mezés, or as a main course with cheese and bread.*

Shellfish and crustaceans, especially lobster and crab, are the prize catch of the Mediterranean. Delicious straight from the sea, they are traditionally char-grilled or pan-fried, sprinkled with fresh herbs, sea salt, olive oil and lemon juice.

OLIVES AND OLIVE OIL IN GREEK COOKING

Greece produces the largest variety of olives in the world and is also a major exporter. Greek olives can be brine-cured, dry-cured in rock salt, oil-cured or water-cured, methods that have been used for thousands of years. Olives are also pressed to extract rich olive oil. The best quality olive oil, extra-virgin, is made by pressing just-ripe olives only.

Arní me vótana *is a country casserole of lamb on the bone, herbs and early summer vegetables: beans, carrots, tomatoes and potatoes.*

Throúmpes

Ionian green

Nafplíou

Choriátiko choirinó *is a pork chop marinated in olive oil, lemon juice, sea salt and oregano, then grilled. It is often served with a salad of chórta (wild greens).*

Kalamátas

Cracked green

Amfissas

Sýka Mavrodáfni *is a dessert of dried figs, which are simmered in Mavrodaphne wine and spices, and served with slices of mature kefalotýri cheese.*

Extra-virgin oil from the Máni

Tin of blended olive oil for everyday use

Kaïmáki *is a very thick cream. It is served with sweet pastries and occasionally rice puddings or, as here, with walnuts drenched in honey.*

What to Eat in Central and Northern Greece

MAINLAND GREECE, with its long and chequered history, is a place where regional food boundaries are blurred and a variety of cooking traditions coexist. The meat and fruit dishes of Thessaloníki reveal a Jewish influence; the spices, sausages and oven cooking of Ioánnina stem from Ottoman times; while a love of sheep's cheese, pies and offal came to Métsovo and the Epirus mountains with the Vlachs from Romania.

Fresh local produce in Thessaloníki bazaar

CENTRAL AND WESTERN GREECE

The regional specialities of cheese, pies, grilled or spit-roasted game and offal are often flavoured with local mountain herbs.

Spicy meat pie

Chórta (wild greens) coil pie

Olive pie

Leek pie

Píttes, or pies, are a speciality of Epirus. Fillings range from game or offal to cheese and vegetables, often combined with rice or pasta.

Saganáki is a mezés or light lunch of kaséri or kefalotýri cheese, cut in slices, fried in olive oil, and served with lemon.

Skordaliá me psári kapnistó, found in inland areas, is a mezés of smoked fish with a garlic and walnut sauce and sharp, cracked green olives.

Fasoláda is an oven-baked dish of large white kidney beans, vegetables, herbs and olive oil. It is one of Greece's staple dishes.

Spetzofáï is made by quickly sautéeing slices of spicy country sausage with herbs and vegetables.

Bourthéto is a western coast speciality. Small fish are baked in an open dish and covered in a thick, spicy tomato sauce.

Glykó kástano is a chestnut pudding with honey and orange-blossom flavouring.

Výssino, a sweet snack made from morello cherries in a thick syrup, is served with slices of aged kaséri cheese.

GREEK CHEESES

Greece produces sheep's, cow's and goat's cheeses. Each type of cheese is made according to local traditions and usually named by taste and texture, not place of origin.

Feta in olive oil

Métsovo

Kefalotýri

Graviéra

Kaséri

NORTHERN GREECE

The spicy food of the North is the legacy of the 1922 Greek immigrants from Asia Minor. The Balkan influence is obvious in pickles, walnuts and yoghurt.

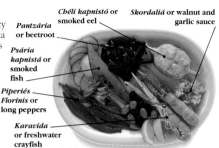

Chéli kapnistó or smoked eel

Skordaliá or walnut and garlic sauce

Pantzária or beetroot

Psária kapnistá or smoked fish

Piperiés Florínis or long peppers

Karavída or freshwater crayfish

Pasatémpo *means "to pass the time" – the purpose of this dish of lightly roasted sunflower and pumpkin seeds and pistachio nuts.*

This regional platter of mezédes is made up of small traditional dishes of contrasting colours, textures and flavours.

Pigeon *or other small game birds are served grilled with fáva (yellow lentil purée) and purslane salad.*

Soutzoukákia, *a speciality of Thrace and Macedonia, are meat patties flavoured with coriander, pepper and cumin.*

Tas kebab, *a country dish of slowly casseroled goat, kid, mutton or beef, is so tender it can be cut with a fork.*

Gemistá *are vegetables stuffed with rice, pine nuts and herbs and slowly oven baked.*

Damáskina, *prunes, are filled with kaïmáki cream in a honey and Mavrodaphne wine syrup.*

Filo pies *are pastries filled with chopped pistachios, cinnamon and honey.*

WHAT TO DRINK IN GREECE

Wine has been part of Greek cultural life from the earliest times. It is usually served with food. Major wine-producing areas include Attica, Macedonia and the Peloponnese. Mavrodaphne is a fortified dessert wine produced in Pátra. Asprolíthi is a dry white wine. Both are examples of excellent modern wines. Traditional Greek specialities include *tsípouro*, distilled from the stems, pips and skins of crushed grapes; retsina, which is wine flavoured with pine resin *(see p147)*; and the strong, aniseed-flavoured spirit, ouzo.

Asprolíthi wine **Mavrodaphne wine** **Ouzo** **Tsípouro**

Choosing a Restaurant

THE RESTAURANTS in this guide have been selected across a wide range of price categories for their good value, traditional food and interesting location. This chart lists the restaurants by area, starting with Athens. Use the colour-coded thumb tabs, which indicate the areas covered on each page, to guide you to the relevant section of the chart.

	AIR-CONDITIONING	OUTDOOR TABLES	LIVE ENTERTAINMENT	LOCAL WINES
ATHENS				
ACROPOLIS: *Strofí* €€ Rovértou Gkálli 25, 11742. **Map** 5 C3. **[** *210 921 4130.* The rooftop views of the Acropolis attract a constant stream of diners. The menu features all the mainstays of a Greek taverna. ● *lunch; Sun.* ⬗	●	▩		▩
EXARCHEIA: *Mpármpa Giánnis* € Emmanouíl Mpenáki 94, 10681. **Map** 2 F3. **[** *210 330 0185.* This popular taverna offers such dishes as octopus and macaroni, baked cod and tomatoes, and seasonal cooked vegetables. ● *Sun evening; Aug.*		▩		▩
EXARCHEIA: *Yiántes* € Valtetsíou 44, 10681. **Map** 2 F3. **[** *210 330 1369.* Set in a beautiful garden, this taverna offers wonderful dishes, such as chicken stuffed with grapes, all made with organic produce.	●	▩		▩
EXARCHEIA: *Rosalia* € Valtetsíou 58, 10681. **Map** 2 F2. **[** *210 330 2933.* This busy taverna is especially popular in summer, when eating takes place outside. The food is simple, but good.		▩		▩
EXARCHEIA: *Ama Lachei* €€ Kallidromíon 69, 10681. **Map** 3 A2. **[** *210 384 5978.* The well known *mezedopoleío* is about as authentic as they get. It is situated in the heart of Exárcheia, well off the usual tourist track. ● *lunch; Sun.*		▩		▩
EXARCHEIA: *La Crêperie* €€ Ippokratous 148, 10681. **Map** 2 F4. **[** *210 646 8493.* Generously filled sweet and savoury crêpes, washed down with a very good house wine, make this a pancake-lover's dream.				▩
KOLONAKI: *The Food Company* € Corner of Anagnostopoúlou & Dimokrítou, 10673. **Map** 3 A4. **[** *210 363 0373.* Anyone in need of wholesome, tasty food offered at excellent prices should go to this café, which is run by two American women. On offer are unusal salads, great pasta and delicious cakes. ● *1–15 Aug.*		▩		
KOLONAKI: *Filíppos* €€ Xenokrátous 19, 10675. **Map** 3 C5. **[** *210 721 6390.* This Kolonáki favourite offers all the standard taverna fare. Roast chicken with lemon potatoes and *ntolmádes* are particularly good. ● *Sat evenings, Sun; Aug 15.*		▩		▩
KOLONAKI: *Lykóvrysi* €€ Plateía Kolonakíou, 10673. **Map** 3 B5. **[** *210 361 6712.* A popular meeting place, the Lykóvrysi serves a few Greek dishes such as *fasouláda* (bean soup) alongside traditional international dishes.	●	▩		
KOLONAKI: *Dimókritos* €€€ Dimokrítou 23, 10673. **Map** 3 A5. **[** *210 361 3588.* The excellent food in this stylish taverna includes cuttlefish cooked in red wine, tongue with lemon sauce, and a wide range of starters. ● *Sun; Aug.*	●			▩
KOLONAKI: *To Kafeneío* €€€ Loukianoú 26, 10675. **Map** 3 B5. **[** *210 722 9056.* Excellent *mezédes* are served at this up-market Kolonáki *mezedopoleío*. Also featured are some of the better new-generation Greek wines. ● *Sun; Aug.*	●	▩		
KOLONAKI: *Vivliothíki* €€€ Plateía Kolonakiou 18, 10673. **Map** 3 A5. **[** *210 363 7897.* The lunches at this smart, French-style brasserie include smoked salmon, steak tartare, pasta and salads. ⬗	●	▩		▩

Average prices for a three-course meal for one, including a half-bottle of house wine, tax and service:
€ up to 12 euros
€€ 12–18 euros
€€€ 18–24 euros
€€€€ 24–32 euros
€€€€€ over 32 euros

AIR-CONDITIONING
Restaurant with air-conditioning.

OUTDOOR TABLES
Tables for eating outdoors, often with a good view.

LIVE ENTERTAINMENT
Dancing or live music performances on various days of the week.

LOCAL WINES
A specialized selection of local Greek wines.

	AIR-CONDITIONING	OUTDOOR TABLES	LIVE ENTERTAINMENT	LOCAL WINES
KOLONAKI: *Academy of Food and Wine* €€€€ Akadamias 24, 10673. **Map** 2 F5. **[** 210 364 1434. Good quality food and wines, presented with great flair and attention to detail, are served here. ● *lunchtimes; Sun.*	●			▨
KOLONAKI: *Dekaoktó* €€€€ Souidías 51, 10676. **Map** 3 C5. **[** 210 723 5561. A dozen candlelit tables, seductive *mezédes*, perfectly grilled fish and a good wine list make for a romantic place to dine.	●			▨
KOLONAKI: *Kíku* €€€€€ Dimokrítou 12, 10673. **Map** 3 A5. **[** 210 364 7033. The city's finest Japanese restaurant has all the ingredients you would expect: understated decor, perfect *sushi* and *sashimi*. ● *lunch; Sun; mid-Jul–mid-Aug.*	●			▨
KOLONAKI: *Sale e Pepe* €€€€€ Aristippou 34, 10673. **Map** 3 B4. **[** 210 723 4102. A chic Italian restaurant with a sophisticated menu. Specialities include ravioli stuffed with white truffles and foie gras in pancetta and leek sauce. ● *Sun.*	●			▨
MAKRYGIANNI: *Socrates' Prison* €€ Mitsaíon 20, 11742. **Map** 6 D3. **[** 210 922 3434. Close to the Herodes Atticus theatre, this popular taverna offers mainly Greek cuisine. The carafe wine is excellent. ● *Sun; 10–31 Aug.*	●	▨		▨
MONASTIRAKI: *Ipeiros* € Agíou Filíppou 16, 10555. **Map** 5 C1. **[** 210 324 5572. Well located near the flea market and the Ancient Agora, this good-value lunch-time taverna serves large portions of local food. ● *evenings; Easter Sun; mid-Aug.*		▨		▨
MONASTIRAKI: *Thanásis* € Mitropóleos 69, 10555. **Map** 6 D1. **[** 210 324 4705. This is a favourite pit stop for some of the best and cheapest grilled food in the city. Try the kebabs of spiced meat, onions or tomato and parsley wrapped in grilled pitta bread. ● *1 Jan, Easter Sun, 25 Dec.*	●			
MONASTIRAKI: *Cafe Avissynía* €€€ Plateía Avissynías, 10555. **Map** 5 C1. **[** 210 321 7047. Tables are always packed for the accordionist and singer who perform every weekend. During the week, when the café is quieter, is a better time to sample the unusual Macedonian dishes. ● *evenings; Aug.*	●	▨	●	▨
OMONOIA: *Andréas* €€ Themistokléous 18, 10678. **Map** 2 E3. **[** 210 382 1522. Set in a small alley off Themistokléous, this *ouzerí* specializes in seafood such as octopus, shellfish, anchovies and fried squid. ● *Sun; 1–20 Aug.*		▨		
OMONOIA: *Athinaikón* €€ Themistokléous 2, 10678. **Map** 2 E3. **[** 210 383 8485. This old establishment serves a wide range of well-executed and delicious fish and meat *mezédes*. Meals are accompanied by carafes of ouzo and wine. ● *Sun; Aug.*	●			▨
OMONOIA: *Ideal* €€€ Panepistimíou 46, 10678. **Map** 2 E3. **[** 210 330 3000. Since 1922, this much-loved institution has been serving excellent Greek and international cuisine. Specials include milk-fed veal with aubergine, stuffed courgettes and *agkináres a la políta* (artichokes in lemon juice). ● *Sun.*	●			▨
OMONOIA: *Néon* €€ Omónoia Square 1, 10431. **Map** 2 E3. **[** 210 523 6409. All-day eating at this self-service chain restaurant includes a salad bar, fresh pasta, grills and typical oven-baked Greek dishes.	●			

For key to symbols see back flap

<table>
<tr><td colspan="3">

Average prices for a three-course meal for one, including a half-bottle of house wine, tax and service:
€ up to 12 euros
€€ 12–18 euros
€€€ 18–24 euros
€€€€ 24–32 euros
€€€€€ over 32 euros

</td></tr>
</table>

AIR-CONDITIONING
Restaurant with air-conditioning.

OUTDOOR TABLES
Tables for eating outdoors, often with a good view.

LIVE ENTERTAINMENT
Dancing or live music performances on various days of the week.

LOCAL WINES
A specialized selection of local Greek wines.

	AIR-CONDITIONING	OUTDOOR TABLES	LIVE ENTERTAINMENT	LOCAL WINES
PANGRATI: *O Vyrínis* — € Archimídous 11, 11636. **Map** 7 B3. ☎ *210 701 5169.* Always busy, especially in summer, this taverna serves simple but tasty food at very reasonable prices. ● *lunchtime; Sun.*		▨		▨
PANGRATI: *Kallimármaron* — €€€ Effóriónos 13, 11636. **Map** 7 B2. ☎ *210 701 9727.* Situated behind the Kallimármaro stadium, this relaxed restaurant provides hearty Greek cooking. Try the unusual *kókoras* (cockerel) with macaroni or wild boar with garlic sauce. ● *Mon; mid–31 Aug.* 🗲		▨		▨
PANGRATI: *Pergoúlia* — €€€ Márkou Mousoúrou 16, 11636. **Map** 7 A4. ☎ *210 923 4062.* A British/Greek couple run this cosy taverna, which offers a fixed-price, three-course meal with unlimited house wine. ● *Sun.*				▨
PANGRATI: *The Sushi Bar* — €€€ Plateía Varnáva, 11636. **Map** 7 B4. ☎ *210 752 4354.* Choose between several Japanese snacks or have a more substantial meal at this tiny but popular sushi bar.		▨		
PANGRATI: *Spondí* — €€€€€ Pýrronos 5, 11636. **Map** 7 B4. ☎ *210 752 0658.* This award-winning restaurant in a Neo-Classical house serves food with Greek and Pacific influences. Dishes include steamed grouper. ● *lunch; Mon; Aug.* 🗲	●	▨		▨
PLAKA: *O Damígos* — € Kydathinaíon 41, 10558. **Map** 6 E2. ☎ *210 322 5084.* This basement taverna specializes in salt cod and garlic sauce, chunky chips and salad. The chilled retsina is excellent. ● *Jul & Aug.*				▨
PLAKA: *To Geráni ("Scholarcheío")* — € Tripódon 14, 10557. **Map** 6 E2. ☎ *210 324 7605.* A popular restaurant set in a Neo-Classical house with balcony seating and walls crowded with Greek ephemera. Try the sausages flambéed in ouzo and *saganáki* (fried cheese).	●	▨		
PLAKA: *Byzantinó* — €€ Kydathinaíon 18, 10558. **Map** 6 E2. ☎ *210 322 7368.* Excellent daily specials such as the *chtapódi krasáto* (octopus) and baked vegetable dishes entice the locals to this old-fashioned taverna. 🗲	●	▨		
PLAKA: *Eden* — €€ Lysíou 12, off Mnisikléous,10556. **Map** 6 E1. ☎ *210 324 8858.* Housed in a Neo-Classical building with modern interior, this is Athens' oldest vegetarian restaurant. Food is made with organically grown produce. 🗲	●			
PLAKA: *Symposion* — €€ Mnisikléous 24, 10556. **Map** 6 D1. ☎ *210 325 4940.* This lively *ouzerí* serves traditional Greek food such as *ntolmádes*. Retsina is served from the barrel and live *rempétika* music is played every day. 🗲	●	▨	●	▨
PLAKA: *Xynoú* — €€ Aggelou Géronta 4, 10558. **Map** 6 E2. ☎ *210 322 1065.* Favoured by the old Athenian aristocracy, who enjoy the simple setting and food. Unsophisticated murals and a strolling trio of guitarists add to the charm of this simple taverna. ● *lunch; Sat, Sun; Jul.*		▨	●	▨
PLAKA: *Dáfni* — €€€€ Lysikrátous 4, 10557. **Map** 6 E2. ☎ *210 322 7971.* Garish frescoes adorn the walls of this converted Neo-Classical mansion. Stick to the simple dishes, such as swordfish or *keftédes* (pork or beef meatballs). ● *lunch; Nov–Apr: Sun.* 🗲	●	▨	●	▨

PSYRRI: *Evripos* €€€
Navárchou Apostóli 3, 10554. **Map** 1 C5. 210 323 1351.
Housed in former royal stables, the Evripos serves *mezedopoleío* and unusual
dishes such as ostrich with damsons and *penne* in vodka sauce. ● *Mon.*

PSYRRI: *Tavérna tou Psyrrí* €
Aischýlou 12, 10554. **Map** 2 D5. 210 321 4923.
With an owner from the Cycladic island of Náxos, the food in this taverna
relies heavily on the island's delicious vegetables, meat and fish. End the
meal with a slice of Náxos *graviéra* cheese. ● *Sun evenings; 15–20 Aug.*

PSYRRI: *To Díporto* €
Sokrátous 9, 10552. **Map** 2 D4. 210 321 1463.
This archetypal taverna, hidden beneath an olive shop, serves a few delicious
dishes each day such as *revíthia* (chickpeas), *fasouláda* (bean soup), grilled
sardines, and always a meat stew. Open to 8pm only. ● *Sun; Easter Day; 25 Dec.*

PSYRRI: *Plateía Iróon* €€
Plateía Iróon 1, 10554. **Map** 1 C5. 210 321 1915.
Good food and drink along with *rempétika* music contribute to the
noisy, amiable atmosphere of this small café.

PSYRRI: *Stoá* €€
Evripídou 63, 10554. **Map** 2 D4. 210 325 1513.
Tucked away in an alley, this old taverna has been serving warming
beef stews, grills and soups for many years. Birds in a large cage and
faded Aegean photographs amuse the clientele. ● *Aug.*

PSYRRI: *Faós* €€€
Lepeniótou 26 (first floor), 10554. **Map** 1 C5. 210 324 7833.
This stylish bar and restaurant offers modern food accompanied by live music
on Friday nights and Saturday afternoons. Pricey wines are more than com-
pensated by the tasty and imaginative cuisine served here. ● *Mon, Sun dinner .*

PSYRRI: *Kouzina* €€€€
Sarri 44, 10554. **Map** 1 C5. 210 321 5534.
Grilled lamb with noodles and orange chicken with basmati rice are two un-
usual dishes served at this cosy taverna. Roof garden. ● *lunch except Sat; Mon.*

SYNTAGMA: *Delfoí* €€
Nikis 13, 10557. **Map** 6 F1. 210 323 4869.
This discreet restaurant offers a large selection of fine grills, slow-
baked stews and a variety of salads. ● *Sun.*

SYNTAGMA: *Kentrikón* €€
Kolokotróni 3, 10562. **Map** 2 E5. 210 323 2482.
This quiet, understated restaurant offers a wide spectrum of Greek dishes,
such as lamb in lemon sauce, pilaffs and grilled liver. ● *evenings; Sun.*

SYNTAGMA: *Palia Vouli* €€€€
Plateía Karytsi 7, 10561. **Map** 2 E5. 210 323 4803.
This piano bar/restaurant offers a wide range of wines by the glass as well as
food, including a few interesting *mezédes*. ● *Sun lunch; Jun–mid-Sep.*

SYNTAGMA: *Diros* €€€
Xenofontos 10–12, 10557. **Map** 6 F1. 210 323 2392.
This charming restaurant specializes in good, home-cooked Greek dishes
such as *lamb jardinière* and *avgolémono* (rice and egg soup). ● *Easter Day.*

SYNTAGMA: *GB Corner* €€€€€
Hotel Grande Bretagne, Plateía Syntágmatos, 10563. **Map** 6 F1. 210 333 0000.
This is a long-established restaurant serving high-class Greek and
international food. The service is impeccable.

THISEIO: *Kírki* €€
Apostólou Pavlou 31, 11851. **Map** 5 B1. 210 346 6960
Forty different *mezé* are offered at this *mezedopoleío*, which is a great place to
sit and watch the world go by or enjoy the views of the Acropolis.

THISEIO: *Pil Poul* €€€€€
Corner of Apostólou Pávlou & Poulopoúlou, 11851. **Map** 5 B1. 210 342 3665.
Fashionable Mediterranean cooking and views of the Acropolis draw the
crowds to this busy and expensive restaurant. ● *Sun.*

For key to symbols see back flap

Average prices for a three-course meal for one, including a half-bottle of house wine, tax and service:
€ up to 12 euros
€€ 12–18 euros
€€€ 18–24 euros
€€€€ 24–32 euros
€€€€€ over 32 euros

AIR-CONDITIONING
Restaurant with air-conditioning.

OUTDOOR TABLES
Tables for eating outdoors, often with a good view.

LIVE ENTERTAINMENT
Dancing or live music performances on various days of the week.

LOCAL WINES
A specialized selection of local Greek wines.

	AIR-CONDITIONING	OUTDOOR TABLES	LIVE ENTERTAINMENT	LOCAL WINES
AROUND ATHENS				
ANAVYSOS: *O Vláchos* €		▨		▨
Leofóros Anavýsou, 19013. **Road map** D4. 22910 54669. Meat grills, dips such as *tzatzíki* (yoghurt and cucumber) and other standard Greek fare can be enjoyed at this traditional taverna with a wooden interior. The vine-covered patio is a pleasant place to dine during the summer.				
GLYFADA: *O Tzórtzis* €€	●	▨		
Konstantinoupóleos 4, 16675. **Road map** D4. 210 894 6020. Situated in Glyfáda, 2 km (1 mile) north of Vouliagméni, this classic taverna survives amidst Glyfáda's blaring fast-food joints. *Biftéki* (hamburgers), chicken and fried courgettes are some of the specialities.				
KALLITHEA: *Valentína* €€		▨		
Lykoúrgou 235, 17675. **Road map** D4. 210 943 1871. In the area of Kallithéa, 2 km (1 mile) southwest of the Acropolis, this tiny taverna with its ethnic Pontian cuisine and chilled vodka is popular with Russian diners. Food includes pickles, breads and stuffed cabbage leaves.				
KIFISIA: *O Mpókaris* €€	●	▨		
Acharnón & Sokrátous 17, 14561. **Road map** D4. 210 801 2589. This famed garden taverna specializes in grills, *stifádo* (sausage stew) and traditional aromatic pies. Try the house rosé and white wines which are excellent. ● *Mon–Sat lunch; Aug.*				
KOROPI: *To Alsos* €€		▨		
Leofóros Lavríou 21, 19400. **Road map** D4. 210 664 2714. Situated in Koropí, 6 km (4 miles) south of Paianía, this grill-house offers perfectly roasted lamb and pork, served with large helpings of salads and vegetables, in a quiet garden setting.				
MAROUSI: *Altamíra* €€€€	●	▨		▨
Perikléous 28, 15122. **Road map** D4. 210 612 8841. Mexican, Arabic and Asian cuisines meet in a mad culinary mix at this popular restaurant in Maroúsi, 15 km (9 miles) north of Athens. ● *lunch; Sun; 1–15 Aug.*				
MOUNT PARNITHA: *O Vláchos* €				▨
Leofóros Párnithos, Párnitha, 13671. **Road map** D4. 210 246 3762. Situated in Párnitha, in the foothills of Mount Párnitha, this atmospheric taverna offers traditional Greek cuisine. Specializes in meat grills.				
PIRAEUS: *Alli Skála* €€	●	▨		
Serífou 57, Kamínia, 18541. **Road map** D4. 210 482 7722. Real home cooking and a courtyard filled with banana trees distinguish this elegant restaurant. The food is outstanding and includes cuttlefish, offal dishes and stuffed peppers with caper leaves. ● *lunch; Sun.*				
PIRAEUS: *Vasílenas* €€€		▨		
Aitolikoú 72, 18545. **Road map** D4. 210 461 2457. This restaurant offers a perfect introduction to Greek cuisine, with 16 dishes brought to the table in succession. ● *lunch; Sun; 1–20 Aug.*				
PIRAEUS: *Kóllias* €€€	●	▨	●	▨
Stratigoú Plastíra 3, Taboúria, 18756. **Road map** D4. 210 462 9620. In typically Aegean surroundings, superb fish and starters such as *garidósoupa* (prawn and tomato soup) are on offer. ● *Sun; 1–15 Aug.*				
PIRAEUS: *Dourámbeis* €€€€€	●	▨		▨
Aktí Protopsálti 27, 18533. **Road map** D4. 210 412 2092. Opened in 1932, this is arguably the best fish restaurant in Piraeus. All the fish comes from the islands of Ios, Náxos and Páros, and is served with delicious salads. ● *lunch; Aug.*				

PIRAEUS: *Varoúlko* €€€€€
Deligiórgi 14, 18533. **Road map** D4. 210 411 2043.
Reservations are necessary at this backstreet restaurant. The innovative
chef, Leftéris Lázarou, prepares such dishes as prawns and artichokes,
seafood *ntolmádes*, and mussel and lentil salad. *Sun; Aug.*

VARI: *Ta Vláchika* €€
Leofóros Váris 35, 16672. **Road map** D4. 210 895 6141.
One of the best of the many meat restaurants in Vári, 2 km (1 mile) north of
Vouliagméni, Ta Vláchika specializes in spit-roast kid, lamb and suckling pig.
Try the oven-roasted goat and *kokorétsi* (piquant heart and liver sausage).

VARKIZA: *Esplanade* €€€
Leofóros Poseidónos 16, 16672. **Road map** D4. 210 897 1760.
An old-fashioned waterfront café that offers Greek and international
dishes, as well as a patisserie, ice creams and drinks.

VOULIAGMENI: *Lámpros* €€€€€
Leofóros Poseidónos 20, 16671. **Road map** D4. 210 896 0144.
Located at the water's edge since 1889, this famed restaurant has
a variety of seafood, salads and meat dishes. A good wine list
complements the freshly grilled mullet and sea bream.

THE PELOPONNESE

ANCIENT CORINTH: *Archontikó* €€
On shore road, 20100. **Road map** C4. 27410 27968.
A family-run concern where the *mezédes* such as *sieftalíes* (charcoal-grilled
minced pork sausages) are more daring than the main courses. Fair-sized
portions are accompanied by excellent house rosé. *lunch; Easter period.*

ANDRITSAINA: *O Giórgis* €
Main square, 27061. **Road map** C4. 26260 22004.
Situated near the Temple of Bassae, this well-respected, tree-shaded
taverna produces standard oven-cooked food.

GEROLIMENAS: *Akrogiáli* €
Town beach, 23071. **Road map** C5. 27330 54204.
The ground-floor restaurant of this modern, 1970s hotel is a veritable
oasis when touring the Inner Máni. The restaurant specializes in
fish dishes but meat grills are also on offer.

GYTHEIO: *Drakoulakou* €
Vasiléos Pávlou 13, 23200. **Road map** C5. 27330 24086.
An exception amongst the tourist-orientated tavernas along the
waterfront in Gýtheio, the Drakoulakou often has a small crowd
at the front admiring its arresting display of fish on ice.

GYTHEIO: *Saga Fish Tavern* €
Tzanni Taznnetaki, 23200. **Road map** C5. 27330 23220.
This tavern is in a wonderful situation on the beach – enjoy your dish of prawns
saganaki or grilled fish seated on the wooden veranda looking out to sea.

KALAMATA: *I Kríni* €
Evangelistrías 40, 24101. **Road map** C5. 27210 24474.
Expect a warm welcome at this old, family-run taverna. The menu offers a
range of fresh fish and good, home-style cooking. *lunch; Sun.*

KARDAMYLI: *Léla's* €€
Off main square, near the old factory, 24040. **Road map** D5. 27210 73541.
The food at one of the oldest tavernas in Kardamýli, 34 km (21 miles) south of
Kalamáta, has remained largely unchanged in its traditional style. Greek oven
dishes with German draught beer are on offer, as well as sea views.

KORINTHOS: *Anaxagóras* €€
Agíou Nikoláou 31, 20100. **Road map** C4. 27410 26933.
Situated in Kórinthos, 6 km (4 miles) northeast of Ancient Corinth, this local
favourite offers a mix of seafood, meat and *mezédes* as well as a limited
range of oven dishes such as baked aubergines.

KORONI: *Kagkelários* €
Waterfront, 24004. **Road map** C5. 27250 22648.
Of four adjacent quayside eateries, this has the most imaginative menu.
Mussels, sea urchins, prawns and small local fish are reasonably priced.

Average prices for a three-course meal for one, including a half-bottle of house wine, tax and service:
€ up to 12 euros
€€ 12–18 euros
€€€ 18–24 euros
€€€€ 24–32 euros
€€€€€ over 32 euros

AIR-CONDITIONING
Restaurant with air-conditioning.

OUTDOOR TABLES
Tables for eating outdoors, often with a good view.

LIVE ENTERTAINMENT
Dancing or live music performances on various days of the week.

LOCAL WINES
A specialized selection of local Greek wines.

	AIR-CONDITIONING	OUTDOOR TABLES	LIVE ENTERTAINMENT	LOCAL WINES
METHONI: *I Klimatariá* € Plateía Polytechníou, 24006. **Road map** B5. **(** *27230 31544.* Regarded as one of the best restaurants for its gourmet preparation of Greek dishes, the menu includes a wide variety of vegetarian dishes. ● *Nov–mid-May.*	●	■		■
MONEMVASIA: *I Matoúla* €€ Main through road, 23070. **Road map** C5. **(** *27320 61660.* For many decades this was the only taverna in Monemvasía. All traditional dishes can be enjoyed under a giant fig tree in the garden.		■		
NAFPLIO: *Omorfi Póli* € Corner of Kotsonopoúlou 1 & Vasilíssis Olgas, 21100. **Road map** C4. **(** *27520 25944.* A varied menu of Greek casseroles and grills with generous portions. Booking is necessary as there are only 15 indoor tables. ● *Mon–Fri lunch.*		■		■
NAFPLIO: *O Vasílis* € Staïkopoúlou 22, 21100. **Road map** C4. **(** *27520 25334.* Of all the competing restaurants along Staïkopoúlou, this is one of the oldest and the best for hearty Greek food. ● *Oct–Mar: Tue; 15–30 Nov.*	●	■		■
NAFPLIO: *Ta Fanária* € Corner of Staïkopoúlou 13 & Soútsou, 21100. **Road map** C4. **(** *27520 27141.* This long-running favourite offers seating under vines. It is best visited at lunch when dishes, including good *mousakás*, emerge fresh from the oven. There is also good bulk retsina from Mégara. ● *15–30 Nov.*		■		■
NAFPLIO: *Zorbás* € Staïkopoúlou 30, 21100. **Road map** C4 **(** *27520 25319.* This family-run taverna prepares all the standard Greek dishes. Try the delicious home-made fish soup or the octopus.	●	■		
NEOS MYSTRAS: *O Mystrás* € Main square, 23100. **Road map** C5. A traditional taverna in Néos Mystrás located 1 km (0.5 miles) east of the Byzantine site of Mystrás. This establishment serves mountainous portions of the tastiest vegetable stews in the Peloponnese, as well as olives and various grilled meats.		■		■
OLYMPIA: *Praxitelous* € Spiliopoúlou 7, 27065. **Road map** B4. **(** *26240 23570.* The emphasis here is on traditional, local food such as *bourekia* and *tisoras*, served in a very Greek atmosphere. Situated in Olympia, 150 m (500 ft) east of Ancient Olympia, you can enjoy your meal outside in the garden.		■		■
OLYMPIA: *Ta Kotópoula* € Linária, 27065. **Road map** B4. **(** *26240 22130.* This is a simple and traditional family-run taverna. Typical specialties include grilled meats and delicious, home-cooked Greek dishes.		■		
PATRA: *Lavýrinthos* € Poukevíl 44, 26223. **Road map** C4. **(** *2610 226436.* This taverna offers unusual interpretations of regular Greek dishes. Food is accompanied by wine from the various barrels decorating the taverna. ● *Sun.*				■
PYLOS: *O Grigóris* € Georgíou Krasánou, 24001. **Road map** C5. **(** *27230 22621.* During the summer, tasty oven casseroles are served in the rear garden. Charcoal-grilled fish is available on request.		■		
SPARTI: *Elysé* € Konstantínou Palaiológou 113, 23100. **Road map** C5. **(** *27310 29896.* This elegant restaurant with pastel-pink decor offers a good range of traditional Greek oven casseroles and grills.		■		■

CENTRAL AND WESTERN GREECE

AGIOS IOANNIS: *Ostriá* €€
On shore road, 37012. **Road map** D3. **(** 24260 32132.
Situated in Agios Ioánnis, 25 km (16 miles) north of Miliés, this restaurant serves mouthwatering examples of typical Pílio dishes such as rabbit stew *(kounéli kokkinistó)* and wild greens pie *(chortópita)*. ● *Mon–Fri lunch; Oct–Apr.*

ARACHOVA: *Karathanásis* €€
Delfón 56, 32004. **Road map** C3. **(** 22670 31360.
A family-run taverna in the heart of Aráchova, 11 km (7 miles) east of Ancient Delphi, offering simple grills and stews with fresh bread. ● *Easter Day.*

ARACHOVA: *O Karmalis* €
Delfón 51, 32004. **Road map** C3. **(** 22670 31541.
This restaurant in Aráchova, 11 km (7 miles) east of Ancient Delphi, serves "mountain" food staples such as beef, chicken, pasta, goat and pork. The salads are ample and liberally sprinkled with herbs. ● *Jul–Aug.*

IGOUMENITSA: *To Chorió* €
Igoumenitsa–Sagiada Road, 46100. **Road map** B3. **(** 26650 26931.
The cuisine offered at this charming taverna, located 4 km (2 miles) from the centre, includes rabbit *stifado* (a type of onion stew) and baked lamb.

IOANNINA: *Kípos* €
Karaïskáki 20, 45444. **Road map** B2. **(** 26510 78287.
This pleasant taverna stands out for its fresh approach to traditional Greek dishes, flavouring the ever-popular pork and lamb with traditional herbs and spices. ● *12–28 Aug.*

IOANNINA: *Própodes* €
Nisí, 45500. **Road map** B2. **(** 26510 81803.
A good island restaurant, well worth the short boat trip to eat in the evenings. Eel and crayfish from the local lake are on offer as well as trout from fish farms in the mountains. ▨

IOANNINA: *To Manteío* €
Plateía Neomártyros Georgíou 15, 45221 **Road map** B2.
Enjoy charcoal-grilled meats and *souvláki* on the vine-canopied terrace of this taverna. Fruit or halva are on the house. ● *Easter Day, 26–27 Jul, 25 Dec.*

KALAMPAKA: *Metéora* €
Plateía Dimarcheíou, 42200. **Road map** B2. **(** 24320 22316.
Wholesome Greek food prepared by the owner's wife and the usual menu of salads, *mousakás* and grills can be enjoyed here. ● *mid-Nov–mid-Mar.*

KALAMPAKA: *O Kípos* €
At entrance to village, 42200. **Road map** B2. **(** 24320 23218.
Set in a traditional old house with a fire during winter, this restaurant offers good Greek cuisine at reasonable prices. There is a large choice of starters and salads as well as home-made desserts. ● *Mon in winter.*

KASTRAKI: *Metéora* €
On Kastráki–Metéora road, 42200. **Road map** B2. **(** 24320 22285.
Close to the Metéora rocks, this simple taverna is set in an old house and serves traditional Greek cuisine. All food is freshly made and there is a fire in winter as well as a garden for the summer months. ● *main public hols.*

KASTRAKI: *Parádeisos* €
On the main road to the Metéora, 42200. **Road map** B2. **(** 24320 22723.
This modern grill-house, within close proximity to Metéora, offers all the standard Greek fare. There is a beautiful, flower-filled garden.

MAKRINITSA: *Pántheon* €
Main square, 37011. **Road map** D3. **(** 24280 99324.
Views over Vólos, 14 km (9 miles) north, would be reason enough to sit here, but locals also drive up here to sample Pílio cooking, such as the spicy sausage, pepper and tomato stew known as *spetzofáï.*

METSOVO: *Athínai* €
Main square, 44200. **Road map** B2. **(** 26560 41332.
The menu in this traditionally decorated, family-run taverna includes game dishes when in season, but also features vegetarian specialities such as leek pie and bean soup.

For key to symbols see back flap

	AIR-CONDITIONING	OUTDOOR TABLES	LIVE ENTERTAINMENT	LOCAL WINES

Average prices for a three-course meal for one, including a half-bottle of house wine, tax and service:
€ up to 12 euros
€€ 12–18 euros
€€€ 18–24 euros
€€€€ 24–32 euros
€€€€€ over 32 euros

AIR-CONDITIONING
Restaurant with air-conditioning.

OUTDOOR TABLES
Tables for eating outdoors, often with a good view.

LIVE ENTERTAINMENT
Dancing or live music performances on various days of the week.

LOCAL WINES
A specialized selection of local Greek wines.

	AIR-COND.	OUTDOOR	LIVE ENT.	LOCAL WINES
METSOVO: *Galaxías* Main square, 44200. **Road map** B2. 📞 26560 41123. Housed in a traditional stone building with wooden ceilings and a veranda overlooking the square, the menu features regional cuisine including *kokorétsi* (grilled offal kebab) and beef cooked in a clay pot. 🍴	€	▨		▨
METSOVO: *To Metsovítiko Salóni* Tositsa, next to post office, 44200. **Road map** B2. 📞 26560 42142. A smart restaurant decorated in Métsovo mountain style, with rugs and wall hangings. The menu features Métsovo specialities such as *spetzofáï*, with seasonal game dishes and the local red wine, *katói*.	€	▨	●	▨
MILIES: *Paliós Stathmós* Old railway station, 37010. **Road map** D3. 📞 24230 86425. This smart restaurant-cum-guesthouse has an Italian chef who produces delightful food, such as beef in lemon sauce, in the equally delightful setting of the old railway station. ● *Mon lunch; Nov.*	€	▨		▨
PAPIGO: *Giorgios Ioannides* Papigo, 44010. **Road map** B3. 📞 26530 41124. Home-made pies are one of the delicious specialities on offer at this charming taverna. Authentic regional cooking served in a traditional Zagorian-style stone house.	€	▨		▨
PARGA: *Floísvos* Mavrogénous 10, 48060. **Road map** B3. 📞 26840 31624. The menu of this restaurant may offer few surprises but the food is reliable, good value for money and enhanced by stunning views of the Ionian coastline. ● *mid-Oct–May.*	€	●	▨	●	▨
PARGA: *Vílla Noúli* Sarakini, 48060. **Road map** B3. 📞 26840 35239. Fresh fish is a speciality at this waterfront restaurant. Daily specials vary, but expect to see snapper, mullet, tuna and swordfish. ● *Nov–Mar.*	€	▨	●	

NORTHERN GREECE

	AIR-COND.	OUTDOOR	LIVE ENT.	LOCAL WINES
ALEXANDROUPOLI: *Klimatariá* Polytechníou 18, 68100. **Road map** E1. 📞 25510 26288. This restaurant is noted for its large menu which covers all the basic Greek dishes such as *mousakás* and stuffed peppers, as well as fresh fish and regional specialities such as *katsikáki* (baked goat). 🍴	€	●	▨	▨
ALEXANDROUPOLI: *Neráïda* Kýprou 5, 68100. **Road map** E1. 📞 25510 22867. One of several eating places around Plateía Kýprou, this smart restaurant is a popular choice and specializes in seafood.	€	▨		▨
KASTORIA: *Omónoia* Mitropóleos 97, 52100. **Road map** B2. 📞 24670 23964. This busy restaurant, situated on a small square in the upper town, has a changing menu. It serves all the regular dishes as well as some vegetarian options such as bean stew. The fish soup is strong and filling.	€	▨		▨
KAVALA: *Michalákis* Kassándrou 1, 65403. **Road map** D1. 📞 2510 221185. This pleasant taverna offers meat and typical Greek dishes, such as stuffed tomatoes. Fresh fish also features on the menu.	€	●		▨
KAVALA: *Pános Zafíra* Karaolí Dimitríou 20, 65302. **Road map** D1. 📞 2510 227978. Renowned for its seafood, this restaurant offers delicious dishes such as *gàvros* (fresh anchovies). 🍴	€	▨		▨

LITOCHORO: *Damaskiniá*   €
Vasiléos Konstantínou 4, 60200. **Road map** C2. 23520 81247.
Situated in Litóchoro, 21 km (13 miles) south of Katerína, this lively taverna
offers good, home-cooked Greek fare. Meals include grilled fish and stews.

NEA FOKAIA: *Kostís*   €€€
At traffic lights, 63077. **Road map** D2.
Situated in Néa Fókaia, 17 km (11 miles) south of Néa Moudaniá, this
restaurant transforms basic dishes such as feta with the addition of onions
and red peppers. Battered cod with *skordaliá* (garlic sauce) is a speciality.

NEOS MARMARAS: *Ta Péfka*   €
Waterfront, 63081. **Road map** D2. 23750 71763.
Set among pine trees in Néos Marmarás, 52 km (32 miles) southeast of Néa
Moudaniá, this restaurant serves unusual dishes such as *mýdia saganáki*
(mussels in red sauce) and octopus *mezédes*. Mon & Tue.

PEFKOCHORI: *Toronéos*   €
Pefkochóri beach, 63085. **Road map** D2. 23740 61495.
Basic Greek staples are enhanced by specialities such as stuffed squid
or fried pumpkin in this welcoming taverna in Pefkochóri, 42 km
(26 miles) south of Néa Moudaniá. 20 Oct–20 Apr.

THESSALONIKI: *Agorá*   €
Kapodistríou 5, 54625. **Road map** C2. 2310 532428.
Backstreet family *ouzerí* offering good Greek cuisine. Salads are generous
and meat and fish dishes deliciously grilled. Sun lunch; 26 Jul–19 Aug.

THESSALONIKI: *Ta Koumparákia*   €
Egnatía 140, 54622. **Road map** C2. 2310 271905.
This simple Greek grill, with its friendly service and good, simple food
is a reliable and popular choice. Wed; Christmas Day, Easter Day, 1 May.

THESSALONIKI: *Ta Spáta*   €
Aristotélous 28, 54623. **Road map** C2. 2310 277412.
This grill-house is almost always busy and specializes in spit-roasted
chicken. It also serves hearty peasant salads.

THESSALONIKI: *Tiffany's*   €€
Iktinou 3, 54622. **Road map** C2. 2310 274022.
This modern-style restaurant serves a wide selection of both Greek
and international food, from *hanoum bourek* to plain burgers.

THESSALONIKI: *To Makedonikó*   €
Georgiou Papadopoúlou 32, 56625. **Road map** C2. 2310 627438.
This taverna is situated in the historic part of Thessaloníki's old town, near
the castle, and is famous for its *keftedakia scharas* (grilled meatballs). Tue.

THESSALONIKI: *Tsarouchás*   €
Olimbou 78, 54646. **Road map** C2. 2310 271621.
This restaurant features traditional *patsás*, a soup made from lamb innards. If that
doesn't appeal, there are other home-cooked Greek dishes on offer here, too.

THESSALONIKI: *Aristotélous*   €€
Aristotélous 8, 54623. **Road map** C2. 2310 233195.
A smart, lively *ouzerí* serving some unusual food such as spicy feta and
pepper dip, or cuttlefish stuffed with feta. Sun evenings; 7–20 Aug.

THESSALONIKI: *Chamádrakas*   €€€
Manoúli Gagíli 13, 55132. **Road map** C2. 2310 447943.
Choose your own lobster at this family-run, seafront taverna. There is a large
selection of Greek cuisine as well as home-produced wine. 1 Jan.

THESSALONIKI: *Ta Nisiá*   €€€€
Proxénou Koromilá 13, 54623. **Road map** C2. 2310 285991.
A popular spot, this taverna specializes in fresh fish and game dishes.
Imaginative combinations, such as shrimps and bacon, and a good dessert
menu are on offer. The walnut pie is a regular feature. Sun evenings.

XORTIATIS: *Plátanos*   €
Agías Paraskevís 1, 57010. **Road map** D2. 2310 349260.
Situated in Xortiátis village, 18 km (11 miles) east of Thessaloníki, this taverna
is worth the visit for its local specialities such as *teingerosarmás* (oven-baked
lamb offal) and *exochikó* (pork baked in tomatoes). Easter Day.

For key to symbols see back flap

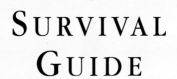

SURVIVAL
GUIDE

PRACTICAL INFORMATION

REECE'S APPEAL is both cultural and hedonistic. Its physical beauty, hot climate and warm seas, together with the easy-going outlook of its people, are all conducive to a relaxed holiday. It does pay, however, to know something about the nuts and bolts of Greek life to avoid unnecessary frustrations – when to visit, what to bring, how to get around and what to do if

Soldier in ceremonial dress

things go wrong. Greece is no longer the cheap holiday destination it once was, though public transport, vehicle hire, eating out and hotel accommodation are still relatively inexpensive compared with most other European countries. Tourist information is available through the many EOT offices *(see p300)*, which offer plenty of advice on the practical aspects of your stay.

WHEN TO VISIT

HIGH SEASON in Greece – late June to early September – is the hottest *(see p49)* and most expensive time to visit, as well as being very crowded. December to March are the coldest and wettest months everywhere, with reduced public transport, and many hotels and restaurants closed for the winter.

Skiing in Greece is possible from January to April, with around 20 mainland resorts to choose from *(see p310)*.

Spring (late April–May) is one of the loveliest times to visit – the weather is sunny but not yet debilitatingly hot, there are relatively few tourists about, and the countryside is ablaze with brightly coloured wild flowers and fresh, brilliant greenery *(see pp22–3)*.

WHAT TO BRING

MOST OF LIFE'S comforts are available in Greece, although it is advisable to take a good map of the area in which you intend to stay *(see p319)*, an AC adaptor for

your electrical gadgetry *(see p301)*, sunglasses and a sun hat, mosquito repellent, any medical supplies you might need and a high factor (15 and up) suntan lotion.

Apart from swimwear, light clothing is all you need for most of the year, though a sweater or light jacket for the evening is also recommended, and is essential in May and October. During winter and spring, rainwear should be taken, as well as warm clothes. Many religious buildings have dress codes that should always be adhered to *(see p301)*.

ΕΛΕΓΧΟΣ ΔΙΑΒΑΤΗΡΙΩΝ
PASSPORT CONTROL

Greek airport passport control sign

VISA REQUIREMENTS

VISITORS FROM EU countries, the US, Canada, Australia and New Zealand need only a valid passport for entry to Greece (no visa is required), and can stay for a period of up to 90 days. For longer stays a resident's permit must be

obtained from the **Aliens' Bureau** in Athens, or the local police in remoter areas.

Any non-EU citizen planning to work or study in Greece should contact their local Greek consulate a few months in advance about visa requirements and work permits.

CUSTOMS

VISITORS ENTERING Greece from within the EU are no longer subject to any customs controls or other formalities. Limits for duty-paid goods have been similarly relaxed in recent years, though anything valuable should be recorded in your passport upon entry if it is to be re-exported. Visitors coming from non-EU countries may be subject to the occasional spot check on arrival in Greece.

However, visitors should be aware that the unauthorized export of antiquities and archaeological artifacts from Greece is treated as a serious offence, with penalties ranging from hefty fines to prison sentences.

Any prescription drugs that are brought into the country should be accompanied by a copy of the prescription for the purposes of the customs authorities *(see pp302–3)*.

On 30 June 1999, the intra-EU Duty and Tax Free Allowances, better known as Duty Free and mainly affecting such luxury items as alcohol, perfumes and tobacco, were abolished. EU residents can now import greater amounts of these goods, as long as they are for personal use.

Visitors on the beach in high summer

◁ **The attractive harbour of Paralía Astros, south of Náfplio**

A family arriving at Athens airport

TRAVELLING WITH CHILDREN

CHILDREN ARE much loved by the Greeks and welcomed just about everywhere. Baby-sitting facilities are provided by most hotels on request, though you should check this before you book in (see p261).

Concessions of up to 50 per cent are offered on most forms of public transport for children aged 10 and under, but in some cases it is 8 and under.

Swimming in the sea is generally safe for kids, but keep a close eye on them as lifeguards are rare in Greece. Also be aware of the hazards of overexposure to the sun and dehydration.

WOMEN TRAVELLERS

GREECE IS A VERY SAFE country and local communities are essentially welcoming. Foreign women travelling alone are usually treated with respect, especially if dressed modestly (see p301). However, like elsewhere, hitchhiking alone in Greece carries potential risks and is not advisable.

STUDENT AND YOUTH TRAVELLERS

WITHIN Greece itself, no concessions are offered on ferry, bus or train travel, except to students actually studying in Greece. However, there are plenty of deals to be had getting to Greece, especially during low season. There are scores of agencies for student and youth travel, including **STA Travel**, which has 120 offices worldwide. IYHF (International Youth Hostel Federation) membership cards are rarely asked for in Greek hostels, but to be on the safe side it is worth joining before setting off. Most state-run museums and archaeological sites are free to EU students with a valid International Student Identity Card (ISIC); non-EU students with an ISIC card are usually entitled to a 50 per cent reduction. There are no youth concessions available for these entrance fees, but occasional discounts are possible with a "Go 25" card, which can be obtained from any STA office by travellers who are under 26.

International student identity card

FACILITIES FOR THE DISABLED

THERE ARE FEW facilities in Greece for assisting the disabled, so careful planning is essential – sights that have wheelchair access are indicated at the beginning of each entry in this guide. Organizations such as **Holiday Care Service**, **RADAR** and **Tripscope** are worth contacting for advice. Also, agencies such as **Can Be Done Tours** and **OPUS 23** organize holidays specifically for disabled travellers.

A sign directing access for wheelchairs at a Greek airport

DIRECTORY

GREEK TOURIST OFFICES (EOT)

Greek National Tourist Board Internet Site
W www.gnto.gr

Athens
Amerikis 2, 10564 Athens.
[210 331 0692 or 331 0561.
FAX 210 325 2895

Australia
51–57 Pitt St, Sydney, NSW 2000.
[(2) 9241 1663.

Canada
2nd Floor, 91 Scollard Street, Toronto, Ontario M5R 1G4.
[(416) 968-2220.

United Kingdom and Republic of Ireland
4 Conduit St, London W1R 0DJ.
[020-7734 5997.

USA
Olympic Tower, 645 Fifth Ave, New York, NY 10022.
[(212) 421-5777.

USEFUL ADDRESSES

Aliens' Bureau
Leofóros Alexándras 173, Athens.
[210 647 6000.

Can Be Done Tours
11 Woodcock Hill, Harrow HA3 OXP.
[020-8907 2400.

Holiday Care Service
2nd Floor, Imperial Buildings, Victoria Rd, Horley RH6 7PZ.
[01293-774 535.

International Student and Youth Travel Service
First Floor, Níkis 11, 10557 Athens.
[210 322 1267.

OPUS 23
Sourdock Hill, Barkisland, Halifax, West Yorkshire HX4 0AG.
[01422 375999.

RADAR
12 City Forum, 250 City Road, London EC1V 8AF.
[020-7250 3222.

STA Travel
86 Old Brompton Rd, London SW7 3LQ.
[020-7361 6161.

Tripscope
The Courtyard, Evelyn Rd, London W4 5JL.
[020-8580 7021.

Holiday Essentials

The EOT's Greek tourism emblem

FOR A CAREFREE holiday in Greece, it is best to adopt the philosophy *sigá, sigá* (slowly, slowly). Within this principle is the ritual of the afternoon siesta, a practice that should be taken seriously, particularly during the hottest months when it is almost a physiological necessity. Almost everything closes for a few hours after lunch, reopening later in the day when the air cools and Greece comes to life again. The shops reopen their doors, the restaurants start filling up and, at seafront locales, practically everyone partakes in the *vólta*, or evening stroll – a delightful Greek institution.

TOURIST INFORMATION

TOURIST INFORMATION is available in many towns and villages in Greece, either in the form of government-run **EOT** offices (Ellinikós Organismós Tourismoú, or National Tourist Organization of Greece), municipally run tourist offices, the local tourist police *(see p302)*, or privately owned travel agencies. The EOT publishes an array of tourist literature, including maps, brochures and leaflets on transport and accommodation – be aware though that not all of their information is up-to-date and reliable. The addresses and phone numbers of the EOT and municipal tourist offices, as well as the tourist police, are listed throughout this guide.

GREEK TIME

GREECE IS ALWAYS 2 hours ahead of Britain (GMT), 1 hour ahead of European countries on Central European Time (such as France), 7 hours ahead of New York, 10 hours ahead of Los Angeles and 8 hours behind Sydney.

As Greece is now part of the EU, it follows the rule that all EU countries must put their clocks forward to summertime, and back again to wintertime on the same days, in order to avoid any confusion when travelling between countries. This should lessen the chance of missing a ferry or flight due to confusion over the time!

Entry ticket to an archaeological site

OPENING HOURS

OPENING HOURS tend to be vague in Greece, varying from day to day, season to season and place to place. It is therefore advisable to use the times given in this book as rough guidelines only and to check with local information centres for accurate times.

State-run museums and archaeological sites generally open from around 8:30am to 2:45pm (the major ones stay open as late as 8 or 9pm in the summer months).

Mondays and main public holidays *(see p48)* are the usual closing days for most tourist attractions. Locally run and private museums may be closed on additional public holidays and also on local festival days.

A *períptero*, or kiosk, with a wide array of papers and periodicals

Monasteries and convents are open during daylight hours, but will close for a few hours in the afternoon.

Opening times for shops are covered on page 308, pharmacies on page 303, banks on page 304, post offices on page 307 and OTE (telephone) offices on page 306.

Most shops and offices are closed on public holidays and local festival days, with the exception of some shops within tourist resorts.

The dates of major local festivals are included in the Visitors' Checklists in each main town entry in this guide.

ADMISSION CHARGES

MOST STATE-RUN museums and archaeological sites charge an entrance fee of between 1.5 and 6 euros. Reductions are available, however, ranging from around 25 per cent for EU citizens aged 60 years and over (use your passport as proof of age) to 50 per cent for non-EU students armed with an international student identity card (ISIC) *(see p299)*.

Though most museums and sites are closed on public holidays, the ones that do remain open are free of charge.

EVENTS

THE ENGLISH-LANGUAGE paper *Athens News* has a What's On column, gazetting events all over the city and also those of special interest to children. The tourist office in Amerikis Street has a free monthly English-language magazine, *Now in Athens*, which details cultural events and entertainment in Athens, as does the weekly Greek-language *Athinorama* *(see pp118–21)*.

A list of Greek festivals and cultural events is given on pages 44–8, but it is worth asking your nearest tourist office about what's happening locally. Other forms of entertainment include the outdoor cinema in summer, which is very popular with the Greeks; most films are in English with Greek subtitles. There are also

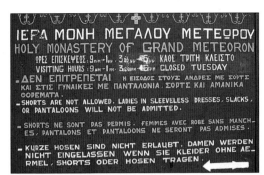

A sign about dress codes at a monastery in Metéora, central Greece

bars, discos and nightclubs in the resorts, as well as tavernas and *kafeneía* (coffee shops), found in every village and often the centre of social life.

RELIGION

GREECE IS ALMOST entirely Greek Orthodox. The symbols and rituals of the religion are deeply rooted in Greek culture and are visible everywhere. Saints' days are celebrated throughout Greece *(see p48)*, sometimes on a local scale and sometimes across the entire country.

The largest religious minority are the Muslims of Thrace, though they constitute less than 2 per cent of the country's total population. Places of worship for other religions are mostly situated within Athens and its environs.

ETIQUETTE

LIKE ANYWHERE ELSE, common courtesy and respect is appreciated in Greece, so try speaking a few words of the language, even if your vocabulary only extends as far as the basics *(see pp348–52)*.

Though formal attire is rarely needed, modest clothing (trousers for men and skirts for women) is *de rigueur* for visits to churches and monasteries.

Topless sunbathing is generally tolerated, but nude bathing is officially restricted to a few designated beaches.

In restaurants, the service charge is always included in the bill, but tips are still appreciated – the custom is to leave between 10 and 15 per cent. Public toilet attendants should also be tipped. Taxi drivers do not expect a tip, but they are not averse to them either; likewise hotel porters and chambermaids.

PHOTOGRAPHY

PHOTOGRAPHIC FILM is readily available in Greece, though it is often quite expensive in tourist areas and close to the major sights.

Taking photographs inside churches and monasteries is officially forbidden; within museums photography is usually permitted, but flashes and tripods are often not. In most cases where a stills camera is allowed, a video camera will also be fine, but you may have to pay an extra fee. At sites, museums or religious buildings it is best to gain permission before using a camera, as rules do vary.

A Greek priest

ELECTRICAL APPLIANCES

Two-pin adaptor, for use with all British appliances when in Greece

GREECE, LIKE OTHER European countries, runs on 220 volts/50 Hz AC. Plugs have two round pins, or three round pins for appliances that need to be earthed. The adaptors required for British electrical appliances are difficult to find in Greece so bring one with you. Similarly, transformers are needed for North American equipment.

CONVERSION CHART

GREECE USES the metric system, with two small exceptions: sea distances are expressed in nautical miles and land is measured in *strémmata*, the equivalent of about 0.1 ha (0.25 acre).

Imperial to Metric
1 inch = 2.54 centimetres
1 foot = 30 centimetres
1 mile = 1.6 kilometres
1 ounce = 28 grams
1 pound = 454 grams
1 pint = 0.6 litres
1 gallon = 4.6 litres

Metric to Imperial
1 millimetre = 0.04 inches
1 centimetre = 0.4 inches
1 metre = 3 feet 3 inches
1 kilometre = 0.64 miles
1 gram = 0.04 ounces
1 kilogram = 2.2 pounds
1 litre = 1.8 pints

DIRECTORY

EMBASSIES IN GREECE

Australia
Dimitríou Soútsou 37,
11521 Athens.
[210 645 0404.

Canada
Gennadíou 4, 11521 Athens.
[210 727 3400.

Republic of Ireland
Vassiléos Konstantínou 7,
10674 Athens.
[210 723 2405.

New Zealand
Kifissías 268, Xalandri.
[210 687 4700.

United Kingdom
Ploutárchou 1,
10675 Athens.
[210 723 6211.

USA
Vasilíssis Sofías 91,
10160 Athens.
[210 721 2951.

Personal Health and Security

Gᴿᴇᴇᴄᴇ ɪs ᴏɴᴇ of the safest European countries to visit, with a time-honoured tradition of honesty that still survives despite the onslaught of mass tourism. But, like travelling anywhere else, it is still advisable to take out a comprehensive travel insurance policy. One place where danger is ever present, however, is on the road. Driving is a volatile matter in Greece, and it now has the highest accident rate in Europe. Considerable caution is recommended, for drivers and pedestrians.

Fire service emblem

PERSONAL SECURITY

Tʜᴇ ᴄʀɪᴍᴇ ʀᴀᴛᴇ in Greece is very low compared with other European countries. Nevertheless, a few precautions are worth taking, like keeping cars and hotel rooms locked, watching your handbag in public, and not keeping all your documents together in one place. If you do have anything stolen, contact the police or tourist police.

POLICE

Gʀᴇᴇᴄᴇ's ᴘᴏʟɪᴄᴇ are split into three forces: the regular police, the port police and the tourist police. The tourist police are the most useful for holiday-makers, combining normal police duties with tourist advice. Should you suffer a theft, lose your passport or have cause to complain about shops, restaurants, tour guides or taxi drivers, your case should first be made to them. As every tourist police office claims to have at least one English speaker, they can act as interpreters if the case needs to involve the local police. Their offices also offer maps, brochures, and advice on finding accommodation.

LEGAL ASSISTANCE FOR TOURISTS

Eᴜʀᴏᴘᴇᴀɴ ᴄᴏɴsᴜᴍᴇʀs' associations together with the European Commission have created a programme, known as **EKPIZO**, to inform tourists of their rights. Its aim is specifically to help holiday-makers who experience problems with hotels, campsites, travel

A policeman giving directions to holiday-makers

agencies and so forth. They will furnish tourists with the relevant information and, if necessary, arrange legal advice from lawyers in English, French or German. Contact the main Athens branch for their local telephone numbers.

MEDICAL TREATMENT AND INSURANCE

Bʀɪᴛɪsʜ and other EU citizens are entitled to free medical care in Greece on presentation of an E111 form (available from most UK post offices), and emergency treatment in public hospitals is free to all foreign nationals. Be aware, however, that public health facilities are limited in Greece and private clinics are expensive. Visitors are strongly advised to take out comprehensive travel insurance – available from travel agents, banks and insurance brokers – covering both private medical treatment and loss or theft of personal possessions. Be sure, too, to read the small print: not all policies, for instance,

will cover you for activities of a "dangerous" nature, such as motorcycling and trekking; not all policies will pay for doctors' or hospital fees direct, and only some will cover you for ambulances and emergency flights home. Paying for your flight with a credit card such as Visa or American Express will also provide limited travel insurance, including reimbursement of your air fare if the agent happens to go bankrupt.

HEALTH PRECAUTIONS

Iᴛ ᴄᴏsᴛs ʟɪᴛᴛʟᴇ or nothing to take a few sensible precautions when travelling abroad, and certain measures are essential if holidaying in the extreme heat of high summer. The most obvious thing to avoid is overexposure to the sun, particularly for the fair skinned: wear a hat and good-quality sunglasses, as well as a high-factor suntan lotion. If you do burn, calamine lotion is soothing. Heat stroke is a real hazard for which medical attention should be sought immediately, while heat exhaustion and dehydration (made worse by alcohol consumption) are also serious.

Be sure to drink plenty of water, even if you don't feel thirsty, and if in any doubt invest in a packet of electrolyte tablets (a mixture of potassium salts and glucose) available at any Greek pharmacy, to avoid dehydration and replace lost minerals.

Port policeman's uniform   **City policeman's uniform**

An ambulance with the emergency number emblazoned on its side

Fire engine

Police car

Always go prepared with an adequate supply of any medication you may need while away, as well as a copy of the prescription with the generic name of the drug – this is useful not only in case you run out, but also for the purposes of customs when you enter the country. Also be aware that codeine, a painkiller commonly found in headache tablets, is illegal in Greece.

Tap water in Greece is generally safe to drink, but in remote communities it is a good precaution to check with the locals. Bottled spring water is for sale throughout the country, and often has the advantage of being chilled.

However tempting the sea may look, swimming after a meal is not recommended for at least two hours, since stomach cramps out at sea can

Pharmacy sign

be fatal. Underwater hazards to be aware of are weaver fish, jellyfish and sea urchins. The latter are not uncommon and are extremely unpleasant if trodden on. If you do tread on one, the spine will need to be extracted using olive oil and a sterilized needle. Jellyfish stings can be relieved by vinegar, baking soda, or by various remedies sold at Greek pharmacies. Though a rare occurrence, the sand-dwelling weaver fish has a powerful sting, its poison causing extreme pain. The immediate treatment is to immerse the affected area in very hot water to dilute the venom's strength.

No inoculations are required for visitors to Greece, though tetanus and typhoid boosters may be recommended by your doctor.

PHARMACIES

GREEK PHARMACISTS are highly qualified and can not only advise on minor ailments, but also dispense medication not usually available over the counter back home. Their premises, *farmakeía*, are identified by a red or green cross on a white background. Pharmacies are open from 8:30am to 2pm, but are usually closed in the afternoon and on Saturday mornings. However, in larger towns there is usually a rota system to maintain a service from 7:30am to 2pm and from 5:30 to 10pm. Details are posted in pharmacy windows, in both Greek and English.

EMERGENCY SERVICES

IN CASE OF EMERGENCIES the appropriate services to call are listed in the directory below. For accidents or other medical emergencies, a 24-hour ambulance service operates within Athens. Outside Athens, in rural towns and on the islands, it is unlikely that ambulances will be on 24-hour call. If necessary, patients can be transferred from local ESY (Greek National Health Service) hospitals or surgeries to a main ESY hospital in Athens by ambulance or helicopter.

A complete list of ESY hospitals, private hospitals and clinics is available from the tourist police.

DIRECTORY

NATIONWIDE EMERGENCY NUMBERS

Police
100.

Ambulance
166.

Fire
199.

Road assistance
104.

Coastguard patrol
108.

ATHENS EMERGENCY NUMBERS

Tourist police
171.

Doctors
1016 (2pm–7am).

Pharmacies
For information on 24-hour pharmacies:
107 (central Athens).
102 (suburbs).

Poison treatment centre
210 779 3777.

EKPIZO BUREAU

Athens branch
Valtetsiou 43–45,
10681 Athens.
210 330 0673 / 330 4444.

Banking and Local Currency

Eurocheque logo

G REECE HAS NOW CONVERTED to the common European currency, the euro, which replaces the former drachma. Changing money from other currencies into euros is straightforward and can be done at banks or post offices. Even in small towns and resorts you can expect to find a car-hire firm or travel agency that will change travellers' cheques and cash, albeit with a sizeable commission. Larger towns and tourist centres all have the usual banking facilities, including a growing number of cash machines (ATMs).

Visitors changing money at a foreign exchange bureau

BANKING HOURS

A LL BANKS ARE OPEN from 8am to 2pm Monday to Thursday, and from 8am to 1:30pm on Friday. In the larger cities and tourist resorts there is usually at least one bank that reopens its exchange desk for a few hours in the evening and on Saturday mornings during the summer season.

Cash machines, though seldom found outside the major towns and resorts, are in operation 24 hours a day. All banks are closed on public holidays (see p48) and may also be closed on any local festival days.

BANKS AND EXCHANGE FACILITIES

T HERE ARE BANKS in all major towns and resorts, as well as exchange facilities at post offices (which tend to charge lower commissions and are found in the more remote areas of Greece), travel agents, hotels, tourist offices and car-hire agencies. Always take your passport with you when cashing travellers' cheques, and check exchange rates and commission charges beforehand, as they vary greatly. In major towns and tourist areas you may find a foreign exchange machine

Foreign exchange machine

for changing money at any time of day or night. These operate in several languages, as do the ATMs.

CARDS, CHEQUES AND EUROCHEQUES

V ISA, MASTERCARD (Access), American Express and Diners Club are the most widely accepted credit cards in Greece. They are the most convenient way to pay for air tickets, international ferry journeys, car hire, some hotels and larger purchases. Cheaper tavernas, shops and hotels as a rule do not accept credit cards.

You can get a cash advance on a foreign credit card at some banks, though the minimum amount is 44 euros, and you will need to take your passport with you as proof of identity. A credit card can be used for drawing local currency at cash machines. At a bank or ATM, a 1.5 per cent processing charge is usually levied for Visa, but none for other cards.

Cirrus and Plus debit card systems operate in Greece. Cash can be obtained using the Cirrus system at National Bank of Greece ATMs and the Plus system at Commercial Bank ATMs.

Travellers' cheques are the safest way to carry large sums of money. They are refundable if lost or stolen, though the process can be time-consuming. American Express and Thomas Cook are the best-known brands of travellers' cheques in Greece. They usually incur two sets of commissions: one when you buy them (1–1.5 per cent) and another when you cash them. Rates for the latter vary considerably, so shop around

before changing your money. Travellers' cheques can be cashed at large post offices (see p307) – an important consideration if you are travelling to a rural area or remote island.

Eurocheques, available only to holders of a European bank account in the form of a chequebook, are honoured at banks and post offices throughout Greece, as well as many hotels, shops and travel agencies. There is no commission charged when cashing Eurocheques, though there is an annual fee of about £8 for holding a European account and a fee of about 2 per cent for each cheque used. All fees are debited directly from the account.

DIRECTORY

To report a lost or stolen credit card call the following numbers collect from Greece:

American Express
(00 44 1273 696933.

Diners Club
(00 44 1252 513500.

MasterCard
(00 800 11887 0303.

Visa
(00 800 11638 0304.

To report lost or stolen travellers' cheques call the following free-phone numbers from Greece:

American Express
(00 800 44 127569.

Thomas Cook
(00 800 44 128455.

Visa
(00 800 44 128366.

THE EURO

INTRODUCTION OF the single European currency, the euro, is taking place in 12 of the 15 member states of the EU. Austria, Belgium, Finland, France, Germany, Greece, Ireland, Italy, Luxembourg, the Netherlands, Portugal and Spain chose to join the new currency; the UK, Denmark and Sweden stayed out, with an option to review their decision. The euro was introduced in most countries, but only for banking purposes, on 1 January, 1999. Greece adopted it on 1 January 2001. In all countries, a transition period saw euros and local currency used simultaneously.

In Greece, euro notes and coins came into circulation on 1 January 2002 and became the sole legal tender at the beginning of March 2002.

Bank Notes

Euro bank notes have seven denominations. The 5-euro note (grey in colour) is the smallest, followed by the 10-euro note (pink), 20-euro note (blue), 50-euro note (orange), 100-euro note (green), 200-euro note (yellow) and 500-euro note (purple). All notes show the stars of the European Union.

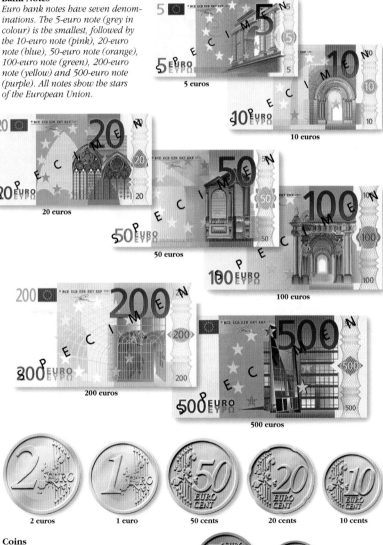

5 euros

10 euros

20 euros

50 euros

100 euros

200 euros

500 euros

2 euros   1 euro   50 cents   20 cents   10 cents

Coins

The euro has eight coin denominations: 2 euros and 1 euro (both silver-and-gold); 50 cents, 20 cents, 10 cents (all gold), 5 cents, 2 cents and 1 cent (all bronze). The reverse of each coin is the same in all Eurozone countries; the obverse is different in each country.

5 cents

2 cents

1 cent

Communications

Post office logo

THE GREEK NATIONAL telephone company is the OTE (Organismós Tilepikoinonión Elládos). Telecommunications have improved dramatically in recent years, and now there are direct lines to all major countries. These are often better than local lines, but the rates are among the highest in Europe. Greek post is reasonably reliable and efficient, especially from the larger towns and resorts; faxes are also easy to send and receive. The Greeks are avid newspaper readers, and in addition to a vast array of Greek publications, there are also a few good English-language papers and magazines.

TELEPHONES AND FAXES

PUBLIC TELEPHONES can be found in many locales – hotel foyers, telephone booths, street kiosks, or the local OTE office. Long-distance calls are best made in a telephone booth using a phonecard – available at any kiosk in a variety of different values. Alternatively, they can be made at a metered phone in an OTE office, where you can also make reverse-charge calls. OTE offices are open daily from 7am to 10pm or midnight in the larger towns, or until around 3pm in smaller communities. Call charges are variable, but in general local calls are cheap, out-of-town domestic calls are surprisingly expensive, and long-distance calls are extortionate. You can ring the operator first to find out specific rates, as well as for information about peak and cheap times, which vary depending on the country you are phoning.

Ship-to-shore and shore-to-ship calls can be made through INMARSAT; for information on this service call the marine operator from Greece on 158.

Faxes can be sent from OTE offices, a few city post offices, and some car-hire and travel agencies, though expect to pay a heavy surcharge wherever you go. The easiest way to receive a fax is to become friendly with your nearest car-hire or travel agency – both will usually oblige and keep faxes aside for you – otherwise the OTE office is the place to go.

A public phone

RADIO AND TV

WITH THREE state-owned radio channels and a plethora of local stations, the airwaves are positively jammed in Greece, and reception is not always dependable. There are many Greek music stations to listen to, as well as classical music stations such as ER-3, one of the three state-run channels, which can be heard on 95.6 FM. Daily news summaries are broadcast in English, French and German, and with a shortwave radio you will be able to pick up the BBC World Service in most parts of Greece. Its frequency varies, but in the Greater Athens area it can be heard on 107.1 FM. There is another 24-hour English-language station, Galaxy, which is on 92 FM.

Greek TV is broadcast by two state-run, and several privately run, channels, plus a host of cable and satellite stations from across Europe. Most Greek stations cater to popular taste, with a mix of dubbed foreign soap operas, game shows, sport and films. Fortunately for visitors, foreign language films tend to be subtitled rather than dubbed.

Satellite stations CNN and Euronews televise international news in English as it breaks around the clock. Guides that give details of the coming week's television programmes are published in all the English-language papers.

USING A PHONECARD TELEPHONE IN GREECE

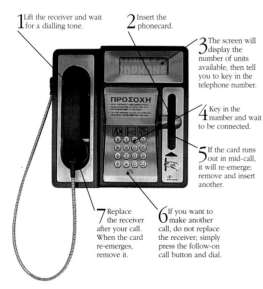

1 Lift the receiver and wait for a dialling tone.

2 Insert the phonecard.

3 The screen will display the number of units available, then tell you to key in the telephone number.

4 Key in the number and wait to be connected.

5 If the card runs out in mid-call, it will re-emerge; remove and insert another.

6 If you want to make another call, do not replace the receiver; simply press the follow-on call button and dial.

7 Replace the receiver after your call. When the card re-emerges, remove it.

A pictorial telephone card

Red post box
for express mail

Yellow post box
for all other post

Eleftherotypía,
Eléftheros Týpos and
Kathemeriní.

NEWSPAPERS AND MAGAZINES

THE TRUSTY corner *períptera* (kiosks), bookshops in larger towns and tourist shops in the resorts often sell day-old foreign newspapers and magazines, though the mark-up is substantial. Much cheaper, and also widely available, is the English-language paper published in Athens, *Athens News*, which is printed every day except Monday. The *Odyssey*, a bi-monthly, glossy magazine, is available in most resorts as well as the capital. These two publications are excellent sources of information on local entertainment, festivals and cultural goings-on, while also providing coverage of domestic and international news. The most popular Greek language newspapers are

POST

GREEK POST offices *(tachydromeía)* are generally open from 7:30am to 2pm Monday to Friday, with some main branches staying open as late as 8pm (main branches occasionally open for a few hours at weekends). All post offices are closed on public holidays (*see p48*). Those with an "Exchange" sign will change money in addition to the usual services.

Post boxes are usually bright yellow; those with two slots are marked *esterikó*, meaning domestic, and *exoterikó*, meaning overseas. Bright red post boxes are reserved for express mail, both domestic and overseas. Express is a little more expensive, but cuts delivery time by a few days.

Stamps *(grammatósima)* can be bought over the counter at post offices and also at *períptera*, the latter usually charging a 10 per cent commission. Airmail letters to most European countries take three to six days, and anywhere from five days to a week or more to North America, Australia and New Zealand. If you are sending postcards allow additional time for reaching any destination.

Stamp
machine

The poste restante system – whereby mail can be sent to, and picked up from, a post office – is widely used in Greece. Mail should be clearly marked "Poste Restante", with the recipient's surname underlined so that it gets filed in the right place. A passport, or some other proof of identity, is needed when collecting the post, which is kept for a maximum of 30 days before being returned to the sender.

If you are sending a parcel from Greece to a non-EU country, do not seal it before going to the post office. The contents will need to be inspected by security before it is sent, and if the package is sealed they will unwrap it.

The main post offices in the centre of Athens are indicated on the Street Finder map, at Plateía Omonoías, Plateía Syntágmatos and on Aiólou.

DIRECTORY

Domestic Calls

☏ 151 *(domestic operator).*
☏ 131 *(directory assistance for local calls anywhere in Greece).*

International Calls

☏ 161 *(international operator and directory assistance).*

International Calls from Greece
Dial 00, the country code (a list is given below), the local area code (minus the initial 0) and then the number itself.
Australia *61.*
Ireland *353.*
New Zealand *64.*
UK *44.*
USA & Canada *1.*

International Calls to Greece from Abroad
Dial the international access code (a list is given below), 30 (country code), the area code minus initial 0 and then the number itself.
Australia *0011.*
Ireland, UK & New Zealand *00.*
USA & Canada *011.*

Athenians reading newspapers on a clothes line at a street kiosk

Shopping in Greece

Sнopping in Greece can be entertaining, particularly when you buy directly from the producer. In smaller villages, embroiderers, lace makers and potters can often be seen at work. Most other goods in Greece have been imported and carry a heavy mark-up. For information on shopping in Athens see pages 114–17.

Souvenir shop window in Párga, central Greece

VAT AND TAX-FREE SHOPPING

Aлмоsт always included in the price, FPA *(Fóros Prostitheménis Axías)* – the equivalent of VAT – is about 18 per cent in Greece.

Visitors from outside the EU staying less than three months may claim this money back on purchases over 117 euros. A "Tax-Free Cheque" form must be completed in the shop, a copy of which is then given to the customs authorities on departure. You may be asked to show your receipt or goods as proof of purchase.

OPENING HOURS

Aллоwing for plenty of exceptions, shops and boutiques are generally open on Monday, Wednesday and Saturday from 9am to 2:30pm, and on Tuesday, Thursday and Friday from 9am to 1:30pm and 5pm to 8pm. Department stores remain open Monday to Friday from 9am to 8pm and Saturday from 9am to 3pm. Supermarkets, found in all but the smallest communities, are often family-run and open long hours, typically Monday to Saturday from 8 or 9am to 8 or 9pm. Sunday shopping is possible in most tourist resorts and also in some of the suburban shopping malls in Athens. The corner *períptero* (street kiosk), found in nearly every town, is open from around 7am to 11pm or midnight, selling everything from aspirins to ice cream, as well as bus tickets and phonecards.

"Brettos" distillery and liquor store, in Athens

MARKETS

Most towns in Greece have their weekly street market *(laïkí agorá)*, a colourful selection of fresh fruit and vegetables, herbs, fish, meat and poultry – often juxtaposed with shoes and underwear, fabrics, household items and sundry electronic equipment. In the larger cities, the street markets are in a different area each day, usually opening early and packing up by about 2pm, in time for the siesta. Prices are generally cheaper than in the supermarkets, and a certain amount of bargaining is also acceptable, at least for non-perishables. This guide gives market days in the information under each town entry.

Tax-free shop symbol

In Athens, there is a famous Sunday-morning flea market around Plateía Monastirakíou and its radiating streets, which should not be missed if you are in the city *(see p87)*.

FOOD AND DRINK

Culinary delights to look out for in Greece include honey, olives, olive oil, pistachios, herbs and spices. There are also various cheeses, including feta, and the sweet breads and biscuits of the *zacharoplasteío* (cake and pastry shop). Greece is also renowned for several drinks, including ouzo (an aniseed-flavoured spirit), retsina (a resinated wine), brandy and the firewater *tsípouro*.

SIZE CHART

Women's dresses, coats and skirts

Greek	44	46	48	50	52	54	(size)
GB/Australian	10	12	14	16	18	20	(size)
US	8	10	12	14	16	18	(size)

Men's suits, shirts and jumpers

Greek	44	46	48	50	52	54	56	(size)
GB/US	34	36	38	40	42	44	46	(inches)
Australian	87	92	97	102	107	112	117	(cm)

Women's shoes

Greek	36	37	38	39	40	41	(size)
GB	3	4	5	6	7	8	(size)
US/Australian	5	6	7	8	9	10	(size)

Men's shoes

Greek	39	40	41	42	43	44	(size)
GB/Australian	6	7	7 ½	8	9	10	(size)
US	7	7 ½	8	8 ½	9 ½	10 ½	(size)

What to Buy in Greece

TRADITIONAL handicrafts, though not particularly cheap, do offer the most genuinely Greek souvenirs. Handicrafts cover a range of items from finely wrought gold reproductions of ancient pendants to rustic pots, wooden spoons and handmade sandals. Some of the country's best ceramics can be found in the markets and shops of Athens' northern suburb, Maroúsi. Brightly coloured embroidery and wall-hangings are produced in many villages throughout Greece, where they are often seen hanging out for

Rugs for sale at Aráchova

sale, along with thick *flokáti* rugs, which are handwoven from sheep or goat's wool. These are made mainly in the Píndos Mountains and can also be found at Aráchova, near Delphi *(see p221)*. In the small, rural communities, crafts are often cottage industries, earning the family a large chunk of its annual income. Here, there is room to engage in some bartering over the price. The *Shopping in Athens* section, on pages 114–17, indicates places within the capital where traditional crafts may be bought.

Gold jewellery *is sold in larger towns or cities. Modern designs are found in jewellers such as Lalaounis, and reproductions of ancient designs in museum gift shops.*

Icons *are generally sold in shops and monasteries. They range from very small portraits to substantial pictures. Some of the most beautiful, and expensive, use only age-old traditional techniques and materials.*

Ornate utensils, *such as these wooden spoons, are found in traditional craft shops. As here, they are often hand-carved into the shapes of figures and produced from the rich-textured wood of the native olive tree.*

Kombolóï, *or worry beads, are a traditional sight in Greece; the beads are counted as a way to relax. They are sold in souvenir shops and jewellers.*

Kitchenware *is found in most markets and specialist shops. This copper coffee pot (mprîki) is used for making Greek coffee.*

Leather goods *are sold throughout Greece. The bags, backpacks and sandals make useful and good-value souvenirs.*

Ornamental ceramics *come in many shapes and finishes. Traditional earthenware, often simple, functional and unglazed, is frequently for sale by the roads on the outskirts of Athens and the larger towns.*

Specialist Holidays and Outdoor Activities

Mountain walker

MANY ORGANIZED TOURS and courses cater for the special interests of visitors to Greece. You can follow in the footsteps of the apostle Paul or visit ancient archaeological sites with a learned academic as your guide; you can improve your writing skills, draw wild flowers or paint the Greek landscape. Sailing and windsurfing holidays are available, as well as walking tours, and botanical and birdwatching expeditions. Many holidays are offered with food and accommodation included in the price.

mountain areas of Agrafa and Stereá, offering a harsh landscape to explore at the southern end of the Píndos range. **Waymark Holidays** offers a similar service in these and other regions, using its own hiking leaders and tour guides. *The Mountains of Greece: A Walker's Guide* (published by Cicerone Press) is a good source of general information and also describes some of the routes.

Visitors on a tour of the ancient remains at Olympia *(see pp170–72)*

ARCHAEOLOGICAL TOURS

FOR THOSE interested in Greece's ancient past, a tour to some of the famous archaeological sites can make a fascinating and memorable holiday. You can choose from an array of destinations and itineraries, all guided by qualified archaeologists. As well as visiting ancient ruins, many tours also take in Venetian fortresses, Byzantine churches and frescoes, museums and monasteries en route to the archaeological sites. **Filoxenía** provide tours with Minoan, Roman and medieval interests, while **Ramblers Holidays** organize tours of Classical sites.

WRITING AND PAINTING

WITH ITS vivid landscape and renowned quality of light, Greece is an inspirational destination for artistic endeavour. Courses in creative writing, and drawing and painting, are available at all levels and are conducted by professional tutors, well established in their craft. **Filoxenía** organize a range of holidays around the activities of painting and art history.

NATURE TOURS

MUCH OF the Greek countryside is rich in birdlife and noted for its spring flowers. The shorelines are also good for wildlife. Specialist tour operators, such as **Peregrine Holidays**, **Peregrine Adventures** and **Sunbird**, offer package holidays that guide visitors through the ornithology and botany of northern Greece and the Peloponnese. The **Hellenic Ornithological Society** can also be contacted for advice on birdwatching in Greece.

WALKING

GREECE IS A PARADISE for walkers, particularly in the spring when the countryside is at its greenest, the wild flowers are in bloom and the sun is not yet too hot.

The best locations for walking are in the mountain ranges of the Taÿgetos in the Peloponnese *(see p195)* and the Píndos range in central Greece *(see p206)*. **Trekking Hellas** arrange walking holidays in these regions, as well as a tour to the remote

SKIING

THERE ARE several ski centres throughout the mainland, including some within easy reach of Athens – the closest being Mount Parnassus, near Delphi *(see p221)*. Depending on snow conditions, the season runs from the start of January to the end of April.

Costs are low compared with other European resorts, though facilities are quite basic. For more information on skiing in Greece, contact the **Hellenic Skiing Federation**, or pick up a copy of the EOT's booklet entitled *Mountain Refuges and Ski Centres*; it is free from tourist offices, and describes all the major ski centres.

WATERSPORTS

WITH ITS extensive and varied coastline, warm weather and crystal-clear seas, it is not surprising that so many water-lovers are

Holiday-makers learning the skills of windsurfing in coastal waters

Holiday-makers sailing off the Greek mainland coast

attracted to Greece. Facilities for watersports are numerous: everything from windsurfing and water-skiing to jet-skiing and parasailing are available in the larger resorts, and many of the places that rent equipment will also give instruction.

Inland, kayaking, whitewater rafting and canoeing holidays are organized by **Trekking Hellas**.

SCUBA AND SNORKELLING

THE AMAZINGLY clear waters of the Mediterranean reveal a world of submarine life and ancient archaeological remains.

Snorkelling can be enjoyed almost anywhere along the coast, though scuba diving is restricted. Greece is highly protective of its antiquities,

and it is forbidden to remove them, or even to photograph them. A list of places where oxygen equipment may be used is available from the Greek Tourist Office (EOT) (see p299), or write to the **Department of Underwater Archaeology** in Athens.

SAILING HOLIDAYS

SAILING HOLIDAYS can be booked through charter companies either in Greece or abroad. The season runs from April to late October, and itineraries range from a few days to several weeks.

Charters fall into four main categories. Bareboat charter, without a skipper or crew, is available to anyone with sailing experience (most

charter companies require at least two crew members to have a basic skipper's licence). Crewed charters range from the modest services of a paid skipper, assistant or cook to fully crewed yachts with every imaginable luxury. Chartering a yacht as part of a flotilla – typically in a group of 6 to 12 yachts – provides the opportunity of independent sailing with the support of a lead boat contactable by radio. **Sunsail** and Thomas Cook offer this kind of holiday, as well as a combined holiday, mixing cruiser sailing with shore-based dinghy sailing and windsurfing. You can contact the **Hellenic Yachting Federation** for more details.

CRUISES AND BOAT TRIPS

GREECE'S UNIQUE combination of natural beauty and fascinating history makes a cruise holiday both relaxing and stimulating. Running from April to October, a variety of options are available, ranging from the luxury of a large liner, accompanied by learned guest speakers, to inexpensive mini-cruises and boat trips. The former can be booked through operators such as **Swan Hellenic**, while the latter are organized locally and best booked at a travel agent on the spot.

DIRECTORY

Department of Underwater Archaeology
Kallispéri 30,
11742 Athens.
[210 924 7249.

Filoxenía
Sourdock Hill,
Barkisland, Halifax,
West Yorkshire,
HX4 0AG,
England.
[01422 375999.

Hellenic Ornithological Society
Vasileos Irakleion 24,
10682 Athens.
[210 822 7937.

Hellenic Skiing Federation
Karagiórgi Servías 7,
10563 Athens.
[210 323 4412.

Hellenic Yachting Federation
Akti Possidónas 51,
Moschato.
[210 940 3111.

Peregrine Holidays
41 South Parade,
Summertown, Oxford OX2
7JP, England.
[01865 511642.

Peregrine Adventures
5th floor, 38 York Street
Sydney, Australia
[02 92 90 27 70

Pharos Travel and Tourism
23 W. 31st Street, New
York, NY 10001 USA
[800-999 5511
FAX 212 736 3921

Ramblers Holidays
Box 43, Welwyn Garden
City, Hertfordshire,
AL8 6PQ, England.
[01707 331133.

Sunbird
PO Box 76, Sandy,
Bedfordshire SG19 1DF,
England.
[01767 682969.

Sunsail
Port House,
Port Solent, Portsmouth
PO6 4TH,

England.
[02392 222222.

Swan Hellenic Cruises
Richmond House,
Perminus Terrace,
Southampton SO14 3PN,
England.
[0845 355 5111.

Trekking Hellas
Tsimiski 71,
54624 Thessaloníki.
[2310 222128.
W www.trekking.gr

Waymark Holidays
44 Windsor Road,
Slough,
Berkshire SL1 2EJ
England
[01753 516 477.

TRAVEL INFORMATION

RELIABLY HOT, SUNNY WEATHER makes Greece an extremely popular destination for holiday-makers, particularly from the colder parts of northern Europe. During high season (May to October) there are countless flights, bringing millions to the shores of Greece. For those with more time, it is also possible to reach Greece by car, rail and coach. Travelling on the Greek mainland is easy enough. There is an extensive bus network reaching even the tiniest communities, with frequent services on all major routes. Greece's rail network is skeletal by comparison and, aside from the intercity expresses, service is much slower. Travelling around by car offers the most flexibility, allowing the visitor to dictate the pace, and to reach places that are not accessible by public transport. However, road conditions are variable, and in remoter parts can be rough, pot-holed and dangerous *(see p320)*. Some of the larger centres and popular tourist destinations can also be visited by plane from Athens and Thessaloníki.

Olympic Airways passenger aeroplane

GETTING TO GREECE BY AIR

THE MAIN AIRLINES operating direct scheduled flights from London to Athens and Thessaloníki are **Olympic Airways** (the Greek national airline) and **British Airways**. Athens now has a new airport, Elefthérios Venizélos, which handles all international and domestic flights. The old airport (Hellinikon) is no longer used.

From Europe, there are around 20 international airports in Greece that can be reached directly. On the mainland, only Athens and Thessaloníki handle scheduled flights. The other mainland international airports – Préveza, Kalamáta and Kavála – can be reached directly only by charter flights. From outside Europe, all

Travellers with airport shopping

scheduled flights to Greece arrive in Athens, although only a few airlines offer direct flights – most will require changing planes, and often airlines, at a connecting European city.

There are direct flights daily from New York operated by Olympic and **Delta**.

From Australia, Olympic Airways operates flights out of Sydney, Brisbane and Melbourne. These generally necessitate a stop-off in Southeast Asia or Europe, but there are two direct flights a week from Australia, which leave from Melbourne and Sydney. Flights from New Zealand are also via Melbourne or Sydney. Other carriers with services from Australasian cities to Athens include **Singapore Airlines** and **KLM**.

Athens' new international airport nearing completion in 2001

Check-in desks at Athens' new Elefthérios Venizélos Airport

CHARTERS AND PACKAGE DEALS

CHARTER FLIGHTS to Greece are nearly all from within Europe, and mostly operate between May and October. Tickets are sold by travel agencies either as part of an all-inclusive package holiday or as a flight-only deal.

Although they tend to be the cheapest flights available, charters do carry certain restrictions: departure dates cannot be changed once booked and there are usually minimum and maximum limits to one's stay (typically between three days and a month). And if you plan to visit Turkey from Greece, bear in mind that charter passengers can only do so for a day trip; staying any longer will forfeit the return ticket for your flight home from Greece.

Booking agency in Athens

FLIGHT TIMES

FLYING TO ATHENS from London or Amsterdam takes about 3.5 hours; the journey time from Paris and Berlin is around 3 hours – the trip from Berlin being a little quicker. From Madrid it takes just over 4 hours and from Rome a little under 2 hours. There are direct flights to Athens from New York, which take 10 hours, although a non-direct flight can take more than 12. From Los Angeles the flight's duration is from 17 to 19 hours, depending on the European connection. From Sydney, via Bangkok, it is a 19-hour flight.

AIR FARES

FARES TO GREECE are generally at their highest from June to September, but how much you pay will depend more on the type of ticket you decide to purchase. Charters are usually the cheapest option during peak season, though discounted scheduled flights are also common and worth considering for longer visits or during the low season, when there are few charters available. Reasonable savings can also be made by booking an APEX (Advance Purchase Excursion) ticket well in advance but, like charters, these are subject to minimum and maximum limits to one's stay and other

Departure gate symbol

restrictions. Budget travellers can often pick up bargains through agents advertising in the national press, and cheap last-minute deals are also advertised on Teletext and Ceefax in the UK. Whoever you book through, be sure that the company is a fully bonded and licensed member of ABTA (the Association of British Travel Agents) or an equivalent authority – this will ensure that you can get home should the company go bankrupt during your stay; it also should ensure that you receive compensation. Note that domestic flights in Greece are subject to an airport tax *(see p314)*.

ATHENS' NEW AIRPORT

GREECE'S LARGEST and most prestigious infrastructure development project for the new millennium opened to air traffic in 2001. Located at Spata, 27 km (17 miles) north-east of the city centre, Athens' brand new airport now handles all the city's passenger and cargo flights. It has two run-ways, designed for simulta-neous, round-the-clock operation, and a Main Terminal Building for all arrivals and depar-tures. Arrivals are located on the ground floor (level 1) and departures on the first floor (level 2). The smaller Satellite Build-ing is accessed along an underground corridor with moving walkways. The airport has been designed to allow for a 45-minute connection time between two scheduled flights.

The airport's modern business and service facilities include a shopping mall, restaurants and cafés in the Main Terminal Building and a four-star hotel in the airport complex. Car-rental firms, banks, bureaux de change and travel agencies are in the arrivals area.

TRANSPORT FROM ATHENS AIRPORT

A NEW SIX-LANE highway is being built to link the airport to the Athens City Ring Road, while metro and

Light, space and accessibility are features of Athens' airport

rail networks that extend to the airport are planned for the future. From the airport, the E95 bus runs to and from Plateía Syntágmatos in the city centre every 15 minutes with a journey time of about one hour. Bus E96 runs to and from Piraeus every 20 minutes, taking about 100 minutes. Tickets for both journeys cost around 3 euros. These tickets are in effect one-day travel cards and can also be used to travel around the city *(see p325)*. A taxi-ride into town costs 12–15 euros.

One of the smaller planes in Olympic's fleet, for short-haul flights

Athens' new airport, designed in the blue and white national colours

FLIGHT CONNECTIONS IN GREECE

As well as having the largest number of international flights in Greece, Athens also has the most connecting air services to other parts of the country. Both international and domestic flights now arrive at and depart from the main terminal at the city's Elefthérios Venizélos airport. Thessaloníki also handles scheduled flights,

but only from within Europe. Greece's other international airports are served by charters only, mostly from the UK, Germany, the Netherlands and Scandinavia.

DOMESTIC FLIGHTS

Greece's domestic airline network is extensive. **Olympic Airways** and its affiliate, **Olympic Aviation**, operate most internal flights,

though there are also a number of private companies, such as **Aegean/Cronus Airlines**, providing services between Athens and the major island destinations. Fares for domestic flights are at least double the equivalent bus journey or deck-class ferry trip. Tickets and timetables for Olympic flights are available from any Olympic Airways office in Greece or abroad, as well as from most major travel agencies. Reservations are essential in peak season.

Olympic Airways operates direct flights from Athens to eight mainland towns, including Thessaloníki, Ioánnina and Alexandroúpoli, and to over two dozen islands. A number of inter-island services operate during the summer, and about a dozen of these fly year round *(see p313)*.

A small airport departure tax is charged on domestic flights of between 62 and 466 air miles. For "international" flights (that is, those over 466 air miles) the tax is doubled.

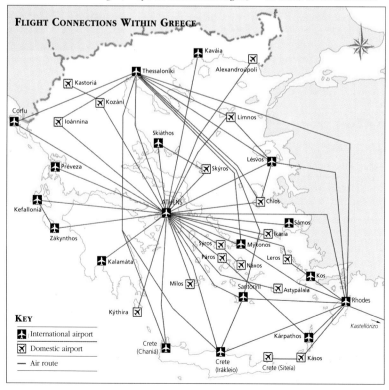

FLIGHT CONNECTIONS WITHIN GREECE

KEY
✈ International airport
☒ Domestic airport
— Air route

Island	Distance	Flying Time	Island	Distance	Flying Time
Corfu	381 km (237 miles)	40 minutes	Crete (Chaniá)	318 km (198 miles)	45 minutes
Rhodes	426 km (265 miles)	45 minutes	Santoríni	228 km (142 miles)	40 minutes
Skýros	128 km (80 miles)	40 minutes	Kos	324 km (201 miles)	45 minutes
Skiáthos	135 km (84 miles)	30 minutes	Mýkonos	153 km (95 miles)	30 minutes
Límnos	252 km (157 miles)	45 minutes	Páros	157 km (98 miles)	35 minutes

DIRECTORY

ATHENS AIRPORT

Elefthérios Venizélos – Athens International Airport
5th km Spata-Loutsa Ave.,
10904 Spata.
[210 353 0000.
FAX 210 369 8883.
W www.aia.gr

OLYMPIC AIRWAYS

Arrivals and Departures
[210 353 0000.
144.

Athens Office
Syngroú 96,
11741 Athens.
[210 926 7251.

Thessaloníki Office
Kountouriótou 3,
Thessaloníki.
[2310 368 666.
W www.olympic-airways.gr

OTHER AIRLINES

Aegean/Cronus Airlines
Leof. Vouliagménis 572,
16451 Athens.
[2801 112 0000.
W www.airgreece.com
W www.aegeanair.com

Air Canada
Ziridi 10,
15124 Athens.
[210 617 5321.
W www.aircanada.ca

Air France
Leof. Vouliagménis 18,
16674 Athens.
[210 960 1100.
W www.airfrance.com

British Airways
Vouliagménis & Themistokleous 1,
16674 Athens.
[210 890 6666.
(Phone for details of Qantas Airline services).
Thessaloniki:
[2310 220 227.
W www.british-airways.com

Delta Airlines
Othonos 4,
10557 Athens.
[210 331 1668.
W www.delta.com

Easyjet
[210 967 0000.
W www.easyjet.com

KLM
Vouliagménis 41,
16675 Athens.
[210 911 0000.
W www.klm.com

Singapore Airlines
Xenofóntos 9,
10557 Athens.
[210 372 8000.
W www.singapore air.com

United Airlines
Syngroú 5,
11743 Athens.
[210 924 2645.
W www.ual.com
(reservations).

PRIVATE AIRLINES (FOR DOMESTIC TRAVEL)

Greek Air Ltd
Efxenia Pontou 45,
Ano Glyfada.
[210 992 8108.

Interjet
Leof. Vouliagménis 6,
16674 Athens.
[210 940 2151.

Olympic Aviation
Syngrou 96,
11741 Athens.
[210 936 5565.
(reservations),
(or via Olympic Airways).

TRAVEL AGENCIES IN ATHENS

American Express Travel Services
Ermoú 2,
10225 Athens.
[210 324 4975.

Blue Star Ferries
Attica Premium,
Attica Posidonos.
[210 414 1141.

Ginis Vacances
3rd floor,
Ermoú 23–25,
10563 Athens.
[210 325 0401.

International Student and Youth Travel Service
1st floor,
Níkis 11,
10557 Athens.
[210 322 1267.
@ isyts@travelling.gr

Oxygen Travel
Eslin 4,
Athens.
[210 641 0881.
@ angeki@eexi.gr

OLYMPIC AIRWAYS OFFICES ABROAD

Australia
37–49 Pitt Street,
Suite 303,
Level 3,
Underwood House,
Royal Exchange,
Sydney,
NSW 2001.
[(02) 9251 1047.

Canada
80 Bloor Street,
Suite 503,
Toronto,
Ontario
M5S F2V1.
[(416) 920 2452.

UK
11 Conduit Street,
London
W1R OLP.
[(020) 7399 1500.
[0870 606 0460
(reservations).

USA
645 Fifth Avenue,
New York,
NY 10022.
[(212) 838-3600.

Travelling by Train

REECE'S RAIL NETWORK is limited to the mainland, and the system is fairly skeletal by European standards. With the exception of intercity express trains, service tends to be slow. In compensation, non-express tickets are very inexpensive (much less than coaches in fact) and some lines are pleasurable in themselves, travelling as they do through rugged and beautiful countryside. Fast and efficient intercity trains operate on some of the major lines, though tickets for these trains are more expensive. An overnight sleeper service is also available on the Athens–Thessaloníki and Thessaloníki–Alexandroúpoli routes.

Greek railway's OSE logo

via Belgrade; the line via Alexandroúpoli splits, going to Sofia and Istanbul; and the line to Flórina continues to Skopje. Intercity express trains run from Athens to Thessaloníki, Alexandroúpoli, Vólos and Kozáni; and from Pireaus to Pátra, Kyparissía and Thessaloníki. From Thessaloníki express trains run to Kozáni, Alexandroúpoli and Vólos.

First- and second-class carriages of a non-express train

TRAVELLING TO GREECE BY TRAIN

RAVELLING TO GREECE by train is expensive, but may be useful if you wish to make stopovers en route. From London to Athens, the main route takes around three and a half days. The journey is through France, Switzerland and Italy, then by ferry from the Adriatic ports of Bari or Brindisi, via the Greek island of Corfu, to the port of Pátra, and finally on to Athens.

The other route is through the region of the former Yugoslavia, and does not necessitate a ferry crossing. The train travels overland via Budapest in Hungary, on to Belgrade and Skopje to arrive in Greece at Thessaloníki.

TRAVELLING AROUND GREECE BY TRAIN

REECE'S RAIL NETWORK is run by the state-owned **OSE** (Organismós Sidirodrómon Elládos), and Athens forms the hub of the system. A north-bound line from Laríssis station links Athens and Thessaloníki, with branch lines to Chalkída (Evvoia);

Vólos; Kardítsa, Tríkala and Kalampáka; and Edessa and Kozáni. The southern narrow-gauge railway runs from Athens' Peloponnísou station to towns in the Peloponnese, linking Athens to Kalamáta via Pátra and Pýrgos, or via Argos and Trípoli. Some routes are extremely pictur-esque, two of the best being the rack-and-pinion line be-tween Diakoftó and Kalávryta in the Peloponnese *(see p168)*, and the elevated section of line between Leivadiá and Lamía in central Greece.

From Thessaloníki there are three lines. The Polýkastro line continues to Budapest,

TRAIN TICKETS

RAIN TICKETS can be bought at any OSE office or railway station, plus some authorized travel agencies. It is worth getting your ticket – and reserving a seat at no extra charge – several days in advance, especially in summer when there are often more passengers than seats. A 50 per cent surcharge is levied for tickets issued on the train.

There are three basic types of ticket: first class, second class and intercity express. The first two are at least half the price of the equivalent coach journey, though service tends to be slower; tickets for intercity express trains are more costly but worth it for the time they save. A 20 per cent reduction is offered on all return journeys, and a 30 per cent discount for groups of six or more. In addition, a Greek Rail Pass is available which allows the user 10, 20 or 30 days of unlimited rail travel on first and second class trains, anywhere in Greece. The only exclusion

Athens' Lárissis station, for trains to northern Greece

Peloponnísou station ticket window

with this pass is travel on the intercity express trains, which is not included in the fixed price. InterRail and Eurail passes are both honoured in Greece, though supplements are payable on some lines.

TRAIN STATIONS IN ATHENS

ATHENS HAS two train stations, virtually next door to each other, about a 15-minute walk northwest of Plateía Omonoías. Lárissis station, on Deligiánni, serves northern Greece (Thessaloníki, Vólos and Lárisa), the Balkans, Turkey and western Europe. Additionally, tickets for OSE coaches abroad are sold here, and there are baggage storage facilities. Peloponnísou station is a five-minute walk to the south over a metal bridge that crosses the railway tracks. This serves trains for the Peloponnese, including Pátra which is the main port for ferries to Italy. Lárissis station is served by the metro, and by trolleybus No. 1 from Plateía Syntágmatos. Alternatively, taxis are abundant in Athens and fares are inexpensive compared with most other European cities.

The distinctive front end of an intercity express train

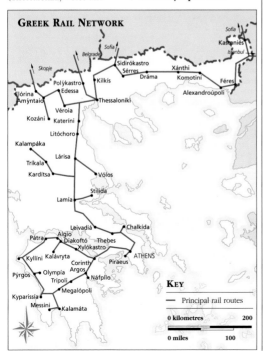

GREEK RAIL NETWORK

Sofia
Skopje
Belgrade
Sidirókastro
Sofia
Kastaniés
Istanbul
Polýkastro
Kilkís
Sérres
Xánthi
Dráma
Komotiní
Féres
Flórina
Amýntaio
Edessa
Véroia
Thessaloníki
Alexandroúpoli
Kozáni
Kateríni
Litóchoro
Kalampáka
Lárisa
Tríkala
Kardítsa
Vólos
Stilída
Lamía
Leivadiá
Chalkída
Aígio
Pátra
Diakoftó
Thebes
Kalávryta
Xylókastro
Kyllíni
Corinth
Piraeus
ATHENS
Pýrgos
Olympía
Argos
Trípoli
Náfplio
Kyparissía
Megalópoli
Messini
Kalamáta

KEY

— Principal rail routes

| 0 kilometres | 200 |
| 0 miles | 100 |

DIRECTORY

OSE OFFICES

Athens
Sína 6.
📞 210 362 4402.
Karólou 1 (information).
📞 210 529 7777.

Thessaloníki
Aristotélous 18.
📞 2310 598112 or 598115.

Lárisa
Papakyriazi 137.
📞 2410 590239.

Vólos
Iásonos 42.
📞 24210 28555.

RECORDED INFORMATION

📞 145 (departures from Athens to other Greek destinations).
📞 147 (departures from Athens to international destinations).

RAILWAY STATIONS

Athens
Lárissis station.
📞 210 823 1514.
Peloponnísou station.
📞 210 513 1601.

Thessaloníki
📞 2310 517517.

Pátra
📞 2610 639108 or 639109.

Lárisa
📞 2410 236250.

Vólos
📞 24210 24056.

RAIL TRAVEL FROM THE UK

Rail Europe (InterRail)
French Rail House,
10 Leake Street,
London SE1 7NN.
📞 08705-848 848.
🖥 www.raileurope.co.uk

Campus Travel (Eurotrain)
52 Grosvenor Gardens,
London SW1W OAG.
📞 020-7730 8832.

Travelling by Road

Road sign to port

TRAVELLING AROUND GREECE by car gives you the flexibility to explore at your own pace. There are express highways between Athens, Thessaloníki, Vólos and Pátra, which are very fast, though tolls are charged for their use. The maps in this guide categorize the roads into four groups, from the express routes in blue to non-asphalt roads in yellow *(see back flap)*. The road system is continually being upgraded, and most routes are now surfaced.

An express recovery vehicle

You have priority

You have right of way

Do not use car horn

Wild animals crossing

Hairpin bend ahead

Roundabout ahead

TRAVELLING TO GREECE BY CAR

Owing to political upheaval in the former Yugoslavia, the most direct overland routes to Greece are currently not recommended. The **AA** and **RAC** can supply up-to-date information on the advisability of routes and, for a small fee, will compile individual itineraries. It is worth asking their advice on insurance needs and on any special driving regulations for those countries en route.

In order to drive in Greece, you will need to take a full, valid national driving licence, and have insurance cover (at least third party is compulsory). **ELPA** (the Automobile and Touring Club of Greece) also offer useful information on driving in Greece.

RULES OF THE ROAD

Driving is on the right in Greece and road signs conform to European norms. There may be exceptions on small rural back roads, where the names of villages are often signposted in Greek only.

The speed limit on national highways is 120 km/h (75 mph) for cars; on country roads it is 90 km/h (55 mph) and in towns 50 km/h (30 mph). The speed limit on national highways for motorbikes up to 100 cc is 70 km/h (45 mph), and 90 km/h (55 mph) for larger motorbikes.

Although usually ignored, the use of seatbelts in cars is required by law, and children under the age of ten are not allowed to sit in the front seat. Parking and speeding tickets must be paid at the local police station or your car-hire agency.

CAR HIRE

There are scores of car-hire agencies in every tourist resort and major town, offering a full range of cars and four-wheel-drive vehicles.

A line of mopeds for hire

International companies such as **Budget**, **Avis**, **Hertz** and **Europcar** tend to be more expensive than their local counterparts, though the latter are generally as reliable.

The car-hire agency should have an agreement with an emergency recovery company, such as **Express**, **Hellas** or the **InterAmerican Towing Company** in the event of a vehicle breakdown. Also, be sure to check the insurance policy cover: third party is required by law, but personal accident insurance is strongly recommended. A valid national driving licence that has been held for at least one year is needed, and there is a minimum age requirement, ranging from 21 to 25 years.

Sign for car hire

MOTORBIKE, MOPED AND BICYCLE HIRE

Motorbikes and mopeds are readily available for hire in all the tourist resorts. Mopeds are ideal for short distances on fairly flat terrain, but for travel in more remote or mountainous areas a motorbike is essential.

Whatever you decide to hire, make sure that the vehicle is in good condition before you set out, and that you have adequate insurance cover; also check whether your own travel insurance covers you for motorbike accidents (many do not).

Speeding in Greece is penalized by fines, drink-driving laws are strict and helmets are compulsory.

Though less widely available, bicycles can be hired in some tourist resorts.

Rack of bicycles for hire at a coastal resort

The hot weather and tough terrain make cycling extremely hard work but, on the positive side, bikes can be transported free on most Greek ferries and buses, and for a small fee on trains.

PETROL STATIONS

PETROL STATIONS are plentiful in towns, though in rural areas they are few and far between – always set out with a full tank to be on the safe side. Fuel is sold by the litre, and the price is comparable to most other European countries. There are usually either three or four grades available: super (95 octane), unleaded, super unleaded and diesel, which is confusingly called *petrélaio* in Greece.

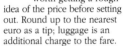

Unleaded and super petrol

Filling stations set their own working hours in Greece. Generally they are open seven days a week, from around 7am or 8am to between 7pm and 9pm. Some stations in the larger towns remain open 24 hours a day.

TAXIS

TAXIS PROVIDE a reasonably priced way of making short trips around Greece. All taxis are metered, but for longer journeys a price can usually be negotiated per diem, or per trip. Also, drivers are generally amenable to

Dual-language road sign, found on most routes

dropping you off somewhere and returning to pick you up a few hours later.

In Athens taxis are plentiful and can simply be hailed. In smaller towns it is best to find one at a taxi rank, which is likely to be either in the centre or by the bus or train station. Most rural villages have at least one taxi, and the best place to arrange for one is at the local *kafeneío* (café). In Greece taxis are often shared with other passengers; each pays for their part of the journey. Although taxis are metered, it is worth getting a rough idea of the price before setting out. Round up to the nearest euro as a tip; luggage is an additional charge to the fare.

HITCHHIKING

GREECE IS A RELATIVELY safe place for hitchhiking but, like anywhere else, there are potential risks. Women especially are advised against hitching alone.

If you do hitchhike, finding a lift is usually easier in the less populated, rural areas, than on busy roads heading out from major towns and cities.

MAPS

NOT TOO MUCH reliance should be given to maps issued by local travel agents and car-hire agencies. Visitors intending to do much motoring are advised to bring with them the GeoCenter regional road maps (1:300,000 range), the single-sheet Freytag & Berndt maps (1:650,000), or to buy regional Road Editions maps when in Greece.

DIRECTORY

MOTORING ORGANIZATIONS IN THE UK

AA Continental Road Service
[0870 550 600 (in UK).

RAC
[0800 550055 (in UK).

MOTORING ORGANIZATIONS IN GREECE

ELPA (Ellinikí Léschi Periigíseon kai Aftokinítou)
Ground Floor, Athens Tower, Mesogeíon 2–4, 11527 Athens.
[210 606 8800.
[174 (information).
[104 (road assistance).

Express Service
[154.

Hellas Service
[1507.

InterAmerican Towing Company
[168.

CAR HIRE AGENCIES IN GREECE

Avis
Leofóros Amalías 48, 10558 Athens.
[210 322 4951.

Budget
Syngroú 8, 11742 Athens.
[210 921 4771.

Dionysus Rent a Car
Syngrou 25, 11742 Athens.
[210 924 3310.

Eurodrive
Syngroú 38, 11742 Athens.
[210 924 6820.

Europcar
Syngroú 4, 11742 Athens.
[210 924 8810.

Hertz
Leofóros Vouliagménis 576A, 16451 Argyroúpoli.
[2801 11 100 100.

Quick Rent a Car
Syngroú 318, 11742 Athens.
[210 957 1302.

Travelling by Coach and Bus

GREECE'S BUS SYSTEM is operated by KTEL (Koinó Tameío Eispráxeon Leoforeíon), a syndicate of privately run companies. The network is comprehensive in that it provides every community with services of some sort. In rural villages this may be once a day or, in remoter places, once or twice a week. Services between the larger centres are frequent and efficient. Time permitting, bus travel is a good way of experiencing the country.

International coaches also connect Greece with the rest of Europe, though fares do not compare well with charter bargains during the summer holiday season.

EUROPEAN COACH SERVICES TO GREECE

COACH JOURNEYS from London to Athens take many days and are not as cheap as a bargain air fare. However, if you are not in a hurry, it is cheaper than taking the train.

Eurolines is a very reliable company, with a huge network of European destinations. Its coaches have reclining seats, toilets and washing facilities, and there are frequent short stops en route. Tickets can be booked in person, or by telephone using a credit card. Eurolines coaches stop at Thessaloníki, with express coach services going from there to Athens. Alternatively, you could take the bus as far as Naples or Brindisi in Italy and then take the ferry across to Greece.

Top Deck is an adventure tour operator used mainly by young travellers. Tours to Greece take about 20 days, with many stops on the way.

UK COACH OFFICES

Eurolines
52 Grosvenor Gardens, Victoria, London SW1.
☎ 020-7730 8235.

Top Deck
125 Earls Court Road, London SW5 9RH.
☎ 020-7370 4555.
🌐 www.topdecktravel.co.uk

TRAVELLING IN GREECE BY COACH AND BUS

THE GREEK coach and bus system is extensive, with services to even the remotest destinations and frequent

Domestic coach, run by KTEL

express coaches on all the major routes. Large centres, such as Athens, usually have more than one terminal, and each serves a different set of destinations.

Ticket sales are computerized for all major routes, with reserved seating on modern, air-conditioned coaches. It pays to buy your ticket at least 20 minutes before the coach is scheduled to depart, as seats often get sold out on popular routes, and Greek coaches have a habit of leaving a few minutes early.

In the villages of the countryside, the local *kafeneío* (café) often serves as the bus and coach station. You can usually buy your ticket from the proprietor of the *kafeneío*, who may also have a timetable. Otherwise it is possible to buy a ticket when you board.

K.T.E.Λ. NOMOУ

KTEL logo

COACH TOURS

IN THE RESORT AREAS, travel agents offer a wide range of excursions on air-conditioned coaches accompanied by qualified guides. These include trips to major archaeological and historical sites, other towns and seaside resorts, popular beaches and specially organized events. Depending on the destination, some coach tours leave very early in the morning, so they are best booked a day in advance.

COACH SERVICES FROM ATHENS

FROM ATHENS there are frequent coach services to all the larger mainland towns, apart from those in Thrace, which are served by coaches from Thessaloníki. Athens' Terminal A is situated 4 km (2 miles) northeast of the city centre at Kifisoú 10 *(see p325)*. The terminal serves Epirus, Macedonia, the Peloponnese and the Ionian islands of Corfu, Kefalloniá, Lefkáda and Zákynthos (ferry crossings are included in the price of the ticket). It takes 7.5 hours to Thessaloníki, and 7 hours to the port of Párga.

Terminal B is at Liosíon 260, north of Agios Nikólaos metro station, but most easily reached by taxi. It serves most destinations in central Greece, including Delphi, which takes 3 hours, and Vólos, which takes 6. Coaches to destinations around Attica, including Soúnio, Lávrio, Rafína and Marathónas, leave from the Mavrommataíon coach terminal in Athens, a short walk north from the National Archaeological Museum on the corner of Leofóros Alexándras and 28 Oktovríou (Patisíon).

Eurolines international coach

Travelling by Sea

Greek catamaran

Greece has always been a nation of seafarers and, with its hundreds of islands and thousands of miles of coastline, the sea plays an important part in the life and history of the country. Today, it is a major source of revenue for Greece, with millions of tourists descending each year for seaside holidays in the Mediterranean and Aegean. The Greek mainland and islands are linked by a vast network of ferries, hydrofoils and catamarans.

TRAVELLING TO GREECE BY SEA

There are regular year-round ferry crossings from the Italian ports of Ancona, Bari and Brindisi to the Greek ports

Passengers on the walkways of a car ferry leaving dock

of Igoumenítsa in Epirus and Pátra in the Peloponnese, plus summer sailings from Venice and Trieste. Journey times and fares vary greatly, depending on time of year, point of embarkation, ferry company, type of ticket and reductions (for young people, students or rail-card holders). Dozens of shipping lines cover the Italy–Greece routes, so it is best to shop around. In summer, reservations are advisable, especially if you have a car or want a cabin.

GREEK FERRY SERVICE

The government is implementing stricter checks on ferries, which should result in higher safety standards. However, ferry service schedules and departure times are

Dane Sea Lines funnel

notoriously flexible. From the smaller ports, your only concern will be getting a ferry that leaves on the day and for the destination that you want. Check the timetable on arrival for frequency and times of services, as schedules are changed each week.

Matters get more complicated from Piraeus, Greece's busiest port. Each of the many competing companies have agents at the quayside. Tickets and bookings (essential in high season) should be made through them, or at a travel agency. Greece also has a network of hydrofoils and catamarans. They are twice as fast as ferries, though twice as expensive. As well as serving the islands, many stop at ports along the mainland coast. Most depart from Rafína, but those going to the Peloponnese coast leave from Piraeus, nearly all from Zéa port. Advanced booking is usually essential.

The Greek tourist office's weekly schedules can serve as a useful guideline for all departures, and some of the English-language papers also print summer sailings.

If you are travelling out of season, expect all services to be significantly reduced and some routes to be suspended.

PIRAEUS PORT MAP

This shows where you are likely to find ferries to various destinations.

Piraeus Port Authority:
[C] 01 422 6000.
Coastal Services Timetables: [C] 143.

KEY TO DEPARTURE POINTS

▨	Argo-Saronic islands
▨	Northeast Aegean islands
▨	Dodecanese
▨	Cyclades
▨	Crete
▨	International ferries
▨	Hydrofoils and catamarans
	For key to symbols see back flap

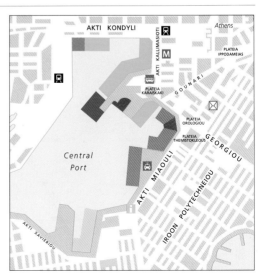

Getting Around Athens

Trolleybus stop sign

THE SIGHTS OF ATHENS' city centre are closely packed, and almost everything of interest can be reached on foot. This is the best way of sightseeing, especially in view of the appalling traffic congestion, which can make both public and private transport slow and inefficient. The expansion of the metro system, though not yet complete, already provides a good alternative to the roads for some journeys. However, the bus and trolleybus network still provides the majority of public transport in the capital for Athenians and visitors alike. Taxis are a useful alternative and, with the lowest tariffs of any EU capital, are worth considering even for longer journeys.

Orange and white regional bus for the Attica area

One of the large fleet of blue and white buses

BUS SERVICES IN ATHENS

ATHENS IS SERVED by an extensive bus network. Bus journeys are inexpensive, but can be slow and uncomfortably crowded, particularly in the city centre and during rush hours; the worst times are from 7am to 8:30am, 2pm to 3:30pm and 7:30pm to 9pm.

Tickets can be bought individually or in a book of ten, but either way, they must be purchased in advance from a *períptero* (street kiosk), a transport booth, or certain other designated places. The brown, red and white logo, with the words *eisitíria edó*, indicates where you can buy bus tickets. The same ticket can be used on any bus or trolleybus, and must be stamped in a special ticket machine to cancel it when you board. There is a penalty fine for not stamping your ticket. Tickets are valid for one ride only, regardless of the distance and, within the central area, are not transferable from one vehicle to another.

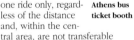

Athens bus ticket booth

USEFUL ROUTES IN ATHENS

Work continues on the Metro extension to Kerameikós, which is due to be in operation by 2006.

Botanikós (open 2006)

Plateía Omonoías

National Historical Museum

National Archaeological Museum

National Gallery of Art

Ancient Agora

Plateía Syntágmatos

Lykavittós Hill

Acropolis

Benáki Museum

Museum of Cycladic Art

Pláka

KEY

—	Bus A5
—	Bus 230
—	Trolleybus 1
—	Trolleybus 3
—	Trolleybus 7
—	Trolleybus 8
—	Trolleybus 9
—	Minibus 60
—	Minibus 100
M	Metro

ΜΟΝΑΣΤΗΡΙΟΝ
Monastirion

Monastiráki metro sign

ATHENS BUS NETWORKS

THERE ARE FOUR principal bus networks serving greater Athens and the Attica region. They are colour coded blue and white; red; orange and white; and green. Blue and white buses cover an extensive network of over 300 routes in greater Athens, connecting districts to each other and to central Athens. In order to reduce Athens' smog, some of these are being replaced with green and white "ecological" buses running on natural gas. A small network of minibuses with red stop signs operates in the city centre only.

Orange and white buses serve the Attica area *(see pp142–3)*. On these you pay the conductor and, as distances are greater, fares are also more expensive. The two terminals for orange and white buses are both situated on Mavrommataíon, by Pedío tou Areos (Areos Park). Though you can board at any designated orange stop, usually you cannot get off until you are outside the city area. These buses are less frequent than the blue and white service, and on some routes stop running in the early evening.

Green express buses, the fourth category, travel between central Athens and Piraeus. Numbers 040 and 049 are very frequent – about every 6 minutes – running from Athinas, by Plateía Omonoías, to various stops in Piraeus, including Plateía Karaïskáki, at the main harbour.

TROLLEYBUSES IN ATHENS

ATHENS HAS a good network of trolleybuses, which are orange-yellow or purple and yellow in colour. There are about 19 routes that criss-cross

the city. They provide a good way of getting around the central sights. All routes pass the Pláka area. Route 3 is useful for visiting the National Archaeological Museum from Plateía Syntágmatos, and route 1 links Lárissis railway station with Plateía Omonoías and Plateía Syntágmatos.

Front view of an Athens trolleybus

ATHENS' METRO

THE METRO, which has three lines, is a fast and reliable means of transport in Athens. Line 1, the original line, runs from Kifissiá in the north to Piraeus in the south, with central stations at Thiseío, Monastiráki, Omónoia and

Victoria. The majority of the line is overland and only runs underground between Attikí and Monastiráki stations through the city centre. The line is used mainly by commuters, but offers visitors a useful alternative means of reaching Piraeus *(see p325)*.

Lines 2 and 3 opened in 2000 and form part of a huge expansion of the system, most of which will be completed in time for the 2004 Olympic Games. The new lines have been built 20 m (66 ft) underground in order to avoid material of archaeological interest. Sýntagma and Acropolis stations have displays of archaeological finds.

Line 2 runs from Sepolia in northwest Athens to Dafní in the southeast, passing through Omónoia and Sýntagma in the centre. Line 3 currently runs from Sýntagma to Ethniki Amyna in the northeast. Its extension from Sýntagma to Monastiráki is due for completion by the end of 2002.

One ticket allows travel on any of the three lines and is valid for 90 minutes in one direction. This means you can come out of a station, then go back and continue your journey within the time limit. A slightly cheaper ticket is sold for single journeys on Line 1. Tickets can be bought at any metro station and must be validated before entering the train – use the machines at the entrances to all platforms. Trains run every five minutes from 5am to 12:30am on Line 1, and from 5:30am to midnight on Lines 2 and 3.

Archaeological remains on display at Sýntagma metro station

DRIVING IN ATHENS

DRIVING IN ATHENS can be a nerve-racking experience, especially if you are not accustomed to Greek road habits. Many streets in the centre are pedestrianized and there are also plenty of one-way streets, so you need to plan routes carefully. Finding a parking space can also be very difficult. Despite appearances to the contrary, parking in front of a no-parking sign or on a single yellow line is illegal. There are pay-and-display machines for legal on-street parking, as well as underground car parks, though these usually fill up quickly.

In an attempt to reduce dangerously high air pollution levels, there is an "odd-even" driving system in force. Cars that have an odd number at the end of their licence plates can enter the central grid, also called the *daktýlios,* only on dates with an odd number, and cars with an even number at the end of their plates are allowed into it only on dates with an even number. To avoid this, some people have two cars – with an odd and even plate. The rule does not apply to foreign cars but, if possible, avoid taking your car into the city centre.

No parking on odd-numbered days of the month

No parking on even-numbered days of the month

Yellow Athens Taxi

ATHENIAN TAXIS

SWARMS OF YELLOW taxis can be seen cruising around Athens at most times of the day or night. However, trying to persuade one to stop for you can be difficult, especially between 2pm and 3pm when taxi drivers usually change shifts. Then, they will only pick you up if you happen to be going in a direction that is convenient for them.

To hail a taxi, stand on the edge of the pavement and shout out your destination to any cab that slows down. If a cab's "TAXI" sign is lit up, then it is definitely for hire (but often a taxi is also for hire when the sign is not lit). It is also common practice for drivers to pick up extra passengers along the way, so do not ignore the occupied cabs. If you are not the first passenger, take note of the meter reading immediately: there is no fare-sharing, so you should be charged for your portion of the journey only, (or the minimum fare of 1.5 euros, whichever is greater).

Athenian taxis are extremely cheap by European standards – depending on traffic, you should not have to pay more than 2.5 euros to go anywhere in the downtown area, and between 4.5 and 7.5 euros from the centre to Piraeus. Double tariffs come into effect between midnight and 5am, and for journeys that exceed certain distances from the city centre. Fares to the airport, which is out of town at Spata, are between 12 and 15 euros. There are also small surcharges for extra pieces of luggage weighing over 10 kg (22 lbs), and for journeys from the ferry or railway terminals. Taxi fares are increased during holiday periods, such as Christmas and Easter.

For an extra charge,. (1–2.5 euros), you can make a phone call to a radio taxi company and arrange for a car to pick you up at an appointed place and time. Radio taxis are plentiful in the Athens area. Listed below are the telephone numbers of a few companies:

Express
℡ 210 993 4812.
Kosmos
℡ 1300.
Hellas
℡ 210 645 7000.

WALKING

THE CENTRE OF ATHENS is very compact, and almost all major sights and museums are to be found within a 20- or 25-minute walk of Plateía Syntágmatos, which is generally regarded as the city's centre. This is worth bearing in mind, particularly when traffic is congested, all buses are full, and no taxi will stop. Athens is still one of the safest European cities in which to walk around, though, as in any sizable metropolis, it pays to be vigilant, especially at night.

Sign for a pedestrianized area

Visitors to Athens, walking up Areopagos hill

ATHENS TRANSPORT LINKS

THE HUB OF ATHENS' city transport is the area around Plateía Syntágmatos and Plateía Omonoías. From this central area trolleybuses or buses can be taken to the airport, the sea port at Piraeus, Athens' two train stations, and its domestic and international coach terminals.

Bus E95 runs between the airport and Syntágmatos and bus E96 between the airport and Piraeus (see p313).

Buses 040 and 049 link Piraeus harbour with Syntágmatos and Omonoías in the city centre. The metro also extends to Piraeus harbour and the journey from the city centre to the harbour takes about half an hour.

Trolleybus route 1 goes past Lárissis metro station, as well as Lárissis train station, with the Peloponnísou station (see p316) a short walk away from them. Bus 024 goes to coach terminal B, on Liosíon, and bus 051 to coach terminal A, on Kifisoú (see p320).

Though more expensive than public transport, the most convenient way of getting to and from any of these destinations is by taxi. The journey times vary greatly but, if traffic is free-flowing, from the city centre to the airport takes about 40 minutes; the journey from the city centre to the port of Piraeus takes around 40 minutes; and the journey from Piraeus to the airport takes about 90 minutes.

Bus from the port of Piraeus to Athens' city centre

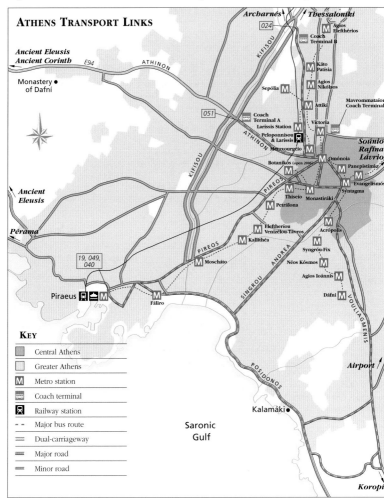

ATHENS TRANSPORT LINKS

Archarnés
Thessaloníki

Ancient Eleusis
Ancient Corinth

Monastery of Dafní

Ancient Eleusis

Pérama

Piraeus

Souníon
Rafína
Lávrio

Airport

Kalamáki

Saronic Gulf

Koropí

KEY

- Central Athens
- Greater Athens
- Ⓜ Metro station
- Coach terminal
- Railway station
- - - Major bus route
- Dual-carriageway
- Major road
- Minor road

General Index

Acknowledgments

DORLING KINDERSLEY would like to thank the following people whose contributions and assistance have made the preparation of this book possible.

MAIN CONTRIBUTORS
MARC DUBIN is an American expatriate who divides his time between London and Sámos. Since 1978 he has travelled in every province of Greece. He has written or contributed to numerous guides to Greece.

MIKE GERRARD is a travel writer and broadcaster who has written several guides to various parts of Greece, which he has been visiting annually since 1964.

ANDY HARRIS is a travel and food journalist based in Athens. He is the author of *A Taste of the Aegean*.

TANYA TSIKAS is a Canadian writer and travel guide editor. Married to a Greek, she has spent time in Crete and currently lives in Oxford.

DEPUTY EDITORIAL DIRECTOR Douglas Amrine

DEPUTY ART DIRECTOR Gillian Allan

MANAGING EDITOR Georgina Matthews

MANAGING ART EDITOR Annette Jacobs

ADDITIONAL ILLUSTRATIONS
Richard Bonson, Louise Boulton, Gary Cross, Kevin Goold, Roger Hutchins, Claire Littlejohn.

DESIGN AND EDITORIAL ASSISTANCE
Hilary Bird, Elspeth Collier, Catherine Day, Jim Evoy, Emily Green, Emily Hatchwell, Leanne Hogbin, Kim Inglis, Lorien Kite, Esther Labi, Felicity Laughton, Andreas Michael, Rebecca Milner, Ella Milroy, Lisa Minsky, Robert Mitchell, Adam Moore, Jennifer Mussett, Tamsin Pender, Jake Reimann, Simon Ryder, Rita Selvaggio, Claire Stewart, Claire Tennant-Scull, Amanda Tomeh.

DORLING KINDERSLEY would also like to thank the following for their assistance: The Greek Wine Bureau, Odysea.

ADDITIONAL RESEARCH
Anna Antoniou, Garifalia Boussiopoulou, Anastasia Caramanis, Michele Crawford Magda Dimouti, Shirley Durant, Panos Gotsi, Zoi Groummouti, Peter Millett, Eva Petrou Ellen Root, Tasos Schizas, Garifalia Tsiola, Veronica Wood.

ADDITIONAL PHOTOGRAPHY
Stephen Bere, John Heseltine, Steven Ling, Clive Streeter, Jerry Young.

ARTWORK REFERENCE
Ideal Photo S.A., The Image Bank, Tony Stone Worldwide.

PHOTOGRAPHY PERMISSIONS
DORLING KINDERSLEY would like to thank the following for their assistance and kind permission to photograph at their establishments:

Ali Pasha Museum, Ioannina; City of Athens Museum; Museum of Greek Folk Art, Athens; V Kyriazopoulos Ceramic Collection; Kavala Modern Art Gallery; National Gallery of Art, Athens; National War Museum, Athens; Nicholas P Goulandris Foundation Museum of Cycladic and Ancient Art, Athens; Theatrical Museum, Athens; University of Athens Museum; Polygnotos Vagis Museum, Thassos. Also all other cathedrals, churches, museums, hotels, restaurants, shops, galleries, and sights too numerous to thank individually.

PICTURE CREDITS
t = top; tl = top left; tlc = top left centre; tc = top centre; trc = top right centre; tr = top right; cla = centre left above; ca = centre above; cra = centre right above; cl = centre left; c = centre; cr = centre right; clb = centre left below; cb = centre below; crb = centre right below; bl = bottom left; b = bottom; bc = bottom centre; bcl = bottom centre left; br = bottom right; bottom right above = bra; bottom right below = brb; d= detail.

Works of art have been reproduced with the permission of the following copyright holders: Vorres Museum *Water Nymph* (1995) Apostolos Petridis 150t.

The publisher would like to thank the following individuals, companies and picture libraries for permission to reproduce their photographs:

AISA ARCHIVO ICONGRAFICO, Barcelona: Museo Archeologique Bari 57tr; Museo Archeologique Florence 54tl; AKG, London: 173t, 259; Antiquario Palatino 53bl; *Bilder aus dem Altherthume*, Heinrich Leutemann 228c; British Museum 95br; Edward Dodwell 87cr; Erich Lessing Akademie der Bildenden Künste, Vienna 54c; Musée du Louvre 53tl; National Archeological Museum, Athens 26–7(d), 27t; Staatliche Kunstsammlungen, Albertinum, Dresden 31crb; Liebighaus, Frankfurt/Main 33c; Museum Narodowe, Warsaw 145b; Staatliche Antikensammlungen und

Glyptotek, München 4, 52b; Mykonos Museum 55t; ALLSPORT: Mike Hewitt 120t; ANCIENT ART AND ARCHITECTURE: 29cl, 30t, 34t, 34ca, 35cl, 37t, 56cb, 56b(d), 246cb, 254c; ANTIKENMUSEUM BASEL UND SAMMLUNG LUDWIG: 60–1, 185br(d); APERION: John Hios 184c; Kamarias Tsigamos 118c; APOLLO EDITIONS: 185t; ARGYROPOULOS PHOTO PRESS: 45t, 45ca, 47t, 47cb, 47b, 48cb; CENTRE FOR ASIA MINOR STUDIES: Museum of Greek Popular Musical Instruments Fivos Anoyianakis Collection 104t; ATHENS INTERNATIONAL AIRPORT: 312cr/b, 313cr, 314.

BENAKI MUSEUM: 25b, 36ca, 39t, 39c, 41ca, 65br, 78–9 all; PAUL BERNARD: 33t; BIBLIOTHEQUE NATIONAL, Paris: Caoursin folio 175 38–9(d); BODLEIAN LIBRARY, Oxford: MS Canon Misc 378, 170v, 34cb; BRIDGEMAN ART LIBRARY, London: Birmingham City Museums and Art Galleries *Pheidias Completing the Parthenon Frieze,* Sir Lawrence Alma-Tadema 58t; Bradford Art Galleries and Museums *The Golden Fleece* (c.1904), Herbert James Draper 220br; British Museum, London *Cup, Tondo, with Scene of Huntsmen Returning Home* 29cr, *Black-necked Amphora, Depicting Boxers and Wrestlers* (c.550–525 BC) Nidosthenes 173cra; Fitzwilliam Museum, University of Cambridge *Figurine of Demosthenes,* Enoch Wood of Burslem (c.1790) (lead glazed earthenware) 57t; Giraudon, Louvre, Paris *Alexander the Great,* portrait head (3rd century BC) Greek (marble) 32tr; House of Masks, Delos *Mosaic of Dionysus Riding a Leopard* (c.AD 180) 35t; Guildhall Art Library *Clytemnestra,* John Collier 179c; Louvre, Paris *Double Bust of Aristophanes and Sophocles* (15th century) 56t; National Archaeological Museum, Athens *Bronze Statue of Poseidon* (c.460–450 BC) photo Bernard Cox 52ca; Private Collection *Two-tiered Icon of the Virgin and Child and Two Saints, Cretan School* (15th century) 38cl; © THE BRITISH MUSEUM: 26clb, 27cb, 28t, 30cb, 31clb, 53tr(d), 53br, 55c(d), 60tl, 61tl, 61tr, 97b, 173cla(d), 185bl.

CAMERA PRESS, London: ANAG 43tl, 43bl(d); Wim Swaan 62–3, 243t; BRUCE COLEMAN LTD: Udo Hirsch 236b; Dr Eckart Pott 257c; Hans Reinhard 22t, 23cla, 206b.

C M DIXON PHOTO RESOURCES: 27ca; Staatliche Antikensammlung und Glyptotek, München 32tr; MARC DUBIN: 17t, 21bca, 168b, 206t, 208cr, 253t, 253br; L DUPRÉ: Bibliotheque des Artes Decoratifs 24(d).

ECOLE NATIONALE SUPERIEURE DES BEAUX ARTS, Paris: *Delphes Restauration du Sanctuaire Envoi Tournaire* (1894) 30–1; EKDOTIKI ATHINON: 19br, 26crb; ELIA: 186c; ET ARCHIVE: British Museum 185c; National Archaeology Museum, Naples 32ca; EUROPEAN COMMISSION: 305; MARY EVANS PICTURE LIBRARY: 241b.

FERENS ART GALLERY: Hull City Museums and Art Galleries and Archives *Electra at the Tomb of Agamennon* (1869), Lord Frederick Leighton 55b; FOLK ART MUSEUM, Athens: 110t, 110b.

GIRAUDON, Paris: Laruros Versailles Chateau *Le Batille de Navarin,* Louis Ambroise Garneray 200t; Louvre, Paris 60c, *Scene de Massacres de Sio,* Delacroix 40ca(d); Musee Nationale Gustave Moreau *Hesiode et Les Muses* Gustave Moreau 56ca; Musee d'Art Catalan, Barcelona 95bra; National Portrait Gallery, London *Portrait of George Gordon Byron,* Thomas Phillips (1813) 149tr(d); NICHOLAS P GOULANDRIS FOUNDATION MUSEUM OF CYCLADIC AND ANCIENT GREEK ART: 65tr, 74–5 all.

ROBERT HARDING PICTURE LIBRARY: David Beatty 44br; N A Callow 263t; Tony Gervis 44cla, 44bl; Adam Woolfitt 46c; HELIO PHOTO: 254b; HELLENIC POST SERVICE: 43cla; MICHAEL HOLFORD: British Museum 32cb, 52t; HULTON GETTY COLLECTION: 41cb(d); Central Press Photo 42clb(d); HUTCHISON LIBRARY: Hilly Janes 98t.

IDEAL PHOTO SA: N. Adams 116cl; T Dassios 45br, 175t, 232, 252t, 252bl, 252br, 253cl, 262b; C. Vergas 48b,178b; IMAGES COLOUR LIBRARY: 99b; IMPACT PHOTOS: Caroline Penn 45bl.

KOSTOS KONTOS: 26cr, 42cra, 42cla, 45crb, 119b, 120b, 140, 152tr, 153tl, 153ca, 153b, 170t, 175c, 178c, 184t, 189tr, 303t, 315t.

ILIAS LALAOUNIS: 309cla. LAMPROPOULOS: 114c MAGNUM PHOTOS LTD: Constantine Manos 44t; MANSELL COLLECTION: 52–3; MUNICIPAL ART GALLERY OF ATHENS: *Despinis TK* Mitarakis Yannis 88t.

NATIONAL GALLERY OF VICTORIA, Melbourne: Felton Bequest (1956) *Greek by the Inscriptions Painter Challidian* 54b; NATIONAL HISTORICAL MUSEUM, Athens: 38t, 40t, 40–1(d), 41t, 42b, 173clb, 188c(d), 194c; NATIONAL TOURIST ORGANISATION OF GREECE: George Boutos 46b; NATURAL IMAGE: Bob Gibbons 23rb; Peter Wilson 237cr; NATURE

PHOTOGRAPHERS: S C Bisserot 236c; Brinsley Burbridge 23clb, 23br; N A Callow 22b; Andrew Cleave 23bc, 237b; Peter Craig Cooper 237cl; Paul Sterry 23t, 23cra, 225cr; ANTONIS NICOLOPOULOS: 311t.

OLYMPIC AIRWAYS: 312t; ORONOZ ARCHIVO FOTOGRAFICO: 211b; Biblioteca National Madrid *Invasions Bulgares Historia Matriksiscronica FIIIV* 36cb(d); Charlottenberg, Berlin 54tr; El Escorial, Madrid *Battle Lepanto Cambiaso Luca* 38cr(d); Museo Julia 53c(d); Musee Louvre 60b; Museo Vaticano 61bl, 221tr.

ROMYLOS PARISIS: 14t, 104b, 136–7, 218b; City of Athens Museum 40cb; PICTURES: 12, 14b, 44crb, 310c; POPPERFOTO: 42crb, 43cra, 43br, 98b, 180t, 262t; MICHALIS PORNALIS: 218c, 219cb, 219b; PRIVATE COLLECTIONS: 5t, 216t, 217t, 217b.

REX FEATURES: 15c; Argyropoulos/Sipa 48t; Sipa/C.Brown 43tr.

SCALA, Florence: Gallerie degli Uffizi 28b; Museo Archeologico, Firenze 29t; Museo Mandralisca Cefalu 30ca; Museo Nationale Tarquinia 61br; Museo de Villa Giulia 28–9, 60tr; SPATHARIO SHADOW THEATRE MUSEUM: 151c; SPECTRUM COLOUR LIBRARY: 244b; MARIA STEFOSSI: 118b; THEODOROS-PATROKLOS STELLAKIS: 154b; CARMEL STEWART: 279c; TONY STONE IMAGES: Aperion 152tl(d).

TAP SERVICE ARCHAEOLOGICAL RECEIPTS FUND HELLENIC REPUBLIC MINISTRY OF CULTURE: A Epharat of Antiquities 5b, 43cb, 58b, 94bl, 94br, 95t, 95c, 96b, 98c, 99cr, 100t, 100c; Acropolis Museum 96t, 97t, 97c; Ancient Corinth Archaeological Museum 166c; B Epharat of Antiquities 82, 141b, 144 all, 146c, 146bl, 146br, 147tl, 147c, 148c, 148b; Byzantine Museum, Athens 67t, 76 all; D Epharat of Antiquities 139c, 139bl, 162–3 all, 164–5, 167bl, 177b, 178t, 179t, 179b, 180c, 181c; Delphi Archaeological Museum 50–1, 228t, 230tl, 231t, 231b; E Epharat of Antiquities 174cb; Elefis Archaeological Museum 156b; 11th Epharat of Byzantine Antiquities 237tr; 5th Epharat of Byzantine Antiquities 19tl, 19cl, 37c, 190–1, 192t, 192b; 1st Epharat of Byzantine Antiquities 139cra, 152c, 153cb, 222–3 all; I Epharat of Antiquities 138ca, 205t, 226–7, 228b, 229c, 230tr, 230b; IB Epharat of Antiquities 211t, 212c; IO Epharat of Antiquities 256c; IST Epharat of Antiquities 241c; Keramikos Archaeological Museum 89t, 89cr, 89br, 91t, 91car; Marathon Archaeological Museum 145c; National Archeological Museum, Athens 3c, 26t, 28tr, 65tl, 68t, 68c, 68b, 69t, 69c, 69b, 70–1 all, 99t, 155t, 157cr; 9th Epharat of Byzantine Antiquities 248c, 248b; Pireaus Archaeological Museum 155t; 2nd Epharat of Byzantine Antiquities 19tr; 6th Epharat of Byzantine Antiquities 13t, 19cr; 7th Epharat of Byzantine Antiquities 19bl, 218tl, 219ca; Thebes Archaeological Museum 221t; Thessaloníki Archaeological Museum 31t, 139t, 233t, 242b(d), 244t, 246t, 246ca, 246b, 247all; Γ Epharat of Antiquities 88c, 88b, 89cl, 89bl, 90t, 90b, 91t, 91cla, 91cb, 91b, 156t, 156c, 157cl, 157bl, 157bc; Z Epharat of Antiquities 138cb, 170c, 170b, 171t, 171b, 172 all, 201c, 201b, 310c; TRIP PHOTOGRAPHIC LIBRARY: Marc Dubin 250–1; YANNIS TSAROUHIS FOUNDATION: Private Collection *Barber Shop in Marousi* (1947) 42tr.

WADSWORTH ATHENEUM, Hartford Connecticut: T Pierpont Morgan Collection 189b; WERNER FORMAN ARCHIVE: 36t; ALAN WILLIAMS: 49t; PETER WILSON: 59bl, 92–3, 94t, 100b, 106–7, 214–5, 216c; WOODFIN CAMP & ASSOCIATES: John Marmaras 254t; ADAM WOOLFITT 45clb.

Front Endpaper: all special photography except Rt IDEAL PHOTO SA: T Dassios and Rbl KOSTOS KONTOS (d).

JACKET
Front - DK PICTURE LIBRARY, TAP SERVICE ARCHAEOLOGICAL RECEIPTS FUND HELLENIC REPUBLIC MINISTRY OF CULTURE Rob Reichenfeld br; Peter Wilson bl; GETTY IMAGES, Walter Bibikow main image. Back - DK PICTURE LIBRARY, Joe Cornish b; Rob Reichenfeld t. Spine - GETTY IMAGES, Walter Bibikow.

All other images © Dorling Kindersley. For further information see: www.dkimages.com

Phrase Book

THERE IS NO universally accepted system for representing the modern Greek language in the Roman alphabet. The system of transliteration adopted in this guide is the one used by the Greek Government. Though not yet fully applied throughout Greece, most of the street and place names have been transliterated according to this system. For Classical names this guide uses the k, os, on and f spelling, in keeping with the modern system of transliteration. In a few cases, such as Socrates and Philopappus, the more familiar Latin form has been used. Classical names do not have accents. Where a well-known English form of a name exists, such as Athens or Corinth, this has been used. Variations in transliteration are given in the index.

GUIDELINES FOR PRONUNCIATION

The accent over Greek and transliterated words indicates the stressed syllable. In this guide the accent is not written over capital letters nor over monosyllables, except for question words and the conjunction ή (meaning "or"). In the right-hand "Pronunciation" column below, the syllable to stress is given in bold type.

On the following pages, the English is given in the left-hand column with the Greek and its transliteration in the middle column. The right-hand column provides a literal system of pronounciation and indicates the stressed syllable in bold.

THE GREEK ALPHABET

Α α	A a	**arm**
Β β	V v	**vote**
Γ γ	G g	**y**ear (when followed by e and i sounds) **no** (when followed by ξ or γ)
Δ δ	D d	**th**at
Ε ε	E e	**egg**
Ζ ζ	Z z	**zoo**
Η η	I i	bel**ie**ve
Θ θ	Th th	**th**ink
Ι ι	I i	bel**ie**ve
Κ κ	K k	**k**id
Λ λ	L l	**land**
Μ μ	M m	**man**
Ν ν	N n	**no**
Ξ ξ	X x	ta**x**i
Ο ο	O o	**fox**
Π π	P p	**port**
Ρ ρ	R r	**room**
Σ σ	S s	**s**orry (zero when followed by μ)
ς	s	(used at end of word)
Τ τ	T t	**tea**
Υ υ	Y y	bel**ie**ve
Φ φ	F f	**fish**
Χ χ	Ch ch	lo**ch** in most cases, but **he** when followed by a, e or i sounds
Ψ ψ	Ps ps	ma**ps**
Ω ω	O o	f**o**x

COMBINATIONS OF LETTERS

In Greek there are two-letter vowels that are pronounced as one sound:

Αι αι	Ai ai	**egg**
Ει ει	Ei ei	bel**ie**ve
Οι οι	Oi oi	bel**ie**ve
Ου ου	Ou ou	l**u**te

There are also some two-letter consonants that are pronounced as one sound:

Μπ μπ	Mp mp	**b**ut, sometimes nu**mb**er in the middle of a word
Ντ ντ	Nt nt	**d**esk, sometimes u**nd**er in the middle of a word
Γκ γκ	Gk gk	**g**o, sometimes bi**ng**o in the middle of a word
Γξ γξ	nx	a**nx**iety
Τζ τζ	Tz tz	han**ds**
Τσ τσ	Ts ts	i**t's**
Γγ γγ	Gg gg	bi**ng**o

IN AN EMERGENCY

Help!	Βοήθεια! Voitheia	vo-**ee**-theea
Stop!	Σταματήστε! Stamatiste	sta-ma-t**ee**-steh
Call a doctor!	Φωνάξτε ένα γιατρό Fonáxte éna giatró	fo-**nak**-steh **e**-na ya-tr**o**
Call an ambulance/ the police/the fire brigade!	Καλέστε το ασθενοφόρο/την αστυνομία/την πυροσβεστική Kaléste to asthenofóro/tin astynomia/tin pyrosvestiki	ka-**le**-steh to as-the-no-**fo**-ro/teen a-sti-no-**mia**/teen pee-ro-zve-stee-k**ee**
Where is the nearest telephone/hospital/ pharmacy?	Πού είναι το πλησιέστερο τήλέφωνο/νοσοκο-μείο/φαρμακείο; Poú einai to plisiés-tero tiléfono/ nosoko-meio/farmakeio?	poo **ee**-ne to plee-see-**e**-ste-ro tee-le-pho-no/no-so-ko-**mee**-o/far-ma-k**ee**-o?

COMMUNICATION ESSENTIALS

Yes	Ναι Nai	neh
No	Οχι Ochi	**o**-chee
Please	Παρακαλώ Parakaló	pa-ra-ka-l**o**
Thank you	Ευχαριστώ Efcharistó	ef-cha-ree-st**o**
You are welcome	Παρακαλώ Parakaló	pa-ra-ka-l**o**
OK/alright	Εντάξει Entáxei	en-**dak**-zee
Excuse me	Με συγχωρείτε Me synchoreíte	me seen-cho-r**ee**-teh
Hello	Γειά σας Geiá sas	y**ee**a sas
Goodbye	Αντίο Antío	an-d**ee**-o
Good morning	Καλημέρα Kaliméra	ka-lee-**me**-ra
Good night	Καληνύχτα Kalinýchta	ka-lee-n**ee**ch-ta
Morning	Πρωί Proí	pro-**ee**
Afternoon	Απόγευμα Apógevma	a-**po**-yev-ma
Evening	Βράδυ Vrádi	vr**a**th-i
This morning	Σήμερα το πρωί Simera to proi	s**ee**-me-ra to pro-**ee**
Yesterday	Χθές Chthés	chthes
Today	Σήμερα Simera	s**ee**-me-ra
Tomorrow	Αύριο Avrio	**av**-ree-o
Here	Εδώ Edó	ed-**o**
There	Εκεί Ekei	e-k**ee**
What?	Τι; Tí?	tee?
Why?	Γιατί; Giatí?	ya-t**ee**?
Where?	Πού; Poú?	poo?
How?	Πώς; Pós?	p**o**s?
Wait!	Περίμενε! Perímene!	pe-r**ee**-me-neh

USEFUL PHRASES

How are you?	Τί κάνεις; Τί káneis?	tee ka-nees
How do you do?	Πολύ καλά, ευχαριστώ Polý kalá, efcharistó	po-lee ka-la, ef-cha-ree-sto
How do you do?	Πώς είστε; Pós eíste?	pos ces-te?
Pleased to meet you	Χαίρω πολύ Chairo polý	che-ro po-lee
What is your name?	Πώς λέγεστε; Pós légeste?	pos le-ye-ste?
Where is/are...?	Πού είναι; Poú eínai?	poo ee-ne?
How far is it to...?	Πόσο απέχει... ; Póso apéchei...?	po-so a-pe-chee?
How do I get to...?	Πώς μπορώ να πάω...? Pós mporó na páo...?	pos bo-ro-na pa-o?
Do you speak English?	Μιλάτε Αγγλικά; Miláte Angliká?	mee-la-te an-glee-ka?
I understand	Καταλαβαίνω Katalavaino	ka-ta-la-ve-no
I don't understand	Δεν καταλαβαίνω Den katalavaino	then ka-ta-la-ve-no
Could you speak slowly?	Μιλάτε λίγο πιο αργά παρακαλώ; Miláte ligo pio argá parakaló?	mee-la-te lee-go pyo ar-ga pa-ra-ka-lo?
I'm sorry	Με συγχωρείτε Me synchoreite	me seen-cho-ree teh
Does anyone have a key?	Έχει κανένας κλειδί; Echei kanénas kleidí?	e-chee ka-ne-nas klec-dee?

USEFUL WORDS

big	Μεγάλο Megálo	me-ga-lo
small	Μικρό Mikró	mi-kro
hot	Ζεστό Zestó	zes-to
cold	Κρύο Krýo	kree-o
good	Καλό Kaló	ka-lo
bad	Κακό Kakó	ka-ko
enough	Αρκετά Arketá	ar-ke-ta
well	Καλά Kalá	ka-la
open	Ανοιχτά Anoichtá	a-neech-ta
closed	Κλειστά Kleistá	klee-sta
left	Αριστερά Aristerá	a-ree-ste-ra
right	Δεξιά Dexiá	dek-see-a
straight on	Ευθεία Eftheia	ef-thee-a
between	Ανάμεσα / Μεταξύ Anámesa / Metaxý	a-na-me-sa/me-tak-see
on the corner of.....	Στη γωνία του... Sti gonía tou...	stee go-nee-a too
near	Κοντά Kontá	kon-da
far	Μακριά Makriá	ma-kree-a
up	Επάνω Epáno	e-pa-no
down	Κάτω Káto	ka-to
early	Νωρίς Norís	no-rees
late	Αργά Argá	ar-ga
entrance	Η είσοδος I eisodos	ee ce-so-thos
exit	Η έξοδος I éxodos	ee e-kso-dos
toilet	Οι τουαλέτες /WC Oi toualétes /WC	ee-too-a-le-tes
occupied/engaged	Κατειλημμένη Kateiliméni	ka-tec-lee-me-nee
unoccupied/vacant	Ελεύθερη Eléftheri	e-lef-the-ree
free/no charge	Δωρεάν Doreán	tho-re-an
in/out	Μέσα /Έξω Mésa/ Exo	me-sa/ek-so

MAKING A TELEPHONE CALL

Where is the nearest public telephone ?	Πού βρίσκεται ο πλησιέστερος τηλεφωνικός θάλαμος; Poú vrisketai o plisiésteros tilefonikós thálamos?	poo vrees-ke-teh o plee-see-e-ste-ros tee-le-fo-ni-kos tha-la-mos?
I would like to place a long-distance call	Θα ήθελα να κάνο ένα υπεραστικό τηλεφώνημα Tha ithela na káno éna yperastikó tilefónima	tha ee-the-la na ka-no e-na ee-pe-ra-sti-ko tee-le-fo-nee-ma
I would like to reverse the charges	Θα ήθελα να χρεώσω το τηλεφώνημα στον παραλήπτη Tha ithela na chreóso to tilefónima ston paralipti	tha ce-the-la na chre-o-so to tee-le-fo-nee-ma ston pa-ra-lep-tee
I will try again later	Θα ξανατηλεφωνήσω αργότερα Tha xanatilefoníso argótera	tha ksa-na-tee-le-fo-ni-so ar-go-te-ra
Can I leave a message?	Μπορείτε να του αφήσετε ένα μήνυμα; Mporeíte na tou afísete éna mínima?	bo-ree te na too a-fee-se-teh e-na mee-nee-ma?
Could you speak up a little please?	Μιλάτε δυνατότερα, παρακαλώ; Miláte dynatótera, parakaló?	mee-la-teh dee-na-to-te-ra, pa-ra-ka-lo
Local call	Τοπικό τηλεφώνημα Topikó tilefónima	to-pi-ko tee-le-fo-nee-ma
Hold on	Περιμένετε Periménete	pe-ri-me-ne-teh
OTE telephone office	Ο OTE / Το τηλεφωνείο O OTE / To tilefoneio	o O-TE / To tee-le-fo-nee-o
Phone box/kiosk	Ο τηλεφωνικός θάλαμος O tilefonikós thálamos	o tee-le-fo-ni-kos tha-la-mos
Phone card	Η τηλεκάρτα I tilekárta	ee tee-le-kar-ta

SHOPPING

How much does this cost?	Πόσο κάνει; Póso káni?	po-so ka-nee?
I would like.....	Θα ήθελα... Tha ithela...	tha ce-the-la...
Do you have.....?	Έχετε...; Echete...?	e-che-teh
I am just looking	Απλώς κοιτάω Aplós koitáo	a-plos kee-ta-o
Do you take credit cards/travellers' cheques?	Δέχεστε πιστωτικές κάρτες/travellers' cheques; Décheste pistotikés kártes/travellers' cheques?	the-ches-teh pee-sto-tee-kes kar-tes/ travellers' cheques?
What time do you open/close?	Ποτέ ανοίγετε/ κλείνετε; Póte anoigete/ kleinete?	po-teh a-nee-ye-teh/ klee-ne-teh?
Can you ship this overseas?	Μπορείτε να το στείλετε στο εξωτερικό; Mporeite na to steilete sto exoterikó?	bo-ree-teh na to stee-le-teh sto e-xo-te-ree ko?
This one	Αυτό εδώ Aftó edó	af-to e-do
That one	Εκείνο Ekeino Ακριβό	e-kce-no

expensive	Ακριβό Akrivó	a-kree-**vo**
cheap	Φθηνό Fthinó	fthee-**no**
size	Το μέγεθος To mégethos	to **me**-ge-thos
white	Λευκό Lefkó	lef-**ko**
black	Μαύρο Mávro	**mav**-ro
red	Κόκκινο Kókkino	**ko**-kee-no
yellow	Κίτρινο Kitrino	**kee**-tree-no
green	Πράσινο Prásino	**pra**-see-no
blue	Μπλε Mple	**bleh**

TYPES OF SHOP

antique shop	Μαγαζί με αντίκες Magazi me antikes	ma-ga-**zee** me an-**dee**-kes
bakery	Ο φούρνος O foúrnos	o **foor**-nos
bank	Η τράπεζα I trápeza	ee **tra**-pe-za
bazaar	Το παζάρι To pazári	to pa-**za**-ree
bookshop	Το βιβλιοπωλείο To vivliopoleío	to vee-vlee-o-po-**lee**-o
butcher	Το κρεοπωλείο To kreopoleío	to kre-o-po-**lee**-o
cake shop	Το ζαχαροπλαστείο To zacharoplasteío	to za-cha-ro-pla-**stee**-o
cheese shop	Μαγαζί με αλλαντικά Magazi me allantiká	ma-ga-**zee** me a-lan-**dee**-**ka**
department store	Πολυκατάστημα Polykatástima	Po-lee-ka-**ta**-stee-ma
fishmarket	Το ιχθυοπωλείο/ ψαράδικο To ichthyopoleío/ psarádiko	to eech-thee-o-po-**lee**-o /psa-**ra**-dee-ko
greengrocer	Το μανάβικο To manáviko	to ma-**na**-vee-ko
hairdresser	Το κομμωτήριο To kommotirio	to ko-mo-**tee**-ree-o
kiosk	Το περίπτερο To períptero	to pe-**reep**-te-ro
leather shop	Μαγαζί με δερμάτινα είδη Magazi me dermátina eídi	ma-ga-**zee** me ther-**ma**-tee-na **ee**-thee
street market	Η λαϊκή αγορά I laïkí agorá	ee la-ee-**kee** a-go-**ra**
newsagent	Ο εφημεριδοπώλης O efimeridopólis	O e-fee-mee-ree-tho-**po**-lees
pharmacy	Το φαρμακείο To farmakeío	to far-ma-**kee**-o
post office	Το ταχυδρομείο To tachydromeío	ta-chee-thro-**mee**-o
shoe shop	Κατάστημα υποδημάτων Katástima ypodimáton	ka-**ta**-stee-ma ee-po-dee-**ma**-ton
souvenir shop	Μαγαζί με "souvenir" Magazi me "souvenir"	ma-ga-**zee** meh "souvenir"
supermarket	Σουπερμάρκετ/ Υπεραγορά "Supermarket"/ Yperagorá	"Supermarket" / ee-per-a-go-**ra**
tobacconist	Είδη καπνις Eidi kapnis	**Ee**-thee kap-nees
travel agent	Το ταξειδιωτικό γραφείο To taxeidiotikó grafeío	to tak-see-thy-o-tee-**ko** gra-**fee**-o

SIGHTSEEING

tourist information	Ο ΕΟΤ O EOT	o E-OT
tourist police	Η τουριστική αστυνομία I touristiki astynomía	ee too-rees-tee-**kee** a-stee-no-**mee**-a
archaeological	αρχαιολογικός archaiologikós	ar-che-o-lo-yee-**kos**

art gallery	Η γκαλερί I gkaleri	ee ga-le-**ree**
beach	Η παραλία I paralía	ee pa-ra-**lee**-a
Byzantine	βυζαντινός vyzantinós	vee-zan-dee-**nos**
castle	Το κάστρο To kástro	to **ka**-stro
cathedral	Η μητρόπολη I mitrópoli	ee mee-**tro**-po-lee
cave	Το σπήλαιο To spílaio	to **spee**-le-o
church	Η εκκλησία I ekklisía	ee e-klee-**see**-a
folk art	λαϊκή τέχνη laïkí téchni	la-ee-**kee** **tech**-nee
fountain	Το συντριβάνι To syntriváni	to seen-dree-**va**-nee
hill	Ο λόφος O lófos	o **lo**-fos
historical	ιστορικός istorikós	ee-sto-ree-**kos**
island	Το νησί To nisí	to nee-**see**
lake	Η λίμνη I límni	ee **leem**-nee
library	Η βιβλιοθήκη I vivliothíki	ee veev-lee-o-**thee**-kee
mansion	Η έπαυλις I épavlis	ee **e**-pav-lees
monastery	Μονή moní	mo-**ni**
mountain	Το βουνό To vounó	to voo-**no**
municipal	δημοτικός dimotikós	thee-mo-tee-**kos**
museum	Το μουσείο To mouseío	to moo-**see**-o
national	εθνικός ethnikós	eth-nee-**kos**
park	Το πάρκο To párko	to **par**-ko
garden	Ο κήπος O kípos	o **kee**-pos
gorge	Το φαράγγι To farángi	to fa-**ran**-gee
grave of.....	Ο τάφος του... O táfos tou...	o **ta**-fos too
river	Το ποτάμι To potámi	to po-**ta**-mee
road	Ο δρόμος O drómos	o **thro**-mos
saint	άγιος/άγιοι/αγία/ αγίες ágios/ágioi/agía/agies	**a**-yee-os/**a**-yee-ee/a-yee-a/a-yee-es
spring	Η πηγή I pigí	ee pee-**yee**
square	Η πλατεία I plateía	ee pla-**tee**-a
stadium	Το στάδιο To stádio	to **sta**-thee-o
statue	Το άγαλμα To ágalma	to **a**-gal-ma
theatre	Το θέατρο To théatro	to **the**-a-tro
town hall	Το δημαρχείο To dimarcheío	To thee-mar-**chee**-o
closed on public holidays	κλειστό τις αργίες kleistó tis argies	klee-sto tees ar-**yee**-es

TRANSPORT

When does the .... leave?	Πότε φεύγει το ....; Póte févgei to...?	**po**-teh **fev**-yee to...?
Where is the bus stop?	Πού είναι η στάση του λεωφορείου; Poú eínai i stási tou leoforeíou?	poo **ce**-neh ee sta-see too le-o-fo-**rce**-oo?
Is there a bus to..?	Υπάρχει λεωφορείο για....; Ypárchei leoforeío gia...?	ee-**par**-chee le-o-fo-**ree**-o yia...?
ticket office	Εκδοτήρια εισητηρίων Ekdotíria eisitirión	Ek-tho-**tee**-reea ee-**see**-tee-**re**-on
return ticket	Εισητήριο με επιστροφή Eisitírio me epistrofí	ee-see-**tee**-**ree**-o meh e-pee-stro-**fee**
single journey	Απλό εισητήριο Apló eisitírio	a-**plo** ee-see-**tee**-**reeo**

English	Greek	Phonetic
bus station	Ο σταθμός λεωφορείων / O stathmós leoforeíon	o stath-mos leo-fo-ree-on
bus ticket	Εισητήριο λεωφορειου / Eisitírio leoforeíou	ee-see-tee-ree-o leo-fo-ree-oo
trolley bus	Το τρόλλευ / To tróley	to tro-le-ee
port	Το λιμάνι / To limáni	to lee-ma-nee
train/metro	Το τρένο / To tréno	to tre-no
railway station	σιδηροδρομικός σταθμός / sidirodromikós stathmós	see-thee-ro-thro-mee-kos stath-mos
moped	Το μοτοποδήλατο / το μηχανάκι / To motopodílato / To michanáki	to mo-to-po-thee-la-to/to mee-cha-na-kee
bicycle	Το ποδήλατο / To podílato	to po-thee-la-to
taxi	Το ταξί / To taxí	to tak-see
airport	Το αεροδρόμιο / To aerodrómio	to a-e-ro-thro-mee-o
ferry	Το φερυμπότ / To "ferry-boat"	to fe-ree-bot
hydrofoil	Το δελφίνι / Το υδροπτέρυγο / To delfini / To ydroptérygo	to del-fee-nee / To ee-throp-te-ree-go
catamaran	Το καταμαράν / To Katamaran	to catamaran
for hire	Ενοικιάζονται / Enoikiázontai	e-nee-kya-zon-deh

STAYING IN A HOTEL

English	Greek	Phonetic
Do you have a vacant room?	Εχετε δωμάτια; Echete domátia?	e-che-teh tho-ma-tee-a?
double room with double bed	Δίκλινο με διπλό κρεββάτι / Díklino me dipló krevváti	thee-klee-no meh thee-plo kre-va-tee
twin room	Δίκλινο με μονά κρεββάτια / Díklino me moná krevvátia	thee-klee-no meh mo-na kre-vat-ya
single room	Μονόκλινο / Monóklino	mo-no-klee-no
room with a bath	Δωμάτιο με μπάνιο / Domátio me mpánio	tho-ma-tee-o meh ban-yo
shower	Το ντουζ / To douz	To dooz
porter	Ο πορτιέρης / O portiéris	o por-tye-rees
key	Το κλειδί / To kleidí	to klee-dee
I have a reservation	Εχω κάνει κράτηση / Echo kánei krátisi	e-cho ka-nee kra-tee-see
room with a sea view/balcony	Δωμάτιο με θέα στη θάλασσα/μπαλκόνι / Domátio me théa sti thálassa/mpalkóni	tho-ma-tee-o meh the-a stee tha-la-sa/bal-ko-nee
Does the price include breakfast?	Το πρωινό συμπεριλαμβάνεται στην τιμή; / To proinó symperilamvánetai stin timí?	to pro-ee-no seem-be-ree-lam-va-ne-teh steen tee-mee?

EATING OUT

English	Greek	Phonetic
Have you got a table?	Εχετε τραπέζι; Echete trapézi?	e-che-te tra-pe-zee?
I want to reserve a table	Θέλω να κρατήσω ένα τραπέζι / Thélo na kratiso éna trapézi	the-lo na kra-tee-so e-na tra-pe-zee
The bill, please	Τον λογαριασμό, παρακαλώ / Ton logariazmó parakaló	ton lo-gar-yas-mo pa-ra-ka-lo
I am a vegetarian	Είμαι χορτοφάγος / Eimai chortofágos	ee-meh chor-to-fa-gos
What is fresh today?	Τί φρέσκο έχετε σήμερα; / Ti frésko échete simera?	tee fres-ko e-che-teh see-me-ra?

English	Greek	Phonetic
waiter/waitress	Κύριε / Γκαρσόν / Κυρία (female) / Kýrie/Garson"/Kyría	Kee-ree-eh/Garson/Kee-ree-a
menu	Ο κατάλογος / O katálogos	o ka-ta-lo-gos
cover charge	Το κουβέρ / To "couvert"	to koo-ver
wine list	Ο κατάλογος με τα οινοπνευματώδη / O katálogos me ta oinopnevmatódi	o ka-ta-lo-gos meh ta ee-no-pnev-ma-to-thee
glass	Το ποτήρι / To potiri	to po-tee-ree
bottle	Το μπουκάλι / To mpoukáli	to bou-ka-lee
knife	Το μαχαίρι / To machairi	to ma-che-ree
fork	Το πηρούνι / To píroúni	to pee-roo-nee
spoon	Το κουτάλι / To koutáli	to koo-ta-lee
breakfast	Το πρωινό / To proïnó	to pro-ee-no
lunch	Το μεσημεριανό / To mesimerianó	to me-see-mer-ya-no
dinner	Το δείπνο / To deípno	to theep-no
main course	Το κυρίως γεύμα / To kyríos gévma	to kee-ree-os yev-ma
starter/first course	Τα ορεκτικά / Ta orektiká	ta o-rek-tee-ka
dessert	Το γλυκό / To glykó	to ylee-ko
dish of the day	Το πιάτο της ημέρας / To piáto tis iméras	to pya-to tees ee-me-ras
bar	Το μπαρ / To "bar"	To bar
taverna	Η ταβέρνα / I tavérna	ee ta-ver-na
café	Το καφενείο / To kafeneío	to ka-fe-nee-o
fish taverna	Η ψαροταβέρνα / I psarotavérna	ee psa-ro-ta-ver-na
grill house	Η ψησταριά / I psistariá	ee psee-sta-rya
wine shop	Το οινοπωλείο / To oinopoleío	to ee-no-po-lee-o
dairy shop	Το γαλακτοπωλείο / To galaktopoleío	to ga-lak-to-po-lee-o
restaurant	Το εστιατόριο / To estiatório	to e-stee-a-to-ree-o
ouzeri	Το ουζερί / To ouzerí	to oo-ze-ree
meze shop	Το μεζεδοπωλείο / To mezedopoleío	To me-ze-do-po-lee-o
take away kebabs	Το σουβλατζίδικο / To souvlatzidiko	To soo-vlat-zee-dee-ko
rare	Ελάχιστα ψημένο / Eláchista psiméno	e-lach-ees-ta psee-me-no
medium	Μέτρια ψημένο / Métria psiméno	met-ree-a psee-me-no
well done	Καλοψημένο / Kalopsiméno	ka-lo-psee-me-no

BASIC FOOD AND DRINK

English	Greek	Phonetic
coffee	Ο καφές / O Kafés	o ka-fes
with milk	με γάλα / me gála	me ga-la
black coffee	σκέτος / skétos	ske-tos
without sugar	χωρίς ζάχαρη / choris záchari	cho-rees za-cha-ree
medium sweet	μέτριος / métrios	me-tree-os
very sweet	γλυκύς / glykýs	glee-kees
tea	τσάι / tsái	tsa-ee
hot chocolate	ζεστή σοκολάτα / zesti sokoláta	ze-stee so-ko-la-ta
wine	κρασί / krasí	kra-see
red	κόκκινο / kókkino	ko-kee-no
white	λευκό / lefkó	lef-ko
rosé	ροζέ / rozé	ro-ze

raki	Το ρακί	to ra-kee
	Το rakí	
ouzo	Το ούζο	to oo-zo
	Το oúzo	
retsina	Η ρετσίνα	ee ret-see-na
	I retsína	
water	Το νερό	to ne-ro
	Το neró	
octopus	Το χταπόδι	to chta-po-dee
	Το chtapódi	
fish	Το ψάρι	to psa-ree
	Το psári	
cheese	Το τυρί	to tee-ree
	Το tyrí	
halloumi	Το χαλούμι	to cha-loo-mee
	Το chaloúmi	
feta	Η φέτα	ee fe-ta
	I féta	
bread	Το ψωμί	to pso-mee
	Το psomí	
bean soup	Η φασολάδα	ee fa-so-la-da
	I fasoláda	
houmous	Το χούμους	to choo-moos
	Το houmous	
halva	Ο χαλβάς	o chal-vas
	Ο chalvás	
meat kebabs	Ο γύρος	o yee-ros
	Ο gýros	
Turkish delight	Το λουκούμι	to loo-koo-mee
	Το loukoúmi	
baklava	Ο μπακλαβάς	o bak-la-vas
	Ο mpaklavás	
klephtiko	Το κλέφτικο	to klef-tee-ko
	Το kléftiko	

NUMBERS

1	ένα	e-na
	éna	
2	δύο	thee-o
	d´yo	
3	τρία	tree-a
	tría	
4	τέσσερα	te-se-ra
	téssera	
5	πέντε	pen-deh
	pénte	
6	έξι	ek-si
	éxi	
7	επτά	ep-ta
	eptá	
8	οχτώ	och-to
	ochtó	
9	εννέα	e-ne-a
	ennéa	
10	δέκα	the-ka
	déka	
11	έντεκα	en-de-ka
	énteka	
12	δώδεκα	tho-the-ka
	dódeka	
13	δεκατρία	de-ka-tree-a
	dekatría	
14	δεκατέσσερα	the-ka-tes-se-ra
	dekatéssera	
15	δεκαπέντε	the-ka-pen-de
	dekapénte	
16	δεκαέξι	the-ka-ek-si
	dekaéxi	
17	δεκαεπτά	the-ka-ep-ta
	dekaeptá	
18	δεκαοχτώ	the-ka-och-to
	dekaochtó	
19	δεκαεννέα	the-ka-e-ne-a
	dekaennéa	
20	είκοσι	ee-ko-see
	eikosi	
21	εικοσιένα	ee-ko-see-e-na
	eikosiéna	
30	τριάντα	tree-an-da
	triánta	
40	σαράντα	sa-ran-da
	saráranta	
50	πενήντα	pe-neen-da
	peninta	
60	εξήντα	ek-seen-da
	exínta	
70	εβδομήντα	ev-tho-meen-da
	evdominta	

80	ογδόντα	og-thon-da
	ogdónta	
90	εννενήντα	e-ne-ncen-da
	ennenínta	
100	εκατό	e-ka-to
	ekató	
200	διακόσια	thya-kos-ya
	diakósia	
1,000	χίλια	cheel-ya
	chília	
2,000	δύο χιλιάδες	thee-o cheel-ya-thes
	d´yo chiliádes	
1,000,000	ένα εκατομμύριο	e-na e-ka-to-mee-ree-o
	ένα ekatomm´yrio	

TIME, DAYS AND DATES

one minute	ένα λεπτό	e-na lep-to
	éna leptó	
one hour	μία ώρα	mee-a o-ra
	mía óra	
half an hour	μισή ώρα	mee-see o-ra
	misí óra	
quarter of an hour	ένα τέταρτο	e-na te-tar-to
	éna tétarto	
half past one	μία και μισή	mee-a keh mee-see
	mía kai misí	
quarter past one	μία και τέταρτο	mee-a keh te-tar-to
	mía kai tétarto	
ten past one	μία και δέκα	mee-a keh the-ka
	mía kai déka	
quarter to two	δύο παρά τέταρτο	thee-o pa-ra te-tar-to
	d´yo pará tétarto	
ten to two	δύο παρά δέκα	thee-o pa-ra the-ka
	d´yo pará déka	
a day	μία μέρα	mee-a me-ra
	mía méra	
a week	μία εβδομάδα	mee-a ev-tho-ma-tha
	mía evdomáda	
a month	ένας μήνας	e-nas mee-nas
	énas minas	
a year	ένας χρόνος	e-nas chro-nos
	énas chrónos	
Monday	Δευτέρα	thef-te-ra
	Deftéra	
Tuesday	Τρίτη	tree-tee
	Tríti	
Wednesday	Τετάρτη	te-tar-tee
	Tetárti	
Thursday	Πέμπτη	pemp-tee
	Pémpti	
Friday	Παρασκευή	pa-ras-ke-vee
	Paraskeví	
Saturday	Σαββάτο	sa-va-to
	Savváto	
Sunday	Κυριακή	keer-ee-a-kee
	Kyriakí	
January	Ιανουάριος	ee-a-noo-a-ree-os
	Ianouários	
February	Φεβρουάριος	fev-roo-a-ree-os
	Fevrouários	
March	Μάρτιος	mar-tee-os
	Mártios	
April	Απρίλιος	a-pree-lee-os
	Aprílios	
May	Μάιος	ma-ee-os
	Máios	
June	Ιούνιος	ee-oo-nee-os
	Ioúnios	
July	Ιούλιος	ee-oo-lee-os
	Ioúlios	
August	Αύγουστος	av-goo-stos
	Avgoustos	
September	Σεπτέμβριος	sep-tem-vree-os
	Septémvrios	
October	Οκτώβριος	ok-to-vree-os
	Októvrios	
November	Νοέμβριος	no-em-vree-os
	Noémvrios	
December	Δεκέμβριος	the-kem-vree-os
	Dekémvrios	